SO-ADT-706

Praise for the work of Judith Weston:

"[*Directing Actors* is] a must read for any director working with actors. It is filled with constructive information that would serve not only the neophyte but also the skilled professional director."
— *DGA Magazine*

"I was repeatedly struck by her deep insight into the craft. The advice she offers would benefit any beginning acting student, and could even lead the most experienced actor to discover further layers of a character. This is the best kind of writing about acting."
— *Backstage West/Drama-Logue*

"*Directing Actors* is a terrific book — informative, exciting, even inspirational."
— Joe Ruben, director
Return to Paradise, Money Train, Sleeping With the Enemy

"Everything you taught me was more than useful. I am deeply grateful."
— Alejandro González Iñárritu, director
Amores Perros

"Judith's course is probably the single best thing you could do for yourself as a director."
— Brian Roberts, director
Everybody Loves Raymond, The Drew Carey Show, King of Queens, Lizzie McGuire

"Judith Weston's 'Acting for Directors' (seminar and book) gave me my first real insight into the work of the actor and the relationship between actor and director. Practical, scary and inspiring, it taught me to think in new ways and turned out to be the ideal introduction to the impossible task that lay ahead."
— Henry Bean, writer-director
The Believer

"Her overview of styles and methods is invaluable to anyone who has to deal with actors."
— Zak Penn, writer
X2: X-Men United, Behind Enemy Lines, Inspector Gadget, Last Action Hero

"Judith's methods (pardon the word) are so thoughtful, humane, and insightful, that I couldn't help but drink them in like a tonic."
— John Markus, writer-producer
Larry Sanders Show, The Cosby Show

"Especially when directing episodic TV, where speed is so important, we need a concise language to communicate not only with the crew but especially with our actors. And for some odd reason, this language is still a 'foreign' language to most of us. This class should be mandatory for every director, new or veteran, who has the desire to explore his craft deeper and bring out better performances in his actors."
— Winrich Kolbe, director
"24", Angel, Prey, Star Trek: Voyager, Next Generation, Deep Space Nine

"In preparation for my first movie, I studied Judith's book *Directing Actors* until the pages were shredded, took her weekend workshop, followed by her six-week workshop, and finally... a private one-day session where we focused only on rehearsal techniques. I still walked onto the set a novice, but I was prepared, I had a game plan, and I was confident. And when James Earl Jones had a question, more times than not, I had an answer."
— Jeff Probst, writer-director
Finder's Fee

"Judith Weston is not a drama teacher, she is an art teacher. She understands that at the heart of great drama is a powerful mystery. What she shows you in her workshops and her book are simple and effective tools that help you get deeper and deeper into that rich, complex, and surprising place."

— David Jacobson, writer-director
Dahmer

"There's no better place to discover new directing tools or to rethink old ones than in Judith Weston's courses. In an environment where growth is deeply supported and new insights never stop coming, this gifted teacher gives you a new way of thinking in her own uniquely warm and candid manner."

— Carlos Avila, director
Price of Glory, Foto-Novelas (PBS)

"Judith's method is wonderful because it is practical. She has given me numerous tools to solve problems on the set and to earn the trust of actors. Her classes and her book are invaluable resources to any director."

— Lawrence Trilling, director
Alias, Ed, Felicity

"I found Judith's book, and later her workshops, bridged a huge gap in my education as a director, helping me better understand the actor's process. Judith clarifies the unique relationship between actor and director. She shows you how to promote an atmosphere of safety, allowing creative spontaneity between you and your actors. The value of this cannot be overstated. When you are free to explore ideas without fearing loss of control, great things can happen."

— Vicky Jenson, co-director
Shrek

"Judith Weston's unique class offers insight into the minds of actors. It presents to the director an extremely valuable channel of communication that can make an award winning performance."

— William Linsman, commercials director
Honda, Pampers, McDonald's, Wendy's, Crest, Chevrolet

"Five stars! 10/10! A MUST SEE!!!"

— Nigel Dick, rock video director
Matchbox 20, Paul McCartney, R.E.M., Guns N' Roses, Britney Spears, Ozzy Osbourne

"Judith gives her full attention to every aspect of directing, and her incisive observations and supportive criticism are invaluable. She offers insight inspiration and practical tools for becoming a better, more confident director. Judith's classes gave me the tools and the confidence to direct tough, professional actors successfully, and to have fun doing it!"

— Anne Makepeace, documentary director
Robert Capa: In Love and War, Coming to Light: Edward S. Curtis and the North American Indians

"Judith Weston took me deep into the breathtakingly exciting, spontaneous, unpredictable and ultimately profound world of the actor."

— Robert Primes, cinematographer
MDs (ASC Outstanding Achievement Award), *Felicity* (Emmy Award)
My Antonia (Emmy Award)

"Judith can and will allow you to see with new eyes."

— Dennis Gassner, production design
The Road to Perdition, O Brother, Where Art Thou?, The Truman Show, Field of Dreams, Bugsy, Barton Fink, Miller's Crossing

the Film director's
intuition

Script Analysis and Rehearsal Techniques

Judith Weston

Published by Michael Wiese Productions
11288 Ventura Blvd., Suite 621
Studio City, CA 91604
tel. (818) 379-8799
fax (818) 986-3408
mw@mwp.com
www.mwp.com

Cover Design: AG Design Company
Book Layout: Gina Mansfield
Index: Bruce Tracy, Ph.D.

Printed by McNaughton & Gunn, Inc., Saline, Michigan
Manufactured in the United States of America

© 2003 Judith Weston

The author would especially like to thank the following writers and copyright holders for permission to use examples from their scripts:

From *Chinatown*; *The Last Detail: Screenplays* by Robert Towne. Copyright © 1974 by Long Road Productions. Used by permission of Grove/Atlantic, Inc.

From *sex, lies and videotape* by Steven Soderbergh. Copyright © 1990 by Steven Soderbergh. Reprinted by permission of Harper Collins Publishers, Inc.

Reprinted from *Clerks and Chasing Amy* by Kevin Smith. Copyright © 1998 by Kevin Smith. Published by Hyperion.

From *Tender Mercies* Copyright © 1980, 1989 by Horton Foote. Reprinted by arrangement with Horton Foote and The Barbara Hogenson Agency.

All rights reserved. No part of this book may be reproduced in any form or by any means without permission in writing from the publisher, except for the inclusion of brief quotations in a review.

Library of Congress Cataloging-in-Publication Data

Weston, Judith, 1946-
  The film director's intuition : script analysis and rehearsal
techniques / Judith Weston.
      p. cm.
  ISBN 0-941188-78-7
1. Motion pictures--Production and direction. 2. Drama--Explication.
3. Motion picture acting. I. Title.
  PN1995.9.P7W47 2003
  791.43'0233--dc21

                                        2003011909

TABLE OF CONTENTS

ACKNOWLEDGEMENTS

The quotations and anecdotes used in this book were found in *The Los Angeles Times, Daily Variety, DGA Magazine, MovieMaker Magazine, IFP/West Calendar, LA Weekly, TV Guide, The New Yorker, Venice Magazine, Filmmaker Magazine, Hollywood Reporter, New York Times, Forbes, LA Film Collaborative, Back Stage West,* and *St. Louis Post-Dispatch.* There are also references from documentaries and television programs including *Inside the Actors Studio, The Charlie Rose Show, A Constant Forge: The Life and Art of John Cassavetes, Easy Riders, Raging Bulls,* and *Woody Allen: A Life in Film.* There are two books I have used quotes from: *Cassavetes on Cassavetes* by Ray Carney, and *Keiślowski on Keiślowski,* edited by Danusia Stok. These two books have also given me inspiration and hope.

I am grateful to Robert Towne, Steven Soderbergh, Kevin Smith, and Horton Foote, and their publishers, for allowing me to reprint excerpts from their screenplays for *Chinatown, sex, lies, and videotape, Clerks,* and *Tender Mercies,* respectively.

An earlier draft of some material in this book appeared in a series of articles I wrote for *MovieMaker Magazine* in 1997-98, under the column *The Right Direction.*

As always, the heroes of the story are my students — both directors and actors. They empower me and give me all my ideas. Further, they give me reasons to continue believing that art can be a source of understanding, joy, and healing. I can't possibly thank them adequately. I received specific help and insights from so many of my students that I couldn't keep track of them all. I'll just mention Todd Malta, Rachel Toles, Mike Dow, Ria Janssen, and Vlamyr Vizcaya — even though the list is far from complete.

The generous, insightful, magnificent readers and copyeditors of this book were Frank Beacham, Marin Gazzaniga, Irene Oppenheim, and John Hoskins. To say that I could not have done it without them is a gross understatement. Frank also made substantive contributions of anecdotes and ideas. Marin had valuable suggestions for the overall organization.

Thank you to Michael Wiese and Ken Lee for support, wisdom, friendship, and making it all possible. And thank you, Michele, BJ, and Gina.

Colleen Malone Engel and Heather Levenson have been my very valued assistants at different times during the writing of this book. My friends, especially Lois Bostwick, Linda Cohen, and Gabrielle Donnelly, have been an unfailing safety net and source of encouragement and humor. In the *Acknowledgments* of my first book I neglected to mention the amazing Judith Claire, who has provided me with business counseling since 1988.

The pressures of writing a book while running a business and carrying a full load of teaching and traveling inevitably involve health issues. I am grateful to Dr. Carol Stoll, Dr. Jorge Moreno, Dr. Cynthia Watson, Eileen Poole, and Sarah Novack. And to my family — who have been unfailingly kind and generous — and extremely understanding of how little time I've been able to devote to them.

The best thing that has happened to me since the last time I wrote an *Acknowledgments* page is that my husband, John Hoskins, has left his corporate job and joined me in my business. His companionship, love, and unwavering support during the writing of this book has been the most precious part of it all. I am truly privileged to be allowed to work so close to my heart.

NEW READERS, RETURNING READERS

"If I think I am a hero who is invincible, I will pay for it with my life. I have to be very respectful of the space. The space is something I will never conquer or master. But if I walk it with artistry, with poetry, with meaning, as a piece of theatre, or an opera, which is what I call this walk, then maybe it can inspire you."

— Phillippe Petit
high-wire walker of outdoor terrain

"I knew growing up that I wanted to do something different than anybody else. I wanted to do something that no one else did or could do, and I wanted to do it better than anyone else had."

— Bob Dylan

WHY A SECOND BOOK

In 1988, when I had been teaching acting classes for three years, I began a new course called Acting for Directors. I've taught it continuously since then, hundreds of times — in Los Angeles, where I live, as well as in New York, San Francisco, and many cities of Europe and Canada. Its purpose is to help film and television directors communicate better with actors. Its premise is that experience is the only teacher and empathy is the best technique. In addition to directors, the workshop is attended by writers, producers, editors, cinematographers, and script supervisors. Even executives, managers, and casting directors take this workshop.

Often the goal of the directors taking these courses has been to learn the arcane "language" of actors. My own intention in teaching has always been a more ambitious one — transformation — to take them from the world of result and obligation into the world of process and creative risk; to open up their imaginations and feelings.

Published in 1996, my first book, *Directing Actors*, was based on the course material of the Acting for Directors workshop. In order to make my ideas clear enough to put in print, I was constantly forced to rethink, refine, and expand them. The challenge became to deconstruct the process of acting and examine its elements in a clear and simple way, without diminishing its complexity and ambiguity. A goal of the book

Directing Actors, as of the Acting for Directors workshop, became to make the richness of the craft of acting accessible — or better yet, irresistible — to people who are not normally susceptible to the sentimentality and mysticism which so often characterizes discussions of acting.

At the time I was certain *Directing Actors* was to be the only book I would ever write, so I put everything that I knew or thought into it. This was a strenuous, exhilarating experience I recommend highly — that is, putting everything you know and feel into every project, without holding anything back for a possible sequel.

I think one result of this process was that I became a better teacher. And paradoxically, the other result was that by the time my publisher approached me about writing a second book, I felt that I had more to say. Giving over everything you have to give does not drain one's resources — it replenishes them. I have always found that in the end it is more tiring to "pace myself" than to go ahead and give everything I've got.

In this second book, *The Film Director's Intuition: Script Analysis and Rehearsal Techniques*, I set myself the goal of not repeating any of the material of my first book, *Directing Actors*. This is an entirely new book, with new approaches and ideas, new anecdotes and quotes, new scenes and examples, new exercise and techniques. It also expands on the tools and concepts presented in *Directing Actors*. It is meant to be of service to both my new readers and my returning readers.

DIRECTORS AND ACTORS
This book will continue to explore ways for directors to collaborate more effectively with actors — but it will also treat acting as a metaphor for the director's access to intuition. Actors must work intuitively — trusting intuition is exactly what is entailed when we speak of actors needing to work "in the moment." Directors need access to their own "inner actor."

Access to their own "inner actor" will make directors better able to communicate with actors, and better able to make a movie set a safe place for actors to do risk-taking work. Often directors don't know enough about the delicate emotional mechanisms involved in acting. Even directors who started out as actors can, if they haven't acted in a long time, forget.

But access to their own "inner actor" gives directors much more than communication skills. It helps them as storytellers. It allows them to "improvise in their imaginations." A good storyteller has to commit to an imagined world — I mean, of course, not "has to" but "gets to," since this work is a great joy and privilege. This involves a commitment to imagine, love, and trust characters that seem, at first, completely different from oneself — and who do things we ourselves might never do. It means letting the characters move, speak, and choose out of the imperatives of their subconscious and vagaries of their free will — just like people. An effective director bonds deeply with the characters and the actors who play them, and at the same time allows both actors and characters privacy and independence.

DIRECTORS AND CHARACTERS

Meryl Streep, in her interview on *Inside the Actors Studio*, confided that she thought of her work of bringing a character to life as "presenting a new soul." Her words affected me very deeply — such an extreme way to express her empathy and love for her characters, and to assert that characters in scripts are people! "Imagined people," to be sure, not "actual people," but people all the same, not artifacts to be shuffled and manipulated like cards in a magic trick, to suit the contrivances of plot. I think that if filmmakers could approach characters more as if they were people, we'd have much better movies.

Directors create a bond with the characters in two ways. The first is script analysis, which is the director's and actor's preparation — investigations of subtext and choices that each does all alone with the script before meeting with each other. The second is rehearsal. That's when the director and actors meet each other, put out feelers, test each other, let each other in, communicate and explore and try out their ideas on each other. It's also when the actors meet each other, sniff around, live out their impulses and ideas together, connect and resist, and create relationships. This is where the director and the writer re-meet the characters as embodied by the actors, and hand the characters over to the actors to bring to life.

DIRECTORS AND "STORY SUBTEXT"

Discovering, bringing to life, and shaping the emotional events and story subtext comprise the director's most important job. All his many other filmmaking decisions hinge on it. Shaping the subtext events, with attention to theme, emotional life, blocking and business, pacing, beats, texture of life,

xviii   The Film Director's Intuition | Weston

tone, and of course camera placement, is the central job of the director. Indeed the subtext story *determines* the theme, emotional life, camera placement, production design, and everything else.

Attention to the "story subtext" is, I believe, the missing link in the education and preparation of many filmmakers. And it is *above all* the skill that directors must have — not just to work effectively with actors, but as the basis for all their decisions — lighting, lenses, locations, shot lists, costumes, you name it. Finding the "story subtext" is the focus of my advanced courses for directors — the Script Analysis workshop and the Actor-Director Laboratory — as well as my private consultation with directors. So it made sense for this second book to develop this topic, through a discussion of script analysis and rehearsal techniques.

DIRECTORS AND THE "RIGHT BRAIN"

Actors and writers tend to be "right brain" oriented. Directors tend to be "left brain" oriented. But to be a good director, a director with intuitive abilities as well as leadership skills and the focus and concentration it takes to tell a story with a camera, requires a person to be equally balanced in the left brain and the right brain. A director needs to be able to step back and see whether a scene or a casting or a camera angle is working. But in order to connect to actors, and in order to connect to characters, he also needs to step *in*, and submerge himself in the subjective, experiential, right-brain world.

That's why I go into such detail about the acting process in my books, and insist that directors take my Acting for Directors course before taking other courses with me. It's not because I think that directors should intrude upon the actors' inner lives, or give acting lessons on the set. It's because I think that many directors — and many people in all walks of life — are victims of a mechanistic, "fix-it" mentality that pervades the consumer society. The study of acting, which takes us to our deeper, more primal resources, can give us a refreshing respite from the "bottom-line" mentality and its superficial formulations for box office success.

Directors often find themselves needing a creative shot in the arm as a corrective not only to financial pressures but to the dominating presence of technology in film and television. Immersion in the imagined world from the actor's point of view is exactly that corrective. And don't forget that the tools and principles of acting have specific, practical value for directors in their development of leadership skills. Listening, playing intentions, and operating at the feeling level all help confer on a director genuineness, confidence, and authority.

Acting has been my central obsession for thirty years. I started my career as an actor, and I teach actors, as well as directors. The craft of acting is a laboratory of life, a giant petri dish in which everything about human behavior can be studied, and even, once in a while, understood. Every now and then, acting can bring revelations, and insight into the human condition. Acting is a calling, an obsession, and the noblest of professions. It can be taught without the intimidation and superstition that makes so many products of acting schools numb, frightened, and actorish. And, even though actors are a unique and special brand of person, anyone can learn acting, with proper training. By "proper training" I mean training that includes the letting go of destructive habits and wrong thinking about what acting is. When students finally drop their social mask and give up trying to do it "right," there can be scene work — even by novices — of beauty, insight, and surprise. I've seen it over and over in my workshops.

Harvey Keitel said in an interview that directors should know more about acting and its principles not only in order to be more skilled at their craft, but because it's "better for their life." I believe he was referring to the rewards of empathy and transformation that accompany a deep immersion in the acting process.

HOW TO USE THIS BOOK
I've divided the book into three parts: Part One on Intuition; Part Two on Script Analysis; and Part Three on Rehearsal. But, as you will see, the subject matter is not particularly linear, and the topics of the chapters constantly overlap. Script analysis and rehearsal, both as concepts and as activities, interweave. They are not separate ways of thinking or working. While a director or actor is doing script analysis, they are rehearsing in their imagination. When the two finally meet for rehearsal, imagination takes verbal, physical and emotional form, but the search for insight into the characters and script, the stripping down to what is essential in the script (which is how I think of script analysis), does not cease.

For a director, every decision you make from the first time you read the script up until the moment you send the negative to the cutter involves tools and principles of script analysis — that is to say, the revelation of the story subtext, which is *what story you are telling.* But your real preparation is actually every experience of your whole life. Once, after I had praised a student for beautiful work in a scene for class, the student said, "I've been rehearsing that role for twenty-five years."

The most frequently neglected area of a director's work is the one that I consider the most important — life preparation. Sometimes directors tell me they want to postpone taking a workshop or consulting with me until just before they are about to shoot, so the things they learn will be "fresh." But there's an enormous difference between cramming a few tidbits of jargon into your vocabulary — and actually having these somewhat radical concepts functioning in your "bones." Hence Part One, with chapters on *Intuition, Imagination and Originality*, and operating at *The Feeling Level*. In these chapters I have ventured into the sources of story imagination — how we go about creating an imagined universe and how we take responsibility for our own imagination. The chapter called *Sources of Imagination* even has exercises for you to try if you wish.

Part Two on Script Analysis plunges into the waters of result-oriented versus process-oriented direction. It has step-by-step examples, including scenes from *sex, lies and videotape*, *Clerks*, and *Tender Mercies*. It also contains a *Rehearsal Plan*, a revised and expanded "Verb/Intention" list, and a list of examples of translations from "result" to possible subtext adjustments.

Part Three on Rehearsal includes suggestions for specific rehearsal scenarios. However, every interaction between a director and the actors of her film, no matter how casual it may seem, is experienced by the actors as direction. In a way, all of the time spent between director and actor is "rehearsal." So, in addition to chapters on *Rehearsal Techniques*, *Scene Shaping*, and *Before the Camera Rolls*, I have included a chapter on the touchy topic of *Director's Authority*.

This book is, like the first one, written for film and television directors. But, like the first one, I expect it to be of use to actors, writers, and other film collaborators, as well. It's well known among actors that when they get no substantive direction from the director — or worse, when they do get direction but it is nothing more than instruction on how to arrange faces, limbs, and emotions like furniture in front of the camera — they need to direct themselves. Writers have frequently told me that the principles of my books and workshops resonate with their concerns for constructing compelling stories and vigorous dialogue. And it is one of my dearest hopes that my efforts might encourage producers and executives to trust their instincts and respect the audience.

The purpose of this book is to inspire and challenge you to re-invent your-self for every project. Even accomplished and successful directors need to start from scratch again with each project. I learned that personally from writing this book: the fact that I'd already written one was no help at all in writing this second one! If anything, the success of the first book was like a skin I had to scrape off before I could say something new. I want this book — both through content and example — to give you per-mission to be looser and freer when practicing your craft. But I want as well to inspire you to ask more of yourselves, to dig deeper, to be unafraid of contradictions, resistances, problems. I want to challenge filmmakers to be more truthful about their material and themselves. And finally, I want you to have more fun. Dedication to process, while hard work, is liberating and it's fun; it's life affirming, pleasurable, and exhilarating.

But does the "industry" have time for all this work and all this fun? People who work in film and television sometimes make the suggestion that my methods, while charming, are a kind of luxury in a world domi-nated by the bottom line. Don't believe it. These techniques are good business. They result in better performances that please audiences. As David Mamet says, "There is nothing more pragmatic than idealism." Commitment to process and subtext — to turning yourself inside out — takes time — I won't lie to you. The tools and principles of re-invention take time to learn, and the process itself takes time every time you start a new project. But it's finally much more efficient to pay attention to process than to ignore it.

PART ONE
INTUITION, IDEAS, AND IMAGINATION

1 | INTUITION

"The compromise… is beginning to feel a lack of confidence in your innermost thoughts. And if you don't put these innermost thoughts on the screen then you are looking down on not only your audience but the people you work with, and that's what makes so many people working out there unhappy. These innermost thoughts become less and less a part of you and once you lose them then you don't have anything else."

— John Cassavetes

WHAT IS INTUITION?

What is intuition? It's when you see or feel something that is not apparent to others, that may even be contradicted by ordinary reason and evidence. Years ago a friend complained to me so strongly about her fiancé's lack of culture and refinement that I finally asked if she was sure she wanted to go through with the marriage. She replied, "I've made my choice." Yes — she said, "I've made my choice" instead of, "I love him." The consensus — even among the groom's family — was that he was sweet and unsophisticated, that he was lucky to have won such a prize as her, and that even though she could probably have done better, his absolving virtue was that he adored her. At the wedding, I had an aisle seat. When the groom turned to watch her come down the aisle, I caught sight of his face — and I suddenly *saw* a flicker of something that looked unmistakably like… plain *dislike*! Everyone had it wrong — *he* didn't love her! My intuition was so strong that at the "If anyone knows a reason…" part of the ceremony I could have honestly spoken up and objected to the wedding.

We all have those moments now and then when we "know" something intuitively with much greater certainty than we know what reason tells us "must" be true. Sometimes we don't notice it and only later when someone asks us why we did a certain thing we say, "I don't know. Intuition, I guess." Other occurrences are so powerful and so odd that we attach mystical causes to them, and see these flashes of intuition as coming somehow from outside ourselves. Basically it's an idea that overtakes us without reason — or an action we take without thinking — that turns out to be true. (My friend's husband deserted her within a year.)

If we don't know these things rationally, how do we know them? We know them unconsciously. Our unconscious minds are filled with forgotten information, spontaneous associations, and deep connections — all of which are a kind of knowledge which is available to us, if we can access it and trust it. The forgotten information, spontaneous associations, and deep connections that are the source of intuition are also the raw materials of our creative imaginations.

DIRECTORS NEED INTUITION

"I was able to capture on film things the actors didn't even know they were doing."

— Elia Kazan

"The trick is knowing when to say something and when not to."

— Alan Pakula

It's pretty obvious that directors need to have intuitive abilities in order to communicate with actors. This is because good actors are operating below the social mask. They are "in the moment" — which means that their emotional territory is primarily subconscious. Angelica Huston told a reporter that during filming of the scene in *The Grifters* in which her character cuts her son's throat, the actress was unexpectedly flooded with "a physical memory of holding him in my arms as a baby." She continued, in something of an understatement, "Things take over that you hadn't thought about."

Directors need to communicate with actors on a level that goes below the social mask — on a feeling level. First, they need to read the actors' impulses and feelings — including those that the actors themselves may not know they have. And then they need to respond to what they see. They need to know when to talk seriously with an actor about the performance, or when, instead, to stay light, even tell a joke. They need to know when to engage and push an actor to go further, and when to step back and give the actor time to figure it out himself. They need to know what "tools" to use when — when to use an image, when to use a verb, when to tell a story, or when to ask a question. Even if all a director is sure of is when to say "faster" and when to say "slower" — and if he is right — that's a big help.

Directors need to know how to prepare so that their ideas achieve a level of intuitive truth. This means deep script analysis, until the characters' inner lives and private joys and problems, are human and idiosyncratic, and as real to you as your own. Directors' preparation also means developing and practicing your craft. The craft of directing is well known to include shot composition and understanding of the technology. But it should also include the abilities to see below the surface of a script, to shape and block a scene so the "master shot" can be usable, and to engage the actors in the emotional events of the script. To do these things well, the director must activate his full intelligence, which includes his unconscious knowledge and associations, rather than perform mechanically, by rote or out of obligation to rules or conventional wisdom.

THE COMFORT ZONE
Intuition resides below the surface of easy opinion and formulaic pronouncements. Our powers of intuition and thinking have been eroded by conventional schooling and the popular culture. A lot of what passes for thinking — in and out of the entertainment industry — is really just opinion. Sometimes our opinions are only a rehash of others' opinions. Sometimes what we call our "beliefs" are really just the unchallenged assumptions that enable us to feel comfortable with our choices and self-image. Sometimes gimmicks and trends of no substance seduce us. It's all too easy to fall into a "comfort zone," an emotional and intellectual "automatic pilot" which, for filmmakers, is death to creativity.

An example of mistaking the comfort zone for intuition is a racist, who thinks his automatic suspicions toward people of another color are based on an intuitive impression, when really they are based on prejudice. An example of mistaking the comfort zone for intuition in the arena of filmmaking might be the following: A director must have ideas that constitute a genuine vision, that is, a full and detailed grasp of the essence of a story. But a director can become complacently attached to his "moviola of the mind" — an idealized fantasy of the completed movie which he stubbornly or wistfully runs over and over in his head. It's not at all uncommon for novice directors to mistake such fantasies for vision. Directors are not the only people on a movie set who can mistake automatic pilot for intuition. Sometimes actors will claim to work "intuitively" when they haven't done any real work at all on their characters, and instead automatically give each line its most obvious reading.

INNERMOST THOUGHTS
When so many in the world are consumed with poverty, with grief, with fear for their safety, health, nourishment, and that of their children, I often feel guilty that I have the luxury to even concern myself with what John Cassavetes called, in the quote that begins this chapter, "confidence in my innermost thoughts." And yet I can't deny that it is my deepest personal priority. One's innermost thoughts, in their raw form, are a kind of stream of consciousness, a free-association. When one *listens* to these observations and associations, questions them and sifts through them, one arrives at insight and ideas. Access to "innermost thoughts" is not

given by one's level of education, but by one's level of *attention*. "Attention" is a moment-by-moment observation of everything that comes into one's world, including one's own feelings, responses, and values. Confidence in one's "innermost thoughts" is intuition.

"INTELLECTUALIZED" IDEAS
It's not always easy to tell the difference between what we really think, know, and feel — and what we think we think. Knowing what we really think involves using all our intelligence — including, besides our rational reasoning, our intuitive and subconscious resources. I find that using "all my intelligence" is almost a physical experience. When I am stuck "in my head" with an intellectualized idea or response, I feel differently from when I am operating with all my intelligence — which feels more like "thinking with my whole body." A simple tactic to alert myself that I've gotten "in my head" is to check the physical sensations in my scalp and face. Sometimes just taking a moment to make myself relax and soften the tightened muscles of my scalp, face, and shoulders has a genuine effect on my ability to focus my ideas and come up with a needed insight. Of course sometimes I need more than a moment; sometimes my subconscious intelligence needs a night to "sleep on it"; sometimes a creative problem needs weeks or months of subterranean percolating before its solution chooses to bubble up to the surface.

BEGINNER'S LUCK/BEGINNER'S MIND
When we are feeling intuitive, we feel a kind of courage, a trust in ourselves, a freedom to act on whatever knowledge we have. We don't stop to think about where we got that knowledge, or whether it is indeed adequate. This trust in whatever knowledge and experience one has is the source of "beginner's luck." The beginner with "beginner's luck" is aware that he doesn't know anything, so he has to trust whatever he does know — and, because he is a beginner, he gives himself permission to fail. Further, he feels pleasure at the prospect that *he has everything to learn*. This trust, this permission to be wrong, this pleasure in learning — this *beginner's mind* — can allow the best of his talent to flourish.

PERMISSION TO FAIL
There is no way to be intuitive without risking failure. If we approach a project declaring, "I trust myself. I'm going to nail it. I'm going to do it perfectly" — that's not trust, that's bravado. And bravado is a form of denial; it's pretending that we're not afraid when, in fact, we are. Denial is a little lie to ourselves. And when we lie to ourselves, we shut down our creativity.

If, on the other hand, our mindset is, "I trust that whatever I do will be worth trying" — that is, worth risking — we give ourselves permission to fail. Permission to fail is exactly the same as permission to learn. *There is no creativity, no originality, no success, no progress without risk.* And there is no such thing as creative risk without accepting the possibility of failure. "Risk" *means* you might fail, right? It also means you might have an adventure. For a director, that's the upside of risk — a creative adventure that pays off with a breakthrough idea, a bravura performance, an original story.

After the success of beginner's luck, there is often the drop-back, the sophomore slump, the proof of the adage that "a little knowledge is a dangerous thing." Once a director gains a bit of knowledge and experience, she may start to watch herself, second-guessing her ideas and choices, evaluating them based on other people's expectations rather than on their relation to truth. When this happens she has lost her intuitive abilities. Her impulses shut down. She gets "in her head"; her feelings become frozen and her ideas become intellectualized. She has become more invested in not looking foolish than in learning.

If a director keeps directing, continued experience may lead to expertise, even confidence. Expertise and confidence can give a deep permission to one's intuition. But success can also lull us into complacency — or worse, make us feel that all we have is something to lose. The permission to fail must be constantly renewed. With every new project one must revive one's permission to fail, and recommit to beginner's mind.

IMAGINING FAILURE AS A POSITIVE APPROACH
One way I give myself permission to fail is by making myself imagine and consider every road that a particular decision might take me down — in particular, to face in my imagination every difficulty, every humiliation, every failure that might ensue. Then I do the thing anyway. This is the direct opposite of the approach to career and personal choices that focuses on "making affirmations." It probably sounds depressing and counter-intuitive to many people. To me it's more depressing to live in imaginative ignorance. The principle here is that the converse of fearing failure is not avoiding failure, but facing failure.

I think one of the reasons why people obsessively fear failure is that they don't really let themselves imagine it. When I imagine in detail the possible ways a project could fail, and all the possible consequences, I come up with ideas of what I'll do if any of these scenarios occurs. Ideas about ways to recover from failure give me confidence. But more than that — the very experience of imagining alternate coping scenarios gives me confidence that even if none of those coping scenarios works, I might in the moment come up with yet another way to cope. And even more than that — imagining the very worst thing that might happen takes away its sting.

One reason why the "imagining failure" approach works is that it stands in for the experience that one is lacking in the area one is contemplating tackling. It's a kind of virtual resume. One of the values of actual experience is having survived mistakes and failure. Imagining the failures gives one a kind of imagined — or virtual — experience.

Whenever I do something risky without that "imagining failure" step, I regret it. I get myself in trouble because I was operating not out of courage but bravado. Courage is when you know something is very scary but you do it anyway. Bravado is when you just do it without thinking. Bravado works for some people once in a while, but seldom forever. (It has never worked for me.) People who act with bravado and fail often conclude from that experience that they shouldn't take risks any more — fear of failure comes to rule their lives.

RESPONSIBILITY FOR OUR IMAGINATIONS

There's a prevailing approach to movies and television that if something is wrong with a script or a performance, it should be *fixed*, like a broken toaster. This idea of *fixing* turns the creative process into a mechanical one. The definition of mechanical that applies here is "seemingly uninfluenced by the mind or emotions." Instead of "fixing," *re-imagine*. Re-imagining means going back to square one with the questions: What truth is in front of me that I didn't see before? What is this thing that I am trying to say or accomplish really like? How can I express it more simply, more truthfully?

The struggle to bring your mind and emotions into your work, to look for insight rather than formulaic fixes, does have to do with ethics — with a respect for the audience and a commitment to giving them something of value. And it has to do with happiness, because it will get you making better movies, having more success, and maybe even feeling fulfilled in your success.

THE LESSONS OF "PHYSICAL GENIUS"

The writer of a *New Yorker* article set about to determine what sets physical geniuses — such as Michael Jordan, Wayne Gretsky, cellist Yo Yo Ma, and a top neurosurgeon — apart from other people. Raw talent and constant practice are factors. But the article noted that basketball player Karl Malone, for instance, did not have less athletic ability than Jordan, or practice less obsessively — and yet Jordan was able to *see* opportunities in the heat of a game that other players did not.

The neurosurgeon told the interviewer, "Sometimes during the course of an operation, there'll be several possible ways of doing something, and I'll size them up and, *without having any conscious reason*, I'll just do one of them [italics mine]." This neurosurgeon was considered by his peers to have almost preternatural powers — he could perform more complex, more dangerous surgeries, and do more of them in any given period of time, with less error, than any other surgeon.

The writer of the article speculated that the unique skills of these people have something to do with being able to spontaneously organize incoming sensory impressions into "chunks" or situations, instead of perceiving them as masses of indistinguishable data swimming in front of one. Wayne Gretsky, for instance, would look down the length of the hockey rink and see not a swirl of players, but a number of situations. The writer hypothesized that this ability to organize data is a function of a limber and skillful imagination. My dictionary calls intuition "quick and ready insight," or "the power... of attaining to direct knowledge or cognition without evident rational thought." Thus the ability to make a spontaneous selection from these chunks of data — and to act upon it without pausing to reflect — must be intuition.

Intuition takes us beyond the normal limits of our hard work and our talent. But the letting go, the surrender to spontaneous impulse that characterizes a burst of intuition, must be prepared for with hard work as well as natural talent. In studying characteristics of each of these "physical geniuses," the *New Yorker* article remarked on a "practical-minded obsession with the possibility and the consequences of failure." After any mistake or failure, Jordan, Gretsky, and the neurosurgeon would rethink everything they had done and imagine how they might have done it differently. They also practiced constantly and obsessively. This article reminded me of another article I had read, about the intense training habits of Tiger Woods.

Tiger Woods decided in late 1998 to tighten up his golf swing. He worked with his coach for a year on the minutiae of the mechanics of a golf swing most people would have said was already pretty damn good. During that time he won few tournaments, because a learning curve often involves getting worse before you get better. But he didn't care. He loved to win, but he loved his craft as much or more, and he knew that developing his craft was his insurance for a long-term career. "People have no idea how many hours I've put into this game," he told an interviewer.

Intuition is not the same as automatic pilot. Automatic pilot — a knee-jerk, unthinking response — is a product of unconsidered habit, routine, acceptance of conventional wisdom, and rejection of whatever disturbs the status quo.

CAN ANY OF THIS BE TAUGHT?

"If directors cannot tell the difference between a fake bit of behavior and a true bit of behavior, they have no business directing. It's not something that can be learned. You have to know the difference between truth and fiction. How do you teach somebody the difference? You can't. It's something intuitive, you just know it. It's called perception. Somebody is or isn't perceptive. That's all you have, as a director, the ability to recognize reality in behavior."

— Sydney Pollock

I can't disagree with the sentiments in Sydney Pollock's quote above. There are questions of taste and judgment that bear on filmmaking ability, that the individual himself must take responsibility for without waiting for any teacher to spoon-feed him the answers. But everyone does have intuitive powers, although they may be untapped or undeveloped. Our powers of "perception" and "intuition" can develop and grow, no matter how perfect or imperfect their current state. I think they are more likely to develop and grow if the individual is in an environment that is both challenging and supportive. And I think that any time they are *not* being challenged to grow and deepen, they are automatically doing the opposite — falling into atrophy or rigidity.

2 | THE FEELING LEVEL

> *"Of course I'm playing on emotions. What else should I play on? What else is there other than emotions? What is important? Only that."*
>
> — Krzysztof Keiślowski

Feelings are a huge concern for actors. There is almost nothing (except for physical appearance) that an actor agonizes about more than his feelings. The actor constantly worries, "Do I have the right emotion for the part? For the line? Do I have enough of it? Or too much?" Directors frequently compound the actors' anxieties with an approach to dramatic emotion that is perfunctory and result-oriented. Directors often have a superficial understanding of the character's emotional life, and a superficial understanding of the actor's emotional apparatus.

Directors need to be able to function in the presence of actors in such a way that allows the actors to keep their feelings alive, and at the same time allows the director to keep his own feelings alive. In the best case scenario the director connects to actors, connects to characters, and connects to his story ideas with a combination of imagination and feeling. You could call it "imagining at the feeling level."

The feeling level is the level at which connection, intuition, and all good work happens. The director, as well as the writer and all the actors, must find a personal emotional hook to the story. If the creators of the work have no genuine emotional connection to their material, the audience will not find any either. The script must communicate feeling to the actors and director; the director must communicate feeling to the actors; and actors must, in turn, communicate feeling to the audience.

RESPECT FOR FEELING
"Mr. Gittes… Don't tell me how I feel."

— Evelyn Mulwray, *Chinatown*

The director's relationships with the actors and with the characters are relationships of emotional intimacy. The director needs to feel everything that happens to the characters. Like an actor, a director should always work on a role until she finds something that touches her personally, that makes her feel something. But this is not the same as projecting your own feelings onto the character — or onto the actors. The best way to communicate feelings to actors and to the audience is to have respect for the feelings of actors and of characters.

For instance, in daily social interactions, no one appreciates being told by another what to feel. Telling someone what they should feel is a bad way to start a relationship. As soon as you tell someone what to feel you are implying that their actual feelings are wrong. It's like telling a friend, "You're too angry about this," or "You shouldn't be so hurt," or "I don't understand why you're so nervous; there's nothing to be nervous about." Such instructions can create alienation.

It is likewise dangerous for a director to tell an actor what to feel. Even though they are used to it — even though they may tell themselves what to feel — it's not a good thing. An actor who tells herself what to feel, who manipulates and tortures herself into having the "right" feelings — the feelings she thinks the character is *supposed* to have — invites alienation in her own being. She starts to watch herself, she gets "in her head," she intellectualizes her feelings.

INTELLECTUALIZED FEELING
Intellectualizing our feelings is something we do all the time. Such as when we tell someone "I am angry with you" without showing that anger. The expression of genuine feeling is often inconvenient in the "social" world where we work and play. So, early in life, we learn to make an instant little examination of each feeling and impulse to make sure it is socially appropriate. We learn to squelch it if it's not. Over time we create a social mask. It becomes habitual, an emotional armor that's eventually embedded in our bodies and manifested through body language. Soon we are "in our heads," or "not in touch with our feelings." Emotion becomes an idea rather than an experience.

For example, when a child suppresses anger toward his parents, his love for his parents becomes only partly an expression of genuine feeling. As he grows up, it becomes an *idea* of something he is supposed to feel. Living out of touch with feelings eventually causes a chronic condition where feelings are avoided, especially the unpleasant ones like fear, pain, and anger. Attitude replaces feeling. Depression (the suppression of the unpleasant feelings) becomes epidemic. Sound familiar? It's a description of modern life in our pop culture.

Actors are lucky — they get to have real feelings right in front of people. It's a perk of the job, but — here's the difficulty — it's also a requirement of the job. When an actor responds to pressure to feel a certain feeling, when she is operating out of an *idea* of a feeling instead of out of an authentic feeling, when her feelings become intellectualized, when she is "in her head," watching herself, controlling the result — her work suffers. Self-conscious, intellectualized acting is stiff and obvious — it lacks spontaneity, presence, and transparency.

Although we want actors to be spontaneous and impulsive, that doesn't mean we don't want them to be intelligent. It may sound like a contradiction to say that we want intelligence, but not intellectualization, from actors. The principle here is that a person's full intelligence comes from subconscious resources as well as, or even more than, from conscious reasoning. In order for an actor to have access to these unconscious resources, that is, the level of intelligence that is intuitive rather than intellectualized, his feeling level must be free and disobliged.

Even when playing a character who is out of touch with his feelings, the actor must not be out of touch with his own feelings. (Just as actors need to listen to each other even if the characters do not.) This extends to non-human characters such as robots, clones, vampires, and talking animals. Science fiction or animation succeeds only when the actions of non-human characters become a metaphor for human experience. All successful stories have a sense of event on the human level, whether these stories are naturalistic and full of feeling (as in the work of John Cassavetes) or highly stylized (Stanley Kubrick). In our modern popular culture, attitude has all but replaced feeling. However, audiences still long to return to their core — indeed, "returning to the core" is the theme of many important stories, from *Excalibur*, to *Blade Runner*, to *The Matrix*, to *King Lear*.

ACTORS' TOOLS WORK FOR DIRECTORS, TOO

For much of the rest of this chapter I'll be discussing some tools actors use to activate their inner emotional life. There are two reasons why directors should have intimate knowledge of these tools. One is to understand how actors' intuition works so the director can be a trusted guide in rehearsal and on the set. But the other is their own personal use — to enlist their own emotional life in their creative work.

"CATCHING A CORNER" OF EXPERIENCE

In *Blues for Mister Charlie*, by James Baldwin, a character speaks about the death of his son, a decent but flawed young man, at the hands of a white racist vigilante. Bringing the audience into the experience of this character is an awesome task, a sacred task. How dare we make some superficial guess into this character's emotional state? It would be like coming up to the person at the funeral service and saying, "I know how you feel," when really we couldn't possibly.

How does a filmmaker begin the work of bringing this character to life? An actor may begin by connecting to some experience of racism of his own. Or an experience of loss, or injustice, or moral chaos. I think of this as "catching a corner" of the character's experience. It's a personal metaphor, "the magic as if." The actor creates a metaphor for the character's experience from his own knowledge of life. By being personal and strictly honest with his connections, he respects the character. He also unleashes his unconscious. Paradoxically, by stripping himself emotionally to whatever element of the character's experience he can understand at the simplest, most primal level, he is most available to the author's deepest intent, which is also unconscious. He is also connected to what is universal about this character's story, and thus he makes the character's story available to the audience.

In the process, a choice is being made of what the scene is about. Above, I mentioned "racism," "loss," "injustice," and "moral chaos" as possible choices. Thinking about what the scene — or the moment — is about on this level of feeling is a way to understand characters without drawing an intellectualized emotional map of their psyches. The actor, responding to his personal images of, for instance, moral chaos, feels his own feelings with full commitment. At the same time he speaks the words of the script and performs its actions simply and without interior comment or explanation — even if the words are words he would never say, the actions things he would never do, the character's experience something he has never felt. This moment of paradox is the springboard to the imagination. It is the invitation to play. It is a moment when the actor is captured, almost shaman-like, in the shimmering territory between the real world and the imagined world. Actors describe it as a zone, an altered state, and it is the reason why they themselves may describe what they are doing as "feeling the character's feelings."

Directors and writers should go through this process, too, in order to begin imagining the characters' world and all the events that happen in it. That is, investigate each filmmaking choice via personal metaphor — making associations to the events and choices of the script with what one knows and has seen in life.

MICRO-MANAGING

The "catching a corner" approach is almost certain to cause the actor to have some emotion, or, more likely, a combination of emotions. But the emotion is a by-product, not the goal. Honesty is the goal. The combination of emotions might end up looking from the outside like a cup of grief, a half cup of outrage, a third cup of confusion, and a tablespoon of resignation. Or maybe a larger measure of outrage. Or of resignation. Or, perhaps, a soupcon of guilt.

Directors (or in television, writer-producers) often think it is their job to tinker with the actors' emotional lives as if they were cooks adjusting a recipe, or mechanics adjusting the timing of an automobile — in other words, to micro-manage the emotional result. Micro-managing actors' performances is what some think directing is all about — extracting an extra twinkle here, a more prolonged grimace there. These misguided directors waste time and wreak havoc with the actors' ability to be believable and present because they don't know the difference between "fine tuning" and "micro-managing." Fine tuning is fine; micro-managing the weight and tone of every move and utterance is a descent into hell.

WHY ACTORS SHOULDN'T TRY TO HAVE FEELINGS

1. *Honesty*. When actors push and manipulate themselves into rages and tears, the acting is self-indulgent, overacted, bogus. When they micro-manage their flickers of distaste, or anticipation, or anxiety, in order to be cute and quirky, the acting is boring, predictable — and bogus.

2. *Aesthetics*. We want actors' emotions to be clean, simple; to at least once in a while achieve purity, beauty; to bubble up like a mountain spring, or fall from the heavens like rain. Forced feelings are neurotic. It's not that an actor can't be neurotic. If an actor is playing a neurotic character, it's fine for him to use a substitution of his own *personal* neurosis as a way to stay authentic with the characterization. But forcing feeling is a distinctly *actor's* neurosis, not a personal neurosis — it makes the scene be "about" the actor instead of about the character.

3. *Power*. Once the actor does find genuine emotion, she may try to hold on to it. It's a bad idea to "hold onto" feelings because, well, humans can't do that. Feelings change if you hold on to them. This is especially true of the big emotions, such as rage, sorrow, and terror. In life, if you hold onto the big emotions, they lose their power, they become smaller emotions. If you hold on to rage it turns into resentment or spite; if you hold on to sorrow it turns into self-pity; if you hold on to terror it turns into anxiety.

4. *Storytelling.* If, when the actor does find an honest emotion, she thinks of that as her entire job she ends up "playing" that emotion instead of playing the relationship or the situation or the objective. This means she is not engaged with the other actors in the scene, and not engaged with the events of the script. When this happens, no matter how genuine the emotion, the scene won't work. She is making her emotion what the scene is about. This interferes with the director's ability to tell the story, which is not about the actors' feelings but about the characters' behavior. (The main difference between "playing the emotion" instead of playing the situation, the relationship or the objective, is that playing emotion, like playing attitude, playing tone, playing a rhythm, or playing a line reading, does not include the other actor in the scene. So, as always, *listening* is key.)

5. *Authenticity.* If an actor tries to have a feeling she won't look like the character who has that feeling, because the character isn't trying. If the actor lets herself have whatever feeling she has freely she will, oddly enough, look more like the character, even if it's the "wrong" emotion for the character, *just because she — like the character — is not trying!*

6. *Range.* Feelings can change if they are honest and free. By owning one's feelings, by letting oneself feel them with all their confusion and inconvenience, an actor can be most available to another feeling.

GIVE AWAY ALL YOUR SECRETS
"That's a great gift for the audience when the actors open themselves up."
— John Boorman

The opposite of trying to have feelings is not an absence of feeling. Rather than forcing certain feelings for a performance, actors should embrace those sentiments that come naturally — even if it's anxiety, boredom, or despair. Once an actor opens herself to accepting feelings, once she is free of obligation, then she is *emotionally available.* And her *choices* for the character can affect her. The other actor in the scene can affect her too, that is, she can *listen.* The very words of the text and physical movement of the action have more effect on her. And her private emotional life can then transform into an emotional life informed by the script. Even if the early hunches she actually feels are not "there" yet, not yet entirely fulfilling the script, she should let them live free, let them move through her body as energy. If she is free, then deeper associations to the images and circumstances of the script may bubble up and capture her.

Acting is a kind of confession. The worst thing an actor can do is hide her feelings, hide her secrets. There is a difference between *having* secrets and *hiding* them. It's good for an actor to have secrets, to make subtext choices that are personal — and to maintain privacy, to refrain from gossip with fellow actors about her character. But these secrets only work if she gives them away emotionally during the performance. The secrets should be so strong that the actor can't hide them.

Even if the actor makes the choice, or is directed to make a choice that the character is hiding his feelings, the actor should not hide his feelings. The actor can make a physical adjustment — forbid himself tears, or refrain from raising his voice. And he can trust the words. If the writer has written the words of a character who is hiding his feelings, the audience will get that.

Strangely enough, *not* hiding feelings makes a person more mysterious. Hiding, shutting down feeling and expression, is the norm in everyday life. When people are holding everything back, covering up their feelings, they're actually pretty easy to read — they're ordinary. When an actor gives away his secrets, lets his most private feelings show, he becomes unusual, fascinating, mysterious. Greta Garbo was quintessentially mysterious not because she hid her feelings but precisely because every emotional nuance flooded instantly across her face.

Letting every feeling show the way Garbo did is easier said than done. We don't always know what we really feel. I find I need to spend time figuring out my feelings. The real feelings are usually layers down — often I need to speak the superficial layers out loud in order to get to the deeper layers. Or I need to let them out, physically — to yell, or weep, or hit a pillow or a punching bag with my fists. Some acting coaches recommend therapy to actors whose feelings are stuck or frozen. I know that when I was studying, I always scheduled my therapy sessions for the morning after acting class!

Directors need an emotional connection equivalent to that of actors. At the end of making a movie a filmmaker should feel changed emotionally — and should feel, literally, as though *she has nothing left to hide*.

TURNING PSYCHOLOGY INTO BEHAVIOR

Genuine emotion is private, that is, unique to each individual. So how does a film director do his job of "standing in for the audience"? First, by working on his script analysis until he feels something. Second, by letting himself be an audience while he watches the actors work — he knows the work is good enough when it touches him as an audience. And finally, at all times during script analysis and work with the actors, he turns psychology into behavior.

Mike Nichols has said that he learned what directing is from Elia Kazan's definition: turning psychology into behavior. It is valuable, essential really, for directors, writers, and actors to be astute and tireless observers of the human animal, to possess a voracious fascination with what makes people tick, and have ideas about why people do the things they do. But in order to tell a story for the audience, such ideas about characters' psychology must be turned into behavior.

Danger lurks in the facile "psychological recipe," a formulaic approach that offers no real insight or personal understanding to a dramatic situation. Characters — like people — are not as logical as common psychological recipes make them out to be. Even if a character has a line explaining his psychology (e.g., "I think I must be masochistic," or, "I never learned how to love") the actor should find a subtext to the line. Such a subtext might be, "Maybe this is what she wants me to say before she will forgive me." But even a subtext of "God, I sound like a character in a mini-series" would be better than no subtext at all.

Nancy Marchand once spoke in an interview about the character Livia Soprano in the series *The Sopranos*: "I don't know that she has a master plan. I just think she loves to cause problems." Now, Livia's behavior (she's a very difficult person) surely has complex psychological roots. Maybe she didn't get enough attention as a child. Maybe she witnessed betrayal and lies in her home and determined the world was a dangerous place she needs to protect herself from. Maybe her mother was unable to protect herself against an abusive husband, and Livia became disgusted by such helpless behavior in a woman.

At the end of the first season, when Livia's son Tony goes so against her wishes as to move her to a retirement home, she actually gives her permission to a plan for his murder. From what psychology could such an action originate? *Sopranos* creator David Chase, in the same interview, called Livia's ability to wreak havoc "instinctive" and said that if you asked her whether she had tried to kill her son she would answer "no" because her tyranny allows her to see herself as a perennial victim. This is an insightful description of Livia's dysfunction. Marchand's genius was to translate that insight into the simple behavioral observation, "she loves to cause problems."

IF YOU DO IT, YOU WILL FEEL IT

Acting is very physical. I love my dictionary's definition of *emotion*: "A psychic and physical reaction subjectively experienced as strong feeling and physiologically involving changes that prepare the body for immediate vigorous action." And of course the root word of "emotion" is "motion."

If you start arguing with someone, say about the merits of a particular movie or politician, pretty quickly you will start to *feel* argumentative. You may not have felt argumentative at all prior to the argument; you may have felt quite reasonable; it is the *activity*, the *event* of arguing that made you feel something. This is the principle behind the use of objectives and intentions to create emotional life; it's why good acting, that is, acting that tells the story, should create believable emotional behavior (intention) rather than emotion for its own sake.

For instance, we want a love scene to have feeling, attraction that is not faked. Telling the actor to "be attracted" is not enough. An actor working himself up into an off-screen attraction in order to play a love scene is not such a great idea. Actual attraction between co-stars can backfire, because the demands and anxieties of courtship may distract the actors from the work.

The way to play a love scene if the actors aren't attracted to each other is by each one paying full attention to the other. Physical attraction is very physical, yes? It can be created — or the illusion of it, at least — if each actor gives the other one complete physical attention. The principle here is that everyone's eyes are beautiful if you look into them, everyone's skin is beautiful if you touch sensitively. And what if the opposite happens, and when you look closely at the other person's face, you only see the zits under the makeup? Then you have to look even closer, and look emotionally, as well as physically. Because, of course, attraction is emotional as well as physical. The more closely I look at those who initially put me off, the more I see their fears and vulnerability, or their hidden strengths, and the more beautiful they become to me.

When actors do become captured by a strong emotion, it's not enough for them to sit in front of the camera and show us that emotion; they must *do* something. They are still in a relationship with the other actor(s) in the scene, and the scene will only work, will only have an emotional event, if they are having an effect on each other. In other words, they must do something emotionally to each other. Just look at the difference, in real life, between weeping in a room alone and weeping when another person is present. When another person is present, a person (character) has an objective or need toward that person: perhaps to keep from exposing herself to him; or to get comfort from him; to give him permission to express his grief; possibly even to make him feel guilty or ashamed.

In order to help actors stay away from playing emotion for its own sake, it is helpful for directors to ask actors questions like, "What is happening to the character emotionally?" or "What is the character's response to what has happened?" instead of "How does the character feel?" This little shift in language creates a shift in perception that locates the thinking about the character's emotional life more specifically and physically, and more in terms of behavior.

SUBSTITUTION

"Substitution" is also called "the magic as if." It's a simple way to humanize the text, to endow or invest an object or image or character with life and emotional importance. As a technique, its usefulness is based on the principle that a remembered object or image will carry associations that create behavior. When the actor begins his work on a role, he should choose, as an inner substitution for every off-screen person the character refers to, a real person of his actual acquaintance. That is, hold an image of his own personal acquaintance in his mind rather than an image of a made-up person that he thinks the character is talking about. This will make him look more like the character, even if the person he has substituted is only a little bit like the person his character is talking about.

Substitution is used for the authenticity of a performance. When actors create the "idea" of the thing the character is talking about, e.g. the supermarket they think the character is shopping in, or the failure they think the character has experienced, they are not doing what the character is doing. The character is talking about an experience, or a supermarket, not an idea. So when the actor substitutes an experience or person of his own, he is closer to playing the character.

Substitution confers *choice* or interpretation. It is automatically specific because it is personal (it's sometimes called "personalizing" or "humanizing" the script). But it can also create emotional nuance and power, as well as comic or dramatic adjustment. Substitution of each of the persons, objects, and experiences that the character is referring to is to me the first thing an actor should do.

When I say "personal" I don't mean it always has to be someone you've met; it can be someone you feel you have a personal relationship with even without meeting him, such as a public figure. Say you are playing the role of Mark Antony eulogizing the slain Caesar in *Julius Caesar*, and from your script analysis you come up with three central facts about Caesar in relationship to Antony: 1) Caesar was Antony's personal friend; 2) Caesar was a public figure, emperor of Rome; 3) he was assassinated by people who say they believe he was evil.

You have numerous choices of how to substitute Caesar in your imagination. You can pick a personal friend or relative who has died. Or a public figure you admire deeply whom some people hate. Or a public figure who is universally admired. (Although this last adjustment is at variance with the facts, it could be Antony's belief that Caesar was universally loved, and assassinated by a lunatic fringe.) Or a personal friend — either deceased or living — who is flawed and difficult. Or, if your interpretation of Antony is that he is calculating his own political chances more than eulogizing his friend, you could even choose to substitute for Caesar someone, either public figure or personal acquaintance, whom you actually dislike. Each of these choices creates a different emotional "adjustment." The usual terminology is the "as if": as if Caesar is a personal friend; or, as if he is a man you admired, etc.

One great advantage to this technique for an actor is that when he is playing a character in very extreme circumstances, he doesn't have to torture himself into believing that those circumstances are happening to him. He can substitute some key element of the character's situation, and then let his imagination take over. The personal substitution gives an actor the safe place from which his imagination can take flight.

IT'S THE SAME FOR DIRECTORS
I've been talking about this as if I were talking to an actor, but directors and writers should do exactly this work as well. Mike Nichols calls it the "it's like when…" The writer, while writing, and the director, while preparing, should check every event and reference of the script against their personal experience and observation. For example, when the script involves a betrayal, the director (or writer) should ask himself, "When

have I been betrayed? What happened to me emotionally? What did I do in response?" And conversely, "When have I betrayed someone? What made me do that? What did I think I was doing? What did I want the other person to feel?"

In order to do this work honestly, you must have an interest in self-knowledge. It's hard work, but the payoff is high. You become intimate with the characters and you make the stories your own. This makes your connection to the script authentic and indestructible. For every question that comes up on the set, the director will have some response, or at least some feeling or impulse from which to fashion a response. Specifically, the director is also then prepared with "it's like when…" and "as if" adjustments to suggest to the actors.

Finally, substitution is a springboard to the imagination. It works as a function of concentration. When an actor (or director or writer) tries to think "like the character," there is an effort, a falseness because no one ever knows the innermost thoughts of another. Such concentration — on the "thoughts of the character" — is inherently incomplete. But concentration on one's own images and associations can be complete, because we ourselves know more about our own experiences than anyone else can. This concentration, because it is easy, simple and relaxed, is freeing. From this relaxed place the actor or director who is using this technique is available to the independent, imagined world that the writer has created — and the writer who uses it is available to the independent imagined world of his characters.

GOING THERE
"Once the cameras roll, this is real to me. There's a very dark room in everyone's mind, and when you go there, it's very ugly. I had to be in that room to do that scene."

— Chi McBride of *Boston Public*

"Bjork was not acting anything, she was feeling everything, and that made it extremely hard on herself and everyone else. It was like being with a dying person all the time, and I worked like a hangman, dragging her there. The work was extremely rewarding but extremely painful. As I see it now, it was the only way it could be done."

— Lars Von Trier
director of *Dancer in the Dark*

When the role — or story — is an emotionally challenging role, it's finally about "going there." The emotional place the creative storyteller "goes" must, as I have said, be a place that she knows something about from her own knowledge of life. Her "knowledge of life" includes her own experiences, but also experiences and behavior she has observed in others, *if such observations affected her emotionally*. The ability to adopt the experience of another as her own is a leap of empathic imagination. For instance, if an actor playing a character who has been raped has never been raped herself, but has a friend who has been raped, she can use her connection to her friend as a base for the characterization. This works best if the person you are using for this connection is someone you love, because it only works if your observations of this person affect you emotionally.

But some people can feel connection and even love for someone whose story they read in the newspaper. Some actors "go there" just from reading a script. Their imaginations are that susceptible. They have a great ability to be affected emotionally by events that they imagine. Stella Adler claimed that the ability to be affected emotionally by imagining the character's circumstances is the only skill of an actor, and that using personal memories to create the character's experience is a cheat. "Going there" seems very different from the "substitution" technique. But I'm not sure they are all that different. The artist who is creating an imagined character weaves back and forth between experience (memory) and imagination. The substitution technique is a "magic as if," a metaphor, that jump-starts the imagination — and since we are artists, we are allowed to use metaphor. An actor or director who "goes there" just from reading a script has made this personal metaphor spontaneously. It was accomplished at such lightening speed that he was not even aware of it.

SELF-KNOWLEDGE

There are certain emotional "places" that almost any person of sensitivity (and good actors are sensitive) can go. Loneliness is one that comes quickly to mind. We've all known loneliness. To suggest to an actor that a character is coming from a place of loneliness is not the same as micro-managing the emotional result. The reason why this is different is that confessing one's own loneliness puts one at emotional risk. Such risk protects one from falsity.

A good director of actors has an ability to observe, deduce, or intuit what other places a particular actor that he is working with can go naturally if she gives herself permission. Self-knowledge is helpful for a director wishing to develop this ability. Experiences of abandonment, being left-out, being trapped; guilt, humiliation, self-hatred; the fear of dying alone — are all *sources of feeling* for many characters. All collaborators in the storytelling process — directors, writers, as well as actors — need to have some idea of their own sources of feeling, the experiences that most affected them, the people they care most deeply about, the loss they have never gotten over, the knowledge or memory that makes them vulnerable — their soft spot. A person's deeply held beliefs are his source of feeling as well.

A director who refuses to admit his own fears and longings, his own mistakes and losses, his own sources of joy, and his own deeply held beliefs, is going to have a hard time working with actors when the script is asking them to go to emotional places.

"COURAGE, MON AMI!"

"People like Connie [cinematographer Conrad Hall] and Sam [Mendes] understand how difficult those moments [in very emotional scenes] can be. They create a bond. Once you've been through that kind of moment and been understood and supported, you feel such gratitude and intimacy with them."

— Annette Bening

No actor — no person, really — should ever be made to feel embarrassed or apologetic for having feelings. The best directors of actors can tolerate feeling in themselves, as well as in others. The best directors *communicate* feeling without telling the actors (or audience) what to feel. This means the director should not direct an actor to produce more of the feeling the director thinks should be in the scene. Instead she should, together with the actor, create some description of the emotional situation of the character — stripped-down to the most primal level — and allow the actor to find his own connection — personal or imaginative — to that emotional situation. Then, if the actor seems muted in his emotional expression, the director can invite the actor to let out more of the feelings he has. This is not the same as telling the actor to produce more of the feeling that "should be" in the scene.

SENSORY LIFE

The reason substitution works is that its stimulus for emotional and imaginative connection is sensory instead of intellectual. When an actor speaks about a car, or cat, or supermarket, or wife *of his own* while speaking the words of the character, sensory associations kick in without effort. The sounds, the colors and shapes, the smells, the textures, softness and roughness, etc., etc. This makes him believable. Sensory life gives a performance depth, as well as believability. When Jessica Lange was asked by a student during her *Inside the Actors Studio* interview a question about how she worked, she replied, "I make everything sensory."

There can be sensory memory of an actor's own experience, and there can be sensory research, into experience that the actor imagines. So that an actor who is playing a logger, but who is not, for insurance reasons, permitted to do his own climbing, might imagine sensorially what it would be like to be up in the tops of trees, the physical sensation of the breeze, the sound of the leaves, the faraway sounds of the people on the ground below, the sensation of your body in the harness.

And, during his preparation, the director should imagine this, as well. In preparation for some recent war movies (*Platoon*, *Saving Private Ryan*, *The Thin Red Line*) the actors have gone though boot camp themselves. But actors — as well as the director and writer — who have never been in combat should also take themselves through private sensory images of what it would really look, sound, smell, taste, and feel like to experience bullets and bombs exploding around you, or be a few feet away from a personal friend who is wounded and dying.

Does this mean that the actor who is playing a rape survivor and who has never experienced rape needs to imagine the rape with all the sensory detail of an actual memory? I don't know. She might need only to catch a corner of it. But physical (sensory) detail would be a place to go if she felt she was losing her concentration All imagining should be sensory. Once an actor, director, or writer commits to imagining sensorially, the imagination becomes indestructible. Whether we are playing, or writing, or telling (directing) the story of, say, a caveman, or an alien, or a president, or a housewife, authenticity is achieved through imagining the sensory details of that life.

In modern life we shut out a lot of sensory experience, probably because so much of it is unpleasant — car horns and so forth. We even deprive ourselves of pleasurable sensory moments (such as stopping to smell the roses or playing with our children) because we're so damned busy. An actor gets to let in sensory life; this is yet another way that the imagined world is a genuine, yet *heightened*, version of the real world. And a way that an actor is allowed — and required — to have simpler, freer, less intellectualized emotions than those of the real world.

IT'S ALL "AS IF"

Of course it's all *as if*. As filmmakers, we are not hoping that the audience believes that the actor James Caan actually dies during *The Godfather*, or that his actual feet were chopped off in *Misery*; we only want our audience to suspend their disbelief and care about the story and the characters. It's an imagined reality. In the moment, it is real, an experience rather than an idea of emotion. When the actors *listen* and play off each other, the feeling of the scene becomes a simple and powerful exchange of energy. It may actually feel good even if the emotions of the scene are painful. Besides the exhilaration of the "zone," the opportunity for intimacy and connection without social consequences is another powerful draw of the acting profession.

Actors are commonly thought of as more neurotic than the general population, but Susan Sarandon has said that she thinks acting makes her *less* neurotic. Meryl Streep has said that, "to be an actor is to want to visit those [dangerous] places, use it as therapy, to exorcise things that in my real life I would never want to deal with." Because actors can act out their inner conflicts openly in the imagined world, they may not need to act them out covertly in the real world, as most people do. Angelica Huston said of working again with Jack Nicholson (in *The Crossing Guard*) a few years after the break-up of their love affair, "There was residual stuff from the relationship I felt could be potent. Why fester with that when you can get it out?" Kevin Spacey says, "I think we're healthier than a lot of people; at least we have an outlet, at least we're able to examine stuff and go to places that most people don't have an outlet to do."

Sometimes I think the only directors who really get along with actors are the ones who embrace their own irrational and erratic depths, as actors do. Surely those are the only directors who can empathize with actors — or with characters.

3 | IMAGINATION AND ORIGINALITY

"When you go see a film, after about 10 minutes, you know whether there's a vision there, an intelligence at work."
— John Boorman

"You need to find an idea you fall in love with. You can't do something just to be different."
— David Lynch

"Do I have an original thought in my head?"
— Charlie Kaufman
Adaptation

INSIGHT, IDEAS, AND ENTERTAINMENT

In addition to an emotional hook, a filmmaker needs an idea — a genuine idea — an insight to communicate. In essence, something to say. The idea should be about the human condition rather than merely a "movie" concept. That is, it should be something the film's creator actually believes and cares about, something he knows from his experience and understanding of life. *You cannot make a good movie if you don't believe in what the movie is about.*

Actually, creative filmmakers need ideas in two areas. First, there's the movie's theme or what Lajos Egri (*The Art of Dramatic Writing*) calls its premise — Sidney Lumet calls it "what the movie is about." It is an *insight* into the human condition. This central insight/premise/theme — however you choose to describe it — need not be original. Indeed, it's very unlikely that there are any totally new story ideas left under the sun. So, to make it an "original" story, the central insight must be so strong and personal to you that you *feel* as if you are the first person to have discovered it.

The premise of *Some Like It Hot*, for instance — which I would describe as "there is nothing in the world more foolish than men and women looking for love" — has been used many times. In fact, many wonderful writers — including Shakespeare, Moliere, Preston Sturges — have explored this idea. The reason it's such a workable premise for a play or movie is that everyone knows it is true.

But the reason why *Some Like It Hot* is still fresh, even after 40 years, has a great deal to do with the passionate belief that writer-director Billy Wilder had in that insight. The movie holds up because of

Wilder's certainty — you could call it cockiness — that what he knows about this subject is something that nobody else knows in quite the way that he does. That is the difference between genuine originality and the churning out of films whose only claim to "newness" is their shock value.

There is no substitute for insight and truth. The central truths that make good movies may have to do with observations of human behavior, as in *Some Like It Hot*. A different kind of premise is found in *The Sixth Sense*. Rather than based on an observation of behavior, it's based on insight into human longings and fears. I would say the premise of *The Sixth Sense* is this: the dead can help us and we can help them.

This statement may or may not be true. But the human desire to believe it true is probably universal. M. Night Shyamalan's sensitivity to the bottomless longing of human beings to understand and conquer the horror of death led him to a story of how the living and dead might contact and comfort each other.

Festen (the Danish *Dogme 95* film known in the U.S. as *The Celebration*, and declared by Steven Spielberg to be among his favorite movies of 1998) has a premise that could be equally at home in soap opera as it is in a European art-house movie. In a nutshell: victims of incest pay the emotional costs for the rest of their lives. What distinguishes *Festen* from soap opera is that the filmmakers' commitment to the premise is honest, hard-won, and deeply felt. *Festen* is also distinguished from soap opera by its storytelling methods.

ORIGINAL STORYTELLING

The second area in which you need good ideas is the way the story is told. This covers myriad decisions having to do with, for example, the character-izations; the content and structure of individual scenes and their situations; the structuring of the events of the whole story; the filmmaking style. "Original" storytelling involves some or all of these elements:

1. The characters' behavior and dialogue are human and finely observed;
2. The situations of individual scenes are imaginatively conceived, recognizably human, and full of idiosyncratic detail;
3. The events of the whole story are structured so as to be surprising and yet inevitable;
4. The filmic style derives its visual technique organically from the content.

All the cool and interesting stuff that you want to put in your movie — whether it's a mind-blowing plot twist or a bit of funny dialogue or a certain visual effect — must be driven by the story. In other words, your individual ideas must be connected to the central idea of what the story is about. For instance, you might get an idea to start a movie with a scene of a character in a car going through a car wash while talking on his mobile phone. But if the phone scene has no connection to the story or to developing a character, it is worthless.

The movie *The Sweet Hereafter* begins with such a scene, but the filmmaker has put the character's conversation with his estranged daughter in the car wash for a storytelling reason — in order to help us feel his emotional event, which is his experience of loneliness and dislocation. And that event has a deep connection to the theme or premise of the movie — that child abandonment can come in many forms and leads to deep suffering for the parent, as well as the child.

THE WORK OF IMAGINATION
"I just imagine that there is such an idiot as Osgood Fairchild. That there is such an old fool. Then I proceed."
— Billy Wilder

An "original" storytelling idea or technique is not merely one that has never been used before. Our "ideas" come from our observations of the world around us, and from our own inner stream of consciousness. Original ideas come out of high quality observations. How does one make one's observations higher quality? For one thing, by making them personal — unique, idiosyncratic — something you see that others don't. For another, by being as accurate and truthful as possible with your observations — whether you are observing the world around you, or contemplating your own thoughts and associations. And last but not least, by putting your concentration on the uniqueness of the thing you are seeing.

Directors and writers too often do not fully and deeply imagine the stories they are telling. Frequently they are satisfied with ideas that are rather ordinary and superficial. I often find myself telling the ones I consult with that I want them to work harder at the imagining of the story.

"Active" imagining is different from an idle fantasy. An elementary illustration of the difference might be found when looking through a fashion catalogue. I see a beautiful dress on a model, and imagine myself looking like the model. That's an idle fantasy (an outcome, by the way, the advertisers are hoping for). It's different from imagining myself in the dress — which is more work. I mean, literally, it takes more time and effort to imagine the dress on me than to succumb to the instantly gratifying fantasy of imagining that in this dress I will look like the model. Doing the work of actually imagining how I would look in the dress is what I call active imagining, or internal imagining, or deep imagining, or the imagining of an expert storyteller. I also call it real imagining, or honest imagining.

Besides being more work, real imagining carries more risk of short-term disappointment. But it carries less risk of long-term self-deception. Imagining that I'm the great-looking model in the great-looking dress enables me to feel, in the short term, self-congratulatory about how great I'm going to look when the dress arrives. Once it does arrive and I try it on, I must face my self-deception. If, on the other hand, I do the work of imagining the dress on me, and being honest about its prospects, the picture in my mind might make me give the dress a thumbs down. Then I must do the work of selecting another dress to imagine, be honest about, etc. This is a very elementary example of how one *tests ideas*.

Story imagination — letting yourself actively imagine, feel, and have a vision of the story — is different from succumbing to an idle fantasy of your movie in the "moviola of your mind." It's an interior imagination — imagining the experiences of the story, imagining what it would be like if these circumstances and events happened to *people*. The interior imagining of the story has a relationship to the "exterior" or visual imagining — a filmmaker's all-important "eye" for locations, scenery, camera angles, and optical illusion. For me, the interior imagining always comes first — I don't get even the most preliminary ideas for a story's visuals until I have completely imagined the subtext of the characters' lives. But for most people who are drawn to filmmaking it's the opposite — the visual imagining of the story comes first. And often they don't get around to the "interior" imagining at all. It is this rich and fascinating world of interior imagining that I hope to entice you into, and make you feel at home in.

This interior imagining is what I've been calling "improvising in the mind." When you let the characters of the story improvise in your mind, you let them go, you let them have free will, and you let them have an independent subconscious life. You trust them. The rewards of working this way are tremendous — you'll have an imagination that is independent and indestructible. The demands are also great — a surrender of ego, a commitment to value self-knowledge over self-congratulation, and a lot of work. The process is liberating and exhausting at the same time.

IMAGINATION AND FEELING
"Why dramatize something that means a little bit to you?"
— Alec Baldwin

Imagination and feeling are intimately tied together. The writer or director who imagines honestly keeps doing the work of imagining and testing and thinking until he gets to the level where he *feels* something — that is, something more primal than self-congratulation or self-pity. In order to do work that is more than superficial, you need to work hard enough emotionally, intellectually, and spiritually so that you are actually changed by the work. We've all heard the directive to "write what you know," but writing [or directing, or acting] "what you know" doesn't just mean *what you already know* — it means what you *come to know* by doing the project, what you learn about life and about yourself and about the people you are working with, through doing the work.

Many of the best scripts touch in some central way on mortality. The movie *Groundhog Day*, for example, which appears on the surface to be a wacky romantic comedy, is really about death; it's also about learning, risk, and intimacy. Its premise is a spiritual precept: In order to make any real change in his life, a man must die to himself.

The ingenious device of the script is that a single day in the life of Phil (played by Bill Murray) is played over and over, and that his participation in the events of that single day has consequence for his inner being, but no consequences in the world. This leads him to acts of greater and greater recklessness, beginning with more daring expressions of the rudeness and selfishness he is already known for, progressing to criminal deeds (robbery), and finally to taking his own life (running his car off a cliff) day after day.

Phil has a death wish! His meanness and selfishness are a mask for his deeper self-hatred. But Phil, now isolated from the realities of the people around him, is forced into reflection on the consequences of his acts. He is also forced to examine the same people, places, and events, day after day, until he finally sees past their surface and enters engagement with them. He learns intimacy, and finds self-worth. The script's central device (the same day repeating over and over) gives a fanciful setting to the human truth that real change *takes time*. Phil's conversion into a person who is capable of intimacy and engagement is therefore not unearned and sentimental — it is hard-won and emotionally satisfying.

In order for such a story to work, all the filmmaking participants (director, writer, actors) should consider, on whatever level they can muster, their own mortality, their fear of death, fear of risk and change, their belief or lack of belief in the power of learning, their own intimacy issues — and their own self-hatred. They should investigate these issues until they feel something. Those feelings — whether fear, or shame, or gratitude, or a mixture of those and other feelings — are bound to be very private and personal for each of them.

It used to amaze me that people would complain about the television show *Northern Exposure* that too many episodes featured death. They were missing the point. The show was *about* death — or at any rate, about living with mortality. Unlike *Gilligan's Island* or *Hogan's Heros*, which also featured extreme locations, *Northern Exposure* used the severity and isolation of the location to put its characters into daily confrontation with life and death. Although it featured charmingly wacky characters, it was not *about* a bunch of wacky characters — it was about living with mortality.

The Ice Storm, too, came under criticism because the death of the boy was called too much of a downer for a story about the mores of the '70s. Again, the point was missed. *The Ice Storm* was not *about* the mores of the '70s. It was about the death of a boy — a sudden, random, incomprehensible, unimaginable loss — and all the moments of pettiness, cruelty, foolishness, self-destruction, exploration, and once in a while kindness, that happened to be going on in the lives that would be touched by that loss.

MIKE LEIGH
"Everything is up for grabs if you see it three-dimensionally, and from all possible perspectives, and are motivated by some kind of feeling about it."
— Mike Leigh

Sometimes filmmakers tell me they want to make a film "like Mike Leigh," allowing the actors to improvise the dialogue and situations. I always fear that they expect this approach will be some kind of short-cut to writing a script. I know they will be disappointed. I don't know if there are other filmmakers who have the guts, audacity, charisma — and *skill* — necessary for his difficult and demanding process. Not to mention willingness to spend the amount of time that Leigh does on preparing a project. (Well, John Cassavetes, of course.)

Mike Leigh's method — which he refers to as a way of "assembling the raw materials" with which to make a movie — is in no way a short-cut.

And it's not a way to make a movie, anyway — it's a way to *prepare* to make a movie. Leigh developed his method during years in theater, first as an actor, then during the preparation, as writer-director, of numerous plays. He claims that he always thought of his work in theater as a route to filmmaking — that he was using it to learn how to work with actors and how to create a character and a story. And, along the way, he was creating his preparation process — all so that he could make movies.

One thing I love about Leigh (besides the movies themselves) is that his method is his aesthetic. He says his impulse to make movies came in a life drawing class at art school. "Suddenly I had this clairvoyant flash. I realized that what I was experiencing as an art student was that *working from source* and looking at something that actually existed and excited you was the key to making a work of art." By "working from source" he means modeling all created characters on real people. Both his process and his subject matter are an obsessive fascination with real life and real people. As I understand his process, from my reading in interviews and books, he first chooses a general topic (in the case of *Secrets and Lies*, adoption) and the actors he wants to work with. He then spends hours and hours over a period of two or three months, conferring with each actor privately, one-on-one. He has her make lists of people in her life who interest her somehow, whether she knows them well or not. He questions her minutely on what these people (from the list) are like — and what they *might* be like, what might be going on in their lives and histories that are not apparent to the eye. He offers his own thoughts and associations, as well.

At some point, Leigh chooses one of the characters the actor has been discussing and thinking about, and tells her to focus on that person/character and make it her own. Then, more work to flesh out the chosen character with greater and greater detail. This work is done not only with discussion, but with spending time living as the character — shopping, for instance — in effect, one-person improvisations. This "research" doesn't necessarily get into the filmed story, but it gets into the subtext, giving the performances texture and authority. Only after a certain amount of this work does Leigh begin to arrange improvisations with more than one actor. Actors are strictly forbidden to discuss anything about the project with each other. The goal is to "convert imaginative impulses into practical performances."

This whole process derives from his aesthetic and theme, which is that he wants to show characters expressing themselves in the world, in interaction with others. He works as hard and long as he does with each actor so that each character can be an utterly unique individual. The stories are about the characters' connectedness. The realization of his theme — the importance of connectedness — depends precisely on creating each character's unique, separate, lonely reality.

I'm not actually telling you all this in order to instruct you in how to do it yourselves. Leigh himself has said that although "in the early days, I would tend to proselytize about [my methods], what I actually, specifically do is so idiosyncratic that I suspect it is exclusively useful to me." But there are elements of his process that are fascinating glimpses into the imaginative process itself.

Katrin Cartlidge, who worked with Leigh on a number of projects, said: "I could create an entire history for Lady Macbeth and nobody would ever be the wiser. [My] responsibility is far greater [when working with Leigh]. I'm being invited by Mike to use every ounce of my creative and imaginative soul to provide the fabric that goes into the making of this film." I don't think all she meant here is that if she played Lady Macbeth she wouldn't get to write the lines. When Cartlidge spoke of creating a "history" for Lady Macbeth, I believe she was talking about a process some actors use of answering a list of questions in order to give their characters a "backstory," such as questions about the character's educational and family background and experiences. Filling in the answers to such a list can easily be pointless because it is often merely an intellectual exercise, an effort to come up with something "interesting" or "new." I believe that Cartlidge was saying that through working with Leigh she had complete freedom to base her choices not on what might be interesting or new, but on what she saw in life as truthful, simple, and important.

Leigh's work is an elongated and detailed version of "active imagining." With whatever amount of time you have, this is what every writer, actor, and director should do with every character — use every ounce of one's creative and imaginative soul to provide the fabric of an imagined world.

THE IMAGINED WORLD

In Sydney Pollock's documentary on the work of Sanford Meisner, there is a clip of Meisner saying, "It's all imagination. Do you think Hamlet was *real?*" Meaning that of course he wasn't. I felt funny when I heard this, almost like a child being told there is no Santa Claus, because on some level Hamlet (the character) is real to me. Not as real as the people I see and touch and talk to every day, but as real as people I no longer see or who have died, and whom I can now only visit in my imagination.

The imagined world is as fragile as memory, and as strong. The imagination is independent and idiosyncratic — personal. It chooses its own path, regardless of the demographic it is asked to appease. In order to create, under imaginary circumstances, not an intellectualized idea of an event, but an actual event; not an idea of a relationship, but an actual relationship; not an idea of a person, but an actual person, you need to *take seriously* the willfulness of your — and others' — imaginations.

The size of a person's imagination has to do with its depth of emotional detail — not with how extreme or exotic it is. It doesn't matter whether you are letting your imagination create a "galaxy far, far away" (*Star Wars*) or whether you locate your ten-episode mini-series around the lives of people in one apartment complex (Krzysztof Keiślowski's *Decalogue*).

IMAGINATIVE TRUTH

"Suddenly, there were people — Hamlet, Nick Bottom — who were like me, who had been shamed worse that I had ever been shamed. Suddenly I could create a context for my life through characters."
— Liev Schreiber

In a scene from *Midnight Cowboy* Joe Buck is eating a meal prepared by Ratso Rizzo. Ratso says, "Eat it while it's hot. Hot it ain't bad." Joe replies, "Smells worse hot 'n it did cold." I've used this scene in class a number of times, and always assumed that the subject of this exchange was Ratso's cooking skills. But one evening, on the umpteenth time I'd heard the line, I suddenly realized that Joe and Ratso are eating dog food. I am now as certain that they are eating dog food as if I had asked the writer — or *as if I had actually been there.*

This is an idea of mine that, for me, has attained the level of imaginative truth. If I am an actor playing one of the roles, it wouldn't matter what the director said to me about the scene, or what the property master has put on the plate, it would always — secretly, privately — be dog food. If I am the director, no matter what adjustment the actors privately make to the line, in my mind I will be telling the story of two men who share a meal of dog food. This is my private imaginative truth that allows me to let these — and many other — characters *live* in my imagination.

You must always tell a true story. It can be imaginatively true rather than literally true. When I am rehearsing actors I often ask them to improvise scenes, as well as situations around the written scenes. I do this because improvisation gives me access to an actor's unconscious, and I find that most people have deeper intelligence and better ideas in their unconscious minds than in their conscious minds. Improvisation is a source of imaginative truth.

So, of course, is life. I treat everything I have seen or experienced, or learned from newspapers and documentaries, as well as stories I have witnessed or been told — as a source of metaphor for the imagined truths I find in scripts. Art is also a source of imaginative truth. The deep artists can always be counted on as a source of imaginative truth — anything that I have learned from reading Shakespeare I know is true. The following chapter will take us into some of these sources of imaginative truth.

4 | SOURCES OF IMAGINATION AND INTUITION

"I am open to what is irrational. I open doors to intuition, because rationality is really death. Nothing that happens makes sense anyway."

— Jeanne Moreau

"... A certain psychological state where you're not forcing things to happen, and what comes out of you, or your subconscious, can be very informative about what you really believe."

— Alan Ball

THE UNCONSCIOUS MIND

"Your best work is the result of your unconscious. It knows how to make its points to you, so coax it out."

— Mike Nichols

"Acting is a science, but one in which the unconscious does the homework."
— Sam Rockwell

I trust the unconscious mind more than the conscious. Sometimes I think our psychic and imaginative resources are like a compost bin — the good stuff is down at the bottom. When I am gardening I use a pitchfork to turn over the compost, to aerate it, to bring the rich, composted material to the top. In order to thrive as creative people, we need, in the same way, to turn over and aerate our unconscious resources. This makes the "good stuff" in our subconscious more accessible in our artistic pursuits.

At times, I have been told I have a good imagination and above-average intuitive skills. This always surprises me, because I have never tried to be either imaginative or intuitive. I have had a lifelong goal to see and think clearly — but only for my own pleasure and peace of mind. Along the way I seem to have cultivated certain habits that enable me to trust — and enjoy — my imagination and intuition. There are simple things anyone can do to ignite the creative process. In fact, as children most of us engaged in these activities quite naturally. Only as adults, when forced to "grow up," do most of us abandon the skills that let us run free with ideas.

I've made of list of a few ways we can loosen up and jump-start the imagination. The remainder of this chapter delves into these simple concepts and offers examples of each. There are even daily exercises one can do to limber up the creative thinking process. Here goes:

Let your mind make free associations.

Acknowledge pain.

Turn off the automatic pilot.

Ask questions.

Give yourself inner permission.

Observe. Empathize. Don't pass judgment.

Remember and Recapitulate.

Tell stories.

Take time to think and daydream.

Listen radically.

Give yourself the freedom to do it "wrong."

Steal from everyone.

Don't run away from resistances.

Improvise in your mind.

Think out loud. Read out loud.

Never stop learning.

Spend time with art, nature, children.

Surround yourself with people who have feelings.

Acknowledge mortality.

Take responsibility for your obsessions.

Test your ideas.

Don't stop until you come up with something.

Follow impulses.

Tell the truth. Life is too short to lie.

FREE ASSOCIATIONS

"We all have in our conscious and unconscious minds a great vocabulary of images, and I think all human communication is based on these images, as are our dreams."

— Tennessee Williams

The root word of "imagination" is "image." And the activity of imagining is a making of associations. A person who sees a cloud and is reminded of a butterfly — or who smells a flower and is reminded of one of the deities of ancient Rome — or who hears a firecracker and wonders if a Mafia hit is occurring next door — is known as an imaginative person. The world of free associations *is* the world of the unconscious.

It's a given conventional wisdom that children have better imaginations than adults. Why should this be? It's because children don't have as well developed a social mask as adults, so they express their free associations spontaneously; they don't self-censor them. But adults, who have lived longer and have had more life experiences, have far more images loaded into their emotional storage banks — it stands to reason that the longer we live, the greater the detail and range our imaginations ought to have.

The free, uncensored making of associations is a right-brain activity. It's a permission to be easily distracted, like a child. Adults who are easily distracted on an artistic level are easily *captured* by an imaginative spark. The best writing is full of images — not inserted mechanically, to show off or be clever — but because the writer free-associates naturally with images. The best directors are able to express their ideas (the conceptual, or left-brain part of their thinking) via images and associations (which are right-brain tools). This helps them act as a link between the writer and actor, both of whom use images in a more subconscious, "right-brain" way than most people.

Lots of good directors — as well as other intelligent people — free-associate vigorously and spontaneously. A *New Yorker* profile of Martin Scorsese, for example, described an interview with him as an exercise in free association. Scorsese has wide-ranging interests and an encyclopedic knowledge — and the ability to hop from subject to subject, perceiving an association from one to another that the average person might not.

The use of images and associations and stories is an excellent way to give direction to an actor on the set. It is also a way for a director to "talk good," to speak eloquently and passionately about the project. "Talking good" is necessary to get actors, as well as producers and designers, to want to commit to your project. It's also necessary to get and keep them "on the same page" with you during preparation and shooting.

Free-association has many practical purposes for the artist. Bob Dylan said of his writing, in particular the song "Highlands" on the *Time Out of Mind* album, "It starts off as a stream of consciousness thing and you add things to it. I take things from all parts of life and then I see if there is a connection, and if there's connection I connect them. I learned a long time ago to trust my intuition."

You can expand your ability to free-associate with exercises on your own. One practical purpose of this is to prepare you for script analysis, because one of the activities of script analysis is to see metaphors and make connections with the images of the script. Let's just start with a word. Randomly, the first word that comes into my head. Okay, "butterfly." (I guess I thought of it because I mentioned it a few paragraphs ago.) Make your own free-associations — as long a list as you can — before reading on.

I'll start. Butterfly — social butterfly — Paris Hilton — Gloria Vanderbilt — the role of Mrs. Cornelius Vanderbilt, which I once performed in a play — the play was called *The Tennis Game* — another actress in the production was Sigrid Wurschmidt, who died in her 40s of ovarian cancer — my dear friend Marcia who died in her 40s of breast cancer — the little trailer she lived in when I visited her during her last months in Oregon — the jewelry she gave me... Okay, back to butterfly — Madame Butterfly — opera — Japanese — love betrayed — a Japanese man I once dated — he was a police officer — the diner I worked in where I met him... Again, butterfly — butterfly nets — the one I had when I was a little girl — butterflies caught and killed and mounted in a collection — a butterfly caught in my hands when I was a child — the sensation of wings beating against my palms — I held it against my cheek... Moth — catching a moth with my hands to take it out of the house — the moth dust left on my hands — moths around a kerosene lamp at a campground — sound of crickets — the night sky... Killing a moth with a paper towel — killing other insects — the first time I saw a water bug (a large cockroach) in my New York apartment in the '60s — the '60s! (no telling how many pages of free-association I could write if I started down that road)... Watching a child chase and play with a butterfly — watching a child chase bubbles — enjoying waving the bubble wand for the child, then getting bored when the child didn't want me to stop.

It feels strange to have put that in print — almost as though I've told you too much about myself. I surprised myself with how many of my associations took me into the past, even my childhood, or to confessions of loss. This is what I mean about the emotional cost of our work — it's a willingness to expose ourselves, in order to come up with the raw material that can be shaped to make a story.

Here are some other words you might use in a free-association exercise. Rain. Desert. Lipstick. Blood. Home. Animal. Fingernail. Scar. Sacrifice.

ACKNOWLEDGE PAIN AND EMOTIONAL COST

"I'm not sure it's not better to suffer than not to suffer. I think that in order to really care about yourself, and particularly someone else, you've got to experience suffering and really understand what it is to suffer, so that you hurt and understand what it is to hurt."

— Krzysztof Keiślowski

"[Aspiring filmmakers] should fall in love very deeply, preferably with someone it is never going to work out with, because you will have endless inspiration. You will be open so wide you will be a wound and you can't help but make good stuff."

— Alison Anders

"I don't think anybody is interesting to look at or to listen to unless they've had their heart broken, you know? Especially funny people."

— Jim Carrey

Another term for free association is stream of consciousness. Stream of consciousness is a way into one's truth. Except for when it isn't. Why is it boring to listen to some people's stream of consciousness, to be cornered in a conversation with someone recounting the endless inconsequential details and observations of her life — but entertaining when Robin Williams or Dennis Miller does essentially the same thing, that is, treat us to his stream of consciousness?

The people who are what we call "boring" are using their chatter in order to *hide*; the people who are entertaining are using their chatter in order to *reveal*. What, specifically, are they revealing? Their embarrassing secrets. Their pain.

Our pain is often the truest part of ourselves. Unless we are willing to reveal our pain, our loneliness, our humiliation, we are not really revealing anything of ourselves. Actors, writers, and directors all must be able to speak from their pain. In order to operate at the feeling level you must be able to feel. Unless you're willing to feel painful emotions, you can't really feel anything. Chris Cooper says of raising a disabled child, and spending every day with his triumphs and problems, "Jesse has fueled the characters I've played. He's filled my emotional life."

In order to bring feeling into their work, writers, directors, and actors must be honest about the emotional cost of the characters' actions. A reason for the success of *The Sixth Sense* is its honesty about the emotional cost that would surely occur if we achieved that contact between the living and the dead we so desperately wish for.

Now, don't get me wrong. Playfulness is just as important, just as deep and potent a resource as pain. It's also as hidden, because our true, natural playfulness is often steamrollered by a frenetic seeking of distraction from pain. The ability to be genuinely, un-self-consciously playful is intimately linked to the ability to allow oneself to acknowledge pain.

TURN OFF THE AUTOMATIC PILOT
Bob Dylan has said about his songwriting, "You strip things away until you get at the core of something important." Stripping away means that you question and revise a lot. But you need a reliable and productive *habit* of stripping away. If you're not used to it, you can easily get confused between stripping away — which is good — and second-guessing and over-intellectualizing — which will only paralyze and deaden you.

Automatic pilot — a/l a the comfort zone — takes several forms. Sometimes it's a lapse into routine or laziness. Sometimes it's just not knowing any better, because of having been exposed to mentors and colleagues who think mechanically and conventionally. Sometimes it's fear — either fear of "doing it wrong" if you don't follow conventional wisdom — or fear that if you work really hard at something and it still is no good, that will finally *prove* that you have no talent.

The way that actors can override the automatic pilot of "doing it right" is by over-identifying with their character, by allowing themselves to deeply feel and trust that their own impulses are the character's impulses. This is also true for writers and directors.

Many people in the entertainment industry read scripts on autopilot. We have been stuffed with images and expectations from popular culture. We have become stuck in our own ruts. Often we don't see something new even if it is right in front of us — we only *see* what we have seen before. Both script analysis and rehearsal are impossible unless one looks at everything with new eyes.

ASK QUESTIONS
The activity of thinking is an activity of questioning. You get an idea and let yourself question it. What are its ramifications? What is its basis in what I know as truth? How does it explain or contradict my experience?

What is its opposite, and what information or ideas do I get from considering its opposite? The activity of questioning and thinking will automatically bring us to looking at opposites. "Opposites" are "the other guy's point of view." In order to free yourself from being satisfied with what you think you believe, and instead discover what you really believe, keep questioning and always look for "the other guy's point of view."

When an "imaginative" person overhears a couple arguing in a restaurant, he can't stop his mind from asking such questions as: Are they breaking off an engagement? How did they meet? Have the invitations already been sent? Do they care about each other in any genuine way at all? What else do they argue about? What do they talk about when they're not arguing? Who holds the power in the relationship? What is their *story*?

A student told me about an animated film he once saw, in which two people pass each other on the street — they call out, "Hi, how ya doin'?" "Fine." Then one of them turns around, runs back and, taking the other by the collar, says, "Wait a minute! I want to know everything about you!"

The exercise here is to conduct interviews with people. Find out everything about them. What makes them tick? Why do they do what they do? To begin, make up your list of questions. Figure out what you want to know. Such as: What makes you laugh? What was the favorite job you ever had, and why? Which one of your parents are you most like? What is your strongest childhood memory? What did you think your grown-up life would be like when you were a child? What's the stupidest thing you ever did? What's the most painful thing that has ever happened to you? What makes you fall in love with another person? Have you ever hit someone? Did you ever want to? The process of questioning is like peeling the layers of an onion, with each new layer revealing new information about the person. Some of this will be information you could have intuited about that person. But a whole lot of it will be stuff you would never know unless you ask.

INNER PERMISSION

Then, ask questions of the characters in the script. The questions are more important than the answers. Ask questions of the characters rather than of the writer. I was present when Gerald MacRainey related a story about an accidental meeting, when he was a young actor, with Tennessee Williams in a New Orleans café — at the same time that MacRainey happened to be rehearsing to play Stanley in a production of *Streetcar Named Desire*! MacRainey got up the courage to start a conversation, and finally blurted out,

"I'm working on Stanley, and I wanted to ask you, what's his motivation in…" a certain scene the actor was having trouble with. Mr. Williams appeared amused, causing MacRainey to quickly apologize for asking such a stupid question. "Oh no," said Mr. Williams. "The question isn't stupid. It's just that you're asking the wrong person — I'm not playing the part!" MacRainey said that from the moment this great writer gave him such permission to make the role his own, he never lost his own inner permission again.

BE OBSESSED WITH OBSERVING PEOPLE
"Stare. It is the way to educate your eye, and more. Stare, pry, listen, eavesdrop. Die knowing something. You are not here long."
— Walker Evans

Never be bored by anything a human being does. Sean Penn has observed that an actor is a kind of journalist — a spectator of humanity. If a complete stranger can be motivated to talk about himself long enough, the keen observer can get a peek behind his social mask. Actors and directors can learn far more about characterization from viewing documentaries or reading a daily newspaper than from watching fictionalized films and television programs.

Jane Campion: "There's nothing I like to hear better than hearing what someone does from the moment they wake up to when they go to bed. When I was little I went to my friends' houses and checked out their whole routine for the day. I always got into trouble for looking too hard, for staring too much. I wouldn't even realize I was staring."

Observe people in detail, both physically and psychologically. Notice what they do with their hands, how they hold their shoulders, their hips. If, for example, a man or woman appears stoop-shouldered, see if you can make more specific observations. Does he stumble when attention is given him? Or does he shuffle into a conversation as though hoping not to be annoying? Does he slump in order to appear less tall? Or to hide emotion? Don't limit yourself to merely deciding that he is shy, or lacks self-esteem. Just saying that he is shy or lacks self-esteem is *general*. The insights are in the details.

Take note of how people look at others, and search for the nuances embedded in their responses. Notice the eyes and the clues they often reveal. See if you can tell what's working under the surface — what the person is seeking, expecting, or fearing. Listen for the topics that appear most often in conversation; does your subject talk more about family, or work, or health, or television programs? (These specific observations lead to deeper insights than making the judgment that the person is shallowly obsessed or neurotic with family, work, health, or television.)

Does the person you are observing talk frequently about the faults of others? Or more frequently about her own faults? When she talks about her own faults, it is to make a joke, in order to put others at ease? Or, is it in hope that others will contradict the comment and insist, "No, no, you're wonderful"? Or, is it a form of public self-punishment? Is she accurate, in her assessment of her faults?

These exercises often feed each other. Doing the free-association exercise makes you a better observer. A day after I wrote the "butterfly" free-association above, I was in my garden, and a butterfly landed on a leaf right next to me. Watching it move its wings gently the way they do, I began to wonder, is the movement purposeful, to keep its balance? Is it pleasurable, like an involuntary response to the pleasure of feeding on the leaf, the way babies curl and uncurl their fingers when they are nursing? Or is it an accidental movement caused by the breeze? Just posing such questions — even if I can't answer them — gets me more in the habit of the stripping away that I mentioned above in the "Automatic Pilot" section.

RADICAL REMEMBERING
"I keep persuading younger colleagues to whom I teach scriptwriting or directing, to examine their own lives. The years in which you don't work on yourself like this are, in fact, wasted."
— Krzysztof Keiślowski

"All of my characters are me. I have to be careful about the characters I play because they're going to be me."
— Angelina Jolie

"There's always something of you in every character you play. You're the conduit."
— Julianne Moore

"I think every character you play has to be somewhat like yourself, it comes out of you someplace."
— Robert Duvall

"That's what acting is — you take from your experiences and you put them on the screen."
— Neve Campbell

An interviewer asked Mike Nichols whether he uses his own experience in his work. Nichols replied, "I have no one else's experience available to me." There is no such thing as a blank slate, nor would we want there to be — every person has his story. People (directors, as well as actors) arrive with their emotional baggage. The actor comes to the set with an array of responses, conscious and unconscious, to the material. His associations, his prejudices, his resistances — this is the baggage of his unconscious. It is also the raw material of his craft. The techniques an actor uses — whether he learned them in acting class, or figured them out for himself — are in service of tapping into this rich mother lode.

When Mike Nichols cast Dustin Hoffman (instead of Robert Redford, who was originally the front runner) in *The Graduate*, it was considered, in Hoffman's words, "the most courageous piece of casting in the 20th century." Certainly it was courageous by box office standards. But I think that by emotional standards, it was the safest possible choice — and here I mean "safe" in a good sense, in the sense of a place of emotional sanctuary from which one is free to be creative. Hoffman says of himself at the time, "I was a paralyzed person. I had come from a paralyzed background. [In the role of Benjamin] I was not acting." Nichols apparently recognized this in Hoffman. And also recognized it in himself. For story reasons, the casting proved to work brilliantly. But I believe that the reasons why the decision actually *happened* were deeply personal and emotional. Nichols was drawn to Benjamin's story because he recognized himself in it, and cast Hoffman because he recognized himself in Hoffman.

In *Directing Actors* I mentioned in the chapter on character "spines" that I thought the spine for Michael Corleone was "to please his father." Since the book was published I have seen two separate sources quote Francis Coppola as stating, in response to two very different questions, that a motivating force in many of his artistic choices was to "make my father proud of me." Is the resemblance of Michael Corleone's script-spine to Coppola's own life-spine mere coincidence? I don't think so.

When the director operates out of a commitment that "this film is about me," he stands the most chance of making a film that the people who come to see it will feel is about them. If you as the director ground your work in your own life experiences, then asking for the same commitment from actors won't feel risky anymore; it will feel normal and natural.

Friends of mine who are mothers (especially those who themselves had painful childhoods) tell me that at every stage of their children's lives, they relive their own childhood. "Recapitulation" is a script analysis activity that I recommend for directors as well as actors — to take every event that occurs in the script and relive whatever you know about such an event from your own life.

Sometimes when I tell actors that I want them to use themselves more, they ask me, "Won't all my characters be the same then?" Actually, it's just the opposite. You see, the way to be original is to be specific, and the most reliable way to be specific is to do something only you know. When SLA member Kathleen Soliah was captured by the FBI in 1999, it was noted that in her underground life as Sara Jane Olson she had continued many of the activities and interests of her previous life, such as acting in stage plays, and participating in social causes. Experts in such matters noted that this was probably the reason she had avoided authorities for so many years. An *L.A. Times* article stated that "fugitives who attempt to change their lifestyles too dramatically seldom avoid authorities for long. Those who make it year after year under the weight of an arrest warrant create an identity with its roots in the truth."

Roots in the truth. A commitment that equally applies to creating imaginary lives on film! And where do we find knowledge that has roots in the truth? In everyday experiences, no matter how mundane or boring we may think them at the time. I treasure every lousy job of my past and even every heartache I've endured. Because it means I know a lot about characters who are waitresses or file clerks, or who suffer loss and illness. This is the essential "stuff" that we use to create genuine characters.

The exercise is called "recapitulation." Take the events of your life — each romance, each job, each friendship, each apartment or home you have lived in — and, in solitude, remember as much detail as you can. And let yourself feel all the feelings.

SELF-KNOWLEDGE
"You have to be very honest with yourself to do my job well. And you're not going to like everything about yourself. If you start hiding what you don't like, you're not going to be in the best position to do your job."
                                                          — Jack Nicholson

Is it cheating to use one's own life so completely in the creation of a role or a story? Is it self-indulgent?

Self-knowledge is the difference between self-indulgence and a creative expression of something deeply personal. A self-indulgent person is constantly self-congratulatory — he congratulates himself on his own responses to everything. A person with an interest in self-knowledge *questions* his own responses, notices his own selfishness, his own dishonesty, and uses them in his creations of characters and stories just as he uses his pain and longing.

Gene Hackman said of creating the role of Royal Tannenbaum, "We all have that thing in us where we want to be loved by our family and do the right thing. Many of us are weak and we can't do the right thing because we're just too selfish. I think I know myself well enough to know there are areas in me that are very selfish and insensitive, that are capable of [the insensitive things done by Royal]. I'm not finding that attractive at all, but I think that is probably true. All of us have that. The job of an actor is to get to that." It's also the job of the director.

Liev Schreiber has said that when he discovered acting he found a way to validate his own experience, and — even more importantly — help the audience members to validate their own experience. He seems to be speaking of acting as a means to self-knowledge. This may have helped him in playing Orson Welles in *RKO 281*, because he saw Welles as a man possessed of not only "deep, deep fear and insecurity," but, like Schreiber himself, "a desire to know who he was — hoping that somehow by working he was going to define himself."

EMPATHY
"The characters that I've played, I feel like they're actual women that I've known and that I've learned something from each one."
— Glenn Close

"We have to constantly… stand in the middle of someone else's pain and wonder — shouldn't their pain be ours too?"
— Steven Spielberg

"Enjoying the joys of others and suffering with them — these are the best guides for man."
— Albert Einstein

As important as it is for directors and actors to be personal with their work, it is equally important to go beyond the confines of one's own history, needs and problems, and create something beyond self — a true work of imagination. We must have a ravenous interest in other people, and be willing to acknowledge that there are people (characters) who are very different from ourselves. Willem Dafoe puts it this way: "For an actor, giving over to something that feels outside of yourself is the purest kind of performing." He's speaking of the imaginative leap.

The actor cannot play a character — and the director cannot tell that character's story — unless both can deeply imagine the character's life. This may be accomplished through metaphor to personal experience (the "this is like when a similar thing happened to me" adjustment) or it may be done through empathic imagination.

Empathic imagination is as simple as allowing oneself to imagine and connect to the predicaments and problems of other people, and to care about their problems as much as one's own. Often, filmmakers are too wrapped up in their own problems (Will the deal hold? What's wrong with the lighting? Can you see the rip in that costume?) to actually connect to the problems of the characters.

Empathy is part of the very mixed bag of human emotions. Infants are a mixture of self-centered demands and reaching out (a precursor to empathy). Children are dependent on adults to guide them in navigating a healthy balance between their "self-centered" needs (e.g., for attention, privilege, independence) and their "reaching out" impulses (e.g., the way they love to "help").

As an example, let's say a 12-year-old girl has a friend whose mother dies of cancer. The girl cries every night for weeks. She has natural feelings of empathy, the ability to feel what she imagines her friend feels. Mixed with her empathic feelings are feelings of fear that this will happen to her. She may need adult guidance in figuring out the difference. But sometimes when adults try to give counseling, instead of asking relevant questions to assist the child in examining and understanding what's behind her feelings, they may micro-manage their child's emotional life. The adult "counseling" may identify only the fear, neglecting to identify the empathy. Further, when they try to comfort the fear, they may clumsily succeed in merely discouraging its expression. The child, being told not to give in to fear, to instead shake it off and move on, gets the message that's it's best to bury her feelings. When this happens, empathy gets suppressed as well.

The good news is that since empathy is natural to humans, it, like the imagination itself, can be resuscitated.

Exercise: Pick a person you have observed or had interaction with, that you don't know well, but who has captured your attention. Speak out loud in that person's voice. Start with a physical description of the person (but using "I," e.g., "I am short, my eyes water easily, I chew gum all the time") and move into free-associations to that person's inner life, things you don't actually know, but imagine. ("I have one friend, but I never call her, I wait until she calls me." "Since the illness of my wife, I notice sadness in other people, and I try to cheer them up.")

Exercise: Cut photos of people (not famous) out of the newspaper, leaving off the caption. Imagine the lives, both outward, and inner, of the people in the photos.

Exercise: For each character in your script, after you have thought of some facts, questions, images, possible backstory and possible spines, think of three ways you're like the character, three ways you're not. You could do this by yourself, as part of your script analysis, or you could do it with the actors. Actors of course can do this on their own for their own character. Be honest. Look for negative as well as positive things you have in common.

PASSING JUDGMENT

"I can't judge a character. I don't even know who they are. I can't account for the characters in the end."

— Willem Dafoe

"Even if a character makes the worst moral choice — my God, I could never do that — you have to be willing to risk that the audience thinks it is you, you have to be willing to believe it enough that they think it's you. Being an actor sometimes requires that you ask yourself questions that you would rather not know the answers to."

— Kevin Spacey

"My strongest asset as an actor is that I'm not finally capable of feeling a great separation between myself and other people, and that includes someone like Matthew [in Dead Man Walking]."

— Sean Penn

The issue of passing judgment is often confusing to directors. Some seem to think that not passing judgment equates to treating every character as a "nice" person. Or that it means the audience should find all the characters sympathetic. Not at all. It's a much deeper issue than that. The challenge for the director is to empathically see herself in every character. You can't direct a script unless you do.

Glenn Close has said that her process is one of "falling in love" with the character — surely a fascinating comment from an actor who, in her roles in *Fatal Attraction, Dangerous Liaisons,* and especially as Cruella Da Ville, has played the most famous movie villainesses of her time!

It's not about sympathy, it's about honesty. An actor cannot properly play a character nor can a director tell that character's story unless he can honestly say, "I can imagine a person — a human being — making those choices, living that way." When Kevin Spacey says, as quoted above, that "being an actor sometimes requires that you ask yourself questions that you would rather not know the answers to," he means that when an actor plays a character who is cruel or dishonest or disloyal, the actor has to find those impulses in himself, and that such self-examination can take him outside his comfort zone.

It surely could not have been an easy thing for Mary Tyler Moore to play the mother in *Ordinary People* as honestly, as emotionally stripped as she does. It would be much less painful for an actor to play such a character with a little extra emphasis, a little subtext signal to the audience that says, "We both know what a monster this woman is, don't we?" Instead, the character Beth is played without an ounce of judgment. She is played as a woman who thinks she is doing the best she can. In order to play her that way, the actor must let us see the way the actor herself does the best she can in her own family life.

And the audience, who is not meant to feel sympathy for the character, doesn't. It's a fascinating paradox, but the less judgment the actor puts on an unsavory character, the more the character is revealed to the audience in all her awfulness. It's only then the audience feels sympathy for the main character, Beth's son. When any character is judged, the audience is distanced. But when we see Beth genuinely doing what she thinks is best, we, the audience, are engaged in every painful moment that the boy struggles with his dilemma of whether to seek her love or rise up against her cruelty.

I don't believe an actor can arrive at a performance like Ms. Moore's in *Ordinary People* without extraordinarily sensitive and intelligent support from her director, in this case Robert Redford. The reason why a director must never pass judgment on any character is so that he can speak to each actor from that character's point of view. Supported this way, each actor comes to the interactions of the script with the full force of conviction — and we (the audience) participate in the events, the wins and losses, in the moment. It's not a fixed fight. As any sports enthusiast knows, fixed fights are not very exciting.

A few actors have given us some information into the ideas and insights that allowed them to play apparent villains without judgment. Ben Kingsley told an interviewer that he understood that Don Logan, in *Sexy Beast*, "is an unloved child. I have great compassion for the unloved child. That's who he is. His *cri de coeur* in the kitchen, when he's having the row with Ray, is 'I don't want you to be happy! Why should I?' There is my key line. There is the link that will open the door to my character. And it's said by a weeping child with clenched fists in the corner of the playground."

Kathy Bates has said of her role in *Misery* that she studied Ted Bundy and books on psychopaths, but that it was important both to her and to director Rob Reiner to create a woman who had her own logic, not someone crazy in a general way. After thinking and exploring, she finally saw Annie as a muse, even an angel of mercy, whose life work was to put people out of their misery.

Brian Cox says of creating his character Big John in *L.I.E.*, that it was necessary to find "where the guy's coming from, the guy's point of view... His real desire is to be a father. Here's a man who's a sexual predator of young men, when actually his desire is to be an enabler, to make someone blossom, to make someone grow."

Robert Duvall realized that to play Adolf Eichmann in a made-for-cable movie, he had to make a choice. He knew that one way to play the character without judgment would be to make the choice that Eichmann did not really know what would be the outcome of his work for the Third Reich. But Duvall didn't believe in that choice, and instead made the choice that Eichmann knew exactly what he was doing when he organized the delivery of millions of Jews to concentration camps. When an interviewer asked him, "How do you play someone evil?" Duvall answered, "You have to find the contradictions. With Eichmann, he loved his son. I think when you do play them you have to think the way they thought. They don't think of themselves as bad."

Villains are not the only characters who should not be judged. D J Qualls never thought of his character in *Road Trip* as a geek or a dork. "I knew a lot of kids like this. A lot of the South is almost secluded in a way. Parents are really strict because of fear of the unknown. I knew kids who had no life experience by the time they graduated from high school. That's how I looked at him. I just tried to be open and honest. I didn't play dork shtick." Shawnee Smith says of her character Linda on the television show *Becker*, "She's just open. What sometimes appears as ditzy or airheaded or weird is that she's just open."

In both these cases the actors have gone beyond passing judgment on their characters, they have made a virtue of what others might consider a defect. Chris Cooper says he patterned John Laroche (*Adaptation*) on men he knew in the Ozarks where he grew up, and also the smart, funny lobstermen he has met living in Massachusetts, of whom he says that with proper education they "could have ruled the world and gone on to become CEO's." Mark Ruffalo said of Terry in *You Can Count on Me* that, "These kinds of people are very interesting to me, because they're the people who people write off. They're alienated, they don't feel like they belong in the world. But somewhere in them is a voice. And maybe it takes some time for them to find their way in the world." This is much more than merely not judging — it is tender regard for the character's predicament, and faith in his potential. The actor goes so far as to believe that Terry will turn out okay, eventually. This — fully as much as any other aspect of Ruffalo's talent — makes him the perfect choice for the role.

Judging is superficial. When I judge a character, I am only considering him in relation to my own concerns — I am making a pre-judgment that I wouldn't like to spend time around him. Not much thinking or creativity goes into that choice. The work of imagining his life, "presenting his soul" begins with considering his situation and his needs. Once I do enough work to understand that the selfishness of Phil Connors (*Groundhog Day*) is masking his self-hatred, then I can't judge him. Every character, in his own mind, is doing the best he can.

Our craft demands that we have open minds. You can't be fascinated by characters unless you are fascinated by people. You can't be an artist if you look down on anybody. I'm not saying you can't dislike, even hate, some people — just don't look down on them. And don't make presumptions. Everyone has a story. You don't know people until you know their stories. Too many people avoid whatever makes them not feel important and congratulatory about themselves, and it is from this point of view that they judge others. Such assessments are little more than gossip — a far cry from genuine insight about people. Artists don't see the world that way. The artist recognizes: "That could be me, under different circumstances. That could be me, with a little worse luck."

Of course, if I were playing a person who judges others in order to feel important, or directing the story of such a character, I'd have to be careful not to judge the judger, either. I'd need to make real for myself a spine "to feel important" or "to be well treated." And I could do that — because feeling important and being well treated are also needs of mine.

A judgment is an opinion and people's opinions are less interesting than their stories. I find I get exactly nowhere by judging people. Judging and gossiping are luxuries that I cannot afford. Even in the affairs of everyday life, I never like to issue ultimatums or terminate communications. You never know when new information might make an appearance.

TELL STORIES

When I am directing or teaching, I constantly use examples from my own life and experience to help flesh out an idea. I begin, "it's like when...." Mike Nichols has said that when talking to actors, "I tell stories about myself, to an embarrassing extent." A *New Yorker* profile of Nichols said that "when Nichols teaches at the New Actors Workshop, he uses examples from his own life to clarify a theatrical moment. He treats himself as a metaphor."

One of my students told me that every night at bedtime he asks his small son and daughter for a word. Then he makes up a story around the words they give him. Practice telling stories. Don't forget — the best stories are true stories. And always watch your audience carefully to make sure they are engaged in the story; if they aren't, stop.

TAKE TIME TO THINK AND DAYDREAM
"I think you get better at staring into space."
— Adrian Lyne

Things take the time they take. Nick Nolte had the script for *Affliction* for five years before shooting began. He says he, himself, created some of the postponements, partly because "I didn't feel quite ready to do it." The writer-director Paul Schrader was probably tearing his hair out, but Nolte's performance is so extraordinary — can we be sure the same depth would have been there without the five-year gestation period?

Cellist Yo Yo Ma says of his preparation time, he spends 90% letting his mind wander, and only 10% practicing.

You need time, to think, to daydream. As Virginia Woolf famously advised, one needs a room of one's own. Mike Nichols says that "downtime is the most unacknowledged factor in our work. If you can't solve something," he says, "leave it alone, put it away, come back later. You'll rediscover it. Or discover something else."

Because of financing delays, Sam Rockwell had the script of *Box of Moonlight* for seven years before shooting began. Laura Dern had five years with the script of *Rambling Rose*. Both these performances are truly remarkable for their range, depth, ease, and freedom. Such freedom is the precious dividend of time spent daydreaming.

For an artist, time spent soaking in the tub is not wasted; I get some of my best ideas when I am in warm water. Or when I am walking, or riding in a vehicle. Or doing nothing. I spent my thirties more or less staring at the wall. I'm still not sure whether I chose this or it befell me, but for about six years (from 1979 to 1985) I was in a kind of suspended animation. I had no active career, no husband or kids, no obligations, no money, no computer, not even a TV. I had an undemanding job, acting class, therapy, four friends, and I lived by the beach. Staring at the wall or at the ocean — just thinking — was my entertainment. I absolutely feel that it was those years of dedicated daydreaming that gave me something to say when I turned forty. Now that I have a busy, full life, the only time I get to "just think" is when I have insomnia.

A lack of distraction, or even stimulation, is necessary if you are to visit the innermost reaches of your thoughts. In order to know what you believe, what you care about, what you have to say, you need to give that stuff time to float up to the surface. If your life has built-in stimulations beyond earning a living, such as children to raise, it is all the more important to guarantee yourself significant time away from work, television, meetings, parties, the Internet.

Paul Newman described, in his *Inside the Actors Studio* interview, how as a young actor he would, whenever he was cast in a new role, book a hotel room for three days and lock himself in the room with nothing but the script and a couple of six-packs of beer, just letting his imagination take him wherever it would. He reported that "90%" of the ideas he came up with that way would be nonsense — but "the other 10% was pure gold."

The exercise here is to lock yourself in a quiet room with your script — and stay there until you get past your easy assumptions, past your boredom and frustration, your desire to ask someone else how to direct (or play) the roles, and your obsession with the finished result playing on the movie screen of your mind. If you are in there for an hour or more with no ideas coming to you, just read it over and over — out loud — slowly.

RADICALLY IN THE MOMENT

I like the word radical, both in the sense of going to the root of things, and in the sense of stretching your imagination beyond the confines of conventional wisdom. For example, all the actors in my scene study classes know they are supposed to be "in the moment," that they are not supposed to be watching themselves. But "in the moment" can become a cliché. Finally I started asking the question, what would it mean to be *radically* in the moment? Well, it would mean that one really *does not know* what is going to happen next. When I started asking my actors to give themselves *that much* permission to fail, all the work improved.

Actors should stay in the moment no matter what. Why do you think audiences love outtakes so much? Because the actors are in the moment.

Once a director asked me what she could have done in a situation in which her DP wanted a shot that would require the actor to step over an awkward roll of cable in the middle of an emotional scene. (Out of consideration for the actor's emotional concentration, she had changed the shot. But later she wished she had the shot.) It was in the middle of a class that she asked me this question, and I found it a puzzling one. I was standing there in front of a roomful of people, hoping an answer would come to me, when all of a sudden I thought of Marcello Mastroianni. The image of his face just popped into my head — I don't know why! But I found myself asking the question, What would Marcello — an actor whose instincts were always impeccable — do if he had to step over cable during an emotional scene? The answer was easy — or at least the answer to the question of what he *wouldn't* do. He would certainly never pretend that he wasn't stepping over cable! If the cable is not in the shot, the audience won't know the actor is stepping over it. But if the actor pretends *anything*, the audience will notice that.

Being in the moment means that whatever you are doing *right now* is the most important thing in the world. So you can see how important that would be for directors when they are talking to actors. A director who can make each actor feel that there is nothing more important in the world than their current conversation is going to have a better relationship than a director who has already got his mind on his next task.

RADICAL LISTENING — FOR THE ACTOR'S PERFORMANCE

"Listening in the terms that we use is not listening to the words, but listening to the person."

— Jack Lemmon

"Some actors are predictable. They have it down. Every time, they'll do it the same way. No matter what you say to them, however you're going to say it, they're basically going to give it back to you the same way. They have a preconceived idea of how it should be, and it's very, very hard to shake it."

— Robert De Niro

"[Pacino] really listens to the other actors. If you look at five takes of him looking over somebody's shoulder, you will see different expressions each time."

— Oliver Stone

"Listening is everything. It's where to learn everything. I don't feel I exist until I'm with someone."

— Meryl Streep

"I learned how to listen. In the process, I forgot my fear. You get your performance from the other actor."

— Kathy Bates

A "good listener" in real life is someone who lets the other person's story be more important than his own. An actor who is a good listener lets what is going on with the other actor be more important than his own performance. Sanford Meisner used to say to his new acting students, "You're not going to like hearing this, but the other actor is more important than you." Yes, it's that radical. And that simple. It's a surrender. The way for an actor to look like he is realizing something *right now*, to look like a person who is thinking *right now*, to look like a person who is saying these words for the first time — is by *getting it all* from the other actor — by listening.

The issues for an actor's performance are believability and expressiveness. In order for an actor's emotional life to be believable and naturally expressive, the emotion must seem to come out of impulse, not calculation. One only has impulses if one doesn't try for them or watch for them. As soon as you ask yourself, "Is this an impulse?" — guess what! It isn't. You only have impulses when you surrender, when you abandon self-consciousness.

Yet, it's easy for actors to get confused between listening to their impulses (good) and listening to the sound of their voice (bad). It's hard to "surrender" in a vacuum. It's more feasible if you have something to surrender to. "Self-conscious" means you are aware of yourself. The most perfect description of this is in Anton Chekhov's *The Seagull*, when Nina says, "My acting became terrible. I didn't know what to do with my hands or where to stand or how to control my voice." She is describing the actor's nightmare of total self-consciousness, when all she can do is watch herself, and all she can think about is how she is saying the lines and the wrongness of her every move. The antidote to an actor's self-consciousness is to place her awareness, her concentration, elsewhere. This shift can be to an object or image, physical activity or imaginative adjustment. But the most powerful, the most reliable place to shift her concentration is to another person.

If she doesn't surrender to the other actor, she falls into a fixed attitude; nothing can affect her. In a theatrical sense, she can't be hurt. Allowing ourselves to be affected is nothing less than taking a risk to be altered — to take a loss. On a practical level, it means that if one actor's lines are spoken with a different tone or intention, then the other actor's lines will come out differently too — if she is listening.

Listening is not the same as waiting for the other actor to do something fascinating. It is *active*; it is an *engagement* that places a demand upon each actor. It is *looking for* something to be fascinated by in the performance of that other actor.

RADICAL LISTENING — FOR THE DIRECTOR'S STORYTELLING
"[To be a good director] I really think you need to be a good listener. I listen to the actors, I listen to the writer. I believe you listen and then make a decision."
— Todd Holland

For a director, radical listening is a central key to success, in several ways. **First, a director must be able to discern whether the actors are listening to each other.** When the actors are listening radically, reality is altered — and thus the director's job (which is to create a new, imagined reality) is well on the way to completion. Mark Ruffalo and Laura Linney are completely believable as brother and sister (in *You Can Count on Me*) because, after whatever work they have done to prepare, they both surrender the text and performance to each other — they are excellent listeners. Besides helping their own performances, they have helped the director, who cast them as brother and sister even though they don't look at all alike.

Another example of actors' listening aiding the director's job is found in *Pulp Fiction*. The chemistry in the relationship of the characters played by Samuel Jackson and John Travolta is achieved by their high level of radical listening. The director allows the resulting intimacy of their relationship to create the events of their scene. In the scene after Mr. Wolf (Harvey Keitel) has chastised Vincent (Travolta) for asking him to say "please," there is a little by-play between Jackson and Travolta in which Travolta says to Jackson, "Don't give me that look." Most directors assume that the line "Don't give me that look" won't work without an insert of Jackson giving Travolta "the look." But in that scene there is no such insert. The shot is way pulled back. *The audience knows there is a look because the emotional event of "giving a look" has taken place between the two actors.*

One more example is the scene in *Carnal Knowledge* when Bobbie begs Jonathan to marry her and threatens suicide if he won't. In his *Inside the Actors Studio* interview, director Mike Nichols described the work on this scene, the first three days of which were spent on the angles favoring Bobbie, played by Ann-Margret. Nichols disclosed that Jack Nicholson, whose character Jonathan is intimidating and berating her, played this painful scene at full force every time, even though he was not on camera at all. "By the time we got to Jack's close-up he was hoarse." Then on the program a clip of the scene was shown, and by golly, he *is* hoarse! He has sacrificed himself to give his partner her performance — and to give the director the scene, i.e., its event.

Such magical moments and on-screen relationships do not happen every day. The prevailing wisdom is to reward only actors who "nail" their performance. So when a director recognizes and values the special magic and chemistry that radical listening brings, he not only needs to ask for it, he must also convey to the actors a deep permission for it. Otherwise even the best actors may play it safe with "business as usual" listening — that is, the kind of listening most people do in real life — which is pretty much just enough to stay out of trouble.

How does a director ask for radical listening from the actors? One way is to tell the actors at the beginning of the project, "This script is not about individual performances, it's about relationships." Meg Ryan told an interviewer that director Rob Reiner said to her point-blank on the set of *When Harry Met Sally*, "It's not about you, it's about the other actor." But you don't have to address it directly by referring to the concept of listening — the "term of art." If an actor is not listening, you can discuss the moment that is not happening, or the objective that will capture him enough to make him want to have an effect on the other actor.

The second kind of listening that is important for a director is that he himself listen to what the actors are telling him, what the characters are telling him, and what the story is telling him. Listening radically means that for the duration of the conversation you actually allow the other person's stories, problems, feelings, needs, and ideas to be more interesting and important than your own. So, for instance, it means that the director allows the actors a chance to try their ideas — not just to be polite — but because their ideas might be worthy. It also means that he reads and re-reads the script, not just to confirm his own ideas, but to look for new ones, to look for something he may have missed, to let the characters tell him their stories, instead of imposing one on them.

Listening exercises that you can practice in real life are pretty simple. *Listen to the people in your own life as if what they are saying is the only important thing in the world.* Of course, don't limit yourself to what they are saying with words. Radical listening means listening for subtext. For instance, when an actor says "This role is a challenge," does he mean "I've been waiting for this chance to show more of what I can do," or does he mean, "I'm afraid — maybe I've been miscast"?

This shouldn't imply that the director has to be a mind reader. She can ask questions. For example, when an actor says, "I don't understand this line," there are probably a dozen different things he might mean. Directors often think they have to immediately fix the situation, and start either over-explaining the psychology of the character on this line, or come up with a change of line. But it's so useful to get more information first.

In the case of the statement "I don't understand this line," the first question I would probably ask the actor is, "Is there a word or phrase you don't know the meaning of?" If he says yes, the problem can be solved easily, by together consulting a dictionary. If he says no, my next question is, "What bothers you about it?"

LISTENING TO THE LITTLE VOICE
"Listen to your own inner voice. The only way to make something new is to make something that is personal to you."
— Julian Schnabel

And finally, listen to the little voice inside you — the one that tells you to keep working, or keep looking, or keep rewriting — or just keep waiting for the better idea to come to you. Or, to jump in and do it! The voice that tells you, "This doesn't feel right." Or the voice that tells you, "I know this is right even though no one else agrees." To mix a metaphor, this voice is your vision. This voice is absolutely muffled by desire for fame and money, by need for other people's approval, and by fear of not following conventional wisdom.

DO IT WRONG

Now, of course, "doing it wrong" is not the *goal* — excellence is always our goal. When we investigate choices to make in a scene, we are looking for the one that solves the scene, and brings the script to life. But there are no rules or formulas for such solutions. The key to unlocking this stubborn door is flexibility. Flexibility catapults us into the experience of risk. We try one thing, it doesn't work — we try another! Flexibility is a cornerstone of intuition and imagination. It's, first, an ability to think of more than one way to do something, and second, a willingness to experiment and change your mind when something isn't working.

It's hard to come up with ideas for "opposite" choices unless your mind can freely venture into territory where you're as likely as not to be "wrong." That risky choice — the opposite — has the chance to be miraculous. Taking the chance to be wrong is the very essence of the creative mind. My campaign for the power of opposites got a big boost with *Mulholland Drive*. Even people who didn't like or didn't get the film were enchanted by "Betty's audition" scene. When she prepares the audition in the kitchen the night before, she reads the lines "on the nose," with the obvious choice that the character is self-righteously defending her honor — and the audience can clearly see the banality of the scene. When Betty arrives at the audition, she makes a complete switch to a girl coming on to the man — and the scene is brilliant. That's an opposite!

One of my favorite problem-solving techniques is this. When you can't think of the right answer, think of three wrong answers. I promise it will "unstick" you whenever you are stuck. As soon as you come up with three wrong answers, you will start to test each idea out in your mind. (If you are in rehearsal, you can even try them out.) Soon one of the ideas will start to seem a little less wrong than the others. Or you'll get new ideas. It's a tried and true exercise.

When actors are frustrated, or bored, and the work is at a standstill, I just stop, and call out to the actors, "Okay, let's take the George Costanza adjustment!" — When all else fails, say every line, every syllable, differently from the way you think it should be said.

"NAILING IT"

Whenever I hear an actor say, "I just want to go into that audition and nail it," or a director say, "That actor was great. He nailed it on the first take" — all I can think of is nails in a coffin.

I hear reports of comments that directors, casting directors, and even acting coaches say to actors and I am dismayed at how superficial and deadening they often can be. Of course it's not so surprising — because the end result, the work we see on television and movies, is also often superficial and deadening. Worst of all, this misguided input is the spoken or unspoken expectation that good actors always "nail it" — without rehearsal and without question or complaint.

Good acting is not about "nailing it." It's about connection, commitment, and freedom to play in an imagined world. We can't choose to be perfect — God didn't make us that way. We can, however, choose to be honest. Honesty is the most reasonable yardstick of good acting.

When Ed Asner read for the Lou Grant role on *The Mary Tyler Moore Show*, his first reading with Mary went poorly; he asked to try it again, did brilliantly and got the role. Then, according to Ms. Moore, Asner "took another dip" in rehearsals. In today's television world, an actor who "took a dip" in rehearsals for a pilot would be pretty quickly replaced — which, in the case of Asner, would have been a big mistake.

Many people in the entertainment industry have bought into the false trade-off between rehearsal and spontaneity. If the actor doesn't nail it on every reading, worry sets in — people think he can never get it again. Nobody thinks that about a ball player who strikes out in his first at-bat against a certain pitcher. If the ball player is good, we assume the opposite — that he'll learn from the strike-out and be able to get around the pitcher in his next ups. Rehearsal and spontaneity are not mutually exclusive.

You can't make a mistake in the imagined world. Instead of "nailing it," make your goals learning and play. For a scene with a difficult transitional moment, don't nail down the emotional map but, instead, during script analysis, investigate a number of the possible things that might happen emotionally at that moment. These different responses are then available to the emotional storage banks. During the scene, one will kick in and crop up *in the moment*.

STEAL FROM EVERYONE

There's nothing really new under the sun. And nothing wrong with stealing creative ideas. No one would be foolhardy enough to undertake to perform or direct *Hamlet* without ever having seen a production of it. When a role or project is very complex and challenging, you may need a place to start, some ideas to steal — or at least an idea of what not to do.

"Stealing" helps one feel reassurance. The best place to steal is from art forms different from movies and television — or from real life. The extreme of stealing from real life is getting a chance to play a character who actually lived. I've had two opportunities myself, one in which my character's lines were taken from court transcripts, and another when I got to play Sylvia Plath in the stage play *Letters Home*, in which all my lines were words Plath had actually written in letters to her mother. There is a liberation in getting to play an actual person. It has to do with *knowing the character is there*, that there is a *person* — an intellect, a physical existence, and a soul — behind the words. This reassurance has apparently empowered the performances of Hilary Swank as Brandon Teena in *Boys Don't Cry*, Angela Bassett as Tina Turner in *What's Love Got to Do With It?* — to name only a few.

A major function of script analysis is to give the participants the assurance that the fictional characters and situations are as real as non-fictional ones.

In an interview Ian McKellen said that sometimes he patterns a characterization after a real-life public figure, that, for instance, he based his characterization of Macbeth (in a stage production) on John F. Kennedy, and his characterization of Coriolanus on tennis star John McEnroe. "It's not truly 'based on,' it's just reassuring yourself" that there can be someone like this character. He added that of course in some roles he doesn't have to do that — some roles are close to the things that everyone experiences.

You can steal from yourself. Or from people you know and have deep feelings about. James Stewart said, "The only kind of role I can really play is someone I can understand: a pretty average kind of man, trying to work out some kind of problem the best way he can without calling too much attention to himself. Someone, yeah, like me." Stewart also said about *It's a Wonderful Life*, "I can't say it took much acting. I knew that character — George Bailey. He was my father. I just pretended I was him." Patrick Warburton, too, says he based his role in *The Dish* on his father.

After Whoopi Goldberg shot *The Color Purple* (her first movie role) she disclosed that director Steven Spielberg went over each scene with her, giving her images from movies that he knew Goldberg loved, for example, that a certain scene they were shooting was like a particular scene from *To Kill a Mockingbird.* I think this technique should be used sparingly, that one should prefer associations from life and other arts to associations with other movies. But sometimes it's just the ticket. As a young actor in the '70s, whenever I had tried everything and couldn't figure out a role, when I was at my wits' end and had truly run out of ideas, I would finally ask myself, "How would Liv Ullman play it?"

RESISTANCE
"I am prepared to kill any actor that won't reveal himself."
— John Cassavetes

Here are a couple of stories I've read describing actors' and directors' resistances to roles or scenes. To me they prove that the place we resist is a truth that we think we can't or don't want to face, but that deep inside we know we must. When we do face it, the liberation may be one of the most creative moments in our lives — or occasionally even in cinematic history.

During the shooting of *Carnal Knowledge*, Mike Nichols wanted to cut the scene with Bobbie and Jonathan (discussed earlier in the "Listening" section of this chapter), explaining to writer Jules Feiffer, "It's just so ugly, it's so awful, people are gonna hate it, and they're gonna hate the movie." The scene is emotionally very raw; it stands as one of the great iconic, painful male-female scenes of all time. Feiffer reports, "I just sat in the car listening to [Nichols] go over and over why he couldn't shoot it. Finally, he just looked at me and said, 'No, we've got to do it, because it's true.'"

Director Bob Rafelson says that when it came time to shoot the scene in *Five Easy Pieces*, in which the main character at last speaks to his mute father — the scene that probably got Jack Nicholson his Oscar nomination — Nicholson at first insisted that he couldn't and wouldn't break down and cry in the scene. "He wouldn't budge. I canceled shooting and kept him up for two days, arguing with him. He finally said, 'All right, I'll do the fucking thing, but the dialogue is terrible.' I said, 'Go ahead, rewrite it.' In the car, he improvised the dialogue on the way to the shoot." On the set, Rafelson dismissed the crew, and he, Nicholson, and William Challee (playing the father) were the only ones present. Rafelson says he locked the camera down, and, holding the microphone, turned away while Nicholson played the scene.

Directors faced with actors resisting must make it safe for the actor to go there. Letting it be finally the individual's free choice will get you the best results, but you don't need to back off from your desire to insist that the actor *must not hide*.

We should honor resistances — our own and others' — and not pretend with false bravado that they are not real and important, because underneath the resistances is the good, important, true stuff. Honor the kicking and screaming — cherish it. Then go ahead and do the thing anyway.

IMPROVISATION IN THE MIND

In a later chapter I'll discuss the use of improvisation as a rehearsal technique. But I want to introduce the principles of improv here, because they are also principles of active imagining. Improv is the imagination made physical. To revisit my dress-shopping analogy from the previous chapter, when I imagine myself in the dress I am improvising in the mind; a real improv would involve actions such as actually going to the store and trying it on.

I like to use improv as a teaching technique for actors because it helps keep their imaginations nimble, and it encourages them in their commitment to always work moment-by-moment. I use it for directors because in order for a director to be able to improvise in her imagination, she needs to get in touch with "the actor inside." Improvisation is a pure experience of what Sanford Meisner called the definition of good acting: living truthfully under imaginary circumstances. Improv is a great help for writers, too, to get a feel for dialogue that is natural and spontaneous — freed from the isolated confines of the computer. The written word takes on new and unexpected dimensions when spoken from the mouths of human beings.

A director who consulted with me on a project before shooting wanted particularly to work with improv, so we discussed and invented a number of different improvs she might use in rehearsal. She wrote me later that even though she ended up not having time to actually do the improvs in rehearsal, having thought them up in her mind was an excellent preparation for talking about the characters with her actors. Her e-mail on this subject made me realize that even when there is no time to actually improvise a scene or relationship, "improvising in the mind" is a valuable practice.

In my improvs, I set participants up with a *situation*, or facts, and I make sure to include opportunity for physical activity. Then I give them two rules. The "No Denial" rule means that anything that happens in the improv is true. So no participant can direct or manipulate the scene in any particular direction;

if you are in an improv, thinking, for example, that you and your partner were making dinner together and your partner suddenly remarks that he hates eating breakfast this early, then the meal is breakfast. The "No Obligation" rule means you don't have to agree that it's too early for breakfast; you don't have to continue the discussion about food at all — and you don't even have to talk. Just live truthfully under imaginary circumstances.

It's easier to understand these principles if you have experienced them in actual improvisations. But this work can be done on your own. First, distinguish the facts — the situation — from any personal judgments or theories about the characters. Then, let yourself imagine those facts to be true — as a *life* situation, not a movie situation. Finally, allow your imagination, experience, and observations of human nature to take you where they will, without manipulating the result.

For an exercise, choose two characters from a movie or play you have seen or read more than once. Give them an imaginary situation; don't decide what to expect them to do or feel. Just imagine, say, Vito Corleone and his wife talking in bed together before falling asleep. Let them talk to each other. Let there be silences. Try to avoid cliché.

The rules of improv themselves can be rules to live by. An inner practice of "No Denial" promotes openness, listening, and an uncensored approach to free associations. "No Obligation" means you never say "I had no choice." When we relinquish obligation, we take responsibility for our choices.

IMAGINATION IS PHYSICAL

Daniel Day-Lewis confined himself to a wheelchair on and off camera and had himself carried onto the set for *My Left Foot*. He learned to trap and skin animals for *The Last of the Mohicans*. For his role in *In the Name of the Father*, he had himself shut into a cell, interrogated by real cops, subjected to the regimen of his character. To prepare for the role of Bill the Butcher in *Gangs of New York*, he worked in a butcher shop and trained to throw knives with deadly accuracy. And, of course, to play *The Boxer* he trained as a boxer. "What helps me an awful lot is to somehow get rid of the illusion that one is making a film," he has said. An interviewer asked him what he thought of David Mamet's pronouncement that, "All the knowledge in the world of the Elizabethan era will not help you play Mary Stuart." Day Lewis said quietly, "But it may make you think that it helps you, and that's as good as anything. Whatever it takes to loosen up that place inside you that either gives you something or doesn't."

"That place inside you" being the imagination.

The objects and experiences of our daily life have an effect on us — how could they not? I've read that director Mike Leigh insists on using public transportation, a deliberate decision to stay in touch with the day-to-day life of the people he makes movies about. Eric Rohmer takes the Metro, also to have contact with real life. Actor Khandi Alexander, who played Fran on the made-for-cable mini series *The Corner*, and who had had early training as a dancer, says that her acting coach told her if she wanted to make the shift from dancer to actor, she should take a job as a grocery clerk and live like ordinary people, in order to get rid of her "dancer's walk."

Some actors call it "research" and some other people scoff and call it "too method-y," but to me it only makes good sense to expose oneself to the physicality of a character's world. The objects and images of our world *are* us, to a great extent. Like it or not, we become defined by our gadgets and fashion accessories, as well as the images that bombard us from the television and the street. The process of getting more connected to the characters' problems than to our own problems has to involve loosening ourselves from our own objects and images, and allowing the characters' objects and images, at least temporarily, to be even stronger.

The exercise described in the "Empathy" section where you venture into imagining the inner life of a person on the street or in a photo, should always begin by investigating the person's physical life — the physical sensations that lead to his stance, his walk, his weight, his height, his aches and pains, the slowness or quickness of his speech.

THINK OUT LOUD. READ OUT LOUD.
Reading out loud is a right brain activity; reading silently is a left brain activity. When you read (or memorize) silently, it's easier to think you know how the words will come out when spoken out loud. Reading out loud is more of a risk, more of a letting go. An actor, of course, can't practice a performance by himself, either silently or out loud — there is no performance until there is another person to act with. And people to watch you. (I always amend Meisner's definition of good acting to "living truthfully under imaginary circumstances *while people watch*.")

It's enormously helpful for a writer or director to read her own script out loud — as well as to hear her script read out loud by actors. Peter Weir audio-records the script and listens to it in his car; he says, "You learn a lot about characters by speaking the lines." It's also helpful for a director to hear a script read out loud by the writer (as Sam Mendes had Alan Ball read him the script of *American Beauty*). This can be more helpful than asking the writer for answers to your questions about the script. Instead of asking him what the subtext is, you can listen for it.

By "thinking out loud" I don't mean stubbornly subjecting everyone within earshot to one's opinions. I mean *thinking* out loud — or silently — but in front of people — allowing oneself to go through thought processes in front of another person, without embarrassment. We tend to be very cautious, to restrict ourselves to public utterances that we know, or think, will make us sound cool, clever, etc. Actually allowing ourselves to think out loud in front of another person is risk-taking. It's a liberating and creative experience.

NEVER STOP LEARNING
"There really has to be a feeling of wanting to learn that's more important than wanting to succeed."

— John Cassavetes

I've been talking a lot about ways to make your thinking, imagining, and feeling more visceral and immediate. But, to be an artist, you need more information than just your own pure feeling and pure experience. Education gives one some distance, some objectivity from one's own experience, and helps us put our feelings and experience into a context. In an earlier chapter I described a discussion between David Chase and Nancy Marchand about Livia Soprano. Having had a family involvement with someone like Livia would be a big help in coming up with insights as astute as theirs are — but it's not enough. In order to be able to *look* at that behavior, and put it in a dramatic context, the creative interpreter also needs to have cultivated a world-view that is wider than the confines of his own family. His knowledge that behavior such as Livia's exists in the world would need to be intimate. But his knowledge that there are other possible ways of behaving must be equally intimate.

Lifelong learning is a personal commitment. If you approach the film industry as an opportunity to learn more about craft and life, rather than as your shot at grabbing the gold ring of overnight success, you will have a greater chance of long-term success. Script analysis and rehearsal are about learning and solving — not about fixing and nailing. Learning one's craft cannot be separated from learning about life. We don't gain knowledge without experiencing emotion.

Many people think of education as something to be stuffed into you — something you can *have* and then not need to think about any more. Sometimes people take one of my workshops to get the "fixes" hammered into their brain. They expect training to immunize them from making mistakes in the real world. That's not the purpose of training. The purpose of training, like script analysis, is to give you ideas of things to try, so you can learn by doing, by trial and error.

The real learners are, by definition, risk-takers. Whenever an opportunity arises that is scary, that could fail horribly, if it feels like it might mean a chance to learn something — the student of life will probably do it. We are all a mixture. The part of us that wants to learn and grow is the creative part. The part of us that wants to feel important and be treated well is human, and must be respected, but it's going to hold us back creatively.

Education is an emotional safety net. It's so easy in Hollywood to feel like you're not worth anything. If you are not educated, your world is small. An education in history, literature, art, philosophy — as well as science and psychology — widens your realm of associations. It gives you strength. This is true whether or not you ever go to college. Everyone should finally become his own teacher.

SPEND TIME AROUND ART, NATURE, CHILDREN. SURROUND YOURSELF WITH PEOPLE WHO ARE CAPABLE OF FEELING.
"I'm interested in a lot of things. I would just like to go to a different museum every day and see different pieces of art. I'd like to go to an opera. I've never even been to an opera. I'd like to go to an opera for the first time and, maybe if I didn't actually like it, to go again until I do. I'd like to take a class at The New School. There's so much stuff of so much interest."
— Phillip Seymour Hoffman

"It didn't matter to me whether or not Shadows *would be any good; it just became a way of life where you got close to people and where you could hear ideas that weren't full of shit."*
— John Cassavetes

How do you distinguish the voice of inner vision from the little voice that tells you, for instance, that you're worthless if you haven't amassed riches by the age of thirty? One way to isolate yourself from negative outside voices is to spend time alone. Another way is to be selective in your choice of companionship.

One of the reasons to take acting or directing classes (in my studio anyway) is sanctuary — the opportunity to be around people who have feeling. Lots of people don't want to feel. Then there are people who can feel their own hurt but have no interest in the feelings of others. I have now lived long enough that on three separate occasions in my career I have been told point-blank by people whom I had considered friends that they had no interest in my feelings. That was the end of those relationships, even though, in two of the instances, it took several painful months to accept the truth.

Make sure you spend time around people who have feelings and who respect the feelings of others. The ones who don't can hurt you. Stay away from them. Cultivate the artists of deep feeling: Shakespeare, Rembrandt, Van Gogh, Fellini, Cassavetes, Billie Holliday — even if you have no inclination to emulate their style.

Imagine the feelings of others. Any time people's actions puzzle you, take the time to figure out what is going on with them. Ask yourself questions. Consider as many details of their situations as you can, and imagine yourself in them.

And express your own feelings. I find that when I tell people my feelings, things go much better. When people disappoint me, if I tell them that I'm sad instead of getting all huffy, it goes better.

TELL THE TRUTH
"You make a story [Affliction] because you want to tell that story and you want to find the truth out about it."

— Nick Nolte

You've heard the adage, "truth is stranger than fiction." Most people seem to think this means that in order to make a story seem real onscreen, you must dilute its truth into "movie" truth. I have an opposite interpretation — the most entertaining fiction is based on truth.

Ingmar Bergman calls *Sawdust and Tinsel* "my first true picture. You know," he said, "my lying went on for a long time. Suddenly I understood that I had to stop. I saw that the lies were some sort of filth on my pictures... I had the conscious feeling 'Now Ingmar, you must tell the truth every minute.' "

"Telling the truth" is a pretty grandiose goal. I find it more helpful to encourage myself just to try not to lie. Don't lie. Get yourself out of the habit. I say this to myself as much as to you. Why do we lie? To make things easier for ourselves. To maintain a self-congratulatory self-image. To please others. To get ahead. None of these activities feeds our creativity.

ACKNOWLEDGE MORTALITY
In Carlos Castenedas last book, he said that the sorcerer Don Juan told him that the world is divided into two kinds of people: those who know they will die, and those who refuse to know they will die. Woody Allen, discussing in a taped interview the character Joey in *Interiors*, described her as a person who wants to be an artist, wants the immortality that artistic accomplishment may bring, even though she, tragically, is without talent. My own feeling is that no one is without talent, and that what is holding this character back in life is her belief that the purpose of art is immortality.

TAKE RESPONSIBILITY FOR YOUR OBSESSIONS
Know the themes of your life, and devote yourself to them. Paul Schrader said the reason he and Martin Scorsese could work together was because they shared a "core." "We are both quite moral. We believe decisions have consequences. There is right, there is wrong, and, in the end, there is a price to pay." Sarah Jessica Parker found, in *Sex and the City*, a vehicle for her obsessions with New York, fashion, and friendship. Walt Disney committed himself to an obsession that his successors have at times turned into formula.

Some filmmakers have more than one obsession, but few dramatists are capable of committing to a totally different obsession in almost every project — William Shakespeare, of course. Ang Lee, perhaps. Most filmmakers do best if they take responsibility for their single obsession and commit to it — even if it means making only one single, perfect movie (e.g., Barbara Loden's *Wanda*).

TEST YOUR IDEAS
Don't take any idea at face value. Test each one. Imagine its ramifications in as much detail as you can, to see if they can stand up in the universe you are creating. When improvising thus in the imagination, always compare the details you are imagining to observations and experiences from your own life. Test even the ideas that you don't think you like, before rejecting them. Script analysis is a place to test ideas in your imagination. Rehearsal is a place to test ideas in space and time.

DON'T STOP TIL YOU GET SOMEWHERE.
"I have no filters on my ideas. And I never, never, never give up."
> — Betty Thomas

The best advice I can give you toward developing a quicker intuition and wider-ranging imagination is this: Start. And don't stop.

Never stop. You never know when a good idea is going to hit you — good ideas take whatever time they take. Al Pacino wore glasses in the first day's shooting of *Dog Day Afternoon*. After watching dailies, he told director Sidney Lumet they should re-shoot — he had realized that Sonny should be a man who wears glasses, but who, on the day he's chosen to rob a bank, forgets them.

Michael Richards says he got the real key to playing Kramer "about eight or nine shows in. I had been playing Kramer as if he were slow-witted." Suddenly Richards had an insight — that Kramer was smarter than everyone else — "and I had him."

Sam Mendes continued his script analysis in the editing room of *American Beauty*, taking out a major sequence that he finally felt did not belong to the essence of the story. The story, he said in an interview, "was like shedding its skin, really — like a snake. The movie kind of emerged." Although others of the cast and crew were disappointed, screenwriter Alan Ball agreed: "The movie revealed itself to be something completely different from what I thought it was."

Sometimes when I'm doing script analysis in class or in consultation my students ask me: How do you come up with so many ideas? Well, I've been doing it a long time; it's a habit now. But the main thing is that I just don't stop.

THEN FOLLOW IMPULSES.
Rigorously testing your own ideas until they get simpler and better is not the same as second-guessing them. Don't confuse thinking things through and testing ideas with intellectualizing and second-guessing yourself until you've beaten down your instincts. Once you have thought things through, once you have questioned and tested every idea in every corner of your brain — forget about everything practical and everything "right" and follow your impulse! As playwright Steve Martin has characters say in *Picasso at the Lapin Agile*, creative ideas may swoop; they may fall like rain or land with a crash; they may pop, or even thunk, but "they never seem to flow... Never. Flowing is a myth. Never flow... Well, sometimes."

PART TWO
SCRIPT ANALYSIS

5 | GOALS OF SCRIPT ANALYSIS

"Why make a movie? To create a universe and see whether it can function."

— David Lynch

"The job is the same every time you start. Every time you pick up a script it's the same process, you have to break it down."

— Anthony Edwards

"It's not necessary for a director to know how to write. It helps if he knows how to read."

— Billy Wilder

"You have no idea how inspiring it is to have a director [Norman Jewison] who connects so deeply with the material."

— Greg Kinnear

"[Put] everything [the character] says and everything he doesn't say…under deep scrutiny."

— Billy Crudup

"The goal is to study something over and over again until it speaks for itself."

— Sigmund Freud

Some call it preparation. Or studying the script. Actors may call it making the character their own. Or taking the script off the page. But in the end it is script analysis — and the methods of working with text on the written page vary a great deal. Anthony Hopkins says that his script analysis method is to read the script "about two hundred times" — out loud. Meryl Streep says she rarely reads a script more than once, but rather trusts "the dream that was created in my head the first time I read it." My personal script analysis process incorporates both reading the script a lot and trusting the tangents that it takes me off on. I think of it as "making friends" with the script, becoming more and more intimate, as one does in a nourishing friendship. The goal is to arrive at insights and connection to an imagined world, as preparation to function in this world during rehearsal and shooting.

And editing. Script analysis is not really "over" until the negative is sent to the negative cutter. Script analysis is an imagining of the story and its subtext, its life outside the four corners of the page and the four corners of the movie screen. Every directorial choice (casting, location, camera lens) changes the script slightly (or a lot) and the story needs to be re-imagined accordingly. The actors' voices, their movements, their moment-by-moment choices and impulses, committed to tape or celluloid, are the raw material of the editing room, where the re-imagining continues.

My own process has always felt fairly intuitive. My attempts to present "methods" of script analysis are attempts to analyze and deconstruct my intuition.

STORY ANALYSIS AND CHARACTER ANALYSIS

Story analysis and character analysis are often seen as separate activities — with story analysis of more importance to directors and character analysis of more importance to actors. But I think of them as intertwined. Character analysis — also called characterization — means locating the characters in their emotional reality, psychology, physicality, and, most important, behavior. Story analysis means finding a shape to the individual scenes — and the whole story — by locating the story subtext. To me, ideas about characterization are interdependent with ideas about story structure, because the story is a series of events that happen to people, and the characters are the people they happen to.

A great many directors look no further into characterization than describing what the dialogue "sounds like." This results in cryptic opinions such as "obsessed," "hostile," "disappointed" — or worse, "hostile, yet disappointed," "brave, but worried," or "obsessed, but not too obsessed." Such quick impressions are likely to be superficial, obvious, and what actors call "unplayable" because they are result-oriented. Another common approach to characterization is reflected in a remark by director Jon Turteltaub that, "When you have a guy who's playing a jerk," it's a good idea to cast an actor of movie star likeability. This idea is okay as far as it goes — I just don't think it goes far enough.

One director, when approaching script analysis of a scene for my class, said he first wanted to ask the writer what was the scene's conflict and its resolution, and whose scene it was. Again, he stops short. The director should ask questions that take him into the characters' experience, so that they live, breathe, speak, take action, make mistakes, have histories, rela-tionships, memories, subconscious impulses, and even free will — in his imagination. When we do that, such issues as the scene's events (its "conflict" and "resolution") as well as the focus and needs of the character who is driving the scene will begin to take shape. Solutions will begin to suggest themselves.

The premise of script analysis is that there is more than meets the eye, that there is subtext. The search is for a reality behind the lines. The lines are clues that invite investigation and translation. We are looking not for what the lines describe, but for what they suggest.

HOW FAR TO GO WITH SCRIPT ANALYSIS

In order to have authority in the actors' eyes, directors need an iron-clad connection to the characters and their story. Michael Douglas reports that, prior to shooting, Steven Soderberg had memorized the entire script of *Traffic*. Haley Joel Osment said that M. Night Shyamalan "knew everything that happened in the script [*The Sixth Sense*] like he had written it yesterday." Peter Weir says of directing material written by someone else, "I have to eat the script. It has to become organic. It has to become part of me. It has to become almost as if I did write it."

The goal of script analysis is to fall in love with the story and the characters. Anytime you find yourself thinking characters are shallow and uninteresting, you just don't know them well enough. When you give them detailed attention they will surrender their secrets and become fascinating. If you've written the script yourself it is all the more important — just as it is in a long marriage — to re-ignite the passion by looking at the beloved with new eyes. A director who is also the writer of the project should approach script analysis with beginner's mind — as though he is reading the script for the first time — as though someone else has written it.

I go overboard with script analysis, questioning everything, taking my imagination down many roads. As long as I never judge the characters, and as long as I stay close to my feelings and my knowledge of life, I can daydream the life of the characters endlessly without harm. Asking as many questions as I do panics some directors — they fear it will lead to confusion and a loss of grip on their vision. For me, asking questions does the opposite of producing anxiety — it is calming. Asking so many questions is the crucial first step to locating the characters in the real world, and assuring myself they can exist as imagined people. Without the investigations that the questions generate I become fearful that the characters will remain creations of literature — or (more likely in today's culture) of the marketing department's merchandising franchises.

Don't expect, however, to use all your ideas when talking with the actors. As Constantin Stanislavsky noted, "An actor is not a capon, to be stuffed." The purpose of asking many questions is to stir up unconscious associations and connections and bring them closer to the surface. There, they present a field from which to make choices. The associations and connections — choices — are ready to spontaneously pop out in the form of inventive and intuitive solutions to the challenges presented in rehearsal or on the set.

Like Paul Newman (from the interview I mentioned in the *Sources of Imagination* chapter), I don't expect to use more than 10% of all the ideas and tangents that I come up with in script analysis. Ten percent of my musings and brainstorms will be pretty cool stuff — simple, usable, "playable" candidates for solutions to a character or a scene. And 90% will be blind alleys, overkill, or plain unworkable. But that's just fine — it's all part of the creative process, a good workout for the fertile imagination.

TELL A STORY ABOUT PEOPLE

"My favorite moments in filmmaking have to do with directors who I think of as being an actor's director, where it has to do with behavior, as opposed to something that is highly stylized where you are part of some idea rather than being the idea."

— Gene Hackman

Make sure that your vision is a story about people. Locate your ideas in a human reality. If you are creating, for instance, a story that includes a close friendship between two characters who are not at all alike, envisioning the poignancy and/or hilarity that will ensue from an "odd couple" relationship is not adequate script analysis. You must imagine human reasons why they might have become friends. (If we look at real life, we'd have to say that it is most likely that they grew up together.)

The way to become a good director of actors is to care about the characters and what becomes of them. If your story just happens to have people in it, but is really about violence, stunts, great camera shots, or "gee whiz" special effects — the actors will always know that, and it will be hard for them to stay present. For the best filmmakers, everything to do with storytelling is finally about the characters — their problems, mistakes, passions, victories, and losses. However, that does not require naturalism or conventional story structure. Finding the human center becomes even more important when the storytelling is non-narrative, stylized, experimental, or fragmented — or when the characters are aliens, superheroes, or animated characters.

LOCATING A CHARACTER'S INNER NATURE

"Every actor must create the part differently than every other actor would because it's a marriage of their essence with the character's essence."
— Dustin Hoffman

Sean Penn, who says he took his role in *Carlito's Way* in order to work with Al Pacino, says that Pacino has "no plan. He doesn't get an idea he's married to so much as a character, so you can't mis-serve him. That frees you." What I think Penn means when he says Pacino has "no plan" is that Pacino doesn't map out his character's emotional life in a connect-the-dots fashion. Instead he springboards off some intuition about the character's inner nature, and then lives and behaves spontaneously, moment by moment, in the world created by that intuition. Meryl Streep's statement quoted earlier about trusting "the dream... created in my head" suggests that she works in a similar way.

Artists of this stature find a center, or core, or kernel, or spine to the character. The process of this search sparks subconscious free-associations and connections which, in turn, generate texture of life. Characters created this way seem to have been alive before the film began and continue to be alive after the film is over.

A film project that uniquely illuminates this question of a character's "inner nature" for me is *Twilight: Los Angeles*. Anna Devere Smith created a stage play from videotaped interviews with survivors, participants and commentators of the 1992 Los Angeles riots, in which she played all the parts, using their words. In 2000 it was made into a movie which was shown on PBS.

I hadn't seen the stage play, but in the movie version her performances were interspersed with clips of the taped interviews themselves. My first flash was — how incredibly bold to allow her recreations of these people to be compared point-blank to the originals! Because a person's imitation of someone else would surely be lacking in comparison to the original, wouldn't it? But this was not the case! Somehow Devere Smith's creations were — I don't know how else to say this — *more the person than the actual person*. What she herself said about her process in an interview was, "It's not an impersonation. I am trying to find the place where the reality of another person bangs on the door of my subconscious."

Her words remind me of those of Pablo Picasso, who struggled for months to reproduce a likeness of Gertrude Stein, finally exclaiming, "I can't see you any more when I look at you!" He rubbed out the face and sent Stein away from the studio where she had sat daily for the portrait. He then painted her portrait from memory, and allowed himself to conceive the portrait as a mask. He never painted from sitting subjects again, instead trusting his intuition of the subject's essence. Richard Linklater's *Waking Life* was shot live-action on digital video, transferred to film, and then animated using a process called "rotoscoping" with thirty different animation artists drawing the characters over the live-action film. The director had given each artist freedom within a set of simple guidelines. Here again, each character seemed *more the person than the actual person.*

Each of these artists (whether actor, painter, animator, or writer-director) has perceived something about the inner nature of the person whose persona the artist is creating. The artist allows herself to trust her selection, and commit to it, bring her entire being to it. She doesn't try to imitate each detail of the character's behavior; she finds some key elements that speak to her own inner nature; she then allows the details to emerge from her own being, her own subconscious. The lessons for script analysis are that we should trust our associations and connections with the material more than a micro-managed road map of the character's inner life.

THREE SOLUTIONS TO EVERY SCRIPT ANALYSIS PROBLEM

Insight is the act or result of apprehending the inner nature of things. To hope to catch a glimpse of the inner nature of things, we've got to take more than one look. If we only have one idea, and it happens to work, that's luck. Luck is great, but, to become an artist and a functioning professional, a director must develop reliable intuitive ability.

Intuition occurs when the mind makes an instant irresistible *selection* from a number of possible solutions. In order to be available when that one, startlingly true option — which is your intuition — pops out irresistibly, you need to practice being alert to a whole field of options.

Forcing oneself to come up with at least three ideas for every single script analysis choice puts you in the practice that will lead to greater access to intuition. It is also a simple way to safeguard against the temptations to micro-manage and intellectualize characters' inner lives. Here is a summary of the reasons why I think a director should routinely ask himself to find at least three ideas for every script analysis question:

1. If you only have one idea to choose from, you are not making a choice, but swallowing an assumption. You are only making a *choice* if you have a field of items to choose from.

2. No matter how terrific a director's first idea might be, there's a good possibility that the actor will have a different idea. If it has never even dawned on the director that there could be another way to interpret the scene, hearing the actor's idea can create alienation between them.

3. Every idea should be tested. If it's good, it will stand up to an honest and rigorous comparison to other ideas.

4. That second or third idea may even be better than the first one.

5. What if *none* of the ideas works when tried? The exercise of having made yourself come up with more than one possible choice is a work-out for the imagination, making it stronger and more limber. Now you are better able to come up with new ideas whenever needed.

SOLVING THE SCENE

When I say come up with at least three possible choices, I don't mean that all choices are equally good. The goal is to find the choice that "solves" the scene. Some ideas for choices don't work — they may be pedestrian, or sentimental, clichéd, or an intellectual concept imposed untruthfully on the scene. Some choices lead us down a blind alley, because they originate from an incomplete understanding of the story or the characters.

But — paradoxically — when you know you must come up with three ideas, and are thus freed from needing to find the right answer, you stand a better chance of finding a creative solution! Pressure to find the one right answer is a killer of intuition and creativity. So instead of stalking and obsessing over the right answer, come up with three possible answers. If you can't think of three possible answers, then cook up three completely wrong answers — but just get started.

Then trust your imagination. Let the ideas percolate, play with them, sleep on them, and see which one rises to the surface. In the end, the director wants to go into rehearsal or shooting with a preferred idea — a vision. But to have these other ideas "in your pocket," ready for use if need be, is a calming reassurance that makes you *know imaginatively* that all those layers are in the material. Here's another paradox: "deconstructing" the material this way makes you respect and trust it more.

ACTIVE IMAGINATION
All script analysis ideas must be tested by imagining them in active detail. If clues in the script suggest that two characters have had a previous conversation on a certain subject, imagine the details of that conversation. Who brought it up? Who had the most to say? Who made a joke? Imagine three different scenarios. This process is a "work out" for the director's imagination. Actors — who must imagine the details of a character's life — feel safer around a director with an abundant imagination.

ENGAGE THE ACTORS, ENGAGE THE MATERIAL
Michael Mann reported that Russell Crowe discovered in his preparation for *The Insider* that Jeffrey Wigand was a poor golfer. Crowe considered this a key element in the story he was creating around Wigand. In his mind he was telling the story of a man who couldn't fit into corporate culture. Then Crowe found out that Mann wanted a brief scene in the movie of Wigand hitting balls at a driving range, more proficient at the game than in real life — as well as a scene in which Wigand is described by another man as an excellent golfer. The story in Mann's mind was that of a man driven by self-discipline and loneliness. Mann and Crowe disagreed on this point, and Mann says that Crowe voiced his objections "repeatedly."

Both of these very talented and hard-working artists of cinema were doing exactly what they should do. Each had created specific imaginative detail around a central core understanding of the character. Then, when they got together, they found they had different core understandings! Such "creative differences" can lead to an actor getting a reputation for being difficult — or to a director getting fired — or even to the demise of a project. But they don't have to. When I watched the movie after reading this anecdote, I of course paid special attention to the "golf" scenes. In the scene in which Thomas Sandefur (played by Michael Gambon) describes Wigand's golf game, his assertion that Wigand plays with a two handicap is swiftly corrected by Wigand, to seven.

At this point I checked back with a copy of the script I happened to have — in which Wigand corrects Sandefur by saying his handicap is three! Apparently sometime in between the writing of the script I saw and the shooting, Mann and Crowe came up with a compromise that allowed each to maintain his own vision.

Here's how I know that: because my methods of script analysis applied to the Sandifur scene that was finally used tell me there is room for both interpretations. A golfer with a seven handicap could be considered a very good golfer — or he could be considered to need improvement. In fact, changing this line from the three handicap to the seven handicap is not even a compromise. The real Jeffrey Wigand might be driven and perfectionist enough to have told Russell Crowe that he was a poor golfer when, in fact, he had a seven handicap, which many golfers consider very proficient. So in reality, both Mann and Crowe are right! Therein lies the trick of this stuff!

MAKE IT PERSONAL
"I got very emotionally involved with the major characters. I identified with each of them."

— Curtis Hanson

Script analysis is, in a way, a misnomer, because it has less to do with analyzing and more to do with connecting, with stripping down to essentials, with finding a hook that makes you feel something. Ideas for script analysis choices must come from what we know about life, from finding something primal in the script *that is the same* as something primal in us. This is the power of the metaphor, "It's like when...."

It's not that a director can impose her personal connections on the actor. Personal connections are personal! But if the director makes personal connections, the actor will, too. If, for instance, the character reminds the director of her father, that won't ring any bell for an actor. But it might give him encouragement to connect the character to his own father.

When in doubt, come from love. In two ways: 1) love every character; 2) look at the character in terms of what he loves. John Travolta said he considered his portrayal of the Clinton-esque Jack Stanton in *Primary Colors* a "valentine" to the former president. Lawrence Fishburne said of his research and preparation for playing Ike Turner, a difficult character who did hurtful things, "It starts with love. Ike loves himself, loves his music, loves Tina."

The personal connection can be a thematic connection — as long as it is one that you deeply believe. Denzel Washington said to Hurricane Carter during their meetings prior to shooting the movie *The Hurricane*, "I'm not trying to imitate you. I think this story is bigger than both of us. I think it's about a spiritual transformation and what happens when people reach out to each other."

PREPARATION FOR REHEARSING — OR FOR NOT REHEARSING
There is no point in rehearsal unless you have some plan of what to

rehearse. The "what to rehearse" comes from script analysis — a number of ideas to try out with the actors. Script analysis is not the movie — it's ideas to try.

If you don't have rehearsals, it is equally important to do a good script analysis, to be prepared on the set. John Sayles, for instance, never does rehearsals. Instead he sends the actors one or two page synopses of the backstory, claiming that he doesn't want them to "invent that shit." He feels that "if they know where they're coming from before we even start shooting, then they really can play the moment."

One thing that strikes me about the John Sayles approach is that its purpose is not to give a road map for the performance. He gives backstory — that is, facts and images — to which the actors can make their own associations and connections. His stated purpose is to make it possible for actors to play the moment. In other words, it's a way to get out of the actors' way. This is important, because many directors think of direction as a reason to micromanage and meddle with the actors' inner lives. It seems to me that Sayles' approach must be founded on a willingness of the director to accept whatever ways the actors bring to life the suggestions of the synopsis.

The second thing that strikes me is that in order for this approach to work, you need exceptionally insightful and vivid ideas about the characters, not just vague generalities. And you need to be a really good writer. You should use this approach only if you feel that the written word expresses your thoughts *more revealingly* than face-to-face interaction. This is different from giving the actors printed material because you feel uncomfortable talking to them — i.e., because you want to hide.

/ / / / /

The next two chapters, *Subtext and Choice* and *Process and Result*, will explore concepts that are the foundation of script analysis. The three chapters following that, *Emotional Events*, *Tools of the Storyteller*, and *Question Everything*, investigate the tools of script analysis. The *Emotional Events* chapter has more to do with story analysis, and the *Tools* and *Question* chapters have more to do with character analysis — but as I mentioned earlier, the lines of demarcation between story analysis and character analysis are not rigidly drawn. The next four chapters (beginning with the *Rehearsal Plan* chapter) present script analysis examples: scenes from *sex, lies, and videotape*, *Clerks*, and *Tender Mercies*. Following those chapters is a chapter on *The Whole Script*, plus two appendix-like collections of examples of *Adjustments* and *Intentions*.

6 | SUBTEXT AND CHOICE

> *"Those moments in between the moments, those are the most interesting. What's unspoken, the way we talk around things, the way our actions are inconsistent with what we're feeling, how anger and affection manifest themselves in strange ways at inappropriate times."*
>
> — Stanley Tucci

WHAT IS SUBTEXT?

Language is what we say with our words, and subtext is what we really say, with our body language, with the tone of our voice, with our eyes and expression. Subtext expresses our real feelings — for instance, feelings of impatience or distaste that may lurk beneath small talk and compulsory politeness. Subtext may express our underlying *intention* — as when someone says, "I'm listening to you" with eyes averted and jaw clenched, thus conveying the subtext intention to prejudge and resist the new information. Or when someone says, "Don't fall in love with me" with a look in her eyes that begs for the exact opposite response.

Subtext also comprises the associations we make to the physical world around us and the speech or activity of others — the associations, that is, that we censor and don't reveal (or think we don't reveal). An "association" is what a thing reminds us of. We make deliberate associations, such as keeping a broken plate or a worn garment solely because it reminds us of an important event, or the loved one who gave it to us. But associations may also be unwilling. I once knew a woman whose face reminded me of the Paul Simon lyric "she was a roly-poly little bat-faced girl," to the extent that whenever I was in her presence I could not stop myself silently humming it. And that made it very difficult to talk to her in any normal fashion!

Another example of subtext is the conscious or unconscious concerns that may distract us from the conversation we are supposed to be paying attention to. Hence, a "Freudian slip" — such as calling a current lover by an old lover's name — is an example of subtext slipping to the surface.

In life we start with subtext, our conscious and unconscious intentions and associations, and we end up with language and behavior. In a script, the writer starts with subtext and ends up with language, the printed word. The director and the actor start with language and delve into the subtext. Language is what is written on the page. Subtext is what is not written on the page; it is deduced from the clues in the script and from what we know about life. Intuition plays a big part in accurately reading subtext.

THE IMPORTANCE OF SUBTEXT

Writers like to think that their scripts can be played "as written," that is, with all words and gestures exactly as the writers imagined them, without the interference of actors' and directors' "interpretation." Directors like to think that their directions are clear and straightforward and that they have a right to have them followed to the letter. But *translation* from concept to experience is necessary in all forms and on all levels of artistic expression. Even if a film director feels inadequate to express her ideas in the "playable" terminology of actors, she should at least be aware that actors need time and emotional space to do this work themselves. Otherwise, the direction of actors degenerates into misguided and usually futile attempts to micro-manage the result.

The ability to notice and appreciate subtext is commonly called an ability to "read between the lines." It applies to reading between the lines of a dramatic script. It also applies to reading between the lines of the words people speak — that is, reading their body language and intention. It's easy to see that accurately reading between the lines of a script would be a key job of the director. But it's equally important for a director to be able to read the subtext behind the questions and complaints — and even the compliments — of actors. The skill of mining subtext — of spontaneously and perceptively interpreting the truth behind actions, words, and events — is intuition.

The "subtext level" is another term for the feeling level, the intuitive level. For any art, subtext and its close cousin, metaphor, are the breath of life. Martha Graham, the great pioneer and genius of modern dance, once said, "The secret to dancing is that it is about everything except dancing." The very definition of an artist may be that one sees, feels, intuits, allows, and treasures subtext.

AN EXAMPLE OF LANGUAGE AND SUBTEXT

Language itself is an imperfect tool of communication. But it does matter. For example, when we point out other people's errors:

1. Thank you for bringing me this file. Actually the one I need is different.
2. This is the wrong file. Please go back and bring the right one.
3. How could you be so stupid? Why did you bring this file instead of the right one? Don't you ever listen to instructions?

These different phrasings of the same request reflect different subtext (and possibly subconscious) *intentions*. Person #3 bullies, berates, or punishes the people that work for him. The intention of Person #2 might be something like "to involve everyone in getting the job done properly."

We would probably think of him as someone fair and reasonable who puts attention to the work ahead of personalities and egos. Person #1 could have as his first priority teaching or encouraging those he works with — on the other hand, he might be in the grip of a need to apologize even when it is the other person who has made the mistake.

Actually, Person #2's intention could be anywhere within a pretty wide range; the same words could be spoken with a subtext of demanding that more attention be paid, or dismissing or disparaging the other person's efforts, or criticizing their commitment to the work. On the other hand, the intentions to teach or to encourage could apply to Person #2's phrasing. Which intention comes into play might depend on *facts* or circumstances affecting the relationship — whether, for instance, the worker has made this same mistake before, or whether the speaker has had a bad day. Having the right file might be terribly important, or not very important; there might be plenty of time to fix the mistake, or there might be no time — these are *adjustments* that affect behavior and intention.

Even Person #1's words could be spoken sarcastically, that is, with a complete opposite subtext to their apparent content — in other words, with the intention to ridicule rather than encourage. And Person #3's adjustment might be that the two co-workers are old enough friends that he can make an over-the-top joke about the mistake without giving offense.

Which is more important, the words or the intention, when you are communicating with people you work with? Both, of course. And both are important for characters as well.

SUBTEXT IN THE WRITING

The Hollywood entertainment industry is frightened of subtext. In an unwavering search for risk-free projects, producers and executives badger writers to make a script more "clear," which they mistakenly think is done by taking out the subtext. One movie director with whom I was consulting told me jokingly that he tries to get the writer to make the script "director-proof." Whenever during our consultation I pointed out to him some nugget of subtext, something that I thought made the writing good and the characters complex, he would exclaim, "Wait a second! That's the stuff I want him to take out!" He was only half joking.

The fear is that if a director has to direct dialogue scenes with subtext, he might miss something, or choose the wrong subtext. Or he might not be able to accurately convey the subtext to the actors; he might not find the "magic words" that bring the actor into connection with the subtext, if the actor is not finding it on his own. And then the story might not work.

These are understandable fears. If a director doesn't find the subtext, and use it to create life, the storytelling will either be pushed and over-wrought, or flat and uninvolving. Complex and unusual scripts like *American Beauty* or *The Insider* or *Ordinary People* could so easily have been ruined without the delicate and insightful attention to subtext they received from their directors and actors. I won't name names, but I have come across excellent scripts that were made into very bad movies, even with "A-list" talent and lavish budgets. In each case, the failure resulted because the director paid insufficient attention to developing subtext.

In a rigidly "bottom-line" climate, such costly failures give complexity and subtext a bad name. Too many people start thinking that the turgid and boring dialogue scenes of many movies are proof that dialogue scenes are supposed to be turgid and boring, filler that we have to put up with to get to the good stuff — the special effects. It's a vicious cycle of mediocrity. A sad waste of the imaginative potential of storytelling.

Hollywood avoids the perils of subtext by producing scenes that are "on-the-nose." When we say that a line of dialogue is too "on-the-nose" we mean that it is a line (such as "What's going on here?" or "You just don't get it, do you?") for which it is difficult to find a subtext. I once sat in on a story meeting of a network soap opera; by my estimation, 80% of the "story notes" were requests to the writer that she take out subtext. The producer would ask the writer, "What does this line mean?" She would explain its subtext, and the producer would respond, "Well, change it to that." (The other 20% of objections were to words that had too many syl-lables.) It's almost needless to say that the writing that was being changed was better quality than the resulting "improvements."

What do I mean by "better quality" writing?

<pre>
                      JOHN
                (smiles at Graham)
        Do you pay taxes?

                     GRAHAM
        Do I pay taxes? Of course, I pay taxes,
        only a liar doesn't pay taxes, I'm not a
        liar. A liar is the second lowest form
        of human being.
</pre>

```
                        ANN
                (from the kitchen)
      What's the first?


                      GRAHAM
      Lawyers.
```

The subtext of this exchange, from *sex, lies, and videotape*, by Steven Soderbergh, might be something like this:

```
                       JOHN
      I think you're irresponsible.


                      GRAHAM
      I don't like you either.
```

In the Soderbergh version the subtext is implied, not spoken or explained. This makes the writing richer, the characters more intriguing. And, strangely enough, more like real people. Of course, one thing that makes the Soderbergh version better than the "no subtext" version is that it is clever and imaginative, rather than merely serviceable to the plot — and we may not in our daily lives say things as clever or imaginative as these characters do. But communication between real people is complex, rarely direct, and often unclear even to the participants. Such genuine human interaction is almost always loaded with subtext.

Another thing that makes Soderbergh's version better than my "no subtext" version is that it uses metaphor. Metaphor in writing is a way of giving examples, or "as ifs." A bit like telling illustrative stories instead of simply stating emotional exposition. "Pay taxes" is presumably an example of responsible behavior. The central comparison (a lawyer is like a liar) is a metaphor. (It also has clever alliteration and punchy rhythm, which doesn't hurt.) In a very few lines the writer has created a relationship without the characters having to declare their own intention or psychology. In other words, metaphor is used instead of explanation.

"CHARACTER SUBTEXT" AND "STORY SUBTEXT"

To be compelling to audiences, dramatic performances demand subtext, even if it's absent in the original script. There are two kinds. One kind is "character subtext." This is information about a character which the character may not speak of or even know about himself, such as his emotional and physical history, his relationships, his needs, and the images and associations that form his memories, dreams, wishes, and fears. Then there is "story subtext." The "story subtext" is the *real story* you are telling. It's not just the incidents of the plot. It's not the logline either. It's more complex than what I think most people mean when they use the term "arc." It's the emotional events — it's what happens on a human, emotional level in the imagined universe of the script to the characters that live in it.

The "story subtext" is the director's responsibility; it is the touchstone for every directing decision that is made. "Character subtext" is finally, moment by moment, the responsibility of the actor. It is whatever is going on in the actor's subconscious during the take that is chosen, and it is most believable when it is most private and idiosyncratic. The director is involved with character subtext, because it is the characters who make the choices and mistakes that are the events of the story subtext. So the actor's choices about the character's needs and backstory will have an effect on those events. But there's no way to know which choices are going to work until they happen in the actor's body and imagination.

For actors and writers, commitment to subtext frees them to trust their subconscious, which is where actors and writers perform most effectively. The director is the go-between between the writer and the actor. The director actualizes the subtext events of the script, and turns them into filmable scenic events. The purpose of script analysis is to explore and excavate that subtext level. Rehearsal is an opportunity for the director to open up communication at the subtext level, among the actors and himself.

"IT'S ALL ON THE PAGE"
When people say, in praise of a script, that "it's all on the page," that doesn't mean that all motivations and secrets are explained in writing. It actually means just the opposite — that there is subtext that is surprising, revelatory, and recognizably human. When the writing is good, the purpose of script analysis is to perceive and bring to life the subtext that the writer has allowed to be in the script. This is done by making *choices*.

To me, this is not the same as determining the writer's "intention," because good writing emerges from the writer's unconscious. The writer's conscious "intention" may be quite different from his unconscious creation. Alan Ball says that the questions Sam Mendes asked him, in preparation for rehearsal for *American Beauty*, made Ball see shadings and meanings that he hadn't realized were present in his work. "I'm an intuitive writer. Sam so clearly understood the script that he deepened my understanding of it."

When the script is thin, the actor and director have to make things up, create subtext that may not really be there. Jean Smart, at a Sundance screening of *Guinevere*, said "I only do research when the script is bad." By that she may have meant that with a good script, like *Guinevere*, she could just meditate and open herself to the script and its subtext would come swimming up to meet her. On the other hand, she may have meant that the director of *Guinevere*, Audrey Wells (who was also the writer), had done her script analysis homework, and was able to make revelatory comments that stimulated the actress, causing her to make associations that made the choices her own.

SUBTEXT IN THE ACTING

"Don't play the line, ever. It's like layers. The line is the top. The one you're playing might be the 14th down. You don't play anything on the button, as it were."

— Judi Dench

Actors engage the subtextual level in two ways. First, by being "in the moment." Subtext is subconscious, so the actor can't control it — he can only allow it, get out of its way. When the actor is in the moment, her feelings are transparent. The audience can glimpse below the surface of her face, and see and feel the spontaneous play of thoughts and feelings as they happen. This confers believability; it makes us believe that the actor is the character. It also allows us to believe that the character does exist (in the imagined world), because no character can take on life unless he or she has a subconscious.

The second way that actors engage the subtext of a script is by making "choices." A "choice" is some insight or connection or association to the script on a subtext level. It's not the plot or the words, or even a road map to the character's psychology — it's not something the audience is supposed to "get." It is a secret. It comes out of unconscious needs, feelings and impulses of the character, so it may be something even the character is not aware of. So the choices are often, perhaps even usually, different from the plot, or the obvious reading of a line. Just as language (the tool of the writer) can be too on-the-nose, choices (the tool of the actor) can be on-the-nose, too. *On the nose* means a literal reading of the lines. When, for instance, an actor who is asked what his objective is for the line "What's going on here?" gives the reply, "The character wants to find out what's going on" — that's too on-the-nose.

Well, usually, anyway. The instant I declare anything as solemn truth, I think of an instance where the opposite might be true. If an actor genuinely needed to know something specific, it would probably work fine. It's just that the choice "to find out what's going on here" is one that so easily lends itself to a hackneyed, movie-esque reading. To arrive at a more playable choice we should look at his circumstances, or his relationship with the other character. Examples might be "to demand respect" from the other character, or "to beg" the other character to help.

When professionals praise acting by calling it "committed," they mean the actor is committed to a subtext choice. An actor who plays "on-the-nose" might also be said to be "playing the plot" or "playing the lines," or even "playing the exposition." Playing the plot means that the actor has adopted the story arc as his character spine; for instance, in a story of a character who catches the bad guys, making the spine "to catch the bad guys." Instead, the actor can find more believable behavior from a subtext spine such as, "to make his father proud of him," or "to protect his family."

Playing the lines means that the actor's concentration is placed on making the audience understand the literal meaning of the line; or on convincing the audience that the information in the line is true; or on making sure that the audience knows that he is intelligent enough to understand what the line means. He gives the line an "intelligent line reading" instead of committing to a choice. Rather than play the lines, the actor should play the situation, or play the relationship, or play the objective.

A movie with examples of both playing the lines and playing the subtext is *Independence Day*. The dialogue scenes giving exposition (most of the scenes) are written without subtext, and played without subtext. They are dull. The scenes with Will Smith and Jeff Goldblum together, on the other hand, are lively and fun, because Smith and Goldblum are playing the relationship rather than the lines.

Now you might say that the actors in the "exposition" scenes are working under a handicap — the writing merely services the plot, with no texture of life to get a grip on. Even so, it's their job to search the script for clues for something underneath the lines, something in the relationships, or the character's personal history, that captures them. For instance, making an imaginative choice that the young Press Secretary is the daughter of a man who mentored the President back in his early days in politics. It is appropriate for the director to shape the scene in such a way that calls the actors' attention to the relationships and history of the characters instead of using rehearsal merely to move the actors around like furniture. Of course, whether or not the director does this, the actors should do that work on their own.

Even if the scene is in the movie for the sole purpose of conveying exposition, the actors should play the relationships, should play the personal event, the emotional event of the scene, and not its information. The audience will get the information anyway! In fact, they'll be able to pay better attention to it if they are not distanced and distracted by wooden acting. Playing the relationship is often called "chemistry." But the term "chemistry" makes it sounds like something mystical or lucky rather than what it is, which is craft.

Playing the subtext instead of the plot or the lines is important whether the characters talk a lot or a little. When characters talk a lot, it is crucial to make subtext choices to illuminate the events and transitions of the scene; without these choices to uncover the meaning of long speeches, they just sound like a lot of words. When, on the other hand, the dialogue is spare, something must be going on in the actors' silent faces — that is, subtext. In the films *October Sky* and *Monster's Ball*, for example, the characters speak so little and so simply their speeches are almost symbols or emblems of their feelings. Without the subtext provided (or "endowed") by the actors and directors, these movies would have fallen flatter than a pancake.

CHOICE

"I used to just show up and say let's get on with it. But you get to that point as an actor where you realize you're examining an aspect of the human condition as opposed to just a story that starts on Page 1 and ends on Page 120. And to do that you have to have some other stuff that's loaded up inside you."

— Tom Hanks

"Making choices" is the fun part of acting and directing. It's also the hard part, and the dangerous part. Acting coach *grandes dames* Uta Hagen and Stella Adler both have said that it is through the making of insightful choices that an actor's talent (or lack thereof) is revealed. Sean Penn, speaking of Benicio Del Toro, said, "There are other actors who are willing to do wild things, but they seem in general to be affectations, whereas Benicio finds things that will affect him." When Penn speaks of finding "things that will affect him" he is talking about making strong, specific, personal subtext choices. When he speaks of "actors who are willing to do wild things, but they seem in general to be affectations," he's taking about actors who cop a general attitude and play it *for its own sake.*

The ability of actors to be prompted by compelling private choices is something directors should look for in casting. In fact, most directors don't realize that such an ability is more helpful to the storytelling than whether the actor makes the same choice the director had in mind for the character. Even though the actors' choices affect the director's task of storytelling, that doesn't mean that the actor and director must agree on every choice.

EXAMPLE OF CHOICE — *SLAP SHOT*

A scene in *Slap Shot* shows the guys on the hockey team on a road trip, watching a TV game show together. A male contestant on the TV show is invited to say hello to anyone he wishes in the viewing audience. Ned (Michael Ontkean) offers the comment, "Ten dollars he says the guys at work." Reggie (Paul Newman) responds, "Naw, wife and kids." It almost sounds like a throw-away line, but of course it isn't. Newman has made a choice about the subtext of this line.

Let's approach this line as a script analysis challenge. I can come up with a few ideas of possible choices. The first question I would ask is whether Reggie's central focus is the guy on the television, or his relationship with Ned, or his own problems. If it is the guy on television, what is his adjustment toward him? That he is a good guy who cares about his family? Or a henpecked idiot? Is Reggie admiring the man on television, or making fun of him?

Or, if Reggie's comment has more to do with Ned, how has he perceived Ned's comment? Is he criticizing Ned for looking down on an ordinary working man? Does he wish to remind Ned of Ned's obligations to his own wife? Of course Reggie's comment does not need to be antagonistic to Ned at all; he could be encouraging the game by joining in the bet. Another idea: Is Reggie making the comment mostly to himself? Is "wife and kids" the answer Reggie would give, if asked who he wants to greet from the set of a television show? Is he wishing that he had a wife and kids to say hello to?

This simple exchange has roots in the emotionally pertinent facts of the script. Ned is a college-educated hockey player who looks down on the game and hates his life. Reggie is the captain of the team. Reggie's wife has recently left him. Ned's dark moods and insensitive actions have driven his wife away.

I don't know whether any of the choices I suggested above was the one Newman made. If I am the director of the movie, if the choice is working, it's not really my business what it is. If the choice isn't working, I might make a suggestion for the subtext adjustment based on what I feel is the event of the scene. Is the event of the scene an event in the story of Reggie's war with Ned? Or is it more an event in the story of Reggie's war with himself?

MAKE A CHOICE, ANY CHOICE

When the writing is complex, and it takes a while for the actor to make the full connection — which an actor may also call "filling" it emotionally — it may still be a good idea to start work with a preliminary choice. Making a choice, any choice, is a helpful step in script analysis. Even a wrong choice, if committed to honestly, can be better than no choice, because it gives you, as one of the characters in David Mamet's *American Buffalo* says, "an idea you can deviate from." Like in real life. When you're having trouble making a decision, sometimes the best thing is to go ahead and choose something; the act of making the decision may bring the insight (ultimately helpful even if disconcerting at first) that the opposite decision was the one you wanted to make.

An off-the-wall, arbitrary choice of subtext often works — for the simple reason that the human mind is not always logical; it stops and starts, buckles and leaps, and free-associates. *Opposites* work with top quality writing because the best writers create complex characters who don't usually understand their emotions and are operating out of the subconscious soup of human desire and contradiction (rather than out of a producer's need for a suitable plot contrivance). So making an "opposite" choice can bring to light an insight into the character's needs and predicament.

When the writing is not very complex, it may almost seem not to matter what subtext is given, as long as there is something. So opposite choices can be effective there too. Just saying the line with a subtext different from the one that seems obvious can create an extra layer, a tiny mystery.

In absurdist material (such as Samuel Beckett, Sam Shepard, Hal Hartley, the Coens, sometimes Kevin Smith or Quentin Tarantino) there may be little apparent logic. Opposites can be handy in getting to the reality behind each seeming *non sequitur*. Take, for instance, Beckett's famous opening lines to *Waiting for Godot*: "Nothing to be done." "I'm beginning to come round to that opinion." Sounds like they're depressed, right? An opposite might be to play those lines with the subtext intention to cheer each other up. But there could be human truth in that choice. If their situation is bad, they could be cheering each other up by making fun of how bad it is — or even cheering each other up by taking turns claiming the crown for "most miserable" (you could call this the "Woody Allen adjustment").

The very act of making subtext *choices* — if you look for the human truth in them — frees creativity and sets one on the path of discovering ever more insightful choices, or *solutions* to a scene or a characterization. Don't forget, it's the nature and definition of subtext that you don't see it at first. If a scene seems glib or too easy, then maybe it's your thinking that is making it so, not the writing. Maybe there is a playable *obstacle*, if you just look for it.

CHOICE AND INSTINCT
The subtext choices that fill and animate a good script are based on insight rather than cliché. A choice that gets under the skin of an actor so he doesn't have to think about it any more feels like instinct. It feels like instinct for two reasons: one, because he is not thinking about it and so it occurs in the moment; and two, because it touches the actor on a primal level. When actors speak about a choice that comes from their "instinct" they don't mean it comes easily or without digging. They mean that they have found something in the script that touches the deepest part of them.

Glenn Close says that what she most wants from a director is "the simplest, simplest truth." "Simple" here is another word for primal. In order for the director to have instincts that are simple and primal enough to bring a deep response from an actor, the director must use the script analysis process to strip away his formulaic and clichéd ideas. Only then can he be open to his deeper, primal connections.

Directors often ask me, "Don't you have to nail down a choice eventually?" "Nailing down" the choice is not the right way to look at it. It makes it sound like you tick off the emotional choices on a list and then you have a movie. No. It's not a matter of coming up with a set of "interesting" choices. Of course it's cool to be impulsive, non-linear, or off-kilter with the subtext associations you make to the script. But truth is the yardstick, not "interesting" — and truth is not something to be nailed down.

ACTING WITHOUT SUBTEXT — SOMETIMES IT WORKS
If the actors are in the moment a scene can work even without making an emotional choice. It's like the montage effect. If an actor's face, voice, and body are completely open and available, with no extraneous attitude pasted on, then we (the audience) will believe that his inner life is whatever the lines and action tell us it is.

If the actors are totally (radically) in the moment when they speak the lines and perform the actions, then the lines and actions will be informed with their unpremeditated subconscious associations, and will thus seem to have a subtext even if one has not been chosen. For actors, being in the moment means not thinking about the effect that their performance is supposed to be having on the audience. So anything that diverts their attention from the effect — even thinking about absolutely nothing — can help prevent the performance from becoming self-conscious.

Some actors make a point of never choosing subtext. This may mean they also refuse to rehearse. They may be afraid that working on the script will take away the potential for freshness. They know that good acting should be surprising and they may be afraid they won't be able to say the words "as if for the first time" unless they actually are saying them for the first time. There's no guarantee that this will always work. Because — as the guys in *Ghostbusters* discovered — it is very hard to think about absolutely nothing.

There is always the danger that, without subtext to capture the actor's attention, he will fall into "automatic pilot," which, for an actor, is thinking about how to play the lines. Not making choices can even become a mannerism, especially if the lines must be repeated over and over for coverage.

SUBTEXT IS NOT AN OBLIGATION, IT'S A PRIVILEGE

From the actor's point of view the purpose of making choices is not to provide a road map to the subtext of the script, but to help the actor to *get out of the way of the words*. The purpose of making a choice is to free the actor, not imprison him. It makes it possible for him to not think about how to say the lines, to not watch himself act. I disagree with the idea that the actor is supposed to have the subtext of the character. Instead the actor makes very private choices inspired by his associations to the script, and then lets the character borrow the actor's subtext. Even if the choice is totally arbitrary, say, thinking about what he will have for dinner after the day's shooting, it will be better than if he thinks about how to say the lines and what expressions to have.

But most actors find that the choices that most successfully keep them "captured" enough that they are not watching themselves are choices that connect them imaginatively and personally to the script and the character. My own observation is that any time the actor is not connected to his character, he is basically *worried*. And a playable *intention* or *objective* makes it much easier for an actor to *listen* and *engage* with an acting partner.

Connecting up to a simple, compelling choice keeps an actor from "playing a moment cheap." "Playing a moment cheap" means falling into trademark mannerisms whose subtext is a wink at the audience. Michael Caine says about his performance in *The Quiet American*, that he feels that for the first time he achieved his goal of finally playing a character with "nothing of Michael Caine" in it — that, instead, he gave a performance that was "all the character." What he means is that he feels that in many of his performances he has sooner or later given in to the temptation "play a moment cheap."

Sometimes the choices that provide actors connection to the script may be surprising. Christina Ricci said in an interview, "I feel I'm best when I'm actually thinking of something else. Like if I'm half-naked and I start thinking maybe I should suck in my stomach, the lines always come out better. When I think too much about what I'm doing, I get more nervous." Now, although this may seem like an arbitrary choice, it may actually be a rather sophisticated choice for the material — after all, if Christina is half-naked, that means the character is too; and the character may well be more concerned with sucking in her stomach than with convincing the other character of the truth of her lines.

A "NO SUBTEXT" STYLE
If the script makes emotional sense and tells an honest story, and if the physical action and filmmaking process serve that story, then the movie may still work even if the acting does not plumb all the emotional depths and corners of the script. When directors steer the actors away from subtext choices, they create a *style* to the movie or play. *Simple Men* (Hal Hartley), *Choose Me* (Alan Rudolph), *House of Games* (David Mamet), some of Woody Allen's films, create a style by keeping away from emotional depths. (I've heard that Hartley encourages the actors to say the lines over and over until they have no artificial "meaning.")

Although many young directors have been introduced to this approach through Mamet's book *True and False*, published in 1997, this is not actually a new idea — it's similar to Bertoldt Brecht's "A-effect" (alienation effect). In the 1930s, Brecht declared that he didn't want the actors to get emotional, because he didn't want the audience to get emotional. Rather he wanted the audience to think about the ideas of the play.

INTELLECTUALIZED SUBTEXT

"If you're too worried and too controlling of the gesture, then you're not gonna be addressing your intuitive side, your subconscious, you'll only be able to do what your conscious mind tells you to do. You're gonna be bound by psychology and meaning, not gonna be experiencing the stuff experientially."

— Willem Dafoe

There is a lot to be said for doing whatever is needed to avoid intellectualizing the subtext, or faking some superficial idea of the emotional life. The intellectualizing of subtext, the torturing and manipulating and beating to death of a precious imagination is, for the purposes of this book, something I think of as a kind of crime.

What is "intellectualized" subtext? Actors understand this question experientially, because they feel the painful difference between being "in their head" versus "in the moment." Directors are more perplexed. They watch an actor's performance get progressively more flat and wooden while they (the director) helplessly keep talking and talking. Later they look back and realize, "I talked too much." What this "talking too much" usually amounts to is a micro-managing of the actor's inner life.

Subtext is the unconscious. If we try to create subtext by choosing what exactly it is supposed to be, then we are "intellectualizing" it, or as Willem Dafoe put it, "controlling the gesture." By definition, as soon as we describe unconscious material, it is no longer unconscious. How do we make subtext "choices" so as not to intellectualize them? This is a question for directors and writers, as well as actors. To rephrase it, where do good ideas come from?

First, we constantly go back and check our ideas against our own knowledge of human behavior rather than armchair psychology, judgment, gossip, and glib notions of what would be "interesting" or "dramatic." We push ourselves to be more and more specific about that behavior. We describe that behavior experientially, rather than abstractly. We create narrative around the characters and events — stories, images, associations, and questions — rather than treating characterization and scene structure like a Power-Point presentation.

And, we use language that encourages imagination and free-association rather than passing judgment and over-intellectualizing. Here's where the subtext tools — verbs, facts, images, physical life, and event — also known as intention, association, substitution, situation, adjustment, physicality, and insight — come in. I encourage directors to use this language when analyzing characters and story, and when communicating with actors. I encourage actors to notice when they are being given unplayable result direction, and to take the time to translate it so that they can tap into their own empathic imagination and knowledge of life. And I encourage writers to throw off the shackles of formulaic writing and instead use these tools to let their characters live in their imaginations.

7 | PROCESS AND RESULT

"The means are to the end as the seed is to the tree. As the means, so the end. There is no separation. Indeed the creator has given us control over means, none over the end."
— Mahatma Ghandi

THE DANGERS FOR ACTORS OF ASKING FOR RESULT

A European filmmaker had to shoot a group of women (non-actors) emerging one by one naked from a lake. They were self-conscious, of course, in front of the (male) crewmembers. The results were impossible. Finally the director said to the women, "The story is not about you, it's about the reaction of the people watching you." Immediately the women relaxed; the director got the shot; the results were just what she had hoped for.

This bit of inspired direction put the actors' concentration elsewhere than on themselves. The worst thing that can happen to an actor is to watch herself. Self-consciousness feels so awful to an actor — and the stiffness of performance it leads to looks so amateurish — that in order to avoid it, actors may try to check and control their performance, or in other words, play a result.

Concentrating on the result leads actors into all sorts of bad habits, such as falling into a preconceived line reading that inhibits their ability to listen or be in the moment. Such habits include pushing or "commenting" on their performance, putting a theatricalized "frame" around it — or playing a moment "cheap" by displaying some little crowd-pleasing mannerism rather than surrendering to the reality of the scene. It leads them into concentrating on what they should do to the words to make the lines "work," rather than imagining the human truth of the situation and relationships. When an actor is concentrating on how to move and react and say the words in order to get a certain effect, it creates a "dead spot" or "false moment."

This hurts their performance. Now, the actor's performance is her own responsibility and not the director's. The reason the director needs to concern himself with these issues is that when actors are not in the moment and not connected up to the human truth of the situation and relationships, the resulting "dead spots" must be edited out — and big chunks of script may end up on the cutting room floor!

When the director continually gives direction in "result" terms, the director is taking a hammer to the actor's concentration. Some examples of result direction are:

1. Describing the effect the actor's performance should have on the audience (as in, "The audience should feel relieved here, because your character returned the money without being caught"), or describing the "note [for instance, of pathos, or weirdness, etc.] we want to sound here";

2. Attempting to dial or calibrate the actor's emotional levels (as in, "Could you ramp up the disappointment and take down the anger — just a tad?");

3. Passing judgment on the character (for instance by describing the character as a jerk, an asshole, a princess, or — more subtly — by allowing condescension or distance in your thinking about any of the characters);

4. Gossiping about the character, or intellectualizing the character's psychology. By this I don't mean it's bad to have a deep understanding of what makes people tick — of course that's an excellent skill for a director to have! I mean that a facile description of a character in pop psychology terms can be less helpful than saying nothing at all;

5. Worst of all — and all too prevalent — is the micro-managing of every look, gesture, and line reading. ("Don't forget to raise your eyebrow on that line, like you did on the last take.")

Instead of concentrating on the result, the actor should surrender, first, to the subtext beneath the words, and then to her partner. Instead of asking, how should this be played, the proper question is what is the human truth, what happens, what is this like? The imagining or creating of this human truth becomes what Sanford Meisner called a "river," with the words of the scene boats floating on its current.

"I always felt like a writer who took the role of director just to make sure his dialogue is delivered correctly. In the first two movies I would give my actors line readings because it was all about timing and syncopation and cadence and jokes. In Chasing Amy, *you can't do that because with drama you can't tell someone to cry a certain way. What you have to do is bring them to some comfortable place where you can help them get inside themselves. It's about creating a far more comfortable atmosphere for the actors."*

— Kevin Smith

Meryl Streep developed a problem on the set of *Dancing at Lughnasa* after the dialect coach told her to take the emphasis off a certain word. Streep recalled, "I couldn't remember my lines. I didn't know who I was."

First-time director Callie Khouri reported that actress Ellen Burstyn would sometimes respond to her direction with a withering look, even snapping, "I don't know what you're talking about, I can't even think about it like that, I have no idea what you're saying!"

Michael Duncan told an interviewer that director Frank Darabont came over to him once during an emotional scene and said, "You know, you're doing a helluva job, but can you just turn it down eight percent?" All Duncan could think was, "What the hell is eight percent? What am I supposed to do?" and added, "I still don't know to this day what he meant."

These cases illustrate three different forms of result-oriented direction: Streep was given a line reading. Duncan was asked to "dial" his emotional pitch. Burstyn was probably offered an unplayable psychological explanation. When actors commit as deeply to the imagined world as these do, result-oriented direction and attempts to manipulate the result by force-feeding, micro-managing, or "dialing" a performance become weird and tactless intrusions on their privacy and creativity. The fact that each of these actors managed to do an excellent job anyway is a tribute to their professionalism and their ability to translate result-oriented direction into playable choices.

One thing I was determined to do in my first book, *Directing Actors*, was to face as squarely as possible the question of "result-oriented direction," and the ways that it assaults creativity in directors as well as actors. "Result-oriented direction" is difficult to define, and I wanted to get directors' attention, so in *Directing Actors* I opened with a list of ten examples of "result-oriented" errors, which I knew directors would find shocking because they would be all too familiar. In order to offer alternatives, I organized my suggestions for more "playable" or "specific" direction around a list of five "quick fixes." Calling these suggestions "quick fixes" was, I admit, a bit of a trick, again to capture the attention of directors, who are frequently obsessed with the need to save time. These tools — *verbs, facts, images, physical life*, and *events* — are much more than quick fixes. They are tools of the storyteller. They open up the world of intention, association, metaphor, situation, adjustment, sensation, feeling, impulse, and insight that is also called subtext.

WHAT IF ACTORS ASK FOR A RESULT?

Most actors expect result direction, and some will even say that they prefer it. Those actors who say they prefer it have different reasons. It may be that they distrust directors who intrude on their inner lives in any way. It may be that they really mean that they prefer brief, clear direction over irritating and oppressive circumlocution — and that they cannot discern any real idea or vision behind the "politically correct" jargon. It is very important that the process-oriented tools be used not in order to be politically correct, but to describe a subtext reality that the director feels and believes in. The real reason for using the language of subtext — or "process" — is that it is a more accurate description of characters and their behavior.

Insecurity can make actors want to know what result to "aim" for. Result direction is a short cut, and short cuts are seductive. Think of it as junk food. A steady diet of it makes an actor's work superficial, and cuts him off from deeper sources of intelligence, honesty, and expressive feeling. We don't always want what's good for us, hence the temptation of result direction. And potato chips.

Sometimes, after I have described an adjustment as specifically and simply as I can (that is, using playable terms), an actor says to me, "You mean you want it angry?" Instead of taking the bait, I'll respond, "You know what? I don't know how it will feel. I'm looking for an experience, an interaction, the behavior of these characters toward each other."

Then I might continue talking, maybe along these lines, "Maybe you'll be angry, or maybe this time you'll find the character's disappointment. Maybe the other character's refusal to listen to you will break your heart. Or maybe you'll find you don't care what he thinks anymore. But just concentrate on getting help from him. If reasoning with him doesn't work, then demand it from him. Go ahead and give him hell if you have the impulse. I really don't know how you're going to feel. But make sure he feels sorry for what he's done wrong."

You see, I *am* looking for result but the result I'm seeking is *engagement*, not a particular line reading or facial expression I've previously concocted in my own head. I'm looking for an *event* to occur in the scene, an emotional event. I don't care how the actor gets there as long as it's honest. If I am the director, then my responsibility is to the events that tell the story. It's not my job or my business to tell the actors how to act.

When the result is not controlled, the results may be unpredictable. This is a good thing, not a bad thing. Whenever I ask directors what they think of as "good acting," unpredictability is always at the top of the list. Directors' desire to control the result of a performer's inner life is in contradiction to the results most directors actually prefer.

I've found that some directors think my injunction against telling actors how to feel means I don't want them to refer to emotions at all. That's not the case. If you look at the example I gave earlier, you'll see that I used hot button emotional words and phrases such as "angry," "disappointment," and "break your heart." I use feeling words, because I want to be sure the actors know they have permission to feel. But I put them into the context of intentions (the verbs "reason with him," "demand," "give him hell") and an objective ("make him feel sorry"), to encourage them to connect to the relationship and the event, and not just the emotion. I'm not advocating that directors develop and mechanically execute a particular jargon. I'm suggesting the use of language that creates narrative, association, and intention around the event and the relationship.

I can often achieve this by asking the right questions. An alternate response to the actor's hypothetical "You mean you want it angry?" might be to ask, "What do you think? Do you think she's still trying to reason with him? Or has she had enough of his shenanigans and is ready to give him hell?" Here I turned the responsibility for her emotional life over to her. I have also *translated* her result-oriented formulation into verbs.

I've noticed something when doing rehearsal demonstrations for groups of directors. More than once, after the demonstration, someone has asked me to give an example of how to use verbs when directing. Interesting request, because I was doing that all along! Only I wove the verbs into my normal conversation, making them undetectable as technique.

Of course it doesn't have to be a verb. A director might begin discussion with an actor by calling attention to the imagery in his character's lines, for instance, by noting that Noah Cross initiates conversation with Jake Gittes (in the *Chinatown* scene discussed in the next chapter) using the word "horseshit." Or the director could use a hypothetical fact — the "what if...?" adjustment. Or a metaphor — the "as if..." or the "it's like when..." adjustments.

PROCESS ORIENTATION IS IN THE DIRECTOR'S INTERESTS

The director is the guardian of the story. The actor is the guardian of the moment. Approaching script analysis and communication using process-oriented tools rather than result enables directors to tell their story more simply and powerfully, and without shutting down the actor's ability to stay in the moment.

The tepid shortcuts of the result-oriented approach are a poor substitute for the deep imagining and intuitive thinking that directors need in their arsenal of storytelling skills. The process-oriented tools are keys to the subconscious; they open the door to imagination, intuition, and the feeling level. They enable directors to establish intimacy with the characters and their stories. This intimacy prepares the director for confident and free communication with the actors, and at the same time generates creative ideas for structuring the scenes and events of the story.

The "process-oriented" subtext tools described in the next two chapters are good communication tools for almost any relationship. For instance, when directors (or producers) talk to writers about script changes they want, it's helpful to be able to discuss the script and characters at the level of their subtext rather than at the level of formula. This holds true when talking to any creative person. Recently a production designer told me that taking my Acting for Directors course made her finally understand the irritations she'd encountered interpreting the result-oriented instructions of directors and producers.

8 | EMOTIONAL EVENTS

"Something palpable happening that the audience perceives and that is not the words."
— Mike Nichols

"It is inside, around, and under the words of the script."
— Sydney Pollack

The single most important subtext tool for directors is the *emotional event*. The term is hard to describe except by examples. And it's difficult to learn except by practice. *Events* are not just the incidents of the plot. An *event* is truer than the text. It lurks beneath the surface, as a shift in the emotional lives of the characters. It is the ultimate subtext choice, the central choice the director is responsible for. It's *what happens* in the story.

In life, a moment — an action, an accident, a choice, a mistake, a decision — even a thought, a feeling, or an impulse — can change our lives. The storyteller isolates and elevates these moments, infuses them with images, and drives them by the needs (spines/objectives) of the characters. The central *event* of a scene is the emotional nub of the scene; it's what the scene — or the moment — is about. The movie itself is a succession of events, each one following inevitably from the previous one and leading to the next one, that bring the audience along an emotional journey which we call the story.

An *event* is an emotional transaction. The two simplest examples of emotional events are these: 1) someone gets turned on; 2) someone gets pissed off. In fact, these are probably the emotional events that are most appreciated by audiences. Some others might include: someone hurts someone else's feelings; someone puts something over on someone else; someone thinks he has gotten his point across when really he hasn't. A confrontation is an event. A confession is an event. A seduction. A betrayal. One way to pinpoint the event is to ask the question: At the end of the scene, how are the characters different — or what has changed in their relationship — from the beginning of the scene?

Morgan Freeman has said he wants a director to direct the movie, not the actors. By that I suspect he means that it is the director's job to find and create the event of the scene, rather than be the micro-manager of the actors' inner emotional life.

The *event* will be the touchstone for every creative participant in the production of a film, including the writer, director, actors, cinematographer, and editor. Whenever one of those key players loses their bearings, he or she can always get back on track by asking: ***What is the emotional event, and what do I know about such an event from my understanding of life — from experiences and observations in my own life?***

CENTRAL EVENT; INDIVIDUAL EVENTS; EACH CHARACTER'S PERSONAL EVENT — *CHINATOWN*

There is for each scene a central event, which is the director's storytelling event. There are probably also individual events, leading up to or resulting from the central event. And — each character can also have his or her personal story event, which is the event of the scene from that character's sole point of view. The characters' personal events can be different from each other — and even different from the director's story event.

Let's take a scene with Jake Gittes and Noah Cross, key characters in the movie *Chinatown*, by Robert Towne, reprinted at the end of this chapter. First, let's list the facts that are true before the scene starts. The two men are meeting for the first time, at Cross' ranch. Cross' daughter Evelyn Mulwray has hired Jake to investigate the death of her husband Hollis. Jake has learned that Hollis and Cross were former business partners. Jake is in possession of photos that show Cross and Hollis arguing a few days before Hollis' death.

Emotional events can be described as wins and losses for the characters, and it can be useful to look at the first section of this scene for its wins and losses. Cross begins the conversation with his observations on the smell of horseshit; the shock value of this opening could be seen as his first *win*. He then uses charm to question Jake's reputation and his motives for taking Evelyn as a client — likely a second *win* for Cross. Jake counters with the announcement that he and Evelyn think Hollis was murdered — Jake's *win*. Instead of responding to this announcement, Cross changes to the subject of the fish on Jake's plate, which has been served with the head; Jake returns with, "Fine, as long as you don't serve chicken that way" — a second *win* for Jake. The two men are now at a draw, 2-2.

Each of these "wins" is an event in the scene. In the next section, or beat, is a series of questions from Cross — What do the police say? Who is the investigating officer? Do you know him? Where from? Would you call him a capable man? Honest? You've got no reason to think he's bungled the case? How much are you charging her? And finally — Are you sleeping with her? Jake gets up to leave. That Cross *provokes Jake into leaving* is the next event.

Then Cross says, "You may think you know what you're dealing with, but believe me, you don't." At this point, there is a stage direction, "This stops Jake." Jake says, "That's what the D.A. used to tell me about Chinatown." And then he stays and continues the conversation!

I'm imagining now that I have never seen the movie and am doing a script analysis on this scene. This moment would raise a big question for me: Why does Jake change his mind and stay? In other words, what is the event? I'm going to suggest a few possibilities. Does hearing these words ("You may think you know what you're dealing with, but believe me, you don't.") so powerfully and unnervingly carry Jake back to his memories of Chinatown that *he drops his guard*? Or does he *make a strategic choice to appear to have dropped his guard*? Or is it Cross who has *dropped his guard* first?

What is the subtext of Cross' statement "You may think you know what you're dealing with, but believe me, you don't"? Is it *a warning*? Or is it *an invitation* to include Jake in the insider information Cross is able to impart? If an invitation — does Jake *decide that it might be worthwhile to stay for the information Cross may volunteer*? Or, if Cross' statement is a warning — does it misfire in its intent? Does Cross strike Jake as so overt as to be clumsy? And could that perception of clumsiness *relax Jake and make him feel smarter than the other man*? Or is the event something else altogether? Has Jake been *sucked in by the charisma and showmanship* of Cross?

This event leads us to the third section. Cross next offers to hire Jake to find "Hollis' girlfriend." Instead of replying, Jake asks Cross when he last saw Hollis. This is an event — Jake is *setting Cross up to catch him in a lie* by announcing the existence of the photos. Cross makes a subject shift to the parade going by. In the next few lines, Jake presses the question of what Cross and Hollis were arguing about. When Cross finally answers, "My daughter," that's an event — *he has given in* by acknowledging that there is emotional content to the evidence Jake possesses. The next event is that Cross *places suspicion on Evelyn* by saying, "she's an extremely jealous person. I didn't want her to find out about the girl." Jake's line "Are you worried about that girl, or what Evelyn might do to her?" could be an event — Jake *nailing Cross* for his attempt to insinuate his own daughter is capable of foul play. The last event is that Jake *throws out a challenge* with the parting remark that he is going to "check out some avocado groves."

Now, it's time to think about the central event, and each character's personal event. Jake has held his own against Cross' insinuations, announced that Hollis was murdered, caught Cross in a lie, revealed the existence of the photos, nailed Cross for his intention to accuse his own daughter of foul play. We could thus see the central event of the scene as a victory for Jake, and a humiliation for Cross.

But let's keep looking. This is a very complex scene, with layers and layers of subtext. By casting suspicion on his own daughter Cross has revealed the extent of his ruthlessness. Cross is a man who sizes up other men to see what tactics he needs to control them. Sometimes he does it with easy charm; sometimes with undermining insinuations. When he feels it is called for — or when he is backed into a corner — he strikes with raw venom. Perhaps he expects Jake to cower, and sustains a loss when Jake instead stands up to him and strikes back.

But — maybe Cross doesn't care whether a man cowers before him or not — as long as he gets information he needs to recoup for another day. And Cross *gets a lot of information* from Jake: that the photos exist, that Jake is investigating the avocado groves, that Jake is hotheaded — or foolish, or strategic — enough to let out that information, and that Jake is smart enough to detect Cross's willingness to throw his daughter to the wolves in order to — do what? Protect himself? Get what he wants? This brilliantly written scene takes us tumbling down some suspenseful psychological tunnels. And don't forget that even though Jake has seen through Cross' attempt to plant the seed of Evelyn's guilt — *the seed is still planted.* And that Cross's question "Are you sleeping with her?" verbalizes an image that may have been here-to-fore unconscious for Jake — and which does become realized in a scene soon after this one. Has Cross *set this in motion?*

From a storytelling point of view — that is, from the point of view of the director who is structuring the whole movie — Cross is a man who turns every loss into a win. So the personal event for Cross in this scene might be a loss, a humiliation. It could be a way to direct the actor playing Cross — with an objective "to keep Jake in his place." Playing it this way gives the actor something at stake, an obstacle; it humanizes this difficult character. It also gives the story suspense, lulling the audience into thinking (erroneously, as it turns out) that these antagonists are evenly matched.

VISION

When I tell directors I want them to let go of the result, I don't mean they should let go of their vision. The vision is the event. That's precisely what I want directors to focus on — creating event, rather than executing results.

That doesn't actually mean the actors must always agree with the director or with each other on what the event is. The individual characters may be wrong about what has just happened to them — I mean, that happens to people, doesn't it? Structuring the scene so each character has his own personal event with no knowledge of the story event makes the characters more believable. Jake may think that the event is that he's held his own before this puzzling stranger. Cross may feel he's been made a fool of. Jake may even feel proud of his assertion of the upper hand. But the storytelling event can still be that Jake has stepped precariously out of his depth. He has revealed too much information. He has — and, as we find out later, not for the last time — allowed the memory of what happened in Chinatown to cloud his judgment.

"DOMESTIC" EVENT

The opportunity to dive into these emotional and psychological waters is the reason why I love to live in the imagined world, the reason why these characters are as real to me as actual people. But it can also be helpful to look at the "domestic" event, which is what is happening on the simplest level of day-to-day life. The domestic event locates the scene in the normal world of objects and activities. We must not forget in all our emotional and psychological analysis that these are *two businessmen meeting for the first time*.

STORYTELLING EVENTS AND SPONTANEOUS EVENTS

When a scene is actually performed, there are two levels of event. One is the storytelling events described above. These are the subject of the director's script analysis, and the center of the scene-shaping which is the director's storytelling. The other is the spontaneous events — all the moment-by-moment ways that the actors actually affect each other. This comes from the effects of listening to one another and the ways they make each other smile, laugh, doubt themselves, grow fearful, curious, turned on, or angry. In essence, these tiny, bite-sized "micro" events occur when one actor has a palpable effect on the other. Because these events happen in the moment, they are by definition always surprises. They may even feel to the actors like mistakes. But whenever actors have an effect on each other, the audience reads it as the characters having an effect on each other — and such "mistakes" are usually the best parts of a movie.

ANY EVENT IS BETTER THAN NO EVENT.
What this means is that the scene may still work even if the actor's ideas about the emotional event are completely different from the director's. If something happens honestly, in the moment, between two actors, the audience will believe it is whatever the script tells them it is. For example, if the script tells us that the characters are falling in love, then if one actor makes the other one laugh, in the moment — or even get pissed off, in the moment — we'll believe that the event is a step in their growing intimacy.

The audience doesn't need to *know* what the event is — they only need to *feel* that an event has taken place. In a scene from *All the President's Men*, Woodward (Robert Redford) and Bernstein (Dustin Hoffman) are interviewing Hugh Sloan, the man who had resigned as treasurer of the Committee to Re-Elect the President. The scene is staged with Woodward and Bernstein seated on two sofas perpendicular to each other in a corner arrangement, and Sloan in a lone armchair on the other side of the room. The scene cuts back and forth from a medium single on Sloan, to a wide two-shot of Woodward and Bernstein. At the beginning of the conversation, Sloan says, "I'm a Republican." Cut to the Woodward-Bernstein two-shot: Woodward says, "I am too."

As Sloan continues to speak, the camera holds on an exchange of looks between Bernstein and Woodward. What is their subtext? I'm going to suggest three different subtext possibilities as three ways of locating the event of that exchange of looks.

One possibility is as follows: Bernstein: "A Republican! I had no idea I was working with a Republican!" Woodward: "I can be a Republican and still write this story. All that matters to me is getting the story right."

On the other hand, it could be: Bernstein: "Don't take a chance telling a lie like that. He could say later that we entrapped him." Woodward: "It's not a lie. I was a Republican, once. It was just a long time ago."

A third possibility: Bernstein: "I thought you were too tight-assed to try a trick like that — pretending you're a Republican! You're always on me when I pull those numbers. Good for you, man!" Woodward: "Quit staring at me! You're giving it away."

If I am the director of this scene, I may not need to instruct the actors which particular subtext to adopt. The audience will never know which it is, because there's nothing in the whole rest of the script to tell us whether Woodward is Republican or not. So it's a choice — it's a secret. As a director, I can mention that any of those three (as well as others) are possible, and leave the choice to their own impulse. In fact, perhaps all I need to say is, "Do you guys think Woodward really is a Republican, or not?" And then say, "Don't tell me — or each other — your answer to that. Let's run it and see what happens."

THE THROUGH-LINE

A great way to create all the tiny "spontaneous" events that enrich and enliven a scene is for each actor to have a "through-line." A through-line is a preoccupation. If someone is rude to us that experience can become our preoccupation for the rest of the day. In other words the image of that negative experience is our through-line — or *focus* — for the day. (Don't forget, the "image" for these purposes is not limited to a visual image; in this case it's the sound of the rude person's voice that permeates our emotional storage banks.)

Usually the most playable through-line for a character is phrased as an *objective*, because:

1. For actors, it's what the character wants, so it's simple and playable, and connects the actor to the other actor, instead of to her own self-consciousness;
2. For directors, it creates conflict for drama; dilemma and incongruity for comedy; and thus is very helpful in bringing about an emotional event;
3. For writers, what the characters want and need are an invaluable entrée into their inner life, and when the writer connects to the characters' inner life, the dialogue and actions will start to almost dictate themselves to the writer's imagination.

The through-line is *subtext*, so it may be the character's central *secret*, the one thing he doesn't talk about. Or it may be revealed in one certain line in the character's dialogue — the thing he says that, whether he knows it or not, is an emblem of his central preoccupation or need. One candidate for Cross' most important line is "'Course I'm respectable. I'm old. Politicians, ugly buildings and whores all get respectable if they last long enough." Another candidate is his line, "My daughter." I'll explain a little later in the chapter why I think either of those lines might be central to the character of Cross.

When looking for a through-line, it's important to be able to notice the "elephant in the room," the thing that is clearly the central situation, the "big, fat fact." Sean Penn says that David Rabe, while doing rewrites for *Casualties of War*, told him, "If a woman comes to your room at 3:00 AM, pay no attention to any other aspect of the scene." He means that the male character's adjustment in such a situation will always be that he is certain that she wants sex.

On the most practical level, the through-line can be a lifesaver when shooting scenes or segments of scenes out of sequence. Or when, as in the movie *The Negotiator*, the two sides of the central phone calls were shot completely separately — Kevin Spacey's side of the conversation shot months later than Samuel Jackson's. A sense of objective for both actors can help create the tension of the relationship which is the center of the film.

But the greatest boon is that a robust through-line that captures the actor's heart and imagination can replace the nightmare of micro-managing the actor's performance. When an actor surrenders to a clear, playable, unambiguous through-line, many of the emotional details of the scene will fall effortlessly into place.

BEATS

I find it incredibly helpful to break the scene down by noting what are its topics and subjects. The "beat changes" are simple changes of subject. It is then also useful to note which character changes the subject. For instance, in the *Chinatown* scene, printed at the end of the chapter:

Topic #1, "horseshit," brought up by Cross.
Topic #2, Jake's reputation, brought up by Cross.
Topic #3, murder, brought up by Jake.
Topic #4, breakfast (Cross).
Topic #5, the police investigation (Cross).
Topic #6, Jake's ethics (Cross).
Topic #7 is tricky: It begins with Cross' mid-speech line "Sit down." And goes through "Politicians, ugly buildings and whores all get respectable if they last long enough." I'm going to say that Cross' topic here is his own power and what he is capable of doing to keep it.
Topic #8 is hiring Jake to find Hollis' girlfriend (Cross).
Topic #9, the photos (Jake, interrupted by Cross' observation of the parade).
Topic #10, Evelyn (Cross).

It's then useful to see if I can group these topics into larger beats. When I went through the individual events earlier in the chapter, I came up with this grouping: first section, the first four topics; then (second section), topics five, six, and seven; finally, topics eight, nine, and ten (the third section).

THE IMPORTANCE OF EMOTIONAL EVENT IN DIRECTING THE ACTORS

Studying the scene from this point of view gives me lots of information and lots of ideas — for instance, about the different ways the two men make their respective attacks. Jake is quick — his suggestion of murder, and revelation of the photos seem to come out of the blue — is this a "no-nonsense" approach? Or an impulsive one? Is ambush his preferred strategy? Cross' strategy seems to shift. In the first section he uses sophisticated charm, humor, and indirection. In the second section he behaves like an interrogating attorney or prosecutor. In the third section, he uses an "I'm just an average Joe" approach — the good friend (to Hollis), the concerned protector of a frightened child, the put-upon parent of a wayward daughter.

"Like an interrogating attorney" is an image, or metaphor, that many actors might find playable. "Ambush" is an image, also a verb. But the most important way the actors need to relate to these events and choices is, as always, on the personal level. It's always helpful for a director discussing a scene with actors to ask, after a brief discussion of these ideas, "What strategies do *you* use when you are negotiating with someone who might be dangerous?" And to jump in with stories about the strategies the director himself uses in such situations. The actor does not need to give the director answers to such questions, but he does need to make the personal connection.

After I had written all this discussion of the *Chinatown* scene, I watched the movie again. I was amazed to discover (I had completely forgotten this since my last viewing of the film some years ago) that director Roman Polanski's emotional structuring gives the scene completely to Noah Cross (played by John Huston). The emotional structure is underscored by the staging — Jake (Jack Nicholson) is physically as well as emotionally in the background for the entire scene. None of the emotional events that I suggested above for Jake was highlighted; Jake is portrayed as a neutral observer to the emotional trajectory of Cross. The emotional center of the scene comes when Cross replies to Jake's question, "What was the argument about?" with the line, "My daughter." I had thought of this, when making my list of topics, above, as the beginning of Topic #10, the "Evelyn beat." When I watched the scene I realized, with a shiver, that the "daughter" Cross and Hollis were arguing about was not Evelyn, but Cross' other daughter.

THE IMPORTANCE OF EMOTIONAL EVENT FOR THE AUDIENCE

Structuring the emotional event is the way the director makes the movie accessible for the audience. Even seemingly remote and intellectually demanding subject matter — as in *All the President's Men*, *The Insider*, *The Hours*, *Sense and Sensibility*, or *Judgment at Nuremberg* — can be made accessible without sacrifice of content when the scenes are structured around their emotional events. The structuring of emotional events is necessary no matter what the style and tone of the movie. Directors David Lynch and Robert Altman, who are famous for a loose, "non-narrative" style, are able to craft subtext emotional events with exceptional subtlety.

TEXT OF *CHINATOWN* SCENE

Chinatown, by Robert Towne

142   EXT. BRIDLE PATH - GITTES & CROSS

walking toward the main house -- a classic Monterey. A horse led on a halter by another ranch hand slows down and defecates in the center of the path they are taking. Gittes doesn't notice.

> CROSS
> Horseshit.

Gittes pauses, not certain he has heard correctly.

> GITTES
> Sir?

> CROSS
> I said horseshit.
>   (pointing)
> Horseshit.

                    GITTES
     Yes, sir, that's what it looks like - I'll give
     you that.

143 Cross pauses when they reach the dung pile. He removes
his hat and waves it, inhales deeply.

                    CROSS
     Love the smell of it. A lot of people do but
     of course they won't admit it. Look at the
     shape.

Gittes glances down out of politeness.

                    CROSS
          (continuing; smiling, almost enthusiastic)
     Always the same.

Cross walks on. Gittes follows.

                    GITTES
          (not one to let it go)
     Always?

                    CROSS
     What? Oh, damn near -- yes. Unless the
     animal's sick or something.
          (stops and glances back)
     -- And the steam rising off it like that in the
     morning -- that's life, Mr. Gittes. Life.

They move on.

                    CROSS
          (continuing)
     Perhaps this preoccupation with horseshit may
     seem a little perverse, but I ask you to
     remember this -- one way or another, it's what
     I've dealt in all my life. Let's have
     breakfast.

144 EXT. COURTYARD VERANDA - GITTES & CROSS AT BREAKFAST

Below them is a corral where hands take Arabians, one by one, and work them out, letting them run and literally kick up their heels. Cross' attention is diverted by the animals from time to time. An impeccable Mexican butler serves them their main course, broiled fish.

> CROSS
> You know, you've got a nasty reputation, Mr. Gittes. I like that.

> GITTES
> (dubious)
> Thanks.

> CROSS
> -- If you were a bank president that would be one thing - but in your business it's admirable. And it's good advertising.

> GITTES
> It doesn't hurt.

> CROSS
> It's why you attract a client like my daughter.

> GITTES
> Probably.

> CROSS
> But I'm surprised you're still working for her -- unless she's suddenly come up with another husband.

> GITTES
> No -- she happens to think the last one was murdered.

Cross is visibly surprised.

> CROSS
> How did she get that idea?

                    GITTES
          I think I gave it to her.

Cross nods.

                    CROSS
          Uh-huh -- oh, I hope you don't mind. I believe
          they should be served with the head.

145 Gittes glances down at the fish whose isinglass eye is
glazed over with the heat of cooking.

                    GITTES
          -- Fine, as long as you don't serve chicken
          that way.

                    CROSS
               (laughs)
          Tell me -- what do the police say?

                    GITTES
          They're calling it an accident.

                    CROSS
          Who's the investigating officer?

                    GITTES
          Lou Escobar -- he's a Lieutenant.

                    CROSS
          Do you know him?

                    GITTES
          Oh yes.

                    CROSS
          Where from?

                    GITTES
          -- We worked Chinatown together.

                    CROSS
          Would you call him a capable man?

                    GITTES
Very.

                    CROSS
Honest?

                    GITTES
-- Far as it goes -- of course he has to swim
in the same water we all do.

                    CROSS
Of course -- but you've got no reason to think
he's bungled the case?

                    GITTES
None.

                    CROSS
That's too bad.

                    GITTES
Too bad?

                    CROSS
It disturbs me, Mr. Gittes. It makes me think
you're taking my daughter for a ride -
financially speaking, of course. How much are
you charging her?

                    GITTES
          (carefully)
My usual fee -- plus a bonus if I come up with
any results.

                    CROSS
Are you sleeping with her? Come, come, Mr.
Gittes -- you don't have to think about that to
remember, do you?

Gittes laughs.

                    GITTES
If you want an answer to that question I can
always put one of my men on the job. Good
afternoon, Mr. Cross.

                    CROSS
Mr. Gittes! You're dealing with a disturbed
woman who's lost her husband. I don't want her
taken advantage of. Sit down.

                    GITTES
What for?

                    CROSS
-- You may think you know what you're dealing
with -- but believe me, you don't.

146 This stops Gittes. He seems faintly amused by it.

                    CROSS
Why is that funny?

                    GITTES
It's what the D.A. used to tell me about
Chinatown.

                    CROSS
Was he right?

Gittes shrugs.

                    CROSS
                 (continuing)
... Exactly what do you know about me,
Mr. Gittes?

                    GITTES
Mainly that you're rich and too respectable to
want your name in the papers.

                         CROSS
                    (grunts, then)
          'Course I'm respectable. I'm old.
          Politicians, ugly buildings and whores all get
          respectable if they last long enough. I'll
          double whatever your fees are -- and I'll pay
          you ten thousand dollars if you can find
          Hollis' girlfriend.

                         GITTES
          His girlfriend?

                         CROSS
          Yes, his girlfriend.

                         GITTES
          You mean the little chippie he was with at the
          El Macando?

                         CROSS
          Yes. She's disappeared, hasn't she?

                         GITTES
          -- Yeah.

                         CROSS
          Doesn't that strike you as odd?

                         GITTES
          No. She's probably scared to death.

                         CROSS
          Wouldn't it be useful to talk to her?

                         GITTES
          Maybe.

                         CROSS
          If Mulwray was murdered, she was probably one
          of the last people to see him.

                         GITTES
          You didn't see Mulwray much, did you?

                    CROSS
          -- No --

                    GITTES
          -- When was the last time?

147 Cross starts to reply, then there's the SOUND of a MARIACHI
BAND and some men in formation clear a bluff about a hundred
yards off. They are dressed like Spanish dons on horseback.
For the most part they are fat in the saddle and pass along in
disordered review to the music..

                    CROSS
          Sheriff's gold posse... bunch of damn fools
          who pay $5,000 apiece to the sheriff's
          re-election. I let 'em practice up out here.

                    GITTES
          -- Yeah. Do you remember the last time you
          talked to Mulwray?

Cross shakes his head.

                    CROSS
          -- At my age, you tend to lose track...

                    GITTES
          Well, It was about five days ago. You were
          outside the Pig 'n Whistle -- and you had one
          hell of an argument.

Cross looks to Gittes in some real surprise.

                    GITTES
                 (continuing)
          I've got the photographs in my office -- if
          they'll help you remember. What was the
          argument about?

                    CROSS
                 (a long pause, then)
          My daughter.

                              GITTES
          What about her?

                              CROSS
          -- Just find the girl, Mr. Gittes. I think
          she is frightened and I happen to know Hollis
          was fond of her. I'd like to help her if I
          can.

                              GITTES
          I didn't realize you and Hollis were so fond of
          each other.

148   Cross looks hatefully at Gittes.

                              CROSS
          Hollis Mulwray made this city -- and he made me
          a fortune... We were a lot closer than Evelyn
          realized.

                              GITTES
          -- If you want to hire me, I still have to know
          what you and Mulwray were arguing about.

                              CROSS
                    (painfully)
          Well... she's an extremely jealous person. I
          didn't want her to find out about the girl.

                              GITTES
          How did you find out?

                              CROSS
          I've still got a few teeth in my head,
          Mr. Gittes -- and a few friends in town.

                              GITTES
          Okay -- my secretary'll send you a letter of
          agreement. Tell me -- are you worried about
          that girl, or what Evelyn might do to her?

                    CROSS
          Just find the girl.

                    GITTES
          -- I'll look into it -- as soon as I check out
          some avocado groves.

                    CROSS
          Avocado groves?

                    GITTES
          We'll be in touch, Mr. Cross.

End of scene.

9 | TOOLS OF THE STORYTELLER

"You can learn the right questions to ask in developing a character. You ask yourself where they're from, what they want, what their relationships are like, what their decision-making process is in life and the tools they use to get what they want. Rather than using adjectives — he's angry here, he's sad here — you give the character motivation to pursue something, and as you build the character you give them tools for going about getting what they want."

— Billy Crudup

The way to vibrant, meaningful choices that bring characters and stories alive is to make those choices specific, emotionally compelling, and bold. When I talk about making choices specific, I don't mean specific about the result — such as a line reading or a facial expression — but specific about the source. In this chapter we are going to explore the tool kit of techniques for excavating the world of subtext choice — images, verbs, facts, adjustments, obstacles, and physical life.

This is not to say that you must use each one for every script and every actor. Some actors work really well with intentions (verbs) and don't respond to images at all — and vice versa. Many do very well with adjustments (the *as if* and *what if*) but others find them confusing. Some want no other direction but where and when they should sit or stand — while others feel treated like furniture when all they get is direction about the physical movement. That's why I think it's helpful to be exposed to many different ways of describing the characters' behavior and emotional life — so you have more than one tool to select as needed.

COMMITMENT TO A CHOICE

Let's say we have a script in which a character is on death row. The character claims that he didn't commit the crime, and the script has left it deliberately ambiguous as to whether he did it or not. The writer still needs to make a choice. Did the character commit the crime or not? The character is a person. Something happened to him. Even if the script doesn't overtly tell us, the writer needs to know, in order to write that person's story, that it's the story of a person who committed a crime — or that it's the story of a person who didn't commit a crime.

The director also needs to "know" this. I don't mean the director should necessarily ask the writer. Even though the writer's choices are specific, she has created an *imagined* world. As the shepherd of the story, the director makes choices which structure the story. He does his research, he looks for evidence, he tests his ideas, but in the end everything we know about our characters we know *imaginatively*, right? The next question — Do the writer and director have to agree about whether the character committed the crime? — is not as easy to answer as you might think, even if the writer and director are the same person!

Choice is as personal as that, and as specific to the moment in which it is made. Imagination itself is idiosyncratic, willful, personal. Commitment to a choice (in life as well as art) is not a static condition but a dynamic one, a place from which one learns and grows — and can change one's mind. When actors are in the moment — and thus available to stimuli — their choices may come out slightly different in each take, even if the actor and director have discussed and agreed on the events of the script. This is a good thing — it keeps the performance fresh take after take. But more than that, it's an approach that allows creative insight. In the case of our death row character, for instance, it leads us to the insight that he might remember differently the event that led to his arrest each time he thinks of it.

IMAGES AND ASSOCIATIONS

Human memories are images, as are their fantasies and wishes. Memories flicker and change. Let's say the character has committed the crime. So the *image* of himself pulling the trigger and the other guy's head blown against the wall — his actual memory — would be locked in his emotional storage banks. But he might *wish* he hadn't done it! His fantasy — his wish — the image of himself turning away and not pulling the trigger — could be just as vivid for him.

A documentary filmmaker told me that when he is interviewing people, one way he gets people to talk about their inner life is to ask them to describe images that are meaningful to them. This technique taps into the inner network of someone's conscious and subconscious thoughts. This network of images is powerful information about what makes a person tick. It's an emotional storage bank. What we are interested in, care about, value, wish for, fear, laugh at, dream of, remember, hope for — all are essential raw materials for the director as well as the writer.

The images that are helpful to actors are interior images. Although it may at times be helpful to discuss with actors the image on the screen in order to let them know the parameters of the camera framing, an actor's interior images are a much more important focus. For actors, the interior images evoked by the script are their very own private, internal "special effects."

FOUR LEVELS OF IMAGES — *SMOKE*
Let's imagine four levels of images.

First level: the images in the text, and our free-associations with them. This "first level" of image is the writer's images. To me the best way to understand something about the writer's "intent" is not to ask the writer, but to free associate to the writer's images.

A line from an early scene in the movie *Smoke*, written by Paul Auster, has the character Paul telling a story about Sir Walter Raleigh, who introduced cigars to the court of the first Queen Elizabeth. "Once he made a bet with her that he could measure the weight of smoke...I admit it's strange. Almost like weighing someone's soul." This speech has two major images in it, *smoke* and *soul*. The writer makes one association for us right off the bat, that weighing smoke is like weighing a soul. We also make our own associations with smoke. Where there's smoke there's fire. A smoking gun. Blow smoke up someone's ass. Smoke signals. A smokey voice, or a smokey atmosphere, film noir.

At this point in my free association I am reminded that I used to smoke cigarettes. When I used to smoke, in the '60s, you could smoke anywhere, especially in New York where I lived at the time. Not just offices and restaurants, but airplanes, movie theaters — even elevators! Smoking is, of course, a major health hazard and nuisance. But it's also possible for some of us to think of the days of smoking with nostalgia, as a romantic thing. This takes me to an idea — since the actual title of the movie is *Smoke* — that perhaps a sense of duality and paradox is intended by the author as a theme. Free-associating to the images of the text can give us ideas about the themes of a script.

Second level: the images of the character's life implied by the images of the text. These are the clues, suggested by the images, to his emotional storage bank, that is, to his interests, preoccupations, wishes, and fears, as well as his activities and history. For example, if the character mentions a shovel, he may also own a rake. If he peppers his conversation with allusions to television programs, that means he watches a lot of TV.

The character Paul has just been invited by Auggie, the owner of a cigar shop Paul patronizes, to join a "philosophical discussion about women and cigars." Paul responds with the story, which includes the image "weighing someone's soul." To free-associate with the phrase "weighing someone's soul" — how much is a soul worth? How much is a life worth? Must a soul have weight in order to exist? The questions raised in my free-associations seem to supply evidence that the person using the phrase "weighing someone's soul" may have a certain level of intellectual awareness. I'm beginning to think of him as a person who enjoys thinking about such questions, who spends time staring at the wall, thinking, questioning, free-associating. Auggie's use of the word "philosophical" in Paul's presence adds evidence for the idea that Paul may be known as the "philosopher" of this group.

You may have noticed when I spoke of this character as enjoying "staring at the wall," that I used that exact phrase when describing myself (in an earlier chapter). Maybe that's why I thought of it here. In any case, my being able to free-associate my own experience to the images of the character begins to give my connection to him the weight of *imaginative truth*.

Paul equates "weighing someone's soul" with weighing smoke. Is this a measure of how important smoking is to him? Or, how close he feels to his own soul? His own mortality? And where do women come in, in his associations with "weighing someone's soul"? When he is asked to tell a story about women and cigars, he talks about Queen Elizabeth, an historical figure. My question about what images are *implied* means the images not spoken, that is, in this case, the women in his life who are not historical and literary figures. Who are the women or woman in his life that he does *not* speak about? We find out later that Paul's wife has died; does he imagine that his chronic smoking keeps him close to her soul?

One of the readers of this book in manuscript reminded me that the obvious association most people now have with "women and cigars" is Bill Clinton and Monica Lewinsky. *Smoke* was released in 1995, well before the Clinton scandals of 1998. If we were re-making the movie *Smoke* now (not that I think we should), would those images weave through our subtext of this scene? With the high quality of Paul Auster's writing, we could free-associate endlessly to images. And none of it would do us harm or be wasted. The images would take us deeper and deeper into our own core of feeling and imagination at the same time as they took us deeper into the script and the characters.

Third level: the actor's (as well as writer's and director's) personal associations with the images. For the actor, this is his personal substitution — perhaps the story he would tell if he were invited to join a "philosophical discussion about women and cigars." Yes, I'm saying that in order to play this part, you'd need to be able to improvise a response to this question in your own words, with your own stories and associations. Likewise to direct it! The springboard to the imaginative realm is personal.

Fourth level: the level of artistic metaphor. To give a simple example, when we talk about a character as being "at the end of her rope," we are using this level of metaphor. If the first level is the writer's images, the second level the character's images, the third level the actor's images, then the fourth level is the director's images. Gene Hackman says that during the shooting of his death scene in *Bonnie and Clyde*, director Arthur Penn said to him, "You're like a wounded animal, stumbling around like a bull, dying in the bullring."

Once during a workshop, I was desperate to find a way to push an actor and her partner to go deeper emotionally. Finally, I said, "This scene takes us to the heart of darkness." I then told them why I thought that — my analysis of the scene, and my personal associations to its central event. But it was the metaphor "heart of darkness" (which I had of course stolen from Joseph Conrad) that many in the workshop remembered and wrote to me about for months afterward.

HOW ACTORS USE IMAGES
The root word of imagination is image. Image and association go to the heart of script analysis. An actor lets his mind and imagination surrender to the image. Images can impel an actor's *objective*, i.e., his behavior toward another actor. Or images can become a character's center, as, for instance, a character consumed by guilt is flooded with bad memories. Images are the sensory associations that fill out any actor's choice and make it concrete and specific. Remembering that one had fights with one's sister as a child is a different experience from visualizing the look on her face, hearing (in one's imagination) the sound of her voice.

Let's say we have made the choice that the death-row character did commit the murder. He has a line, "I didn't do it." Either the image of pulling the trigger (his memory) or the image of not pulling the trigger (his wish) could be behind that line. If he is a bad liar, the image that is contrary to his words might make his voice falter, might make him "look guilty." If he is a cool and calculating liar, he might have the image of pulling the trigger behind the words "I didn't do it" — perhaps with an underlying intention of daring the other person not to believe him. But very often when people are lying they are holding an image of the person they wish they were, the person who didn't do the bad thing. It is this *image* they want the other person to believe.

Here's one more idea. The line could be impelled by an image of his mother's disappointed face. "I didn't do it" would then really mean, "I don't want my mother to think that I did it." Here, the actor substitutes his own mother's face when she has been disappointed in him, even though it was over something much less serious than murder. In all of the above examples, the actor needs to make his association to the image *personal*, by substituting personal images from a time when he himself told a lie. Making it personal is the way the actor's performance achieves universality — because we all have lied, haven't we?

I once read a newspaper article about a female rickshaw driver at Universal Amphitheater in Los Angeles. For her manual labor she doesn't get paid a salary, only tips — which are often no more than one dollar. But, she told the reporter, it is worth it just to see the happiness she can give people. She then disclosed that her brother, who sustained brain damage in an accident, had once experienced great pleasure from a rickshaw ride. What this story means to me is that whenever she takes a rickshaw passenger she is really carrying her brother — that's the central image that guides her life. If I were playing her in a movie, I might substitute the image of my own niece or nephew, who are not disabled, or perhaps my mother, who was disabled, or any of a number of disabled friends.

An actor needs to have images behind his words. When the actor playing Noah Cross says the line, "Horseshit," he needs to see and smell a physical image of the thing he is talking about. He needs to do this even if he has made a choice that Cross is not really talking about actual manure, but is saying that line with the intention to intimidate his guest, or to make a comment on modern life.

However, he doesn't stop in the middle of the scene to conjure up the image. He works on creating that image ahead of time. When he speaks the line during the take, the image pops in. Actors use images to stir the imagination and create substitution and personal hooks to the material. Then they let them go, and allow them to bubble up during the scene. The point is not to make the effort to think of them all at the proper moment of the performance, but rather to stir them up ahead of time, like we stir up the compost pile — then let them rise up spontaneously, evoking feelings and impulses in the moment.

HOW DIRECTORS USE IMAGES TO COMMUNICATE WITH ACTORS

As a director, being able to make associations such as the ones I was making above, in relation to the character in *Smoke*, or the murderer, or the rickshaw driver, is invaluable to my ability to imagine characters. And being able to imagine characters helps me in turn to imagine their movements and activities, which leads me to ideas for blocking and structuring of scenes.

Making these associations also helps a director's communication with actors, because he can evoke images that spark the actor's own associations. Angelica Huston, for *The Grifters*, gave herself an image of a fox/vixen caught in a trap, who, to escape, must gnaw off her own foot. Gene Hackman had the following to say about the "wounded bull" image that director Arthur Penn gave him: "Arthur had very simple, specific ideas that helped you do your work." So, you see, actors notice and appreciate it when directors can give them images that stimulate their feelings and imaginations.

The images actors choose also help tell the story. In the *Chinatown* scene described in the previous chapter, Noah Cross replies to the question, "What was the argument [with Hollis Mulwray] about?" with the line, "My daughter." The first time one sees this movie, one assumes that Evelyn is the daughter Cross is referring to. When one views this movie for the second time, it is clear from John Huston's performance that his image behind the words "my daughter" is not Evelyn, but his other daughter, the very girl he is asking Jake to locate. Even though on the first viewing the audience has no inkling of the second daughter, there is a mysterious emotional weight to the line that reverberates subconsciously when the movie's secrets are revealed in later scenes.

Metaphor is important. Sometimes we are way too literal. We are artists, and metaphor is allowed to us. I was very shocked some years ago to find that some people objected to the movie *The Deer Hunter* by insisting that the central event of Russian roulette never actually took place in Southeast Asia. They may be correct, literally. But the Russian roulette is a metaphor, is it not? Are the people who object to it saying that since it did not literally happen, *war is not as bad as that*?

Creating a "soup" of association helps me believe in the world of the script. Using imagery in my language, and personal and imaginative association in the stories that I tell actors about the characters, helps me invite the actors into the world I have imagined. Did I say a "soup"? It's a huge, glorious Milky Way of associations — moving, flashing, sparkling, careening, colliding, sparking off into showers of impulse and insight.

NEED / SPINE / OBJECTIVE / INTENTION / VERB

The terms *need, spine, objective, intention,* and *verb* are sometimes used interchangeably. I think of the *spine* as the character's super-objective or through-line for the script. It is what the character wants out of life, his overwhelming preoccupation, his driving need.

The *objective* is what the character wants or needs in a particular scene. It can also be called a through-line, goal, preoccupation, driving need, or agenda.

The *intention* or *verb* is what the character is doing to get what he wants — his ammunition, his tactics, his strategies, or — as Billy Crudup puts it — his tools for getting what he needs. For example, if he wants the other character to comfort him, he might first invite or ask for that comfort; if that doesn't work, he might beg for it; if that doesn't work he might demand it; if that doesn't work he might accuse the other person of not caring enough to comfort him; if that doesn't work he might try begging again, or cajoling, seducing, even whining. The following rough sketch suggests how these elements relate to each other:

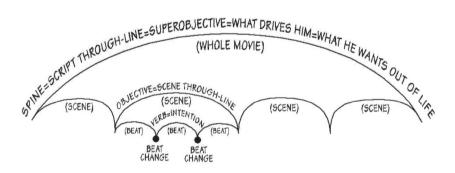

VERBS CREATE A SENSE OF EVENT

We talked about *event* and *through-line* in the last chapter. Subtext choices for the characters' needs or *objectives* are invaluable to creating a sense of event and through-line. When each character in a scene wants something, there is dramatic (or comedic) conflict, and *something happens* — which is the event.

The simplest way to get ideas of a character's objective is to look at his situation or circumstances — his facts — and consider possible responses a person might have to those circumstances. For instance, if a person is alone, he might want company. If he has been poor during his entire childhood, he might be driven by a need for security.

VERBS CREATE CHARACTERIZATIONS

People have habitual ways of dealing with the world which become their emotional tools or strategies. These emotional strategies can be described in terms of dominant or characteristic verbs which express their personality. For instance, some people, no matter what the content of their conversation, seem always to be apologizing; others seem always to be complaining; others challenging; others encouraging. These behaviors become habitual, whether or not they are appropriate or effective. Sean Penn created a character in *The Falcon and the Snowman* who seems to have the dominant verb "to whine."

The character Jim Rockford, from *The Rockford Files*, is a good example of a character with a characteristic range of verbs; he has three: to charm, to complain, and to nail/confront. Thomas Magnum (*Magnum P.I.*) also seemed to employ those same dominant verbs. Maybe those verbs are the dominant verbs of the reluctant hero? Come to think of it, they worked for Cary Grant, too. Each actor (James Garner and Tom Selleck, respectively) put his own stamp on each intention — and each, like Cary Grant, was a relaxed and confident listener.

A few observations about choosing objectives and intentions:

1. People don't always do the right thing to get what they want. A student of mine described her sister as a person who more than anything wants respect but who in every personal and professional interaction falls into flirting — a behavior that creates the exact opposite effect from the one she wants, because it makes people think of her as insubstantial.

2. The objective (through-line) is not the plot. Just because a certain thing happens, that doesn't mean the character wanted it to happen. For example, in real life we frequently want to make things better. But, by my unofficial estimate, fifty percent of our efforts to make things better end up making them worse.

3. People may want something it is unreasonable to expect that they can get, or even that they know they can't have. (No need to give examples of this; we've all seen plenty.)

4. They may want something that if they got it would actually make them unhappy.

5. They may want something even though they already have it. For example, a character can continue to need an apology even after the other character has uttered the sentence, "I'm sorry."

The objective is a tool of concentration; it's not the plot or event that we want the audience to get. If a character comes in to ask a simple favor and in the course of the scene is made to feel guilty for his request, it has never been his *objective* to feel guilty. His objective is to get the favor. An objective that can function as a through-line is one that is true before the scene starts, remains true throughout the scene, and is still true after the scene ends.

The objective is who the character is, under those circumstances. It's an *emotional hook*. An understanding of psychology can help us determine such hooks, and an understanding of behavior helps us turn these hooks into playable objectives. A young man once told me he had a history of picking fights in bars I asked him why, and he said his thinking at the time was, "I just wanted to make something interesting happen." Surely the psychology behind such behavior was more complex than this, and if I am playing this character in a movie, it might be useful to speculate about a need for attention, or to feel important, or to get revenge against authority, or even a need to punish himself. But, on the other hand, maybe the objective "to make something interesting happen" might actually work best — simply because no one, including the young man himself, really knows the secrets of his psyche.

Above all, the thing to remember is that the objective is subtext. It's not anything the audience needs to know in order to follow the plot. It clarifies the emotional events — and thus the plot — but it does not need to service the plot. It is a tool, a way for the actors to engage with each other. When the actors are engaged, they are free to play the moment. And when they play the moment, the words and the events come to life.

VERBS CREATE RELATIONSHIP
People who have needs are vulnerable. Any time you need something from another person, you are in a relationship with that person. Even if

all you want from that person is that he should go away and leave you alone, your wanting something from him puts you in relationship. Having needs and relationships makes a character human, instead of merely an emblem of some character trait or representative of good or evil.

The most useful objectives are simple and have a physical goal, like wanting the other person to smile, or to leave the room. They are *emotional tasks*. A goal such as "wanting respect" can be abstract and thus easy to intellectualize. If "wanting respect" doesn't feel specific enough, it can be helpful to ask, "what could [the other character/actor] do that would let me know that he respects me?" Such as, if he stopped shuffling his papers and looked me in the eye.

The objective usually works best if the actor looks for its success in the eyes or body language of the other actor. If the actor is waiting and hoping to *feel* respected, this will subvert the usefulness of the objective because she has located her concentration in herself, in observing and monitoring her own feelings. It's more useful to ask what do I want the *other* character to feel? *One of the most reliable ways for a director to salvage a foundering scene is to get each actor to concentrate on the other actor's feelings instead of on her own.*

The objective or intention as an expression of relationship is what one *feels* in the presence of the other person. Instead of describing that emotion, we describe the emotional intention toward that person — which is a verb. I may think I want to confront another person, I may even rehearse the confrontation before the meeting. But when I am actually in the person's presence, my need to be liked by him may override the intention to confront. I once read a memoir of someone who had known a person who met Hitler. The man who met Hitler was a Jew, a tap dancer who was brought before Hitler without Hitler knowing he was Jewish; this was in the early days of the Reich. The tap dancer later said, "You could laugh at him from a distance, but up close, let me tell you, you felt a lot better off if he liked you."

Midway through the billiard room scene in *Eyes Wide Shut*, Dr. Bill Harford (Tom Cruise) discovers that Victor Ziegler (Sydney Pollack) was at the masked ball the night before. It's tempting to think that upon arrival at Ziegler's home Harford has the objective to make the house call he's been summoned to, and, after he gets the information about the ball, his objective shifts to finding out what's been going on. But if we make that choice, the scene will be flat, without subtext or emotional content. That's because these objectives are not true subtext choices — they are mere restatements of the plot. If actors play the scene this way, the revelation that Ziegler was at the ball will not have any impact on the audience.

An effective objective for the young man in this scene would be an expression of his relationship to the older man. Two candidates for this choice: The younger man *wants the approval* of the successful "daddy" figure. Or, the younger man's "low-dog" behavior towards the older man masks *a need to compete, to take his place*. As playable choices for the scene, either *to get his approval* or *to compete and take his place* could work, because either choice will impel the actor to react on a moment-to-moment basis, reading the other actor's gesture and expression and reacting accordingly.

INTENTION CREATES DRAMA AND COMEDY

Intention is a condition of aliveness, as well as of relationship, personality, or situation, as described above. When the actor has an intention, it keeps his face and body alive, because he is engaged. Without intention the actor's inner work (images and associations) might not read.

In a later chapter I've included a list of examples of intentions, called *Expanded List of Verbs and Emotional Intentions*, grouped roughly by their emotional purpose. Many of the intentions that are common for the colorful characters and heightened situations of movies and television — such as *accuse, beg, challenge, nail, seduce* — are rare in real life. In real life people stick to less threatening, more socially acceptable verbs. We are more likely to *explain* our feelings of neediness than to reveal them by actually *begging* for help. Instead of *accusing* a wrongdoer, we try to *convince* him to admit he was wrong. *Complaining*, and *teasing* or *entertaining* are socially acceptable in most relationships. But many of the rest of the verbs on the list are risky behavior in the regular world.

An actor who lacks a wider repertoire than the social verbs — *convince, explain, complain*, and *tease* — is probably not going to be very compelling. Likewise an actor who falls back on "to urge," which like convince and explain is likely to pull the actor into the quicksand of "convincing us that the words are true," in other words playing the lines. The objective "to get someone to believe you" is another choice likely to pull the actor into an attitude or a line reading, rather than a connection to the subtext. When the line itself is, "You've got to believe me," it's more important than ever to have an intention behind it that is not "to get the other person to believe me." For instance, it could be *to intimidate* or, an opposite, *to beg*.

My suggestion to directors is that they stay away from describing a character by saying, "she wants to convince him to go away," and instead take a chance on the bolder verbs, such as demand, punish, or berate. Bold choices bring a scene to life. When you describe a character as "wanting such-and-such but knowing she can't get it," you are putting emotional handcuffs on the actor. People (characters) want what they want, whether or not it's rational. Committing to a simple intention, need, or emotional task makes the character (actor) look like a person in a situation rather than like an actor trying to look believable.

TEST YOUR IDEAS AGAINST WHAT YOU KNOW ABOUT LIFE

Finding playable subtext choices is not a matter of turning a dial. If you want to make the switch away from result direction, it won't help to replace one mechanical approach with another, such as plugging in a verb to replace an adjective. The shift from the mechanical notion of "fixing," to the more dynamic activities of observing, thinking, feeling, and imagining with your whole being, is a long-term commitment.

I do have one simple "quick-fix" way to add more verbs to your life, though. You can translate a result-oriented attitude or judgment into a verb by flipping it. Instead of telling an actor to "be angry," suggest "make the other person angry." Instead of "be cheerful," cheer up the other person. Even if you describe the character's emotional task as "to make the other person feel as disappointed as you do," this slight shift in language creates an intention that is more playable than trying to achieve a state of being disappointed.

What is the behavior of a person who is angry? What does she do to the person she is angry at? Perhaps punish him. What do we observe are the characteristics of a charming person? A charming person makes others feel charming. What does a sexy person do? Makes others feel sexy.

EMOTION IS A BY-PRODUCT

The side benefit of committing to intention is that if the actor does something he will feel something. If he sets about to make someone else angry, his own anger will probably kick in. Making someone else feel sexy may make you feel sexy. The great thing about verbs and objectives is that the actor can bring his own feelings — and his own sense of humor — to them. The way that Sean Connery plays "to accuse" is different from the way Gene Wilder plays the same intention.

FACTS (BACKSTORY)
There are facts that are given in the script. These facts are what there is to imagine. For instance, the actress playing the main character's girl-friend in *Cast Away* has to imagine *what it would be like* to lose her fiancé in a plane crash, and four years later, to have him turn up, rescued — after she has married another man.

There can also be imagined facts. An *L.A. Times* column, making fun of the HBO documentary *Project Greenlight*, called Aidan Quinn "method-obsessed" because Quinn asked the director, "In your mind, was [my char-acter] in Vietnam?" This column struck me as a good example of the con-tempt Hollywood has for the craft of acting. Why disparage that question as "method-obsessed"? It's simple common sense for an actor to be inter-ested in his character's history. And a normal and logical element of the director's work to join the actor in this quest. Combat experience in Vietnam is bound to have an impact on the character's relationship with his son, the main character of the film whose progress *Project Greenlight* was chronicling. This is an example of "imaginative" backstory — that is, a fact that is not in the script but which can be intuited or inferred as an element of subtext.

FACTS CREATE SITUATION, PREDICAMENT, AND PROBLEM
It is so much more helpful to talk to an actor in terms of a character's sit-uation or predicament than to judge the character or label his psycholo-gy. Take, for example, a scene in which character A is taking character B to task for having failed at an assignment. Before deciding that char-acter A is ill-tempered or hard to please, wouldn't it be important to ask what exactly is the nature of the job that character B had been assigned? And how many times previously has B failed at assignments?

If the script gives none of these details, the actor makes choices that answer these questions. The director's job is not to oversee or micro-man-age each of these choices, but it can be helpful to call attention to them. For instance, if a moment seems flat, the director might ask, "Have you made a choice about the nature of the conversation your character is referring to here?" The actor may respond, "No, but I will," in which case the director needn't say anything else. Or the actor may respond, "No, I'm confused about this," and thus open up an opportunity to discuss together possible choices.

"CENTRAL" FACTS — *FARGO*
We are looking especially for the *pertinent emotional facts* — the central facts, the ones that have an emotional effect on people. Usually there are

one or two central facts that have the biggest emotional influence on the character's behavior. For instance, two central facts for the character Marge in *Fargo* are 1) she is pregnant with her first child; 2) she is a police chief.

A central fact for Marge's husband, Norm, is that he is a painter or illustrator of wildlife, and submits his work to the U.S. Post Office to be chosen for commemorative stamps. Although we find these things out later in the movie, both these facts are true before the movie starts. Now we ask questions. Does he have a job? Has he recently left a regular job to pursue painting? Or has he always made his living as an illustrator? Do the Postal Service competitions carry a cash stipend, or does he spend all his time on non-income-producing activity? We don't observe him in income-producing activities. We observe him fishing, making breakfast for Marge, watching television with her in bed, telephoning her when she is away on police business.

LET THE FACTS LEAD YOU TO A STORY
The excellence of this script lies in its preferring of such factual details and unanswered questions to insipid generalizations about the state of their marriage. When actors praise a script by saying, "It's all on the page," they are talking precisely about writing like this, where there are many factual details, but the connections are left to be figured out in the actors' imaginations. The writing is "clear," but it is "clear" *because* it has tons of subtext — not because the emotional life is all explained to the audience.

What we get to do now is make choices in order to create (daydream) a story around the facts that we have. First, I make a choice that Marge is indeed the principal or only wage earner. Then I take responsibility for this choice. By "take responsibility for a choice" I mean that I look at what I know about such situations from life. As it happens, my own husband left his corporate job two years ago to work with me as my business manager, and focus on his acting career. So I have material to draw on. Of course we have our occasional miffs and misunderstandings, but mostly, now that we are both doing exactly what we want to do, we are closer than ever.

I vividly recall the hours of emotion and soul-searching — some of it painful — that led to our decision. Thus, from my own experience I *know* Marge and Norm must have had discussions about their unusual financial structure. Of course I don't know what those discussions were (they are not in the script) but I let myself imagine them. I know them *imaginatively*.

Now you may challenge my assertion that I know Marge and Norm have had such discussions; you may respond that Marge and Norm are not the soul-searching type. (My first comment is that you shouldn't stop your script analysis at such a superficial stage as deciding what "type" the characters are.) But, okay — let's say we make the choice to imagine that Marge and Norm's discussion was very short — even as short as this: "I think you should stay home and concentrate on the wildlife painting." "Are you sure you won't mind?" "Yes, I'm sure." "Okay. I'd like to do that." Do you see how this kind of imagining is specific and active, how it leads to a closer connection to the characters than saying that they are not the soul-searching type?

My next script analysis question is: What was the subtext of this conversation? They are considering an unusual and potentially stressful financial structure, especially with a baby coming. Many marriages in such a situation would carry a subtext of resentment and guilt. As I contemplate the possible subtext of this imagined conversation, I am faced with a choice: Are they a close couple, or are they in a marriage riddled with resentment and guilt? If I make the choice that they have closeness in their marriage, then I am going to imagine that a deep current of feeling passed between them during this brief conversation. In other words, my personal knowledge of such a situation strongly suggests that the emotion and soul-searching that is necessary for this decision to be successful, was, in the case of Marge and Norm, subtext rather than spoken. In fact, it suggests it so strongly that finally I (imaginatively) *know* it.

What I've done here is concoct a story, using questions, images, associations, and my own observations of life, to arrive at invented facts. This is my subtext story, my vision. These "invented facts" are as vivid for me as the "real" facts of the script, because I imagine them as very specific events in the lives of the characters. As a director it is my job to spin such stories about all the characters and their relationships. The primary reason for this is so that *I know what story I'm telling*.

The other reason is that telling stories is a great way to give direction. Imagining stories about the characters, especially when fleshed out with parallel true stories drawn from real life experiences and observations, is probably the best way for the director to bring the actor onto "the same page." Ideally, the director's stories have the effect of "priming the pump" imaginatively for the actors, so that they come up with their own stories — which they may or may not share with the director.

But what if the actor playing Marge has her own subtext story, based on her own knowledge of life, and that personal connection leads her to *know* something completely at odds with what I *know* about this story? The asking of my questions and the telling of my story may persuade her to consider stretching her imagination to a character that is different from her own experience. This could work out very well. If she has personally never experienced the closeness that I envision for the Marge-Norm marriage, then it's quite possible that she has longed for it. And being allowed to give expression to that longing in her characterization may be a liberating and creative experience — at least I would certainly try to present it to her as such.

But sometimes the actor's "knowledge" is so certain that I (the director) am finally the one that is persuaded. It can happen. It's an imagined world, after all. In the face of a deeply compelling "knowledge" on the part of the actor, the director sometimes must allow some of his own ideas to be transformed. Of course, as we know in the case of the actual movie *Fargo*, the director cast his own wife in the role. This may well have helped them — with or without discussion of the role — to be "on the same page."

THE BIG, FAT FACT

My favorite facts are the big, fat ones, the ones that are so obvious that directors (and actors) often overlook them, and torture themselves with trying to figure out and create an unplayable psychology. There's a scene in *Being John Malkovich* that directors like to use in class: Craig has succeeded in getting Maxine to meet him at a bar, by "guessing" her name; at the bar she insults him and abruptly leaves.

Catherine Keener says that she and director Spike Jonze had to be vigilant to keep Maxine from one-dimensional nastiness. "I struggled. I really struggled. It was easy to fall into the trap of just being hard and mean." Keener and Jonze of course both knew that if Maxine were played with that moral judgment of her, none of her scenes would work.

Student actors and directors, on the other hand, find it nearly impossible not to judge Maxine, frequently describing her as a "bitch" or "man-hater." But a simple solution is to keep one's attention on the *facts*. In almost the first line of the scene, Maxine asks Craig if he is married, which he is. After calling attention to that fact, I ask the actress, "What's your personal opinion of married men who hit on you and trick you into a date? What kind of treatment do you think they deserve?" Pretty much any actress can then make a simple, primal connection to Maxine's intentions in the scene, to punish and humiliate Craig, and have no need to judge her.

That *Craig is married* is the "big, fat fact." The simplest, most playable choices for a character are based on situation (facts) rather than personality. Even if Maxine does "hate men" it's more playable for her to specifically punish each particular one for each of his specific crimes.

FACTS, IMAGINATION, AND MEMORY

We can't really talk about facts without talking about memory. So-called facts are really clues, because memory is so faulty. Memory is selective. Anything a character claims to remember has a factual reality behind it, even though it may not be literally accurate. Even a lie has some reality, some image or association, behind it. And a "true" story is never *all* the facts. Telling a story doesn't take as long as the event itself being described — and that, of course, means we have left some of the story out.

Facts are most useful because they give rise to questions, which are even more important than facts. Finding the facts of a script is not an academic exercise, it's a jumping off place for association and insight, or what Sanford Meisner called "daydreaming." *The facts are what there is to imagine.* The *facts* are the "imaginary circumstances" which Meisner said the actor must live truthfully under.

ADJUSTMENT — "WHAT IF?"

Facts are suggestive, not rigid. Like images, they create imaginative or personal associations to the facts that have been left out — which are the choices. These imaginative facts inspire what we call "what if?" adjustments. In the published version of the *Chinatown* script, there is a scene (not in the movie) in which Jake arrives at Noah Cross' compound in a small plane. *What if* as soon as the plane dropped him off, it climbed back in the sky and disappeared? The actor playing Jake might imagine the experience of being dropped on a remote island, watching the plane — presumably the only means of departure — leave without him.

ADJUSTMENT — "AS IF..."

An adjustment may be a shift in the actual facts, for example when a scene between a mother and son is played *as if* they are disappointed ex-lovers. An "as if" adjustment may be used to create through-line (as in, "Let's try playing the whole scene as if the other character was just released from a mental institution"). Or it may be used to illuminate the subtext of a line or moment ("When the other actor tells you the plane will be late, it's as if he just told you that your father is dead").

An adjustment doesn't have to be "right" — it just has to work. Take a scene in *The Sixth Sense* in which Malcolm, played by Bruce Willis, is observing his wife being visited by her male coworker. The story fact is that she was widowed six months earlier. Malcolm doesn't know that. From his point of view, she is married. Should she play the scene "as if" she is a six-month widow making her first encounters with the attentions of a man? Or should she play it "as if" she is a neglected wife exchanging signals with another man?

My first thought was that the actress should play it as a widow, because that's the central story of the film — that life has gone on without Malcolm; he is only watching "as if" he were not dead. But on the other hand, if I start deeply imagining what it might be like if I were widowed and a man starting paying me attention only six months later, I might very well feel as if I was still married. If there was pleasure in the exchange, I might wonder whether I was being disloyal. So on reflection, the "disloyal wife" adjustment might work just as well as the "six-month widow" adjustment.

An adjustment can be what the character sees or knows or hears, which is different from what another person might see, know, or hear. For example, a young anorexic woman who looks in the mirror and sees a fat girl when really there is only a thin girl. In *Scenes From a Marriage* Marianne has a line, "one of my children died." Nothing else is said about this. Had she held the child in her arms, watched it suffer? Or was it a miscarriage? For some women, the experience of a miscarriage is the same *as if* it was a living child who died in her arms.

A friend of mine, in his 40's, told me the story of a blind date who, on the phone when they were arranging their meeting, mentioned her daughter was about to graduate from Brown University. He then told me he had been grateful she suggested meeting at the restaurant, because a woman whose daughter went to such a prestigious school would be instantly repelled by his old car. When he heard the statement, "My daughter is graduating from Brown University," he heard a woman say that she expected a prospective date to meet a certain cultural and financial level. But when I heard him repeat this statement, I heard a woman warning a prospective date that she was old enough to have a 22-year-old daughter.

It's natural for people to have different adjustments to the same information. It's completely okay — indeed very useful — for different actors in a scene to have different adjustments to a line or a circumstance. Sometimes it helps if the two actors don't know what each other's adjustment is — if they have secrets. Other times it helps if they do know each other's subtext and respond to that subtext, rather than to the lines.

An "as if" adjustment can be based on observations of the character's behavior. A colleague of Al Gore took acting lessons in order to impersonate George Bush in mock debates to help prepare Gore for the 2000 televised debates. The acting coach studied tapes of Bush, coming up with these observations: "Bush speaks in that halting way, and always seems to be emphasizing the wrong word. There's always this fear in Bush's eyes. And there's the smugness he uses to cover it." The coach then had an idea: "Bush has this look *as if* something smelled really foul near him, but he doesn't want to be impolite about it. As an actor, I'd play him *as if* there were always something that stinks nearby."

ADJUSTMENT — "IT'S LIKE WHEN..."
The "it's like when..." adjustment is another way of making a substitution; it's a way of making sure that everything in the script, scene, or movie is original and truthful. For example, the adjustment for the actress in the *Being John Malkovich* scene could be "this is like when..." she herself was approached aggressively by a particular married man of her own experience. This is a simple one — a "freebie" — because many actresses have had this experience.

But what about a character who has been tricked into giving away classified information about the location of a nuclear warhead? The director, in his script analysis, must ask himself, what is this like from my own experience? Is this like a betrayal? Is it like facing my own stupidity? *Betrayal* and *facing my own stupidity* are both experiences I have had. So even though I have not had the experience of giving away nuclear secrets, I can connect with this character, his problems and choices.

WHAT'S AT STAKE
When a director asks for "more tension" or "more urgency" the scene is almost sure to get less compelling rather than more compelling. The term "higher stakes" is theoretically a way to "ramp up" a performance, give it more tension, more urgency, without asking for that result. "Stakes" are often added with imaginative adjustments. They are secrets, in that they

are not in the script. For instance, if the character is driving his wife to the hospital, the actor could give himself a secret that his mother had died of the same ailment or injury his wife is now suffering.

But this idea is useless if it is abstract and intellectualized rather than personal, that is, if the actor *plays a character* whose wife is ill with the ailment his mother died of. The "intellectualized" adjustment, no matter how insightful, will only hurt the performance. The idea will only work if the actor either has personal experience with such fearful coincidences, or if he is willing to imagine that this is happening to someone dear to him. The only genuine way to give "higher stakes" to a performance is for the actor to be ruthlessly honest about what the character's predicament can emotionally cost a real person — in particular, himself, or people he has closely observed. That is, to make it more personal.

And in order for the director to be able to tell whether the actor is doing this, the director needs to bring personal honesty to his understanding of the characters, to put himself at emotional risk, too.

OBSTACLE or PROBLEM

It can be easy for actors to fight with each other, to say horrible things to each other, to play, to kiss, even to make love in front of a movie crew. In real life such events carry emotional cost. This is why it can be helpful to make mention of the *obstacle* or *problem*.

The scene between Dustin Hoffman and Jane Alexander in *All the President's Men* is a great example of a scene which not only contains an obstacle, but is driven by it. The lines are simple: he asks her questions; she tries to evade them. The information produced by the interview is slight. There is really no scene at all without the obstacles that both actors create. Her obstacles include her loyalty to some of the people she has worked with, and her fears for her own job and safety if she talks to the press. He must press her for information without pushing so hard that she frightens and shuts down. The scene is beautifully played; the game of patience and urgency is palpable, almost physical. He seems almost like a man who is trying to get close to a wounded, wild animal — or talk a potential suicide down from a ledge. (Those are possible imaginative adjustments an actor might use in such a scene.)

Obstacles are inherent to being human, so it is not always necessary to make a choice about the obstacle. If the actor is making his problem real to himself, then there will be an obstacle, just because that is the nature of life. The simplest way for an actor to find a playable obstacle is to locate his need or objective in the other actor. It may sound like it would be easy, even fun, to yell at someone and tell her she's an idiot, but if you're right in front of the person, and letting that person's feelings affect you, then there is automatically an obstacle. Looking for the characters' problem or predicament is another way of locating need and obstacle, and it's a very helpful way to give direction.

An obstacle is likely to be a secret — perhaps, for example, the character doesn't want the other character to know what her objective or agenda is. But I can't emphasize enough the uselessness of an intellectualized obstacle — one that is merely a great idea, but that takes no hold in the actor's personal or imaginative storage banks. I often find it helpful to say to an actor, "There needs to be more obstacle," as an alternative to saying, "It needs to be more real." It's the same thing, really.

PHYSICAL LIFE

My brother's children told me once about a commercial they'd seen which depicted a director directing an actress recording the voice-mail message, "Your business is important to us." After the first take the director asks the actress, "Can you be more sincere?" On the next take he instructs her, "Take a pause after the word business." Neither my brother nor his family has any connection to acting or directing, and of course they wanted my opinion about this commercial. Instead of answering, I asked them their opinion. They all agreed that the last one, in which the director told her to pause after a certain word, came out the best, and that after the first request, to be "more sincere," the actress had actually seemed less sincere.

A direction that can be executed physically, even one as inelegant as "pause here," may work better than a vague emotional result direction like "be more sincere." Of course, "be more sincere" is worse than most result directions, because a person who is trying to look sincere will always seem like a liar. My sister-in-law (a primary school educator) gave a perfect example: a five-year-old who is learning to lie opens his eyes very wide in order to look terribly truthful. Specific physical direction, such as "don't smile," or "don't look at him until this line," can work remarkably well. "Don't smile" works because smiling is often a social response, a social automatic pilot. So "don't smile" can operate as *permission* to feel more genuine feelings.

BLOCKING THE PHYSICAL LIFE

"Blocking" or "staging" is the director's job of creating the physical movement of the scene. The physical movement has an effect on the camera framing and on the emotional life of the characters. Some directors merely move the actors around like furniture to fit the camera frame. Others give specific physical direction in order to illuminate an emotional moment. Actors can tell the difference. One saps their energy, the other releases their energy.

When actors have something physical to put their attention on, it frees them emotionally. Susan Sarandon feels she did her best work in *Thelma and Louise*, in which Geena Davis had most of the lines, and all Sarandon had to do was "drive and listen." She says, "And I realized from that, you can do your best work when you're concentrated on something else."

PHYSICAL TRANSFORMATION

Sometimes a physical transformation is central to the characterization, for instance, Steve Zahn in *Out of Sight*, Billy Bob Thornton in *Sling Blade*, Hilary Swank in *Boys Don't Cry*, Philip Seymour Hoffman in *Flawless*, Willen Dafoe in *Shadow of the Vampire*. But there can be more subtle physical adjustments too. Lisa Kudrow in *The Opposite of Sex* always keeps her teeth a little closed, and it gives her an "uptight" look. The affliction of Edward Scissorhands (Johnny Depp) affects not just his hands, it affects his walk, the way he holds his head. With reference to the physicality of his character in *Jesus' Son*, Billy Crudup said, "The walk was an integral part of building that character. It was important to me that he was a character who was stumbling through life — literally and figuratively — but that he always look forward, hopefully. So he was somewhat stooped, but his face was always open to the world."

Such a specific psychological physicality is also known — especially to theater-trained actors — as gesture. Willem Dafoe calls it finding the character's "mask." It helps turn the emotional choices of spines, images, and adjustments into *behavior*. Skilled actors can make such insightful ideas specific and sensory, rather than merely indicate them superficially.

10 | QUESTION EVERYTHING

"There are no answers, only choices."
— Steven Soderbergh
(from *Solaris*)

Don't be afraid of questions. The pressure to answer every question and "nail down" the emotional map is unhelpful to creativity. The questions are more important than the answers. "Answer" implies getting it right on a quiz; it implies that once you've gotten the right answer, you can mark that question off your list, finished. Rather than answers, we're looking for solutions. A solution is more active than an answer — it's something that works. If it stops working, we look for another solution. Ideas for solutions are arrived at by making choices. A choice is something to try, to commit to — and then change your mind if it doesn't work.

SOME QUESTIONS TO ASK ABOUT THE CHARACTERS

I've listed some questions that frequently come up in script analysis consultations, and that often lead into helpful areas. But — please don't go down the list, ticking off each item by concocting "interesting" answers. To do so would only intellectualize your instincts about the characters, and would make this exercise worse than useless. These are examples of questions which might come up, and could cause you to meditate and day-dream, allowing a soup of association and connection to engage your imagination and make the character more real to you.

The best way to insure that these questions lead you toward engaging intuition rather than dissipating it, is this: Every time you ask one of these or any other questions about the character, ask it also about yourself.

- What are the character's values?
- What are her interests?
- Where is she vulnerable? How can she be hurt? What's at stake for her?
- What is she not saying?
- Whom or what does the character trust?
- Look for ways that the character is facing some unpleasant truth about himself — or refusing to face it.
- Look for ways that he makes mistakes.

- What are his dreams? His hopes? His fears? His longing?
- What is his "soft spot"?
- What has he seen happen to others that he is determined to keep from happening to him?
- What is the character smart about?
- How does he use his intelligence?
- In what way is this character an artist?
- Is the character protecting himself from pain in his past?
- What hunger drives him? (e.g., hunger for affection, for respect)
- What is he looking for in a mate?
- What makes him laugh?
- What might cause him to lose his sense of humor?
- What is the character's biggest problem? His most immediate problem? Long-term problems? In what ways has he dealt with his problems in the past?
- Whom does he look up to?
- What is the biggest thing that has ever happened to him?
- How is the character different at the end of the script (or scene) than at the beginning?
- What is happening to her for the first time in this scene?
- What is she doing in this scene that she has never done before?
- What is she lying about? To others? To herself?
- How much self-knowledge does she have?
- What are her demons?
- What is her blind spot?
- What secrets does she have? Which one is her most important secret?
- What has she been doing just before the scene starts? What would happen next if the scene didn't start now?

MYSTERIOUS LINES — I — SIMPLE MEANING

A mysterious line can be one that simply has an odd construction, or words that need to be looked up in the dictionary. Examples of this abound in Shakespeare, where director and actors must translate the sentence constructions into their more ordinary subtext, line by line, in order for their delivery to be understood by modern audiences. For instance, when the fairy Puck (in *A Midsummer Night's Dream*) says, "Oh what fools these mortals be," he means "People are crazy." It's crucial when performing Shakespeare to keep the simple, human meaning in mind, rather than an awareness that one is speaking great poetry. The best writing often has oblique constructions whose subtext must be mined to have it make any sense at all.

There is a line in *Raising Arizona*, "Do you think his mama will be upset — I mean overly?" In order to be able to say this line un-self-consciously, it needs to be translated into its underlying meaning, which might be, "Do you think his mama will be overly upset?" (I don't mean the line should be changed — the actor speaks the line as written while *thinking* the subtext meaning.) The director needs to be ready to help the actor with information about the meaning of such lines so that actor can hold an image of the simple meaning when she speaks the line. Otherwise the delivery may become stilted, forcing a change to the more mundane version — at a sacrifice of poetry and psychological detail.

MYSTERIOUS LINES — II — KEYS TO PSYCHOLOGICAL DETAIL

A mysterious line is any line that could be interpreted more than one way. It's also any line that irritates or confuses. But it's also any line that jumps out, fascinates, charms, or sparks that "ah-ha" moment. In other words, it's any line that's loaded with subtext. Sometimes I skip around the script, letting mysterious lines jump out at me randomly. But sometimes I go line by line, letting each be mysterious. There will be many examples of mysterious lines in the Script Analysis chapters ahead.

Ask questions about each mysterious line. Determine at least three possible ways to understand it. What is the event (from his past) that is behind the character's actions or choice of words? Or — what image lies behind the words? What issue, problem, thought, belief, or fear? And what event is behind the fear? This is how you make your ideas more specific, and ground them in the human realm. The questions imply a picture of the character's experience.

Questioning every mysterious line generates *lots* of questions — and some possible answers, which I think of as "candidates for solutions." Some directors tell me that this process frightens them; it makes them feel lost; it makes them feel out of control, faced with too many choices. But for me, asking these questions has the opposite effect — it calms me, because it locates the characters in the real world, and makes me feel they could actually exist. Therefore, I gain confidence that solutions exist, even if I don't have them quite yet.

MYSTERIOUS LINES — III — THE KEY LINE

If a line is giving an actor trouble, one way for a director to deal with it, if she doesn't want to change the line, is to encourage the actor to think of that line as the most important line in the script. Seriously. A line cloaked in mystery may become the through-line, the line that's central to unlocking the character, the scene, or the movie. Meryl Streep has said that in every script she takes on there is always one line she really doesn't want to say, but as she works on the role, that line always becomes "the one that locates" the character.

Ben Kingsley called the line in *Sexy Beast*, "I don't want you to be happy! Why should I?" his *key line*. He said, "There is the link that will open the door to my character. And it's said by a weeping child with clenched fists in the corner of the playground." I referred to this statement in an earlier chapter on passing judgment on characters — but the anecdote applies here too. When we investigate these mysterious lines, we're looking for something to *know imaginatively* about these lines. Kingsley saw behind that line the reality (past event) of the weeping child in the playground. That image — of the weeping child with clenched fists in the corner of the playground — *becomes* the line for him. It also became the key — the through-line — that unlocked the character for him. His commitment to that "key" gave him the extraordinary freedom and moment-by-moment reality of that performance.

The key line can be one thing a character says that betrays his central preoccupation or secret. It may or may not be an accurate perception. For Graham in *sex, lies, and videotape*, the line might be, "I'm not a liar."

MYSTERIOUS LINES — IV — WHEN THE SCRIPT GIVES RESULT DIRECTION

Certain lines in a script seem to be telling the actor what to feel. For instance: "I'm elated." "You look like you've seen a ghost." These lines should not be treated as emotional instructions, but as mysterious lines. The subtext of a person who says, "I'm elated" might really be, "I wish I was as elated as I want everyone to think I am." The character who says to another character, "You look like you've seen a ghost" may actually be trying to trap her into a damaging admission, by suggesting she's already given her feelings away.

BOLD CHOICES

Kingsley has also said that he dreamed up his performance for his *Sexy Beast* role on the airplane to the shooting location. It was a bold choice. By that I mean he had an intuition that hit him like a lightening bolt, and he trusted it. He didn't hedge his bets by second-guessing his intuition with tepid qualifications — such as, "and he also wants the money," or "he knows he can intimidate Ray." The purpose of daydreaming as many associations as possible to the mysterious lines is not to dilute our ideas by second-guessing them. It's to open our imaginations so the bold choice — often hidden away in our subconscious — can make its appearance.

What do the performances of Susan Tyrell in *Fat City*, Tom Cruise in *Magnolia*, and Daniel Day Lewis in *Gangs of New York* have in common? Bold choices.

QUESTION THE STAGE DIRECTIONS
Taking out the stage directions is like looking at a picture without the caption. It's provocative. It makes you think. It makes you free-associate. The stage directions I want to take out are the ones that instruct the actor on what to feel (such as "with a shudder," "in a tiny scared voice," "his chest heaving with rage"), because they are more likely to constrict the actor's emotional range than stimulate it. I don't like to be told what to think or what to feel, and that's why when I first read a script I only glance at the stage directions. At some point in my script analysis, I look at them more carefully, but I am looking for their subtext, not their instruction.

Attention should be paid to some stage directions — the ones that refer to an emotional event. The stage direction, "They kiss fully clothed" should get attention; it's a different emotional event from "They kiss tearing at each other's garments." But such references to emotional events should still be translated. For instance, when a stage direction declares that character "A" weeps or gets angry, I translate that to mean that character "B" has *gotten a response* out of character "A."

I'm not suggesting that writers shouldn't put stage direction (also called "narrative") in their scripts. The narrative is needed in scripts that are sent to agents, producers, executives, and financial prospects — or anyone else who needs their imaginations spoon-fed. Directors and actors need to have their imaginations stimulated, not spoon-fed. So take all stage directions with a grain of salt, as an opportunity to ask questions, rather than an occasion of instruction.

Here's an example. In the *Chinatown* scene cited earlier, a stage direction describes Cross as responding with "real surprise" when Jake reveals the existence of the photos. A few lines later Cross is described as looking at

Jake "hatefully." But — in the very next beat, Cross is described as speaking "painfully" when he says Evelyn "is an extremely jealous person. I didn't want her to find out about the girl." Here he is hinting that his daughter might be capable of mayhem towards the girl, and that, as a loving father, it pains him to have to say this. This is a lie, isn't it? These are crocodile tears, designed to manipulate Jake into becoming suspicious of Evelyn. Noah Cross, the character, is an actor. He is *acting* the role of concerned father. What that means for our script analysis is that any of his other feelings and intentions could be acting too.

I am saying something quite radical. *No one* knows the secret inner life of another — and that includes the writer not knowing — at least not literally — the secret inner lives of his characters. The writer creates action, behavior and dialogue, and knows his characters imaginatively. But a character's actual inner life on screen happens moment-by-moment in the actor's body, voice, and impulse.

FINALLY, SOME QUESTIONS TO ASK YOURSELF
- How are you like the character? How are you not like the character?
- How is this script a way for you to tell the world what you know about life?
- What can you figure out about this character that no one else can figure out?
- What truth is there in the script that you know in your heart is true?

11 | REHEARSAL PLAN

I am much better at verbalizing script analysis in person than in writing. In person I can speak and exchange a stream of consciousness — and bounce off the ideas of other people. When it works it feels like the material is giving up its secrets, telling us what it is about, and carrying us on a white-water river of discovery and deepening courage.

I have two rules for my "group" script analysis experiences in workshops and consultations. They are 1) blurt; and 2) don't argue. By "blurt" I mean don't judge and censor your ideas — blurt them out first, and then test and examine them. By "don't argue" I mean carry each idea as far as it will go imaginatively. Even if you rule it out, keep it on a back burner in case you need it later.

The purpose of script analysis is to generate a Rehearsal Plan — a digest of ideas coming out of use of the tools I've been discussing. Three chapters of script analysis follow — of scenes from *sex, lies, and videotape*, *Clerks*, and *Tender Mercies*. For the first — *sex, lies, and videotape* — I'll follow the Rehearsal Plan outline, and for the others I'll do a shorter version. These written examples may seem technical compared to the lively experience of group script analysis that I do in workshops and consultations. If you find them alienating, please blame my writing ability and not the method itself.

I. BEGINNER'S MIND
What are your preliminary ideas? What are your feelings about this scene? Why did you choose (or write) this material? How do you feel about the characters? Which one do you like the best, or feel closest to, and why?

What are your "freebies"? That is, what immediate personal connections to do you have to the material — to the characters and their situations? What do you bring to the table?

What causes you anxiety about working on this scene? What judgments, prejudices, and resistances do you bring to the scene?

II. RAW MATERIAL OF THE SCENE
Facts and Evidence. What are the facts when the scene begins? How do you know or deduce them?

Questions. Make a long list. Questions about the characters, their situation (facts), their behavior. The questions are more important than the answers.

Mysterious (Ambiguous) Lines, Words, or Phrases. Which lines bother you? Which lines fascinate you? Which lines mystify you? If you have time, let every line be a mysterious line. Don't be afraid of ambiguity — embrace it. Come up with at least three possible candidates to explain each mysterious line, phrase, or word.

Images and Associations. Images that are in the text (dialogue and description). Images that are under the text. Associations to the character's world. Your personal associations, imaginative associations. Metaphors.

III. CHOICES AND IDEAS (Always come up with more than one candidate, and consider opposites.)
Objectives and Intentions. What does each character want? Or need? What is he/she doing to get it?

What Just Happened? The pre-scene beat. What has each character been doing just before the scene starts? What is he/she in the middle of?

What's at Stake for each character? What is his/her *problem*? What are candidates for a playable *obstacle*?

Adjustments and Subtext. Adjustments and/or subtext that illuminate particular individual lines. That define the relationships. That define the character's response to his/her situation.

Imaginative Backstory. The "what if?" adjustment.

Issues. Sometimes the emotional event of the scenes is best understood by separating and investigating its issues.

Through-Line. What is the primary focus for each character? Is it a response to his situation? Or a response to his relationship with the other character(s) in the scene? Or a response to his relationship with a character who is not present? What is his/her central need or problem? Or, what is the central adjustment or metaphor of his/her relationship to the other characters and to his/her situation?

IV. RESEARCH: Research you have completed; research yet to be done.

V. SCENE SHAPE
Beats. When does the subject change? Who changes it? Why (three possible reasons)? What happens in each beat (its event or issue)? Investigate each beat as if it is a tiny scene: subtext, intentions, adjustments, "as ifs." As always, think of several candidates, and don't forget opposites.

Central Emotional Event. What is the central emotional event of the scene? As soon as you come up with your vision of the central emotional event, you should ask yourself to think of at least two alternate versions.

Domestic Event. What is the domestic event (i.e. the literal event, the simple texture-of-life event, the thing the characters think is going on)?

Individual Events. What are candidates for all the transitions, decisions, and realizations that the characters go through in response to each other, to outside stimuli, and to their interior life? What are the candidates for *wins* and *losses*? When do they make *mistakes*? When do they get a *new thought*? In order to keep this from leading to a connect-the-dots "emotional map," think of these events as associations.

Physical Life. What is the setting (indoor, outdoor, etc.)? The effects of weather, etc.? Physical characteristics or situations of the characters? What personal objects figure in the emotional life of the characters? How will objects and movement affect the relationships and the emotional event?

VI. PERSONAL CONNECTIONS. For each character: at least three ways you are like him/her; three ways you are not like him/her. And a story to go with each characteristic. Anchor each choice or idea from Section III above with a personal metaphor ("It's like when…").

VII. VISION: What is your vision of the scene? What is the "story subtext"? What is the scene about?

VIII. BLOCKING IDEAS. Blocking diagram. Storyboard? Shot list?

IX. REGARDING THE WHOLE SCRIPT:
What is the script about? (may be phrased as a premise, a theme, a paradox, a revelation, a question with answer, or a spine)

What is each character's spine? What is each character's transformation and when does it occur?

X. PLAN OF ATTACK: You don't have to stick to it, but it's a good idea to have a plan for what you want to cover, and how you wish to conduct your rehearsal. There are some examples in Part Three, *The Lost Art of Rehearsal*.

12 | SCRIPT ANALYSIS —
sex, lies, and videotape

sex, lies, and videotape, by Steven Soderbergh

INT.   JOHN AND ANN MILLANEY'S HOUSE—NIGHT

JOHN, ANN and GRAHAM are eating dinner.

>   JOHN
>   (to Graham)
>   Call the cops. That's the first thing
>   that ran through my mind when I saw
>   you. I thought this is not the same
>   man that rode the unicycle naked
>   through the homecoming parade.

>   ANN
>   (to Graham)
>   You did that?

>   GRAHAM
>   Everybody has a past.

>   JOHN
>   (smiles at Graham)
>   What do you think the Greeks would make
>   of that outfit you're wearing?

>   GRAHAM
>   A bonfire, probably.

John takes a sip of Chivas.

>   GRAHAM
>   (to Ann)
>   This food is excellent.

>   ANN
>   Thank you.

                    JOHN
          Yeah, it's not bad. Usually Ann has
          some serious salt action going. I keep
          telling her, you can always add more if
          you want, but you can't take it out.

                    GRAHAM
               (to Ann)
          You have a family here also?

                    ANN
               (nods, chewing)
          Mother, father, sister.

                    GRAHAM
          Sister older or younger?

                    ANN
          Younger.

John takes a large swig of Chivas.

                    GRAHAM
          Are you close?

Graham sees Ann and John exchange looks.

                    GRAHAM
          I'm sorry. Am I prying again?

                    JOHN
          You were prying before?

                    GRAHAM
          Yes, this afternoon. I was grilling
          Ann about your marriage this afternoon.

                    JOHN
               (smiles)
          Really. How'd it go?

                    GRAHAM
          She held up very well.

Ann laughs.

                    GRAHAM
          (to Ann)
     So I was asking about your sister.

Ann's smile fades. John resumes eating.

                    ANN
     Oh, we get along okay. She's just
     very... She's an extrovert. I think
     she's loud. She probably wouldn't
     agree. <u>Definitely</u> wouldn't agree.

                    JOHN
          (to Graham)
     Are you going to see Elizabeth while
     you're here?

An almost imperceptible reaction by Graham.

                    GRAHAM
     I don't know.

                    ANN
          (interested)
     Who's Elizabeth?

                    JOHN
     Girl Graham dated. Still lives here,
     far as I know.

Graham eats in silence.

                    ANN
     Graham and I were talking about
     apartments and I told him to check the
     Garden District, there are some nice
     little places there, garage apartments
     and stuff.

                    JOHN
          (to Graham)
     Stay away from the Garden District.
     Serious crime. I don't know what kind
     of place you're looking for, but there
     are a lot of studio-type apartments
     available elsewhere.

                     GRAHAM
      I wish I didn't have to live someplace.

                     JOHN
         (laughs)
      What do you mean?

Graham thinks a moment, then puts his keyring with its single
key on the table.

                     GRAHAM
      Well, see, right now I have this one
      key, and I really like that.
      Everything I own is in my car. If I
      get an apartment, that's two keys. If
      I get a job, maybe I have to open and
      close once in awhile, that's more keys.
      Or I buy some stuff and I'm worried
      about getting ripped off, so I get some
      locks, and that's more keys. I just
      really like having the one key. It's
      clean, you know.

Graham looks at the keyring before returning it to his pocket.

                     JOHN
      Get rid of the car when you get your
      apartment, then you'll still have one
      key.

                     GRAHAM
      I like having the car, the car is
      important.

                     JOHN
      Especially if you want to leave
      someplace in a hurry.

                     GRAHAM
      Or go someplace in a hurry.
Ann takes her plate in the kitchen.

                         JOHN
                 (smiles at Graham)
         Do you pay taxes?

Graham also stands, empty plate in hand.

                         GRAHAM
         Do I pay taxes? Of course, I pay
         taxes, only a liar doesn't pay taxes,
         I'm not a liar. A liar is the second
         lowest form of human being.

                         ANN
                 (from the kitchen)
         What's the first?

                         GRAHAM
         Lawyers.

John smiles, thinking. Graham follows Ann into the kitchen.
John shouts after them.

                         JOHN
         Hey, Ann, why don't you go with Graham
         to hunt for apartments? Show him the
         city has changed.

Ann looks at Graham.

                         ANN
         Would you mind?

                         GRAHAM
         No.

                         ANN
                 (shouts back to John)
         Okay, I will!!

John, sitting at the table and now toying with <u>his</u> keyring,
nods.

End of scene.

For this first script analysis scene, I'm going to follow the Rehearsal Plan in the previous chapter. However, I will no doubt end up jumping around among the sections. Script analysis is not a linear process of ticking off a given list of questions, or filling in charts. Instead it's a way to get your juices going and your ideas popping.

There wasn't room to reprint the entire script, but I will assume that readers are familiar with this movie, and I'll mention some facts, clues, and evidence from the rest of the script if it's helpful for investigating this scene. But I won't be analyzing the whole script — just this scene. I will be thinking of this scene as if it is the most important scene in the movie.

Of course this "analysis" is purely a teaching example. And an incomplete one, at that. I'm not suggesting that this is how writer-director Steven Soderbergh interpreted this scene — and I'm definitely not claiming that he should have thought of it in the following ways. It's a wonderful movie, and this exercise should not imply that a single frame of it should be changed.

I. BEGINNER'S MIND
What are your preliminary ideas? What are your feelings about this scene? Why did you choose (or write) this material? How do you feel about the characters? Which one do you like the best, or feel closest to, and why? What do you like and not like about them? What are your "freebies" — that is, what immediate personal connections do you have to the material, to the characters and their situations? What do you bring to the table? What causes you anxiety about working on this scene? What prejudices do you bring to the scene?

This section of the Rehearsal Plan has to do with your first impressions and your "freebies" — the connections that you make strongly on an early reading. Also the prejudices that you bring to the material. In this first stab at collecting my thoughts and feelings, I won't try at all to be "correct" about putting my ideas in a playable form. It's going to be in a diary form, and I'm just going to blurt out my thoughts.

My preliminary ideas, not surprisingly, are influenced by the casting and direction of the actual movie. (This is why, for my Script Analysis workshops, I always choose unproduced scripts.) I can't help remembering the performances, which were very strong. My anxieties, before I even start to work, have to do with the admiration I feel for the actual film of this script, and my fear that I won't be able to bring any fresh insights to it. I like the scene. I chose it for this chapter because I wanted to have at least one three-person scene and because I think the writing is good.

The character I like the most is Ann; in fact, I identify with her quite strongly. The freebies for me about Ann are that I think of her as a stranger in her own world (as I have often thought of myself), sexually fragile (as I have myself been at times), and in the grip of feelings of help-lessness and worthlessness.

What I don't like about John is that he belittles other people. In this scene, he belittles Graham's appearance, his activities in college, his lack of job, and he deliberately brings up a subject (ex-girlfriend Elizabeth) he probably has reason to know will be painful. He belittles Ann's cooking, and her suggestion of a suitable section of town for Graham to look for an apartment. He belittles a whole section of town — the Garden District. And, he is a liar. Now I must look for something to like about him and I guess it would be his intelligence; he's clever and witty. Another thing to like might be that when the subject of Ann's sister comes up, he doesn't join the conversation. He doesn't contradict her or belittle her feelings in public. Perhaps we could find something to like in that he opens his home to his college buddy.

This all goes to keeping from passing judgment. Even though there are a lot of things that John does that I don't like — and try not to do myself — I need to find some things that he does that I also do. So noticing that he opens his home to a buddy he hasn't seen in a long time — that's something I would do, in fact have done. So even though it may not be as central a fact about him as some others that are less appealing, at least it's a place to start, a way to think of him as a human being rather than as a movie villain.

Things I like about Graham: he compliments Ann's cooking, he helps with the dishes, he's interested in her feelings. Then there are other items of information we receive about him — riding naked on the unicycle, dressing poorly, refusing to own keys. Sometimes I like people who do things like that, sometimes I don't. Then there's his statement "I'm not a liar" — my first inclination is to like him for saying that. But then I won-der, couldn't that just as easily be the statement of a pompous ass, as of a genuine seeker of truth? It's a mysterious line!

II. RAW MATERIAL OF THE SCENE:
FACTS, EVIDENCE, QUESTIONS, IMAGES, MYSTERIOUS LINES

These were all preliminary thoughts and feelings. Now let's list some facts and images. We'll begin with facts that are true at the beginning of the scene, whether we learn them in this scene or in another part of the script. Since I expect *sex, lies, and videotape* to be familiar to readers of this book, we'll include facts from other parts of the script.

Here are the facts I know from earlier scenes in the script: Ann and John are married. John is an attorney. Ann has no job outside the home. Ann is in therapy. John is having an affair with Ann's sister, Cynthia, who works as a bartender. John and Graham went to college together; they have not seen each other since Graham dropped out of college nine years ago. Graham has contacted John and asked to stay at his home; John has said yes; Graham arrived early and he and Ann had a conversation before John arrived home from work. Also this afternoon, John spent his lunch hour at Cynthia's apartment, and Cynthia told him she wants to make love with him at his house in his and Ann's bed.

Now I'll make a list of images gleaned from the text of the scene: call the cops; riding a unicycle naked; homecoming parade; the Greeks; bonfire; serious salt action; family; grilling Ann about the marriage; extrovert; Elizabeth; the Garden District; garage apartments; key ring with single key; one key versus many keys; the car; leave someplace in a hurry; go someplace in a hurry; taxes; liar; second lowest form of human being; lawyers; John's key ring.

These images are in the dialogue, except for Graham's key ring with a single key and John's key ring, which were both mentioned in the stage directions. Although I often question or cross out stage directions, these two images I'm going to highlight — they are personal objects of two of the characters. Maybe they will suggest a metaphor for the differences between the two men, or maybe they'll have some other thematic resonance. I'm not certain that I'll stage the scene with both men putting their key rings on the table. I'll highlight them and consider their significance later.

The facts and the images are the bones of the scene. Laying them out in lists gives me a clean picture of the raw material the writer has provided. It provokes questions and associations too.

Now we'll start through the scene, line by line. We'll look at facts, evidence, questions, images, associations, and mysterious lines — all at once. We'll find that asking our questions and making our associations will cause us to weave into the territory of Section III (Choices and Ideas). But that's the way script analysis goes. It's not a linear process.

John and Graham

In John's first speech he says, "Call the cops. That's the first thing that ran through my mind when I saw you. I thought this is not the same man that rode the unicycle naked through the homecoming parade." These are *mysterious lines*. What do they mean? What is their subtext? What reality lies behind them? My first thought was to link the images "call the cops" and "the man that rode the unicycle naked through the homecoming parade" to mean that in college Graham was such a hell-raiser that his very presence in town meant the police should be on alert. The image "riding a unicycle naked in the homecoming parade" could have several associations, and my first association was that it was an act of protest against college institutions.

But the naked unicycle riding could have an opposite connotation. John's next remark is, "What do you think the Greeks would make of that outfit you're wearing?" I deduce from the reference to "Greeks" that they were in a college fraternity together (fraternities are titled with Greek letters) — also from the images "homecoming" and "bonfire," which create associations to college football weekends. So the naked unicycle riding could have been a fraternity prank — something that could be described as a conservative activity, in the sense that college fraternities often are the breeding grounds of business, financial, and political leaders. And when I look more closely at the sentence construction, it seems more likely that John is saying that if Graham was the same unicycle-riding guy as before, then the cops would not have to be called, because all would be well. Whereas the way he is dressed now is very unlike what would be proper for a fraternity brother, and outside John's ideas of what is socially acceptable. In fact, maybe Graham's appearance is so unacceptable as to make him look like a lowlife, even a criminal — hence, "call the cops."

Now I have another fact — that John and Graham were in a fraternity together. And a couple of questions: What was their relationship in college? What other adventures/pranks did they participate in together? Also — what *is* Graham wearing? How bad does he look? Does he smell bad?

Ann and Cynthia

Next in the scene, Graham changes the subject away from his appearance and their college days, to Ann ("This food is excellent.") followed by a series of questions ("You have a family here also?" "Sister older or younger?" "Are you close?" and, "Am I prying again?"). At this point, John joins the conversation and there is a brief exchange on the subject of "grilling Ann about the marriage." Graham returns to the subject of Ann's sister until he gets some actual information about Ann's feelings, with the lines, "Oh, we get along okay. She's just very…she's an extrovert. I think she's loud. She probably wouldn't agree. <u>Definitely</u> wouldn't agree."

This is another mysterious line. The one thing we can say for sure about this speech is that it does have subtext! It refers to a lifetime of specific incidents and issues. What issues have been between the two sisters? (We are now weaving into the area of Section III.) There is a later scene in which Ann objects to Cynthia's vulgar language, Cynthia laughs at Ann's primness, and Ann criticizes Cynthia for not having bought a gift for their mother's birthday. But even the list of issues from the later scene (vulgarity, prudishness, and inconsideration of mother's feelings) may not be all their issues. What else do they argue about? Or, *do* they argue? We see them arguing in the later scene, but that doesn't necessarily mean that they argue often — we shouldn't assume that they do. We could conceivably make the choice that at the time of the dinner table scene we are considering in this chapter, Ann and Cynthia have no history of overt arguing.

If they have had arguments, how often? What subjects? And what issues do they have with each other that they have never verbalized? When Ann describes Cynthia as "extroverted" or "loud," what specifically does she mean? Is she referring to sexual behavior? Her subtext might be that in her opinion Cynthia flirts and behaves lewdly at inappropriate times — the evidence in the later scene supports this idea. Have they been at parties when Ann has been embarrassed by Cynthia's raucous behavior?

Or could "extroverted" and "loud" apply to family gatherings? Does Cynthia over-drink at family gatherings and become obnoxious? Is it possible that Cynthia's choice of job is objectionable to Ann — that it bothers Ann that Cynthia prefers the company of pubcrawlers to the genteel society they were brought up in? Is it possible that Cynthia resents Ann for not having to work? Or looks down on Ann for not being self-respecting enough to work? In an earlier scene, Cynthia refers to Ann as the "beautiful, popular" one. Is it possible that Cynthia always felt like the runt, less loved by their mother, and her obnoxious behavior around Ann is a cry for attention and approval? What is their mother like? Does Ann resemble her? Sleeping with Ann's husband would certainly appear to be the wrong way for Cynthia to get the love and approval of either Ann or their mother — but people often do the wrong thing to get what they want!

It might appear that I've gotten far afield, going on about Cynthia — a character that's not even in this scene! But I'm really thinking about Ann. What is her responsibility for the disastrous condition of her relationship with her sister? I've already mentioned how much I like her, but it's just as important to be honest about the characters' flaws as it is to find something positive about them. It takes two to make a bad relationship. Now I'm coming up with something not so wonderful about her — that she may have ignored her less beautiful, less conformist little sister. Is this snobbery — a kind of class distinction between the two? (And what is their class background, anyway? Was it expected that Ann would marry an up-and-coming lawyer? Or was it expected that both girls would make their living as waitresses and hairdressers? In which case marriage to a lawyer would be a social coup?) How does sex come in? Does Ann demonize her sister's sexuality as a projection of her own anxieties about sex?

All this goes to the search for the subtext to Ann's lines, "Oh, we get along okay. She's just very…she's an extrovert. I think she's loud. She probably wouldn't agree. Definitely wouldn't agree." Is Ann saying things in front of Graham, a stranger, that she has never said to her sister's face? Is John hearing her verbalize these sentiments for the first time?

Stage Directions
Considering characters with flaws leads us neatly to John. At this point in the scene he puts a stop to the conversation between Graham and Ann by interrupting with, "Are you going to see Elizabeth while you're here?"

I haven't said anything yet about stage directions. In this tiny section about Elizabeth there are two: "An almost imperceptible reaction by Graham," and "Graham eats in silence." I haven't crossed them out because I am so appreciative that the author didn't write, "Ann notices his discomfort and comes to his rescue by changing the subject," even though this may well be what happens here — the *beat change* or *transition*. But the stage direction "Ann notices his discomfort…" etc. would be an intellectualization of the transition, not as helpful to the actor as letting her figure it out herself.

So I'm leaving in "An almost imperceptible reaction" and "eats in silence," but not because I want them to be a blueprint for the actor's inner life and facial expressions. I'm *questioning* them. I'm going to *translate* them. I'm not going to ignore them, but I'm going to replace them with ideas for *imaginative backstory*. These stage directions trigger a *question*: What happened between Graham and Elizabeth?

Later scenes in the script give us more information, as does Soderbergh's diary accompanying the published script. Soderbergh writes in the diary that actor James Spader expressed a concern about the motivation for Graham's withdrawal from people and his return to Baton Rouge. Soderbergh and Spader "came up with a backstory involving a child that Graham had fathered with Elizabeth that turned out to be retarded and led to Graham's abandoning Elizabeth due to an inability to deal with the child." Soderbergh was going to change the script to include this information, but later changed his mind. Thank God! This is exactly the kind of detail that is so much better left in subtext. The actor must make a specific choice, and the audience must *feel* that there is subtext to this section — but it does not need to be explained and intellectualized. Later scenes in the final script clarify the emotional history of Graham and Elizabeth, but without giving details. The theme of child abandonment would have been trivialized by sticking it into a script whose story does not support that theme emotionally.

The actor can of course give himself a private subtext that has to do with child abandonment. But it is unlikely to be helpful unless he has some personal experience with that issue. In that case, allowing his personal association to be part of his characterization may work very well to give texture and grounding to the performance. But there is no need for him to think up a child abandonment backstory — to do so would probably only intellectualize his performance.

The stage direction earlier in the scene, "Graham sees Ann and John exchange looks," after Graham's question about whether Ann and Cynthia are close, is another one which I'm not crossing out, but which I'm putting a question mark next to, to remind myself to translate it into *questions*. What — if any — conversations have Ann and John had on the subject of Cynthia? Has John been patient or dismissive when Ann complains about Cynthia's behavior? Is it possible that Ann has seen Cynthia flirt with John?

Ann and Graham
Back to the line-by-line look at the scene. Ann changes the subject from Elizabeth — perhaps to rescue Graham from his embarrassment. Or, perhaps because she herself is already interested in him and doesn't want to hear about his other women? Or, perhaps because the conversation they had this afternoon about sections of the city was pleasurable to her, and free-associates into her mind with the sound of his voice? (I am making myself come up with three possibilities, even though I was pretty satisfied with the first one.)

Now that the conversation has turned to Graham's hunt for an apartment, he suddenly comes out with, "I wish I didn't have to live someplace." This is a mysterious line! Does he mean it literally? Perhaps, but there's not too much evidence for that choice — he does indeed rent an apartment the next day. Does he mean it existentially? — that he doesn't want to be described or categorized by where he lives rather than by who he is in his inner being? Does he mean it spiritually? — that he wishes he could evolve into a being that exists only spiritually and not corporeally? When asked what he means, he goes into a little speech including the line, "If I get a job, maybe I have to open and close once in awhile, that's more keys." Is it a main preoccupation of his to live without responsibilities to other people? (This could be a candidate for his *spine*.) Or is this statement intended as a deliberate provocation to John?

Lawyers and Liars

Graham's meditation on the desirability of having only one key includes his statement, "I like having the car, the car is important," to which John replies, "Especially if you want to leave someplace in a hurry," and Graham returns with, "Or go someplace in a hurry." These are very mysterious lines that take us squarely into the meat of the scene. What does John mean by "Especially if you want to leave someplace in a hurry"? Is this a general expression of his distaste for people who don't like to accept responsibility? Or does it refer to some specific event in his and Graham's past relationship? It is always more helpful to look for a specific past event as a trigger for a line like that, than to think of it as a general statement of the character's feelings and beliefs. In fact this is a good example of what is meant by making choices *specific*.

So I'll skip ahead to do some Research (section IV), and read once more the afternoon scene in which Graham told Ann that he was surprised John was letting him stay at his and Ann's home. Graham says, "We were extremely close until I dropped out...Up until I dropped out, John and I were...very much alike." These lines give some evidence that John may have experienced Graham's dropping out as an abandonment or betrayal. They suggest a context for John's line in our scene, "Especially if you want to leave someplace in a hurry." What about Graham's reply, "Or go someplace in a hurry"? Is it a defense against a charge of irresponsibility? Is it a dig at John's way of life? Is it a statement that if he had stayed in college he would have been making no choice, just letting himself drift into the usual path that all his middle-class friends were taking. Again, is this an existential statement — that his choice is *to make choices*?

In this next section every line is a mysterious one. As I mentioned in the *Subtext* chapter, the image of "paying taxes" might give us an association with duty and responsibility, a subject that seems to have been brought up already. We could still ask questions about the subtext of the line. What is John really asking? Is he asking whether Graham has a job? Or whether Graham is on welfare, in other words, living off the contributions of taxpayers such as John? What *does* Graham live on? Does he have an independent income? Is John implying that Graham lives on illegal — and therefore untaxed — income, as from drug dealing?

Then there are Graham's statements, that lawyers are the lowest form of human being, and that "I'm not a liar." These lines must have feeling and history behind them, even if they are delivered without edge or attitude. In real life we might speak very quietly about matters of great importance — the simplicity of the delivery might even be an indication of how important the issues are. What is Graham's intention on these lines? To make a joke? To make a dig? To get revenge for the digs that John has been making? Or to bring up some old wounds? Has he come back to Baton Rouge to put his fingers in a sore?

The Set-Up
In the last beat of the scene, John suggests that Ann accompany Graham on his apartment search. From the following scenes, we deduce that he does this in order to get her out of the house so he can fulfill Cynthia's request to have sex there. What has given him this impulse? Does the vibe of Ann and Graham's interest in each other give him an impulse to punish her? Does he have an impulse to assert his ownership of the house against this intruder?

More Questions
Now let's go back to some questions raised by the facts. Take, for example, the fact that John is having the affair with Cynthia. I always wonder why married people have affairs — to me, if one wants to have affairs, it makes sense to get a divorce. And, in particular, why does John conduct his affair with Cynthia? Is the taboo itself exciting? Does he feel trapped by marriage? Did he feel corralled into getting married too early? Is he punishing Ann, and if so, for what, specifically? There is evidence in an earlier scene that John's and Ann's sex life has begun to wither, but was that the cause, or the result, of the affair?

It's not enough to say that John is a cheater or a liar — that's a judgment. Was there a breakdown in communication that caused him to feel undernourished and cheated in the marriage? Again, my purpose in investigating these issues is not to make John a sympathetic or likeable character. However, lying and lies are a key theme of this script, and I'm wondering whether the author isn't asking tough questions, such as when is the moment when a breakdown in communication becomes the same as a lie?

Here's another idea: Was Cynthia the instigator of the affair, and John too weak to resist? Could it even be that his driving need (his *spine*) is to hold onto the attention of women the way a little boy tries to hold the attention of his mother?

One can go on and on with questions — for example, is Ann a good cook or not? This may not seem terribly important at first, but I have an impulse to go down this road. Graham calls the food "excellent." John calls it "not bad." These are contradictory statements. So the quality of the cooking makes a difference. If the food is excellent, what is John comparing it to, that makes him grudging in his appreciation? Is his boss's wife a better cook? His mother? Or is the meal in fact only average? It's not uncommon for a dinner guest to praise the cooking more than it deserves. But Graham declares in this very scene that "I'm not a liar." Does that mean that if the meal was mediocre he would say so?

III. CHOICES AND IDEAS:
OBJECTIVES and INTENTIONS, WHAT JUST HAPPENED, WHAT'S AT STAKE, PROBLEM, OBSTACLE.   ADJUSTMENTS and SUBTEXT, IMAGINATIVE BACKSTORY, ISSUES, THROUGH-LINES

What just happened
This scene begins in the middle of a conversation. So *what just happened* is the conversation off-camera before the scene starts. What topics were they discussing? Was it all small talk? Does the scene begin as soon as anything of substance happens? Or could they have been in the middle of a spirited discussion of politics? In rehearsal we could improvise this "pre-scene beat."

Adjustments
Here are some possible adjustments a director could suggest to the actors, based on his script analysis preparation.

1) John's remarks about Graham's appearance. The actor playing John could make one of several different *adjustments* to these lines. It could be a big joke that Graham, once a dapper dresser, now looks so scruffy. Or it could be cause for concern to his friend, that he has let himself go this way. Or it could be insulting to John that Graham would accept a dinner invitation in this condition.

2) The idea of parties when Ann has been embarrassed by Cynthia's raucous behavior is an example of a "what if…?" adjustment. It creates an image to propel the delivery of those lines about Cynthia.

3) When John asks Graham if he plays taxes, I thought of the question: Is John implying that Graham lives on illegal — and therefore untaxed — income, as from drug dealing? Even though there's no

evidence anywhere in the script that Graham has anything to do with drug dealing, it could still be an association in John's mind when he asks this question. While we are working on a scene, it's helpful to consider that scene the most important one in the script.

Imaginative Backstory

Here are some ideas for imaginative backstory that came out of my questions and meanderings in Section II:

Graham might be interested in the philosophy of existentialism.
John might have a mother who is charming but emotionally distant.
Ann might look more like her mother than Cynthia does.

I might bring these ideas up when discussing the characters with the actors — but I might not. For instance, if the actor playing Graham has no interest in existentialism, I would let that idea go. But these ideas are helpful to me as a director anyway, even if they never get used, because they add emotional, psychological, and spiritual detail to the characters — and daydreaming those details helps me allow these characters to live in my imagination. And allowing the characters to live in my imagination gives me authority to tell their story.

Issues

We went over some issues in the relationship of Ann and Cynthia. What issues are between Ann and John? One is the issue of over-salting the food. John says, "I keep telling her, you can always add more if you want, but you can't take it out." How many times have they had this conversation? Why does Ann keep adding salt to her cooking after John has told her he doesn't like it?

Objectives and Intentions

I want to come up with three different candidates for the objectives of each character. Actually I'll use the terms objective and intention somewhat interchangeably. I'll need to imagine I haven't seen the movie, so I can come up with ideas based on analysis of the script, rather than on the performances. Since this is a three-person scene, each character can have a different objective toward each of the other characters. That adds up to a lot of candidates! I'll try to keep it simple.

John. John could have the intention 1) to put Graham down, to make him feel small and worthless. He could even have this intention toward both Graham and Ann. Or, 2) he could have an objective to impress them, or even, 3) to make them like him. I've often noticed that people whose behavior is what we call "obnoxious" are driven by a need to be appreciated and liked — they're just doing the wrong thing to get it.

Graham. Graham has a different objective toward John than toward Ann. His objective toward John could be, 1) to hurt or destroy him. Or, 2) he could be teasing him, trying to get his goat, or even make him laugh. Or, 3) he might want John to wake up, face himself, and rescue himself from complacency and moral laziness. Graham's objective toward Ann could be, 1) to make her feel good about herself, protect her from her brutish husband. Or, 2) to seduce and charm her, or even, 3) manipulate and insinuate himself into her thoughts.

Ann. Ann doesn't say much, so let's gather whatever evidence we have about her. First let's take all her lines and put them together, thus: "You did that? Thank you. Mother, father, sister. Younger. Oh, we get along okay. She's just very...she's an extrovert. I think she's loud. She probably wouldn't agree. Definitely wouldn't agree. Who's Elizabeth? Graham and I were talking about apartments and I told him to check the Garden District, there are some nice little places there, garage apartments and stuff. What's the first? Would you mind? Okay, I will!"

Then, let's look at her situation (facts): she is the hostess at a dinner with two men, one of whom is her husband. She might have an objective to be a good hostess and a good wife, to deflect attention away from herself and onto the men and their interests. Or she might have a need for attention, so deep and unspoken that it takes form in shyness. People whose behavior is "shy" have just as strong needs for attention as anyone else — maybe even stronger. Maybe their needs for attention are so strong that they fear that any expression of those needs will cause an explosion.

Do you see how the "objective" is a way of expressing the characters' relationships to each other? And a way to express personality traits as well? It's a way to describe personality traits with reference to the person's situation rather than by judging them or gossiping about their psychology.

What's at Stake
Asking what's at stake is the same as asking what are the characters fighting for, and what are their obstacles. John could be fighting for his dignity, his self-image, his manhood even. This idea could verge on a judgment, except that I know there are times when I have felt that my self-image was at stake. I haven't necessarily been pleased with the way I behaved in those situations, but at the time I felt I was doing the best I could.

Through-lines
Often the through-line is the same as the character's objective. But in a three-person scene it's more complex. For each character, what is his or

her primary focus? For instance, could Graham's through-line be to take Ann away from John?

IV. RESEARCH
Research includes re-reading the script, even as often as every day. It also means revisiting your personal connections. But also outside research. Another issue between Ann and John is a difference of opinion about the Garden District. Before going much further into this issue, it will help tremendously to find out where and what is the Garden District of Baton Rouge.

V. SCENE SHAPE: BEATS, CENTRAL EVENT, SUB-EVENTS, PHYSICAL LIFE
The topics and the person who introduces them are as follows:
1) Graham's appearance (John)
2) Ann's cooking (Graham)
3) Ann's family (Graham)
4) Graham and Ann's conversation this afternoon (Graham)
5) Cynthia (Graham)
6) Elizabeth (John)
7) Graham's apartment hunt (Ann)
8) keys (Graham)
9) leaving somewhere in a hurry (John)
10) taxes, liars and lawyers (John)
11) Ann helping Graham with apartment hunt (John)

Usually what I do next is try to group these topics into three major beats. These are judgment calls — choices that start to uncover one's vision of the scene. I'm going to say that the first major beat is topic #1, plus the conversation that was going on before the scene started. In other words, topic #1 is the end of a longer conversation, perhaps about old times and how things have changed since they saw each other. The second major beat is topics #2-5: Graham steers the conversation away from himself and John and toward Ann, and to some extent, his relationship with Ann. Topics #6-7 are a transition beat/event: John puts a stop to the conversation about Ann by bringing up Elizabeth, and Ann rescues Graham from the subject of Elizabeth. Topics #8-10 are the third major beat. This is the meat of the scene, the debate about responsibility, loyalty, and ethics. Topic #11 is a "tag" and set-up for the next two scenes.

We touched on the individual events in the discussion under Section II, above. The central event? A strong candidate for central event is the showdown between the two men in the "responsibility, loyalty, and ethics" beat. Who wins? Graham, apparently, when he trumps the discussion with his "liars and lawyers" riff. John fights back, but covertly, by getting the idea to set up his meeting with Cynthia the next day in Ann's own bed. In his own mind he probably feels that he won.

VI. PERSONAL CONNECTIONS

The "salt in cooking" issue reminds me of a story. A close friend went through a painful divorce after fifteen years of marriage. Some years later she mentioned to me quite casually that in the years when they had only one car, her ex was constantly bugging her about leaving the car parked in neutral, instead of in first gear, as he preferred. I couldn't help being curious, and I asked her, did she think it was important to leave the car in neutral? Or was she deliberately needling him, to assert her independence, or to get him back for times when he disregarded her wishes? (She had often complained that his forceful personality did not always leave room for the expression of her own needs.) But she said it was neither one — she just could never remember to do it the way he wanted, and it was puzzling to her that it bothered him.

When people consistently "fail to remember" something like that — well, the term "passive-aggressive" can't help but spring to mind. But "passive-aggressive" is a judgment, and we don't want to judge anyone — not Ann, and certainly not my friend, whom I love dearly. But I do notice that apparently Ann has not over-salted the food tonight... Has she made a special effort for Graham? Is the usual over-salting one small way that she can assert her autonomy in a suffocating marriage?

I was in a suffocating marriage (my first one, when I was twenty) and I did lots of passive-aggressive things to get back at my overbearing husband — that's the main reason why I can never throw a first stone at any other woman. I have also been, during the long years in between my two marriages, in Graham's position, on the outside looking in at other people's relationships, inserting myself when and where I could. It's harder to connect to John, but only until I let myself think of him as a confused person, perhaps a person who has always done what he thought others wanted of him, getting married before he was ready, without enough self-knowledge to bring to a lasting relationship — I was like that in my first marriage.

VII. VISION, STORY, THEME

As you can see from my personal connections, a prominent theme for me in this scene is bound to be the puzzle and challenge of marriage, both for those inside the institution and for those outside of it. There are other themes as well. There is the overtly stated theme of lying, and implied themes of responsibility, loyalty, and ethics. There are hints of themes of abandonment and betrayal.

Now, what is the overall structure, or story of this scene? What is it about? What happens? There's a question we should ask ourselves: Is Ann peripheral to the interaction of these two men, or is she the focus for them both? Are they fighting over her? Or are they focused on each other, vying for alpha dog status, with Ann the near-silent witness and foil? These are two ways to describe a vision of the scene.

Or, you could see the structure as John trying to assert control over the conversation, the dinner table, his marriage, and his life, while Ann and Graham play at their attraction to each other. This would mean there's more at stake for John in the scene than for Graham or Ann. Their through-lines could have more to do with playing and exploring, while John struggles to keep control and assert his manhood. I think this is the vision that I tend toward.

Is abandonment a "soft spot" for John, the place where he is vulnerable? In the relationship between John and Ann, each one probably feels emotionally abandoned by the other. They are paying each other back for hurts that the other one doesn't know he or she has committed. Graham is the wild card thrown into their life. There is no human being who never lies. I think of Graham as a man who has adopted this "I never lie" persona as a way to have nothing to lose. A person with nothing to lose is a destabilizing element in any institution, including marriage. His center is hurt, too. Insisting one has "nothing to lose" is a way of protecting oneself from hurt.

Part of my vision is that I want to make sure this feels like a real marriage, based on what I've known and seen of marriage. I want to depict the human event — the thing that happens when there is a marriage already weakened by serial paybacks for unacknowledged hurts, and into that marriage comes a guy with nothing to lose.

It's funny. Even though this has turned into a long chapter, I still feel that I have only scratched the surface of these characters and their problems. I've got enough, though, to feel ready to meet with the actors, who will in any case do much more to fill in the blanks and bring them to life than I can, on puny paper.

13 | SCRIPT ANALYSIS — *CLERKS*

Clerks, by Kevin Smith

INT: VIDEO STORE. Day

RANDAL pulls a soda from the cooler

>   RANDAL
>   Want something to drink?

>   (OC) DANTE
>   No, thanks.

>   RANDAL
>   Who was on your phone this morning at
>   about two-thirty? I was trying to call
>   for a half an hour.

>   (OC) DANTE
>   Why?

>   RANDAL
>   I wanted to use your car.

He walks by a row of snacks and grabs one without looking at it.

>   RANDAL
>   Snack cake?

DANTE sits in his seat behind the register.
RANDAL grabs a paper and joins him behind the counter.

>   DANTE
>   You don't want to know.

>   RANDAL
>   You called Caitlin again?!

                        DANTE
She called me.

                        RANDAL
Did you tell Veronica?

                        DANTE
One fight a day with Veronica is about
all I can stomach, thanks.

                        RANDAL
What do you two fight about?

                        DANTE
I guess it's not really fighting. She
just wants me to leave here, go back to
school, get some direction.

                        RANDAL
          (*opening paper*)
I'll bet the most frequent topic of
arguments is Caitlin Bree.

                        DANTE
You win.

                        RANDAL
I'm going to offer you some advice, my
friend: let the past be the past.
Forget Caitlin Bree. You've been with
Veronica for how long now?

                        DANTE
Seven months.

                        RANDAL
Chick's nuts about you. How long did
you date Caitlin?

                        DANTE
Five years.

                    RANDAL
Chick only made you nuts. She cheated
on you how many times?

                    DANTE
Eight and a half.

                    RANDAL
          (*looking up from paper*)
Eight and a half?

                    DANTE
Party at John K's-senior year. I get
blitzed and pass out in his bedroom.
Caitlin comes in and dives all over me.

                    RANDAL
That's cheating?

                    DANTE
In the middle of it, she calls me Brad.

                    RANDAL
She called you Brad?

                    DANTE
She called me Brad.

                    RANDAL
That's not cheating. People say crazy
shit during sex. One time, I called
this girl "Mom."

                    DANTE
I hit the lights and she freaks. Turns
out she thought I was Brad Michaelson.

                    RANDAL
What do you mean?

                    DANTE
She was supposed to meet Brad
Michaelson in a bedroom. She picked the
wrong one. She had no idea I was even
at the party.

                    RANDAL
Oh, my God.

                    DANTE
Great story, isn't it?

                    RANDAL
That girl was vile to you.

                    DANTE
Interesting postscript to that story:
Do you know who wound up going with
Brad Michaelson in the other dark bedroom?

                    RANDAL
Your mother.

                    DANTE
Allan Harris.

                    RANDAL
Chess team Allen Harris?!

                    DANTE
The two moved to Idaho together after
graduation. They raise sheep.

                    RANDAL
That's frightening.

                    DANTE
It takes different strokes to move the
world.

                    RANDAL
In light of this lurid tale, I don't
see how you could even romanticize your
relationship with Caitlin - she broke
your heart and inadvertently drove men
to deviant lifestyles.

                    DANTE
Because there was a lot of good in our
relationship.

                    RANDAL
Oh yeah.

                    DANTE
I'm serious. Aside from cheating, we
were a great couple. That's what high
school's all about - algebra, bad
lunch, and infidelity.

                    RANDAL
You think things would be any different
now?

                    DANTE
They are. When she calls me now, she's
a different person - she's frightened
and vulnerable. She's about to finish
college and enter the real world.
That's got to be scary for anyone.

                    RANDAL
          (suddenly recalling)
Oh shit, I've got to place an order.

                    DANTE
I'm talking to myself here.

                    RANDAL
No, no, I'm listening. She's leaving
college, and...?

                    DANTE
        ...and she's looking to me for support.
        And I think that this is leading our
        relationship to a new level.

                    RANDAL
        What about Veronica?

                    DANTE
        I think the arguments Veronica and I
        are having are some kind of
        manifestation of a subconscious desire
        to break away from her so that I can
        pursue the possibility of a more
        meaningful relationship with Caitlin.

                    RANDAL
        Caitlin's on the same wave length?

                    DANTE
        I think it's safe to say yes.

                    RANDAL
        Then I think all four of you had better
        sit down and talk it over.

                    DANTE
        All four?

                    RANDAL
        You, Veronica, Caitlin...
                (*lays paper flat*)
        ...and Caitlin's fiance.

THE HEADLINE of the engagement announcement
reads, BREE TO WED ASIAN DESIGN MAJOR.

End of scene.

I enjoy Kevin Smith's writing. Besides his fresh, natural, inventive dialogue — which most people find attractive in his work — I find his characters and scenes emotionally complex, intellectually stimulating, very human, and constantly surprising. Although Smith's scripts and characters are remarkably well constructed, his directorial approach — a kind of emotionally chaotic "no-direction" directing style — ensures that his fairly careful structuring is never obvious or self-conscious.

Smith himself has said that it was a turning point in his life when his reputation for anarchy and irreverence was busted by a reviewer calling *Clerks* and *Mallrats*, "two very sweet movies about guys who want very badly to be in love." My directorial approach to this scene may be different from Smith's, but I would certainly never want to turn his work into anything sentimental or ponderous. A light touch is an essential counterpoint to the thematic concerns of the scripts — whose deeply felt elements include commitment and love, trust, friendship, commercialism, mortality, and religion versus spirituality.

IMAGES

The facts and images are the "bones" of the scene. Instead of starting out the script analysis with a review of the facts, I'm going to start with images, and get to facts a little later. Listing the images will help us set out the raw material of our scene and the characters' lives. I've organized the images into a few categories, as follows.

The images of Dante and Randal's daily life and relationship: snack cake, soda in the cooler, newspaper, Randal calling Dante at 2:00 in the morning to borrow his car.

Dante's personal images (pertaining to his life and situation): go back to school, get some direction.

The images of Dante's love life: phone call with Caitlin, fight with Veronica, Caitlin frightened and vulnerable, meaningful relationship with Caitlin, Caitlin's fiancé.

Dante's stories and riffs: the story of John K's party; the image of Brad Michaelson and Allan Harris raising sheep in Idaho; the brief riff on algebra, bad lunch, and infidelity in high school.

Randal's images: placing an order, calling a girl "Mom" during sex.

BEATS

Next, structure. I find the most helpful way to approach structure is to look at beats. I'm determining beats by noticing when the subject changes, and the beats in this scene seem to hop back and forth between two subjects: Caitlin and Veronica. The first subject is Caitlin. Who brings it up?

It could be Randal. Randal starts the scene by questioning Dante about his 2:00 AM phone call. His response ("You called Caitlin again?!") when Dante replies, "You don't want to know" could be evidence that he already suspects that it was Caitlin, and is only checking to see how long it will take for Dante to volunteer the information. That would mean that when he asks who was on Dante's phone at 2:30, he is bringing up the subject of Caitlin, since he thinks he knows the answer to his question already.

Or, it could be Dante who brings up the subject of Caitlin, via heavy sub-text to his line, "You don't want to know." In this case, this line would actually begin the second beat. The first beat would be about Randal's daily life and relationship with Dante, which includes snacking, car-borrowing, and middle-of-the-night drug drop-offs. The exclamation point in Randal's line ("You called Caitlin again?!") is not really persuasive of either interpretation — he could be genuinely surprised by the news, or he could be feigning surprise, with the intention to make fun of Dante for his transparency.

The Caitlin beat continues through "She called me." Then Randal changes the subject ("Did you tell Veronica?") to Veronica. Then, with "How long did you date Caitlin?" Randal changes the subject back to Caitlin again.

This next beat (second Caitlin beat) is a long beat, with a few sub-beats — the story of John K's party, the Brad Michaelson-Alan Harris-sheep farm riff, the purpose-of-high-school riff, Caitlin's new vulnerability. But I'm going to say (these are judgment calls, after all) that the "second Caitlin beat" continues through Dante's line "And I think this is leading our relationship to a new level." Randal changes the subject back again: "What about Veronica?" Then, one last Caitlin beat, again brought up by Randal ("Caitlin's on the same wave length?"), which includes Randal's revelation that Caitlin's engagement has been announced in the newspaper.

In every beat the subject is changed by Randal, and the pattern is back and forth between the two subjects: Caitlin and Veronica. The long Caitlin beat in the center of the scene contains Dante's riffs (arias almost) on John

K's party, the sheep farm, and the purpose of high school. If C=Caitlin, V=Veronica, and R=Randal, the structure is R-C-V-*C*-V-C. The starred Caitlin beat is the one with Dante's arias. The C-V-*C*-V-C part is kind of interestingly symmetrical, with the elaborated "aria" beat in the center.

The off-kilter John-K-party-sheep-farm-purpose-of-high-school aria in the middle beat is genius. It keeps the scene from being informational and on-the-nose, and Smith's ability to veer off like this at the drop of a hat is surely a significant part of his writing talent. But it also has an emotional purpose. It's the only time Dante takes charge of changing the subject — but my feeling is that he doesn't change the subject at all. The story of John K's party, the sheep farm riff, and the high school nostalgia are all part of the long Caitlin beat — they are all tangential to his romantic reminiscences of Caitlin, the excitement she generates, and her centrality to his world.

FACTS, EVIDENCE, AND QUESTIONS
A fact: Dante has been communicating with Caitlin without telling Randal. How long? A week? A month? Has Randal suspected it? Has Dante lied about it? It seems to me that Dante's line "You don't want to know" is evidence that they have spoken on the subject and that Randal has expressed his disapproval of Dante's continued infatuation with Caitlin. How often have they had such conversations? What was said in their last conversation? Randal brings up the subject of Caitlin's cheating — is this the first time he has actually brought it out in the open, or has that been the constant topic of all conversations about Caitlin?

POSSIBLE CHOICES
A question that needs to be answered in order to play the scene is this: At what point in the scene does Randal discover the news item about Caitlin's engagement? The stage direction is significant here — he doesn't enter with the newspaper; he picks it up after the soda and snack cake and before he sits down. So at some point in the scene he must see the item on Caitlin's engagement. Is it just before he mentions it? Or is it earlier? Is it as soon as he opens the paper? Does the sight of the item motivate his line, "I'm going to offer you some advice, my friend: let the past be the past. Forget Caitlin Bree"? Or does he notice it sometime during Dante's long mid-scene aria?

It is possible to make the choice that Randal knew about the engagement before the scene starts, and is playing casual with the newspaper, in order to spring the news on Dante at the moment when it will have the biggest effect. Here's another question about Randal: does he have feelings for Veronica? (There is some evidence, later in the script, to support this idea.)

These questions go to the heart of *who Randal is*. One version is a dark Randal, with selfish motives and a cynical view of Dante's romantic prospects. Does it sound like I am judging him? Actually, I'm thinking of the cynical, selfish people I know who are full of energy and make entertaining company. This Randal already knows about Caitlin's engagement and goes to the trouble of playing a trick on Dante. He also has his eye on Veronica, and is constantly checking ("Did you tell Veronica?" "You've been with Veronica for how long now?" "What about Veronica?") to see if Dante is on verge of abandoning Veronica and leaving the field clear for Randal. He's not necessarily a bad guy — he may think of himself as a rescuer; he may think that he is saving Dante from Caitlin (who doesn't love him) and saving Veronica from Dante (who doesn't love her).

But, on the other hand, Randal may not be nearly as future-oriented as all that. This would be the Randal who follows the impulse of the moment, who says and does whatever comes into his head. This Randal opens the newspaper randomly and reads whatever article is in front of him, even if it is the Society Page. This Randal may also be attracted to Veronica, but totally unaware of his feelings or how they affect his relationship with Dante. How does an actor play that? By adopting Randal's conscious objective — to protect and help his friend — rather than his unconscious need to shake Dante down for information, so he can make his own move.

What does Dante want? Even though he's been keeping his revived relationship on the Q.T., he gives up his secret pretty quickly. Although we don't know how long Caitlin's been calling him, or how often, we do know that she phoned him last night and they spoke at least a half hour. What did she say? What subtext was in her voice?

Another fact is that Veronica has just been to the convenience store visiting Dante, and she questioned him about Caitlin. These two facts create images — in this case, they are sounds, rather than visual images — one of Caitlin's voice on the phone in the middle of the night, and the other of Veronica's voice haranguing him a few minutes ago. Dante could be impelled in this scene with Randal by a desire to revisit his daydreams and fantasies about Caitlin — that could work as an objective or through-line. It's probably more playable to state the objective in a way that includes

Randal, so we could say it is "to involve Randal in his daydreams, fantasies, memories, and philosophical ruminations about Caitlin." His focus (through-line) is then the remembered sound of her voice, and the memories and fantasies triggered by talking with her.

Or, is Dante's through-line his relationship with Randal? Is it only in discussing these things with Randal that Dante's life seems real to him?

EMOTIONAL EVENT

The plot point in the scene is the revelation of Caitlin's engagement. But there are still several ways of describing the *emotional event*. Here's one candidate: Through the process of talking out loud with Randal about these things, Dante decides to break up with Veronica and get back with Caitlin. Just as we asked the question about Randal, we should ask about Dante: Has Dante made up his mind before the scene or does he make up his mind during the scene? You should never assume that the character has already made up his mind about any issue he discusses in a scene — it's quite possible that it will be a more dynamic scene if Dante makes up his mind during the scene than if he is just telling Randal something he has already decided. (You don't know that until you try it, though. This is a good time for a reminder that none of these ideas is a movie! They are proposals to try in rehearsal or on set. While mentally experimenting with a number of ideas, your preference, or vision, will emerge — but you don't know whether it works or not until you try it.)

Another candidate for emotional event (based on the choice to play the dark, cynical Randal): Randal plays a trick on Dante. By allowing Dante to hold forth on his plans for getting back with Caitlin and not revealing his knowledge of the engagement, Randal has set Dante up. Is this a mean trick — for instance, to get the best of Dante in an ongoing rivalry? Or to teach him a lesson? The lesson being that Dante should face his delusions about Caitlin.

If we choose the dark Randal, the structure of the scene is C-V-*C*-V-C. If we choose the live-for-the-moment Randal, the structure is R-C-V-*C*-V-C. Except that I can't help noticing how much this author likes symmetry. Maybe the structure is R-C-V-*C*-V-C-R — that is, with another Randal beat at the end! The last beat of the scene might be a silent communication between the two guys — a moment of shared — what? Misery? Vindication? Comeuppance?

How a director finally chooses to describe the emotional event is contingent upon the entire story he is telling, and where that event fits into the big picture. Dante is the main character. A vital choice for the director to make is whether Dante's primary relationship is with Randal, or with Caitlin, or with Veronica. In the whole script, I think there's little doubt that Dante's central relationship is with Randal. That doesn't mean that his preoccupation (through-line) in every scene has to be with Randal. Is his preoccupation in this scene with Caitlin? Or with Randal?

When I am confronted with good writing, I can't help but have these questions. That doesn't mean that I think this script will work if it is played with a heavy handed, over-analyzed subtext — not at all! My only goal in script analysis is to find the simplest, truest understanding, which will allow the scene to play "real," and allow the writer's style and themes to emerge.

14 | SCRIPT ANALYSIS —
TENDER MERCIES

Tender Mercies, by Horton Foote

INT: BEDROOM - NIGHT

Mac? Is that you?

                    MAC
Yes.

                    ROSA LEE
What time is it?

                    MAC
Late. (*a pause*) I'm not drunk. I bought
a bottle but I didn't get drunk. I
poured it all out. I didn't have one
drink.

                    ROSA LEE
Did you have anything to eat?

                    MAC
Nope.

                    ROSA LEE
Are you hungry?

                    MAC
I guess so.

ROSA LEE *gets out of bed.*

                    ROSA LEE
Come on. I'll get you something to eat.
She puts a robe on and goes out to the kitchen. He follows.

                    ROSA LEE
          How hungry are you?

                     MAC
          I'm not very hungry.

                    ROSA LEE
          Want some eggs?

                     MAC
          No.

                    ROSA LEE
          Some chili?

                     MAC
          No. A little soup will do me.

She opens a can of soup. She heats it at the stove.

                     MAC
          I rode by here six or seven times. I
          could see you all sitting here watching
          T.V. Did you see me ride by?

                    ROSA LEE
          No.

                     MAC
          I rode all over town tonight. Started
          twice for San Antonio, turned around
          and came back. Started for Austin,
          started for Dallas. Then turned around
          and came back.

She takes the soup off the stove, puts it in a bowl.

                    ROSA LEE
          You know that song you took over to
          that man in Austin.

                     MAC
          Yes.

                    ROSA LEE
You remember those four boys had a band
that came by to see you the other day?

                    MAC
Yes.

                    ROSA LEE
Well, two of them came by here after
you were gone and left off a poster.
(*She points to it.*) I asked them if
they could read music and one of them
could and so I asked if they would
teach me that song of yours as I
thought I would try and surprise you by
singing it for you when you got home. I
think it's a pretty song, Mac, and so
does he - and he was wondering if you
would let him and his band play it. (*a
pause*) I said I couldn't answer that.
He'd have to ask you. (*a pause*) I said
I would ask you. I said it was an old
song and you might not...

                    MAC
It's no old song. I only wrote it last
week. That's why I got so upset when
Harry said he didn't like it. (*He goes
into the bedroom. He comes out with a
small trunk*) I been writing them all
along. I got even more in here. (*a
pause*) Did you say the boy liked the
song?

                    ROSA LEE
He said he did. I sure like it. What
are the names of the other songs?

                    MAC
One is called, "God Has Forgiven Me,
Why Can't You?", and one is called,
"The Romance Is Over."

He opens the trunk, and we can see sheet music inside. She takes
the music and looks at it.

> MAC
>
> Did you learn the song?

> ROSA LEE
>
> Not good enough to sing it. (*a pause*) I
> wish I could read music. How did you
> learn to read music?

> MAC
>
> I had an auntie taught me. We had an
> old half-busted piano, and she sat me
> down at that piano all one summer when
> I came from the fields, and she taught
> me.

He gets his guitar. He plays a little.

> MAC
>
> I've been missing my music. I may not
> be any good anymore, but that don't
> keep you from missing it.

He plays a little bit of the song she has learned as if trying
to make up his mind about its value. SONNY comes out.

> SONNY
>
> When did you get home?

> ROSA LEE
>
> He got here a little while ago.

> SONNY
>
> I thought you were going to wake me.

> ROSA LEE
>
> I forgot.

MAC continues playing. We sense now he is enjoying it. SONNY
listens for a beat.

                SONNY
Good night.

                ROSA LEE
Good night...

SONNY goes on back to bed. MAC continues playing. He pauses and looks up at ROSA LEE.

                MAC
I don't care if you give that song to those kids to play.

                ROSA LEE
All right.

He continues picking at his guitar.

                MAC
Come on try it with me.

He sings a few chords. She starts to sing. She sings a few phrases. ROSA LEE cries.

                ROSA LEE
I'm sorry. I just got nervous tonight.

End of scene.

Tender Mercies was directed by Bruce Beresford and released in 1983. Horton Foote, who wrote the screenplay, is one of the greatest American dramatists, as well known for his many plays as for his screenplays, including *To Kill a Mockingbird*. I'm expecting some may be unfamiliar with this movie, so I won't concentrate on this scene's place in the whole film, or even refer to other facts from the rest of the script. Instead we'll think of this scene as whole in itself — a moment (event) in the life of a couple. It's very helpful to think of each scene in a script — while you are working on it — as the most important scene in the movie. Thus, the scene's emotional events are moments in the lives of people.

Let's start with a few facts and questions. Mac and Rosa Lee are a couple: the fact that he enters without knocking while she is sleeping is evidence that they live together. It's late at night. In the first beat (through his line "Then turned around and came back") they discuss his absence. Does she know where he has been? There seems to be evidence that she does not. The most significant thing I notice about the first beat is that, without her ever asking, he volunteers information about his absence: that he bought a bottle of liquor but didn't drink it; that he "rode by here six or seven times"; that he started for three cities, but decided to come back. All she does is offer and begin to make him some food, and answer "no" when he asks if she saw him drive by.

This is my evidence that she didn't know where he was, but it also brings up a significant question: what is her subtext? Why doesn't she refer to his absence in any way? Is she so furious with him that she is unable to speak about anything except small talk? Is she afraid of his temper? What was it that sent him out of the house? Was there a fight?

When she answers "No" to his question about whether she saw him drive by, I don't quite believe her. Don't forget — characters can lie, just like the rest of us. Even if they are not deliberately lying to others, they may lie to themselves — or they may not know the truth. Or, they may give a partial answer. In this case, it might be a partial answer. What is the rest of the answer? Mac has said he saw "you all" (which could include other people, but, since this is the south, could be just her) watching TV. I deduce that Rosa Lee (with others?) was in the living room, with the blinds open, in sight of the road. How busy a road? Unless there is a lot of traffic, it seems to me that by just turning her head she could have monitored the times his familiar vehicle passed by. Why didn't she turn her head and watch out the window?

I'm treating her response, "No," as a mysterious line. Here are some possible subtexts; each one could imply a completely different take on their relationship: "No, why should I care what you do any more?" "No, I felt so rejected it didn't even occur to me that you were even coming back." "No, I was superstitious. I was afraid if I watched you wouldn't come." "No, I wasn't worried, I knew you'd come back." "No, I didn't want to intrude on your privacy by watching for you at the window." "No, I didn't look out the window because I didn't want Sonny to know I was worried about you being gone so long." (Sonny, who appears later in the scene, may be the person she was watching TV with.) Or, it could even mean, "Yes, of course I watched at the window, and of course I saw you drive by.

But I don't know if I can talk about these things right now." (In other words, "no" could mean "yes" — an opposite.)

Let's leave Rosa Lee for a minute and look at Mac. Why does Mac tell her that he drove by six or seven times? And that he bought a bottle and poured it out? Why does he tell her he started for San Antonio, Austin, and Dallas? What or who is in those places? Drinking buddies? An ex-lover? The person he is angry with? These are important questions because the actor will need to make specific choices for these references. More questions: How long has he been sober? Has she seen him when he is drunk? Has he made a promise to her about the drinking? Is it even true that he refrained from drinking? Does he smell of alcohol?

I have three different ideas, each expressed in a series of questions:
1) Is his purpose in volunteering this information to forestall her anger? To defend himself against the accusations he is expecting? If he is defending himself, is his strategy to attack her first, for her suspicions? Is he satisfied that his driving by was an adequate substitute for not having telephoned? Did he think of telephoning and decide not to do it? Or did it simply not cross his mind? Is he ashamed of driving by repeatedly, without the guts to come in?
2) Or, is his purpose to reassure her? To save her the humiliation of having to ask him?
3) Or, is he offering a simple account of his actions, without analyzing or perhaps even understanding his feelings and motivations?

Idea #1 is that he is a flawed husband. In this case, we should not judge him as defensive or cowardly, but ask questions that help bring us into his world and experience. Such questions are the way to translate an idea into a human understanding.

I'm actually playing devil's advocate for idea #1. My real feelings about the character are closer to ideas #2 or #3. The reason I list #1 is to give that idea a thorough testing before discarding it. Also in order that I, as director, will be fully prepared in case the actor playing the role is thinking of the character this way.

Another way to look at the first beat is to ask, what is its *event*? Now I have a story to tell you. A couple of years ago a young writer-director taking my class told me that he had just attended Robert McKee's Story Seminar, during which he had gone up to McKee and asked him this question: Since McKee was counseling the screenwriters to "show, don't tell," what did McKee have to say about this scene in *Tender Mercies*? Wouldn't it have been better to show Mac buying and pouring out the bottle, instead of telling us that he did so? The young screenwriting student was surprised when McKee told him gruffly that he'd asked an impertinent and worthless question — he had no right to question anything that such a writer as Horton Foote might choose to do!

I love this story. McKee's answer is not wrong, of course — the instincts of a Horton Foote are worth more than any screenwriting "principle" — or indeed, perhaps all of them put together! But I think the real answer is that buying and pouring out the bottle is not the event — *telling her that he did so* is the event. It's an event in their relationship — possibly a turning point. He opens up to her.

When I use this scene in class, sometimes the women are bothered by Rosa Lee because they think of her as a victim. Is she a victim? It's an important question. The experts tell us that if alcohol is an issue for one person in a family, then it's an issue for everyone in the family. Is this couple climbing out of dysfunction or sinking into it?

The second beat begins with Rosa Lee's line "You know that song you took over to that man in Austin?" The subject of the first beat was a discussion of Mac's absence; she has changed the subject to the song, and his songwriting. With Sonny's entrance, the subject changes back to Mac's absence. After Sonny leaves, Mac changes the subject back to music. Then, with her last line, Rosa brings the subject back to Mac's absence, when she says, through tears, "I'm sorry. I just got nervous tonight."

I often look at the beats first, or at least early in my script analysis, because doing so organizes the scene for me, and gives me lots of information, associations, and ideas. While I'm still looking at the first beat, it's very helpful to notice that its subject is reprised in Sonny's entrance and in the last line, in an A-B-A-B-A structure.

Rosa's last line is the most direct reference she makes to her feelings about Mac's absence. I'm not going to cross out the stage direction "Rosa Lee cries." But — I'm not going to insist that the actress cry. Does that seem contradictory? A stage direction like "she cries" must be paid attention to — even though I don't feel it has to be executed literally. It has to be translated. Whenever someone cries in someone else's presence, it's an event in their relationship. So I want that event. The way that event transpires between the two actors in the moment when they play the scene will be our *translation* of the author's stage direction.

The point at which she lets go and expresses her feelings comes after Mac gives permission to give the song to the boys. In the second beat Rosa Lee speaks about the song — how much she likes it, that the young men in the band like it and want to play it. She asks him about the other songs he's been writing and how he learned to read music. Along the way we're getting information: evidence that they may lack formal education; that he may have had a career in music some time ago; that his recent songwriting has been done in secret. This is a possibly important fact — that he has been writing songs without speaking about it to her — but here's the question: Is it more important that he's been keeping it secret? Or is it more important that he is telling her now?

Then there are the titles of the other songs — "God Has Forgiven Me, Why Can't You?" and "The Romance is Over"! Are we to deduce that the song titles are cruel messages to Rosa Lee? Not necessarily. All we can deduce with certainty from the song titles is that Mac is a writer-singer of country western songs. Artists are allowed to write and perform works that are not exact mirrors of their own lives, aren't they?

You may notice I'm starting to make a case for my vision of the story subtext. The plot point of this scene is that Mac gives permission to give the song to the boys. The emotional event is that Rosa has managed to bring Mac into contact with himself and with his music. She has everything at stake in this scene — the specter of his possible return to drinking puts his health, her peace of mind, their marriage, their children's future — everything — at stake. She chooses to risk everything not on emotional blackmail ("How could you scare me like that? Don't you love me?") but on making him feel that his music matters. Her tears at the end are tears of relief — it might not have worked.

Another way to look at the emotional event is to ask some more questions about Mac. What has he come home expecting? Does he walk in knowing he is going to say what he does say? Is he looking for forgiveness? Consolation? Is he expecting her to ask for an explanation of his absence? Throw him out? Could this be the first time in his life he has spoken so openly to a woman about his feelings? "Speaking to someone about one's feelings for the first time in one's life" definitely qualifies as an emotional event.

For my preferred choice for the subtext of Rosa's mysterious line "No," I have always liked "No, I didn't want to intrude on your privacy by watching for you at the window." But lately I've been leaning toward "No, I didn't look out the window because I didn't want Sonny to know I was worried about you being gone so long." It might be the most playable, because it's the simplest, most ordinary one. It's also off-kilter to the emotional line of the scene, which can give it an extra layer, some texture of life. My preferred choice for why Mac tells her about the bottle and his driving route is going to be the third one: that he gives an account of his actions, without analyzing or perhaps even understanding his feelings and motivations. I think this choice might play against any possibility of melodrama, and thus contribute to the style and tone of simplicity that I would want for the script.

These, however, are exactly the kind of choices that finally must be very private for the actors playing the roles. It's not in the least important whether the actress thinks her subtext is "No, I didn't want to intrude on your privacy by watching for you at the window" — or, "No, I didn't look out the window because I didn't want Sonny to know I was worried about you being gone so long." No matter how interesting I think my idea is about bringing her role as a mother into the scene, if the actress' deep connection is with some other choice, I will let my idea go.

There is a point, however, at which a difference in interpretation could be a problem. What if her ideas for the character ran more along the lines of, "No, why should I care what you do any more?" Finding out that there is such a big gulf in interpretation is exactly a central reason for rehearsal. But not necessarily for despair. It is possible — perhaps by going ahead and letting her try her idea, or at least listening to her reasons for it, and then giving her my reasons and associations for the other interpretation — to get on the same page.

There are more layers to this rich writing. But I'll leave this scene for now with only one more question: What is my personal connection? To encounter and engage this scene and these characters, one must ask oneself some tough questions about one's ability to put another's needs ahead of one's own, and about the times one has despaired of connection and hit bottom with loneliness. I have those stories to tell, and that gives me confidence that I can meet the actor and actress at an emotional place deep enough that I can entrust them — and they can trust me — with the scene.

15 | THE WHOLE SCRIPT:SPINES, MAIN CHARACTERS,AND WHAT THE SCRIPT IS ABOUT

The previous three chapters have been script analysis of individual scenes. I'd like to include in this chapter a few things to think about when tackling a whole script.

A CHARACTER'S SPINE

The "script through-line" or "spine" is the character's greatest need. Like an "objective," which was discussed in the *Tools of the Storyteller* chapter, the spine is not a function of the plot but of the character's personality or essence. It could be thought of as his central personality trait. For example, he may need to be right at all costs, or to be approved of, or to be more successful than his peers, or to please his family. It is often expressed as a verb, an objective, a need. Expressing the spine as a verb can help us view the character as active rather than passive. For example, Meryl Streep has said of Sophie in *Sophie's Choice* — a character paralyzed with inertia, guilt, and despair — that her spine was to put on blinders, to get through the morning.

A workable spine is a tool used by actors (and writers) to help them create characters that seem like real people. People's essential needs do not change overnight. Thus, one test of a workable spine is that it is something that could be true for the character all the way through the script rather than an idea that is in service to twists of the plot. It's still helpful to come up with more than one possible candidate. In script analysis, this means we are considering the priorities of the character. A character may have different priorities (spines) with different people in her life.

Different kinds of spine can have an effect on the style or genre. For instance, in sitcom, the spines of secondary characters often contain the name of the main character. As in "to irritate Drew [Carey] and make his life miserable," or "to make Larry [Sanders] like me."

For drama, the spine of a character is likely to arise from the big emotional facts of her life. For example: She has moved to New York from a life of backwoods poverty (*Breakfast at Tiffany's*). She has lost her husband and child (*Trois couleurs: Bleu*). She is married to a man who doesn't love her (*Far From Heaven*). He has committed his resources and sanity to the making of an independent film (*Living in Oblivion*). Emotional facts lead to emotional needs.

A spine can be an addiction; when a person is addicted to drugs or alcohol, the bottle or the needle becomes his spine; it is the thing he will sacrifice everything else to have. But there are other addictions, for instance to one's position in a family. Edie Falco once said of Carmela Soprano that in spite of her claims of dissatisfaction with her husband, "she's gotten very used to this sort of pedestal, holier-than-thou position she has in the family. That's a very comfortable place for her."

An addiction, or certain other spines, such as "to control everything," or "to feel important," could imply a judgment on the character. So whenever we are considering such a spine, we need to make sure we have looked at the ways that we ourselves need control or to feel important, or are addicted to a certain self-image. We are not making excuses for the character. We want to be honest about the characters' flaws, just as we try to be about our own.

A spine might also be considered a core, a kernel, or a key to a character. It is any insight that frees us to imagine the essence of the character. Kimberly Pierce said that Hilary Swank won the role of Brandon Teena in *Boys Don't Cry* because she tapped into the joy that Brandon felt being a boy. "She loved being Brandon. And that was one thing I knew: Brandon *loved* being Brandon."

An insight into a spine of a character connects with what is most vulnerable, "most exposed" as John Hurt called it, about a character. Ben Kingsley's connection to the image of Don Logan (*Sexy Beast*) as a "weeping child with clenched fists in the corner of the playground" becomes his spine for the performance. The most important test of a spine for any particular character is that the filmmaking collaborators — director, actor, writer — connect to it on a primal level.

The "primal" level is a very private level. So that means automatically that the spines that the director, actor, and writer find and connect to are going to be private and personal. It's not the director's job to legislate conformity and consensus between her perception of the spine and the actor's perception. It's not required that the actor and director agree on the spine, or describe it the same way — or even discuss it verbally at all. But it will be helpful for casting if the director has already connected to the characters' spines at a level of imaginative certainty such as Kimberly Pierce describes having about Brandon.

Even so, the choice of spine for a character is not an absolute — it's a choice. For a particular character, one idea for a spine may work for one actor, and another for another. Even for the same actor in a role, one spine might work on one day of shooting, and another on another. This might sound contradictory to the statements above about the spine being "primal," having to do with a character's "essence" and "core." But this existential mystery is at the heart of script analysis. It's the reason I recommend to directors that they not take their notes to rehearsal. *When you love an idea, set it free!* The work of script analysis is not a movie. It's *preparation* for cultivating ideas and experiences in rehearsal and on the set as you make the movie.

THE SPINE OF A RELATIONSHIP
Consider the film *The Accidental Tourist*. The relationship of Muriel (Geena Davis) and Macon (William Hurt) could be described in the phrase "bug and suppress." She is constantly engaging him, looking for response, to the point that she could be seen as pestering him. He avoids and even refuses engagement to the point that when he is around her he suppresses her energy and high spirits. This is their through-line toward each other.

MAIN CHARACTER
Sometimes, during a script consultation, a director insists that his script has two (or even three or four) main characters. I resist and always urge them to choose just one — not as a way to limit the story, but to expand it. Choosing — committing to — a main character is not limiting, it's liberating. In any case, it's a subtext choice, so it's not anything the audience is supposed to get. Choosing a main character is a tool that gives the director authority to tell the story.

Often the main character is perceived to be the character with the most lines. Not so. Think *Othello* — Iago has many more lines, but Othello is the main character, right? Some assume that the main character has to be the one that makes the "transformation." Or the one who "drives" the action, or is somehow "central" to it. Both these ways of choosing a main character are confusing and unhelpful — not to mention wrong. As to choosing the character who "drives" the action, the *Othello* example again applies. Iago drives the action and is a much more proactive character, but *Othello* is still a story about Othello. As to the "transformation" argument, why can't more than one character have a transformation? And why can't a transformation be subtle?

The main character does not have to be the one whose transformation is the most theatrical. Emma Thompson's character in *Remains of the Day* underwent the most visible transformation, but Anthony Hopkins' character was the main character.

Indeed the main character does not have to be the most theatrical character. In *American Buffalo*, for example, Teach is the most vivid and theatrical character (and has the most lines), and many productions make him the main character, but I think that's a mistake, and that a careful reading of the script points to Donny as the main character. In *The Godfather*, Don Vito is an extremely vivid and compelling character, but the main character is Michael. In *Midnight Run*, 'The Duke,' played by Charles Grodin, is the more colorful and magnetic personality, but Jack (Robert De Niro) is the main character.

Even brilliant filmmakers can be seduced by vivid characters — or vivid performances — as Stanley Kubrick seems to have been, in allowing Peter Sellers to steal his scenes in *Lolita*. As an audience, I totally agree with Kubrick that when it comes to Peter Sellers — the more the better. But as a teacher of script analysis, I feel obliged to mention that the main character in *Lolita* is not Clare Quilty (or Dr. Zempf, also played by Sellers), but Humbert Humbert. The *Lolita* example also reminds us that another wrong way to choose a main character is to assume that the title character must be the main character.

Here's a simple way to pick the main character. Start the sentence "This is a story about…" and see what character your impulse names. You could, without changing the script, conceivably say that *The Godfather* is the story of an aging Mafia boss who, after his eldest son is murdered and his second son proves a disappointment, must bury his hopes that his youngest son might leave the family business for a legitimate law career. But the story Francis Coppola fashioned is that of a bright, sensitive young man who becomes a killer in order to bind himself to the love of his charismatic father, first by choosing to reject his mainstream future in order to avenge his father's attempted murder, and finally by assuming the mantle of Godfather after his older brother is killed.

Is *The Insider* the story of Jeffrey Wigand (Russell Crowe) whose life is destroyed when he tries to do one right thing? Or the story of journalist Lowell Bergman (Al Pacino), a man whose calling card has always been his integrity, and who must watch helplessly as a man he promised to protect is destroyed? Years ago I attended a lecture by story consultant Paul Gray in which he asserted that the main character in *Citizen Kane* was not Charles Foster Kane, but the reporter uncovering the story. In other words, the "story subtext" of *Citizen Kane* begins, "This is the story of a reporter who…"

In *Atlantic City* the two lead characters, Lou and Sally, are equals in charm and charisma, and the choice is difficult. Is it the story of a young woman (played by Susan Sarandon) who, in her quest for self-determination, casually destroys the hopes of a self-deluded older man? Or of an aging man (Burt Lancaster) whose self-delusion and disappointment allow him briefly to find a flicker of hope in the imagined attentions of an ambitious young woman? Making a commitment to one story as the central one will not dull the second story. Instead it frees the filmmaker to tell the story meticulously, honestly, and specifically. It is this level of care, honesty, and particularity that confer on a filmmaker his authority. Each character can still be fascinating. And each member of the audience can make his own choice as to who is the main character

Even if the title has two names, there may still be one main character. Is *Romeo + Juliet* the story of a boy with no real direction in life until he meets this exceptional girl? Or of a girl whose remarkable sensibility brings meaning to the life of a directionless boy, and whose courage brings remorse and painful self-knowledge to her foolish parents?

"Ensemble" movies do exist. *Crimes of the Heart*, *The Three Sisters*, and *Hannah and Her Sisters* are all scripts whose premise can properly be stated only by beginning with the words, "This is the story of three sisters, each of whom…," because each of these scripts is a story of a family dynamic. *The Big Chill* is an ensemble piece, although I can't help feeling a case could be made that the main character is the deceased guy whose funeral they are all gathering for — or even the Glenn Close character who was once his lover and whose home the others camp out in. *Magnolia* is a genuine ensemble piece; each character's story is given scrupulously equal emotional weight. I find *Magnolia* a brave and wonderful film about love and mortality. Its reckless disregard for the "rules" doesn't bother me a bit, and, long as it is, I wish it was longer. But the lack of a main character makes *Magnolia* inaccessible to many people.

What about Butch and Sundance? Thelma and Louise? Is *Men in Black* the story of a veteran who has to put up with a rookie? Or of a rookie who has to prove himself to the veteran? Or is it about the relationship itself?

How do you make the choice? Don't follow formulas or the proclamations of script doctors and studio executives. Follow your heart. Tell the story that you feel obsessed by. Or, follow your impulse. Be mischievous. The idea that the main character of *Citizen Kane* is the reporter sounds just mischievous enough to be worthy of Orson Welles.

And don't tell anyone. There's no need for studio executives to know a director's subtext choices. Telling the actors is discretionary. Most of the time, when the director is talking to the actor playing Romeo, he will say, "this is the story of a boy who…" and when talking to the actor playing Juliet… well, you get the idea. As director Jonathan Demme (*Silence of the Lambs*) said to writer Ted Tally, "Remember that as far as Dr. Chilton is concerned, the entire story is about the embattled director of a mental hospital."

WHAT THE FILM IS ABOUT

Answering the question, "what the movie is about" should also answer a filmmaker's question, "why I chose this project." Discovering "what the movie is about" is a stripping down to essentials. Another way to say the theme or "what the script is about" is to call it what the truth is behind the script. This truth must also be a personal truth for each storytelling collaborator — director, actor, writer.

Gina Prince-Bythewood says about casting *Love and Basketball* that producer Spike Lee wanted her to cast an experienced basketball player in the lead role of Monica. But the director asked herself, "Is this a love story or a basketball story? I finally realized it's a love story first. It doesn't matter how great the basketball is if you don't care about the character or the love story. You can fake basketball but you can't fake a close-up." So Sanaa Lathan was cast for her acting, and engaged in a rigorous training course to learn basketball.

Most directors know deeply what story they want to tell from the inception of the project. But the filmmaker's connection to "what the film is about" can be a process. Jim Brooks says that he didn't know "up front" what the movie *As Good As It Gets* was about, but that "I observed the work that everybody did and finally it meant something to me. And what it meant to me was, 'That which makes us safe imprisons us.' And that life is tough. In the middle it sort of came to me."

Most of the time, in order to get producers, financiers, actors, and others on board your project, you need to be able to say "what it's about" in a snappy way and in around ten seconds — it's your pitch, or log-line. The best pitches are the ones that contain actual truth and personal commitment, and are the product of careful thought and soul-searching. However, at times you may find yourself using a pitch that works with the "suits," but does not exactly match your personal vision. In my opinion that's okay too — Robert Altman claims that he has always done this, that for instance when executives ask him, "Will there be action in the movie?" he always says, "Yes, lots of action!" even though he knows that his private definition of action is different from that of the person he is replying to.

You need to be very, very honest with your private self about these matters, even though you may need to tell producers and financiers something slightly different in order to get the project made. You must constantly renew your connection and commitment to "what the film is about." The way to do this during script analysis preparation is, paradoxically, to read the script as often as possible with beginner's mind — that is, read the script not looking to make sure *your* vision is in there, but looking to see *what* vision is in there. You look for the script's themes, and make them personal to you.

This goes for writer-directors, too. No matter how detailed and committed their vision while writing a script, they should, when the script is finished, take off their writer hat and put on the director hat. They should start from scratch, and approach the script *as if someone else wrote it.*

THEME AS A WAY TO DIRECT ACTORS
"[Milos Forman] made everyone aware of what making [Hair] meant to him personally. It instilled in everyone a sense of something larger than just, 'What am I going to look like in this movie?'"
— Beverly D'Angelo

Julianne Moore, who had been in an earlier film where she felt exploited by having agreed to nudity, said about *Short Cuts* that the nudity "wasn't gratuitous. We were trying to communicate something about marital intimacy and not about sexuality or coyness."

Some actors find their performance by connecting to the script's themes. Stella Adler always counseled actors to play a role by connecting to the themes of the script, rather than to its emotions. In order for the theme to work as a point of concentration for the actor, it must be something that he deeply believes. Should the director discuss theme with the actors? That depends on the actor, the role, and the theme. If the actor does not connect to what the director considers the theme of the movie, then the director's discussions of theme may come across to the actor like an abstraction he is expected to embody — in other words, a result direction. It's part of a director's skill to be able to talk about theme with personal commitment and imaginative range, and to be able to let his passion for the project show — but always with the understanding that no one can adopt someone else's belief. The actor must connect to the script via his own passions and beliefs.

EXAMPLES OF THEME AND PREMISE

Here are ideas about the theme/premise of a handful of movies. Unless otherwise noted, these remarks are based on my own perceptions and conclusions after viewing these films.

Big Night: The people who come into your life randomly (such as family, or a person who eats at your restaurant), and the simplest daily things you do with them, like eating, are more important than dreams of fame and romance.

sex, lies, and videotape: Everyone lies. The only way to not be a liar is to be in a genuinely committed relationship, because in a committed relationship one's lies are exposed, and one is loved anyway.

Life is Beautiful: Protecting our children's imaginations is as important as protecting their lives and physical well-being.

The Negotiator: How do you bullshit a bullshitter?

Crimes and Misdemeanors: Contrary to what we've been told, God doesn't see all. (Woody Allen said this in a televised documentary.)

John Cassavetes said that "the idea in *A Woman Under the Influence* was a concept of how much you have to pay for love."

My own idea about *Dead Man Walking* is that it is not about capital punishment, it's about responsibility and commitment. Its premise: Every soul is worth saving. Or, a single person who makes a call to responsibility and commitment can be heard.

The Thin Red Line is about dying with courage. (I am indebted to F.X. Feeney's article in the *LA Weekly* for help in understanding this rich and multi-layered film.)

The truth behind the television show *Buffy the Vampire Slayer* is that high school is seriously dangerous. (One of my young acting students clarified this for me.)

Happiness: I can think of four possible ways to describe this film's premise: 1) there is no redemption for those who will not look at their own behavior and take responsibility for their own actions. Or, 2) there is no redemption for anyone. Or, 3) there is no human activity so egregious that it cannot be forgiven. Or, 4) where is the line between what can be forgiven and what cannot be forgiven? My own opinion is that #2 is the one embraced by the director.

Mike Myers has said, "The maybe-shouldn't-be-spoken-of truth of what [*Austin Powers*] is about is: You can let somebody take away your power or you can maintain your own power. I'm not having a seminar here. We're going on a nice little journey and having a few laughs. But the journey is rooted in something. My belief is that no one can take away your mojo."

The script for *Cast Away* would never have worked as a movie without a bold commitment to "what the script is about." It seems to have been conceived by director Robert Zemeckis as a story of betrayal. This works emotionally because if the incidents of the plot of the script happened in real life, it could *feel* like betrayal, even though no one was at fault.

One reason I imagine Zemeckis making such a choice is that I read an interview in which he declared, "*Forrest Gump* is not a movie about special effects. It's a movie about grieving." So I know that Zemeckis does this work of looking for the subtext "what the movie is about."

To me *Adaptation* (the script) is also about loss and grief. It doesn't matter that probably most moviegoers don't think of either *Adaptation* or *Forrest Gump* as being about loss and grieving. And it doesn't matter that very likely neither Robert Zemeckis nor Charlie Kaufman told any studio executives that their movies were about grief. These choices are private to the filmmakers. They are necessary to achieve the emotional and imaginative authority needed to tell a coherent story on which audiences can project their own private imaginations.

16 | OBSERVATIONS AND ADJUSTMENTS

Directors have sometimes asked me for "cheat sheets" of verbs and adjustments in order that they can plug in their ideas with "correct" language. I resist this because I don't want directors to "plug in" a mechanical formulation. I want their thinking to become more original, multi-layered, and functional. One doesn't become more adept at process-oriented thinking by memorizing a cheat sheet. Meaningful development of these skills comes only through close observance of human behavior. In order to translate result-oriented constructions into playable ones, we must ask questions about what people *do* emotionally. What are their behavior, experience, needs, and interests?

My ideas for adjustments result from my observations of human behavior (including my own actions and foibles). Instead of making shorthand judgments about a character's personality traits, or superficial guesses about their emotional states, one should make detailed, specific observations of behavior. These observations may lead to playable adjustments. I'll include some examples below. And in the following chapter there is an expanded verb/intention list, organized (somewhat) into categories of emotional situations.

The examples of this chapter include some ways to turn judgments into observations of behavior. When I advise you not to judge characters, I'm not claiming that selfish or obnoxious people don't exist. But to create them believably we need to look more deeply than just the way they appear to others. In the words of a character in one of my favorite short stories, *The Talking Dog of the World* by Ethan Mordden, "There's a reason for everything and sometimes two."

This and the following chapter are not cheat sheets! And they don't cover the whole range of human experience — not even close. It's a collection of a few examples, to put you on a road to coming up with your own ideas and inventing your own solutions.

A SELFISH OR SELF-CENTERED PERSON

The self-centered people that I've observed are all different. Some are driven by a love of comfort and convenience. Some by an overriding need for validation. For some people a driving need for tidiness and order leads them to self-centered behavior. Other people who seem self-centered think of themselves as "one-pointed"; their desire to achieve some goal causes them to screen out the needs of others.

A selfish person doesn't think of himself as selfish; hence he often comes to the conclusion that everybody is selfish, and that people who seem to be unselfish are merely hypocrites. (Shakespeare's Richard III is an example.)

People who don't connect very deeply to the needs of others, and who are unaware of the effect their actions have on others, are not necessarily unpleasant people. They can be rather delightful company because they are always in the moment!

A STUPID PERSON
There are different kinds of "stupid." A person (character) that society calls "stupid" might speak without thinking; or he might ask a lot of questions; or he might misinterpret the responses of others. A "stupid" person might have secret interests that he believes no one else cares about, so he never shares his pursuits and expertise with others; he then seems to have nothing interesting to talk about. Or a person with potential might have become "stupid" from being told over and over as a child that he was stupid when it wasn't actually true.

Everybody is smart about something. A character who does poorly on academic tests might perform excellent card tricks (even if there are no scenes in the script where he does so). Or a character who inadequately reads the responses of other people might be attuned to animals, or plants, or machinery (again, with or without explanation in the script).

The driving need (spine) of a "stupid" person might be to keep up, to be a part of things, or even to impress people (sometimes people can seem stupidest when they are trying hardest to impress others). On the other hand, a person who knows he is "slow" might want above all to prevent his slowness from inconveniencing others.

AN OBNOXIOUS PERSON
What is the behavior of an obnoxious person? He may tell people what to do without authority. He may talk excessively on subjects of little interest to others. He may be a poor listener. Where does obnoxious behavior originate? Sometimes an obnoxious person has had poor role models. The driving need of an "obnoxious" person is often to impress people, even to make them like him — he's just doing the wrong thing to get it.

Women sometimes think the way to impress a man and make him like her is to let him know how smart she is; but some men are turned off by this.

FRUSTRATED
What does someone do when "frustrated"? We should think of "frustrated" not as a state of mind, but an experience. What is the experience? It could be that the character wants to have an effect on someone or something, but there's an obstacle. His subtext could be "why won't this work?" Or, "it's my turn!"

LOW SELF ESTEEM
Noticing what the character makes sacrifices for can be a way of determining spine. The principle here is that everyone needs everything — adventure, security, respect, love, etc. A person that we describe as having "low self-esteem" has needs for respect and power just like anyone — but he will allow those needs to be sacrificed to his needs for approval. Other ways to think of a person with "low self-esteem" is as one who puts other people's needs ahead of his own, or a person deeply invested in making everyone happy.

CLOSED OFF
A person who is "closed off" does what? Keeps others at a distance.

NEUROTIC
A neurotic person is sometimes described as "conflicted." He frequently does the wrong thing to get what he wants. He may find himself apologizing even when it is the other person who has made the mistake. He may think he has expressed his needs when he hasn't. He may instantly regret the expression of any need or desire, however legitimate.

An intention "to get the other person to hit me" is a great way to get at a number of emotional states, most of them "neurotic." A person with the subconscious objective to get another person to hit him might feel guilty and want to be punished. Or he might be so lonely that any attention, even negative attention, would be better than no attention. This might be another behavior of an "obnoxious" person. Or of a character who has a chip on his shoulder, or one who is self-destructive.

When I suggest that a character (or person) has the unconscious objective to get another person to hit him, I don't mean that he is clinically masochistic — or that he wouldn't be upset if someone actually did hit him! As a subtext choice, it's a tool to create behavior. The great need (spine) of his life, as for the rest of us, is probably love and acceptance.

INSECURE
A woman who has just learned that a girlfriend has been dumped might fall into insecurity about the stability of her own love life. So if you want an actress to behave "insecurely," an adjustment might be, "as if you just learned that your best girlfriend has been dumped."

IN DENIAL
This one is easy! If your psychological assessment of a character is that she is "in denial," then the playable adjustment is simple — as if it is all true! If she is in denial about her alcoholism, then as far as she's concerned she isn't an alcoholic.

If a character says something she shouldn't have, for example, gives away someone else's secret, and if your idea about her behavior is that it "slipped out," the character's inner reality might be that she thinks she's saying something innocent. The actor could work with the adjustment *as if* she is saying something else, entirely innocent, such as a comment on the weather.

A "passive aggressive" person is chronically in denial. She does something hurtful and thinks it is helpful. Her playable objective, therefore, is usually "to be helpful."

AN AVERAGE PERSON
What is the spine of an "average" person? My observation is that a lot of ordinary people don't ask much of life except to be well treated. Another spine common in the real world is "to be a good boy (or girl)." The generation that grew up during the Depression spent so many formative years in want that "to keep track of my things" is a compelling concern. Duty, or "doing the right thing," is a spine for many people who live simply.

AMBITIOUS
Instead of saying someone is ambitious, which is general, be more specific about what she wants, what she yearns for. If she currently lives in an apartment, would she be happy owning her own home, or would it have to be on the French Riviera? Would it have to be a better home than her sister's? Another way to describe an ambitious person is to suggest factual detail about the number of hours a week that she works.

DEFENSIVE

A defensive person thinks he is under attack. What, in his perception, constitutes an attack? It could be that the mere occasion of someone looking directly at him feels to him like an attack. It is more helpful to describe such a person this way, i.e., that "whenever someone looks directly at him he perceives an attack," than to say that he is pathologically averse to eye contact, which is a judgment.

You see, it's a question of where one draws his line. For most of us, if someone yelled at us or raised a fist to us, we would perceive that as an attack. Instead of labeling a character "defensive," we note that he draws his line differently.

AGGRESSIVE

Ditto for an "aggressive" person. Everyone has a point at which his temper boils and at which he would consider it self-defense to strike another person. An "aggressive" person draws his line differently.

EXPRESSIONS OF ANGER

Different verbs describe different ways of being angry at someone. "Accusing" means you are still giving the person a chance to mend his ways and win back your good graces. "Punishing" means you have withdrawn the option that the other's change in behavior will make things better. The rawest expression of anger might be to rant and to rage (King Lear comes to mind). An intellectual person, rather than accusing or punishing, might metaphorically bite the other person's head off. Of course some people express anger with a wholesale opposite, even apologizing for their anger, or joking about it. A passive aggressive person gets the other person to start the fight.

BAD GUYS

Here are four ways to play villains:
1. He thinks he is doing the best he can.
2. He draws his line differently from the rest of us. He thinks he is behaving in self-defense. Behavior that the rest of us would not be offended by, or might consider merely annoying, he considers an attack.
3. He is having fun.
4. He is, underneath, a wounded child. In other words, look for the hurt that is behind the vicious behavior.

PSYCHOTIC
Matt Dillon said that when he was playing a schizophrenic in *The Saint of Fort Washington*, he put his focus at all times, even whenever he was speaking, on mentally counting the window panes.

SARCASM AND IRONY
"Belittling" is sometimes the underlying verb when a person is being sarcastic. But sarcasm can be achieved with an intention opposite to the apparent meaning of the words. For example, if someone says, "You're a real shithead, aren't you?" with the subtext intention "to soothe," that would probably come out sarcastic. Irony is achieved by giving a line a contradictory subtext image, such as the firehosing of civil rights freedom marchers under the line, "America has a history of justice and tolerance."

SUSPICIOUS
A "suspicious" person may have a dominant verb "to scrutinize" others; or even "to nail" or "to confront" them. It might be useful to think more specifically about what he suspects others will do — for example, hit him, or say mean things behind his back.

PASSIVE
A passive character may think that by declining to act he is doing something positive, for example causing less trouble to others.

COMPETITIVE
If a person is competitive, her adjustment might be "what if someone is having fun that I'm missing out on?"

CONFIDENT
Another way of saying a character is "confident," might be to say, "She thinks she's sealed the deal." Or, "confident" could equal "as if you own the room."

BEWILDERED
An imaginative adjustment for a person who is "bewildered" might be, "as if I have received a communication that the person I am talking to is an alien from another planet."

IMPERVIOUS TO CRITICISM
A person who is impervious to criticism might have the adjustment to criticism that it's an interesting idea that applies to someone else.

RELUCTANT
If a person is "reluctant," pick, as a subtext, something specific that he'd rather be doing.

SHAME
When an actor plays a character who "feels ashamed," the actor should speak as if he is telling a secret of his very own, something he himself is ashamed of and never tells people. A helpful thing for a director to say is, simply, "this scene is about shame."

SEXUAL IMAGERY
In order to play a character "sexy," an actor might use sexual imagery as the subtext. For example, the song *Honeysuckle Rose*, written and originally performed in the 1920s by Fats Waller, has lines in which the singer is telling his sweetheart that "you're my sugar, you just have to touch my cup." He's talking about a coffee cup, right? In the 1940s when Lena Horne made her crossover recording of this tune, the only way it could be played on white radio stations was if she too made it sound like she meant a coffee cup. But when the song is sung by Diahnne Abbott in the movie *New York, New York*, it's pretty clear that the subtext is sexual.

A MOTHER'S LOVE — BUT FUNNY
In the indie movie *Hit and Runway*, the main character asks his mother, "Was I stupid when I was a kid?" She replies "Not particularly." Her delivery is funny, but also very real. That's because the actress (Rosemary De Angelis) is delivering the subtext and not the line. I wondered what adjustment she used. One possibility is that she gives herself an image of something stupid her own kid has done, or that she herself has done. The subtext of her line might then be: What does it matter that you were stupid as long as I loved you? The delivery of this line by De Angelis is casual, so another possibility is that she replies with the adjustment, *as if* he had asked her whether she likes anchovies.

LOSER
Instead of thinking of a character as a loser, think of him as an underdog.

BRAVE
Bravery is not a mental condition. It's an action — something one does. It's when one feels afraid but does the thing anyway. If there is no emotional cost, then it's not bravery. Instead of telling an actor his character is "brave," suggest that what he does is an act of bravery.

INSULTED
Rather than say "the character feels insulted" or "gets insulted," say "the thing that just happened was an insult."

ANXIOUS
It's good to make adjustments personal, to say "it's like when..." If the character is "anxious," the actor might make the adjustment: this is like when she is waiting to hear about a callback for a big audition.

MISCELLANEOUS
The subtext of a person who is bragging is that he wants the other person to be proud of him. The subtext of a person who is punishing is "I don't forgive you."

If a person is frightened, their subtext intention might be to beg (as in begging for help). The simplest way to get at the emotion of fear is to make it personal: "as if telling a story of something frightening that happened to you." When a person begs or pleads, his subtext is to appeal to the softer side of the other person.

A "cheerful" person cheers up other people. A "gracious" person makes others feel at ease. An "ill-tempered" person punishes everyone. A "bitter" person ridicules other people's hopes.

A "naïve" person might have a dominant verb to dazzle (because the world seems surprising and wondrous to her). To dazzle might also be the dominant intention of a "hopeful" person. But "hopeful," "excited," or "animated" can also be created with a subtext image of something wonderful and amazing that one has experienced, in other words, with the adjustment, "as if telling a story of something wonderful that happened to you."

Saying, "Play it as if you look down on these people" is more helpful than saying, "You look down on these people."

Instead of telling an actor, "You are scared of the knife," it's more helpful to say, "The knife is scary."

The psychological assessment, "He doesn't feel alive unless he is getting hurt," could be translated to the adjustment, "When I see my own blood I get a touch of life."

17 | LIST OF VERBS AND EMOTIONAL INTENTIONS

SECTION I—INTERACTIONS TOWARD THE NEGATIVE SIDE

Retaliation (for a wrong that has been done)
Accuse, blame, punish, retaliate, thrash, shame, scold, reproach, reprove, reprimand, condemn, disapprove, point one's finger

Suppress and Torment (deny another person's freedom and happiness)
Berate, attack, abuse, harass, menace, badger, browbeat, bully, force, intimidate, knife, coerce, pressure, persecute, rag on, crush, clobber, wallop, violate, rape, castrate, destroy, hammer, suppress, torment, confine, weigh down, poison, subdue

Warn and Nag
Warn, admonish, threaten, harangue, remind, nag, find fault

Ridicule and Humiliate
Ridicule, mock, belittle, discourage, disparage, deflate, dampen, demean, deny, disparage, sneer at, vilify, disrespect, undermine, criticize, humiliate, taunt, jeer at, look down on, make a fool of, talk down to, spit upon

Harassment by Unwanted Attention
Stalk, hunt, pry, scrutinize

Confrontation
Nail, pounce, confront, get the jump on, test, invade his space, stare him down, look daggers

Pick a Fight
Goad, bait, prod, provoke, dare, challenge, engage, get his goat, pester, bother, fuss, quibble, contradict, insult, negate, battle, get in the way, interfere

Evasion
Dodge, deflect, stonewall, evade, repulse, push away, fake out, string along, beguile, wean, guard against, shut out, defend against

SECTION II—INTERACTIONS OF A GENERAL FAMILY/BUSINESS SORT

Take Authority
Demand, order, summon, direct, command, compel

Give Instruction
Instruct, lecture, teach, preach, expound

Take Attention
Brag, upstage, bluff, one-up, dramatize, clown, entertain

Stand up for Oneself
Show him the door, let him know who's boss, take charge, let him have it, set him straight, take him down a peg

Rebellion
Rebel, revolt, renounce, reject, challenge, defy

Create Excitement, Enthusiasm and Riot
Incite, exhort, kindle, galvanize, enflame, infuse

Get a Rise Out of People
Startle, shock, shake up, expose, thrill, dazzle, electrify, arouse, awaken, engage, make waves, rock the boat, barge in

Influence Strongly
Plead, beg, entreat, importune, appeal, pray

Influence Subtlely
Convince, persuade, guide, maneuver, massage, cajole, coax, assure, induce, prevail upon, sweet-talk, hustle

Reason and Negotiation
Inform, explain, clarify, justify, reason, negotiate, dicker, bargain, haggle, grapple, cut a deal, conspire, brainstorm, hatch a plan

Giving In
Accommodate, concede, yield, acquiesce, capitulate, tolerate, apologize, back peddle

Whine and Complain
Whine, complain, nag, pout, sulk, mope, gripe, wheedle, steer, manipulate

Get Information That May Not Be Your Business
Pry, quiz, interrogate, insinuate, meddle, intrude, inspect, calculate, diagnose, categorize

SECTION III—INTERACTIONS MOSTLY POSITIVE

Lift up Others
Encourage, empower, help, foster, nourish, support, boost, bolster, build up, crown, reward, honor, stimulate, enliven, cheer, inspirit, treasure, endorse, champion

Give Approval
Accept, approve, affirm, flatter, compliment, vouch for, salute, applaud, praise, appreciate

Show Friendship and Good Will
Make friends, greet, welcome, thank, surrender, confide, attend, give attention, entrust, reach out, befriend, cooperate, open up

Show Mercy and Compassion
Forgive, rescue, heal, comfort, console, take care of, soothe, caress, reassure, cherish, hold, touch, defend, grieve

Placate and Pacify
Lull, pamper, indulge, appease, smooth over, enfold, smother, suffocate, overwhelm, kill with kindness

Playful
Celebrate, tease, tickle, needle, banter, play, please, entertain, clown, amuse, divert, lighten, humor, jolly

Seduce and Charm
Dote upon, drool over, savor, nuzzle, ogle, hypnotize, lure, tantalize, seduce, flirt, entice, woo, fondle, charm, flatter, compliment, butter up, spoil, undress, make love

SECTION IV—INTERIOR VERBS
Reminisce, dream, speculate

PART THREE
THE LOST ART OF REHEARSAL

18 | DIRECTOR'S AUTHORITY

*"[Krzysztof Keiślowski] could shoot as close as he wanted,
shoot in my eyes. He was allowed, because he said what he
wanted, and I understood it. It was like a complicity that
has no boundaries."*

— Juliette Binoche

MONEY AND MACHINERY RULE

*"There is no lens, no trick, that will ever approximate one moment of intimacy
that an actor will offer you, that glimpse into their heart and mind."*

— Anthony Minghella

No matter how much lip-service is given to the importance of a good script
and good acting, it's a sad fact that, once on the set, money and machinery rule. A director who wishes to maintain the integrity of the script and
the acting must be prepared to fight tooth and nail. Your best weapons
will be an iron-clad connection to the material and an organic authority in
relation to the actors. The previous chapters on script analysis (Part Two)
had to do with making that iron-clad connection to the material. This
chapter is about authority in relation to the actors.

True authority in the actor-director relationship requires a whole-heart-
ed commitment from the director to creating trust and intimacy in that
relationship. It requires making that commitment a priority. It's not that
I think that the technical and financial aspects are unimportant — it's
just that pressures on the set become so great that nobody is ever allowed
to forget their importance. During the intensity of day-to-day production
activity, it's very easy to let the importance of the director-actor relationship slip away. It takes vigilance on the part of the director to prevent
that from happening.

AUTHORITY VS CONTROL

*"I know that the best directors that I've worked with, Richard Linklater or
Peter Weir, have been successful at empowering other people. And some of
the least successful directors I've worked with were interested in trying to
control everybody."*

— Ethan Hawke

First-time directors receive dire warnings on the importance of maintaining their authority on the set. Their producers and managers—and even teachers — caution their protégés against actors who "play the experience card." But be honest — have you ever had to work for someone who had less knowledge and experience of the job than you do? Did you feel less than totally thrilled at the prospect?

A first time director who had studied with me called me after a disastrous first rehearsal with an actress who had had a supporting role in *Leaving Las Vegas*. "She wouldn't take any direction from me, she argued with everything. She played the experience card — she kept trying to tell me how Mike Figgis had worked in rehearsal!" Played the experience card? The actress *was* more experienced than the director involved. I was flabbergasted by this attitude; I said, "Why on earth wouldn't you be interested in finding out how Mike Figgis worked on *Leaving Las Vegas*? I sure would!"

Some directors feel that the worst thing that could happen is to be contradicted publicly. That's an illusion. The mere absence of public contradiction does not constitute genuine authority. Authority must be earned. It comes from respect. A willingness for engagement and self-revelation — and an openness to learn something new — are the best ways to earn respect and trust from actors. This is not to say that directors are egomaniacs or control freaks. In my experience, most directors are extremely conscientious, usually to the point of what most people would call driven. More often than not, it's their over-developed sense of responsibility and the constant fear of missing a critical (costly) detail that can cause them to appear controlling of everything and everyone.

Genuine authority, however, transcends panic-induced behavior often found in the heat of production. Here are some characteristics of a person of confidence and authority:
1. Prepares to the best of her ability and resources;
2. Arrives at a vision and commits to it;
3. Able to communicate that vision to others and get their support to carry it out;
4. Takes responsibility for decisions, and protects the people she is supervising;
5. Comes up with a new idea when something isn't working.

It's point #3 that causes panic — directors live in fear that the actors won't do what they are told. Here's some food for thought: Actors don't want to take away a director's authority! It's exactly the opposite. Actors *want* to work with a director who has authority! Actors may *test* that authority — and certain actors will test the authority of any director, no matter how successful and experienced. Sidney Lumet, in his book *Making Movies*, tells the story of Marlon Brando testing him on the set of *The Fugitive Kind*, even though Lumet had already directed a number of movies, including *12 Angry Men*; Mark Rydell said that he was subjected to first-day testing by Kathryn Hepburn on the set of *On Golden Pond*, even though he too was an accomplished, successful director at the time.

But these actors are hoping you will pass the test. Actors *want* a director who is strong, knowledgeable, smart, and confident! They want a director they can trust and count on to do the job. That way they can feel safe in the performance of their own job. The film director's task is to tell the story. The tasks involved in telling a story filmically can be grouped thus:

1. Choose a script, and investigate and imagine its subtext story;
2. Supervise the design elements, and make sure they tell the story;
3. Plan and supervise the shots, and make sure they tell the story;
4. Cast the actors, block out their physical action, and make sure their performances tell the story.

The first three areas concern the actor in that he wants to be sure the director is competent, has good ideas, and can tell a cinematic story. But #4 has a more complicated impact on actors. "Making sure the performances tell the story" is the director's job, whereas "characterization" is the actor's job. However, the choices are bound to overlap and encroach on each other's turf. This is where differences in "interpretation" can arise. But they don't have to! Communication is the key.

LISTEN TO THEIR IDEAS

"[John Madden] makes you feel like a collaborator. He allowed me to have so much scope; then we would talk through and build on that, invent and come up with ideas."
— Joseph Fiennes

"I cast with people who are going to bring a lot to the table, which means they're going to bring their brain and bring creativity to the process."
— Ridley Scott

"Any director you work for, if they're defensive, and they're not able to take your suggestions, and they don't respect what you say — which has happened rarely in my life, rarely, rarely, but it can happen — after a few times, you're gonna say, 'OK. Fine. Fine.' You're gonna shut down."
— Robert DeNiro

"If I listen to [the actors], they not only listen to themselves, they also listen to each other…"

— Ingmar Bergman

"I say as little as possible. We talk for hours but about other things. Or rather I listen to them."

— Krzysztof Keiślowski

"I watch everything, and I have all these tendrils, and I just feel a lot. That's why actors like me, because I really pay attention to them."

— Paris Barclay

"[Mike Nichols] appears to defer to you, then in the end he gets exactly what he wants. He conspires with you rather than directs you, to get your best."

— Richard Burton

"The way I listen is like a three-year old child."

— Ingmar Bergman

The reason a director should listen to an actor's ideas is not politeness. Steven Soderbergh says, "My job is to use people, to suck the brain out of everybody I encounter to make my movie better." In order to "suck the brain" out of all the actors, you need, at a minimum, to pay attention to the ideas that they take the trouble to express to you. Indeed you should seek out their ideas, by asking questions. A confident, prepared director will not be threatened by actors who have ideas.

Listening is not just a good thing when it comes to actors — it is every-thing. Empty flattery and superficial attention make an actor feel lost and alone. Perhaps the term "directing" should be changed to "listening." Just because you've done a good job of explaining something doesn't mean that the person you're speaking to has gotten it. As a director, you have to pay close attention — you have to *feel* the response — in order to be able to tell whether an actor is on the same page with you.

What if you want to go beyond the minimum level of communication need-ed for good performances? What if you want to *collaborate* — or even, as Richard Burton put it, *conspire* with actors — to give them the support to allow the characters and story to live in their bones and speak through their very souls? That would mean *radical listening* — surrendering to the actors, just as they surrender to each other.

Far from being the source of all fear and all danger, actors can then become the director's safety net. This is because directors who are able to listen radically can hear the two all-important cues: 1) actors giving the director permission to push them further, and 2) actors giving the director information about their resistances. When a director has a natural antenna for these signals from actors, directing becomes an intensely creative encounter, and there's no telling where a performance can go. Believe it or not, this antenna can be developed, and become instinctive and intuitive, even for directors who are dedicated "technical" guys. I've seen it happen (although it doesn't happen overnight...).

I find that once I do my script analysis homework, and have some ideas in my head, I acquire the freedom to let go of my ideas, because if the ideas are good, they will come back to me. Then I can be in the moment with the actors, giving them my full attention. When I want them to do something, I can honestly present the idea to them by saying, "Something you just did gave me an idea" — because the idea really did come back to me *in that moment* of watching and connecting to the actors.

People crave to be heard. Anytime a director is having trouble with an actor, the first thing that director should do is give that actor undivided attention for as long as it takes to get to the source of the difficulty. Sometimes the problem will be solved as soon as he gets it off his chest. Other times finding a solution may be more challenging. However, the issue will never be solved if the director is dismissive or inattentive in his behavior toward the actor.

What if the actor presents a problem that the director can't reasonably be expected to solve? Here are two responses that might help: "I'm going to need your help to solve this." Or, "I don't have a solution off the top of my head, but I will figure one out." The idea here is to *stay with* the actor — even if you think the actor's behavior is off-putting or the demands being made are irrational. This is exactly what is meant by "radical listening" — listening even to things that may not be easy or pleasant to hear.

Sometimes directors think there is a choice to be made between, on the one hand, executing their own vision of the script, or, or on the other, listening to the actors' ideas and letting them do what they want. These two objectives are not mutually exclusive — in fact they are intertwined. In order for a director to have the authority needed to achieve his vision, the cast must want to listen. I have found I can never get people to listen to me unless I listen to them.

"STEALTH DIRECTING"
More and more I find that the backbone of my own directing is to *ask questions* and *tell stories*. One of my former directing students calls my method of asking questions and telling stories "stealth directing." It's virtually "invisible" direction because it allows the actors to feel that the ideas are their own. It gives them permission instead of instruction; it empowers them. The great virtue of "stealth directing" is that it creates engagement between the director and the actors. A condition of *engagement* is a creative place from which to work productively and continue to get new ideas. Of course solitude can be a creative place too — but solitude is not available to a director on a movie set!

Asking questions as a directorial technique does not mean that directors can arrive at rehearsal or set unprepared and ask the actors how to play a scene! And it's not that irritating thing that grade school teachers do of asking a question when they know the answer they want the students to come up with. The purpose of asking questions is to engage the actors and discover their ideas and resistances. Don't ask questions if you don't want to hear the response.

Telling stories is a good way for a director to bring actors onto "the same page." Stories flesh out the lives of the characters with human detail and bring texture and layers into the performances. Stories are the persuasive emotional details that bring an idea to life. Start with "It's like when…" or "This reminds me…" These stories should always be true stories. Stories that are true and personal reveal a person's private and subconscious associations and connections to the material. When the director tells his stories, the actors bring their own stories, and thus their own private and subconscious associations and connections, into the work.

A DIRECTOR'S LIFE RAFT — THE WORD "OR"
Whenever you are asking questions or telling stories to actors, watch very closely your audience. If they seem to tire, if their attention wanders, stop. Change the subject. Invoke the word "or" — it can be a life saver. If you're describing some wonderful idea, and you notice the actor's eyes glazing over, just say, "Or — let's just try it." "Or — maybe the other way is best." "Or — what do you think?"

LANGUAGE OF PERMISSION
With stories and questions as the foundation, I can introduce my own ideas casually, prefacing them, for instance, thus: "Why don't we try…" or, "I

was just thinking..." or, "Maybe..." or, "It's okay to..." or, "You know what might work?" I haven't given up my vision — I don't stop until I get what I want. But I'm available if an actor gives me something better first.

Try using, "It's all right to go faster," instead of, "That's too slow." "Let yourself move over next to her on that line," instead of, "Move over next to her on that line." Or, "See if you have an impulse to do such-and-such," instead of, "Do such-and-such." After a good take or rehearsal, "Things are going great," "You're working well," "We're on the right track," or even "It's cooking!" instead of, "That was perfect. Do it again exactly like that." Of course, when directors don't use the language of permission, actors should make this translation for themselves rather than internalizing failure or pressuring themselves to reproduce a performance.

Most people are more comfortable hearing, "I have observed" such-and-such, than, "I believe" such-and-such. When you assert your beliefs, others seem impelled to shoot back their own beliefs instead of listening to yours. Observations are more unique and therefore more fascinating.

But don't use the "language of permission" unless you mean it. When a director uses "correct" terminology or procedure mechanically or patronizingly, actors will always sense the falsity.

HAVE A STRONG VISION THAT YOU ARE UNAFRAID TO COMMUNICATE
"Don't be afraid to tell me what you want, please!"
— John Mahoney

"Any actor — De Niro down to me — is looking for a good director to direct you."
— Ben Stiller

What does Ben Stiller mean when says he wants a director to *direct* him? He doesn't mean that he wants a director to micro-manage his line readings and facial expressions. He wants a director to have done his homework, to have intelligent ideas that might engage an actor on an emotional level, to have insight into the characters and the events of the script, and to have taste and good judgment. And he wants to know that the director can competently stage and photograph the scene so that the emotional events are delivered on screen to the audience.

Most of all any actor wants a director who knows *what the script is about.* The director's connection to the story and to the central emotional event of each scene must be iron-clad. His vision must be one that he believes in deeply, personally, that has attained for him the certainty of *imaginative truth.*

And then he should have several alternate visions — in case the first one doesn't work. I know this sounds like a contradiction. But it is a simple, existential reality. The actor's *imaginative truth* will be different from the director's — just because he is a different person. If both actor and director are passionate about significantly different imaginative truths, it is up to the director to find the solution that allows all genuine connections, revelations, and truths to flourish. (See *The Insider* example from the *Goals of Script Analysis* chapter.)

RESPONSE
All actors need honest and accurate responses from the director after each take. As Susan Sarandon said, if a director is not there to tell her when she's gone over the top, she won't "be able to make mistakes. If I have to watch myself, then I don't think I can come up with any interesting possibilities."

There's a wide range of what is appropriate here. Some actors need constant attention and hand-holding through every choice and nuance. For some actors, on the other hand, a "dream-come-true" director is one who comes up with a single insightful and deeply suggestive sentence — and then disappears while the actor figures things out himself. Of course, coming up with that "single insightful and deeply suggestive sentence" can take a little time, a little brainstorming, a little trial and error — that's what rehearsal is for.

Don't worry about whether or not you are "eloquent." Let yourself take the chance of revealing both your intelligence and your feelings at the same time. Eloquence can occur in surprising forms. It may be a function less of rhetorical skill than of honesty and emotional connection. It may be more likely to happen when one is not trying for it. And don't forget that sometimes silence can be eloquent. Communication can happen with the eyes, with a gesture — with the subtext. A director told me of a time some years ago that he was directing a spot with Sophia Loren. After the second take, Ms. Loren came up to the director and asked, "Was that better?" The director suddenly remembered that after the first take, he had made a gesture of exasperation that Ms. Loren had interpreted (inaccurately) as a comment on her performance. ***Everything that a director does in the presence of an actor is experienced by that actor as direction.***

MAKING ACTORS FEEL SAFE
"The great directors just — it's something to do with making an environment comfortable enough for you to create within."
— Helen Mirren

The director communicates with actors in two ways. One is *personally*, as a colleague and supervisor, but in the special, dependent relationship created by the fact that the director can see what the actor's work looks like when the actor can't. Actors are more vulnerable and more emotional than most people. So the personal communication is automatically an intimate communication. In the best-case scenario actors and director go face-to-face (heart-to-heart really) to break though habit, cliché, mannerism, and resistance, to reach unguarded moments of experience and response.

The director also communicates with actors *imaginatively*, via discussions between director and actor about the character the actor is playing. This is also an intimate communication, because we're not making a widget or a new special effect — we are creating the lives of imagined people, which is a sacred trust.

Making actors feel safe doesn't just mean being nice to them, or indulging or pampering them. Good actors are sensitive — attuned to the ring of truth. False notes, including false flattery, in the interaction of director with actor shut down the relationship. Honesty is key to making actors feel safe.

Add to that the directorial skill of knowing whether or not an actor's performance is working. An actor needs to feel secure that a director will not use a take with an inferior performance in the movie. Only with this confidence can an experienced actor feel free enough not to watch his own performance.

Further, the director is responsible for making the set a place where the craft is respected and the work comes first. The set needs to be a place where the actors are safe to make emotional mistakes — those unplanned impulses that often become the great moments in a film. The actor who takes it upon himself to demand this "safety zone" easily acquires a reputation as difficult — or may even be thought of by the crew as unprepared.

Film crews — left to their own devices — can be unkind to actors, sometimes ridiculing them behind their backs. Actors can sense this and it can poison the working atmosphere on a film set. The director needs to make collaborators of the crew and the cast members. It's a director's responsibility to insure a gossip-free set — a place where both actors and crew feel respected and can respect each other.

In order to feel safe an actor needs to feel that the actors she is working with are serious. The director can protect actors by making sure that everything that happens on a set is *about the work*, not about the defects of others. Kathy Bates complained to Rob Reiner during the shooting of *Misery* that James Caan was not listening to her. Reiner told her the character Caan was playing was a bad listener too — in other words he was telling her to *use it*.

James Brooks says that Jack Nicholson told him on the set of *Terms of Endearment*, "You can say anything to me, don't worry about how you put it, don't worry about sounding stupid." This was a great thing for an actor to say to a director, especially since he really meant it. But Brooks, who was directing his first feature, crossing over from television, soon discovered that meant Nicholson reserved the right to say anything as well. Brooks says Nicholson would approach him with unsettling comments like, "You want to know what the worst direction you gave today was? You want to know what the best direction you gave today was?" For Nicholson, the freedom to speak his mind and to connect and engage with everyone on the set is essential to his feeling safe to work creatively. When the director can tolerate and even rejoice in the actor's freedom to be himself on the set, the actor feels a deep safety from which he can take risks.

But nothing makes an actor feel safer than to believe that the director feels he is *the best choice in the world for this particular role*. Even if you did not choose them yourself, even if you were forced to choose from "the list" of actors approved by the financiers — even if you had to cast the producer's daughter — even if, as in episodic television, the cast has been chosen well before you were chosen — you must make the choice that these are the actors who are best suited to the roles, who have a unique contribution to bring to the roles, and with whom you wish above all to work. If you can't make that choice, you should give yourself permission to decline the project.

Can we be absolutely certain that we would have ever heard of James Dean if in his first leading role he'd had a lesser director than Elia Kazan? So many people, including those who work on movie sets, know very little about acting. There are only two things that most crew members are certain that actors are supposed to be able to do: remember their lines and stay in the camera frame. James Dean consistently neglected both duties — he often improvised lines as well as movement, frequently irritating directors, acting coaches, and even other actors. It took a director of exceptional skills to recognize Dean's potential, and to make the set a place where he could work.

BE FEARLESS ABOUT LOOKING FOOLISH
"When you come to [Curtis Hanson] with a question that he can't answer, he isn't afraid to admit it. That kind of vulnerability makes you feel comfortable."

— Michael Douglas

"I think that there are a lot of directors who prescribe to that sense that they have to pretend they know what's happening at all times. I know from being an actor that everybody sees through that pretty quickly."

— Jon Favreau

Why, if it's so important for directors to be strong and confident, would "vulnerability" make an actor feel comfortable, as Michael Douglas asserts above? Because human beings are vulnerable, and actors feel safer around human beings than around automatons. It's funny — even though actors want directors to be strong, they are not necessarily put off by a director's personal weaknesses. Kenneth Branagh said he found "endearing" Barry Sonnenfeld's willingness to admit his confusion when he didn't know what to do next.

Be a person around actors. Be frank and open. Don't feel you have to hide your real feelings from them. When you get that clutch of fear when someone asks a difficult question, relax, breathe, and respond with candor. Don't pretend to know what you don't know. Try not to spend any time worrying about whether you look foolish.

Don't hold back from interacting with an actor because you're uncertain of the proper vocabulary. Human interaction is not about terminology; and it's certainly not about censoring yourself to make sure you don't express something "wrong." Much more important than using any particular language is to be honest and forthcoming.

There is no way to earn authority without risk. Do what's needed to make the best film possible, even if your actions make you unpopular. You are much more likely to look foolish if your overriding goal is to protect your personal image and not look foolish. In the end the work is what matters.

EMOTIONAL RESPONSIBILITY

At the same time, a director must act as a leader. This demands emotional responsibility — even stoicism. If you are the person in charge, there will be times when your work must come ahead of personal needs. In the case of film directors, "the work" includes paying attention to the feelings of actors. In other words, there are going to be times when you need to comfort others when it is you actually in need of comforting.

Leadership means putting out, emotionally and physically. The budget for *The Pianist* was low, and lead actor Adrien Brody was required to do his own stunts. One stunt, when described to him, was particularly complex and difficult-sounding, and Brody asked if someone could show him how it worked. Director Roman Polansky himself demonstrated the stunt to the actor. Such a deed gives the actor confidence that the stunt is safe to perform, but it also touches him that the director cares enough to take the same risks he is asking of the actor.

The wrangling between Jim Brooks and Jack Nicholson on the set of *As Good As It Gets* was well-known. It was nothing personal, however. It was about the work. And, as Nicholson later said, probably "inevitable given the intensity of the role." At one point, Brooks shut down the set and sent everyone home in the middle of the day. Since Brooks was also a producer of the movie, his action made a strong statement: *I will do whatever it takes to make this work. This is more important than money. It's more important than me winning and looking smart. I'll do anything to meet you emotionally.*

It's a good idea to check in often with the actors and ask them how they are doing. After every take, even, if it feels right. And be sure that you are prepared to hear the answer! The reason for asking actors how they are feeling about their work is that information about their self-doubt, irritations, expectations for their own performance, etc. is incredibly useful for directing the movie.

LET THEM WORK

"Having spontaneity from actors tends to intimidate most directors. [But] Mike [Figgis] looks for that. A confident director lets the actors find their characters and nurture them."

— Nicholas Cage

"[John Madden] is open to your input. He creates a space where you can feel safe. Also, as a director, he knows when not to direct. He knows when to back off and not direct every single second."

— Bruno Kirby

"What Danny [Boyle] does is absolutely let you do your job, which is what most other directors I've worked with seem to forget."

— Ewan McGregor

"I think there are two kinds of directors as far as actors are concerned. They either want you to surprise them, or they don't."

— Dustin Hoffman

"The best directors I've worked with leave you alone."

— Robert Duvall

When actors say they want to be "left alone," they may mean they just don't want to be micro-managed on every line and facial expression. As Angelica Huston says, "I'm not crazy about being minutely dictated to." One of the worst things that can happen in rehearsal is the director hovering over the actors, micro-managing their every look and word — not letting them work. Steven Soderbergh says that he spent the two weeks of rehearsal for *Out of Sight* "watching the actors work," getting ideas for how to interact with them on the set. Derek Luke says that Denzel Washington's direction, for *Antwone Fisher*, was always "carved around freedom."

Letting good actors work means trusting the process. It may also mean letting actors speak their minds, horse around, do their warm-up exercises, laugh too loud, demand attention, be needy. And although I don't think anyone should ever be indulged in abusive behavior, it may sometimes mean letting them pout and storm about a bit.

PROBLEMS AND RESISTANCES

"I would never date a businessman. Put that in print. They're civilians. I'm of the alien nation of actors. I am proud to be an alien, and I'm only really comfortable with fellow aliens."

— Glenn Close

Actors can get downright difficult.   Don Boyd, the director of *My Kingdom*, said that he and Richard Harris, who was playing a character based on King Lear, had "three or four enormous rows." Harris told him that, "If I respect the director then I am going to want them to understand me." That means that Harris would be vocal about his resistances. *Fighting through his resistances to the essence and details of a role* is central to an actor's work.   Some actors need to do that work while *engaged* with another person — the director.   It is disastrous for a director to take it personally when an actor *fights through his resistances* in the director's presence.   It's not a personal attack — it's the job of acting.

The difference between experienced and inexperienced directors is that the inexperienced director hopes there are no problems, while the veteran director expects problems and prepares to address them.   The measure of any successful businessperson is their performance in times of difficulty and stress.   Successful people in any field have another idea ready when something goes wrong.

All this takes intimacy.   Without intimacy, how can the director know whether or not he and the actor are on the "same page"?   No one can read minds.   You must get the actors to *let you in*.   When an actor seems arrogant or petty, his insecurity is probably the root cause.   A director who knows this — who knows that existential uncertainty is at the core of the actor's experience — and knows it not just intellectually, but *feels* it — stands a chance at intimacy with his actors.   Actors tend to feel that only other actors really understand them, and to view everyone else as outsiders — and that includes the director.   It's up to the director to initiate an intimacy, if there is one to be had.

Many actors, out of insecurity, automatically translate any direction into a negative.   If you try to use the language of permission and say, "It's okay to move," what they may hear is "You must move," or "You weren't moving enough."   If the demand or criticism was what you really meant, but were covering up with "correct" language, they will surely spot it.   Once in a class — while discussing how an actor's resistance can offer the opportunity for breakthroughs and intimacy — a director laughingly asked, "What if the bitch *is* ruining your movie?"   It was a revealing comment, since it unmasked the director's contempt for actors.   If you are inclined to such a response, directing actors will for you always be a question of damage control.

DAMAGE CONTROL

"The important thing is to work with actors who like their work and who are willing to explore with me something that we don't know yet."
— John Cassavetes

Producers often instruct writers to make their scripts "actor-proof." That is, a script written in such a simple-minded and "on-the-nose" way that no actor — no matter how lazy or stupid — can be mistaken about the reading each line should be given. Directors, especially young ones, ask me wistfully, "Why isn't it all right for me to just tell them what to do?" By which they mean, "Why can't I move them around like furniture and micro-manage every look, gesture, and line reading to fit the movie in my head?"

Directors also complain that actors don't work hard enough, and don't get excited and engaged in the script and the shooting. When actors are micro-managed and controlled, they become either afraid, or too bored, to try anything before receiving instruction. They may lose all interest in anything the director has to say. At such moments, they may try to "protect" their performance by watching and controlling it, pushing and telegraphing the result.

Or they may fall back on ego-protecting activities, such as insisting on script changes to make their character sympathetic at the cost of the story, or deliberately ruining a take in which they don't care for their own performance. Or choosing to "play the movie star" or "play the franchise" instead of playing the character. Or turning the set into a high school-style competition for who is the top dog, by, for example, calibrating their exit from the trailer in order to be sure they never arrive on the set before their co-stars. Or — this is the worst — muscling into the editing room to choose and insist on the takes that they think showcase their most brilliant line readings and most attractive expressions.

Soon the project is spiraling down in a vicious cycle of damage control. I am frequently asked by directors how to combat such suffocating behavior from actors. My only advice is this — respect the craft and put the work first.

One of my students told me of a directing teacher who gave this advice to young directors: during casting sessions, plant a spy in the waiting room to report on which actors, while off-guard, displayed annoying personality traits. To me such a tactic automatically places the director in damage control mode, and puts the project on the wrong foot. First of all, I would never accept someone else's assessment of whether a person is annoying.

I can often find a way to be interested in people that others consider irritating. But the most important reason to resist tricks and tactics such as this one is this: If a director wants to know an actor's "off-guard" behavior, to know *who each actor is*, then it is that director's job, in a casting session, to put the actors at ease enough to catch a glimpse of who that actor is. As director, it is your right and responsibility to cast people whose humanity is transparent to you.

TRUSTING AND TESTING

"Ben [Stiller]'s not automatically going to just hand himself over to you, saying, 'Here, I'm your puppet. Do what you want.' He's going to engage you and test your insight into the character."

— Jay Roach

"It's incumbent upon a director to give his trust to every actor that he has cast from the very start, but the director isn't owed that same immediate trust. He has to earn it, because the actor is far more vulnerable to the director than the director is to the actor."

— Dwight Yoakam

"The function of the director is to establish an environment of trust for the actors."

— John Boorman

"I think any actor who is reasonably smart is going to want to make sure the person who they're following into battle has done their homework."
— David Fincher

"I still feel that the honorable thing is to believe you're going to die if it doesn't work. As painful as that sounds, to me it's just good manners. I can't imagine what actors would want to work with anyone who didn't feel the same way."

— James L. Brooks

Did you notice what looks like a contradiction between Jay Roach's quote regarding Ben Stiller — and Stiller's own statement earlier in the chapter that he wants a director to direct him? There's actually no contradiction, even though both were being interviewed in connection with the same project, *Meet the Parents*. A good actor makes demands on a director. For one thing, he wants the director to have ideas, and to care. A collaborative relationship involves a constant testing and challenging of those ideas and of each other's stamina and commitment. That's not because actors are out to get directors — it's because the actor-director relationship is an extremely intimate one.

Part of proving yourself strong enough to pass the tests is letting yourself be invigorated instead of apprehensive about the testing process itself. A director who feels relief that an actor does not make demands upon his skill and intelligence is only kidding himself. It may turn out in the editing room that the actor was "walking through" the role.

Edward Norton asks a zillion questions of every director he works with. It's not that the director must have the answers to every one of those questions, but if he wants to work with actors of the caliber of Edward Norton, he should be ready for a high level of engagement and commitment. When an actor asks a lot of questions, he's testing not just the answers you come up with, but whether you respect the questions.

Emma Thompson, in her published diary of the production of *Sense and Sensibility*, speaks of Ang Lee (a theater-trained director) requiring the actors to do preparation exercises in rehearsal, including meditation, physical exercises, and "inner life" exercises. In a *Daily Variety* interview she said that some actors responded to Lee's exercises with the attitude, "We *are* British. We do know how to do Jane Austen!" Thompson goes on to disclose that Lee's response was to "let us know that *he wasn't interested in what we already knew how to do.*"

When an actor tests a director, make no mistake — the director must step up to the plate and respond with full energy and commitment, and must counter the test with a challenge of his own. Ang Lee has an easy-going and self-deprecating demeanor, but he is a demanding director who never lets his actors off the hook.

DIRECTORS CAN GIVE ACTORS PERMISSION TO GO FURTHER

"I want guts, passion. I want to be pushed. It's lonely — you want somebody who's in there to work with you. Not the directors who are just interested in the camera. I want the director there waiting for me."
— Kathy Bates

"[George Roy Hill] is truly a director in the best sense. When you're cookin', he leaves you alone. When you get in trouble, which is where most directors falter, he's the guy that comes in and points you in the right direction and that, believe me, is very unusual."
— Paul Newman

Jennifer Aniston said to director Miguel Arteta, on the set of *The Good Girl*, "Please keep watch over me and don't let me do anything that you've seen before." She was smart to ask him, and she was lucky he was able to do it — even though she also said that, "By the third day I was ready to strangle him. I was frustrated. It was muscles being exercised that have been asleep for years. And it was scary. I found myself crying all the time. He pushed me into uncomfortable places. I didn't realize how uncomfortable I was with experiencing depression or being sad."

Why do good actors sometimes do bad work? *Because no one dares tell them that it's bad.* Directors who don't know enough about acting don't know how to push experienced actors into new territory. So everyone goes for the easiest thing.

It's especially difficult for actors who are identified with a successful, long-running television show, or a successful string of similar characters, to stop "playing the franchise," and create a new, believable persona. The original persona — no matter how excellently done, and no matter how appropriate for the original assignment — must be scraped off. It's almost as though it has become a mask that is stuck to the skin of the actor, and must be peeled off, down to the bone. The actor must re-invent himself.

It's not too extreme to call such a re-invention a life-changing experience. It can be painful. Sometimes life makes these changes for you — as it did for Michael J. Fox, who, in the process of reinventing himself from Alex Keaton of *Family Ties* to Mike Flaherty of *Spin City*, faced fatherhood, Parkinson's disease, and his own alcoholism. But it can also be the director who gives the actor support, permission, and the kick in the pants to make the transformation. Mary Tyler Moore's performance in *Ordinary People*, discussed in an earlier chapter, comes to mind. As does that of Tom Cruise in *Magnolia*. Or James Coburn in *Affliction* — a stunning performance for which Coburn won the Academy Award. Paul Schrader says that when he met with James Coburn about the role of the father in *Affliction*, he came right out and said he didn't want the regulation Coburn persona, the "our man Flint" that Coburn was famous for. "Oh," said Coburn, "you mean you want me to act."

Nicole Kidman thinks of her work with Jane Campion on *Portrait of a Lady* as a turning point in her career. She said Campion said to her, "Go into yourself and give from your soul." Since then, Kidman has said she tries to make herself exposed and vulnerable and insecure early in the rehearsal period. She then feels, "Ok, the director kind of sees me. You either connect or you don't connect."

Don't let actors hide. If you want good acting, ask for it.

Sometimes it's necessary for a director to be blunt. Brendan Gleeson says that when he was working on the role of Martin Cahill in *The General,* he spent a long time researching, listening to stories, looking at footage, getting the externals. "But it was still mimicry and John [Boorman] said, 'It's not really coming from inside.' I had to find out what was going on inside." Dustin Hoffman says that Mike Nichols took him aside a couple of months into shooting of *The Graduate,* when Hoffman was getting listless in front of the camera, and put a scare into him: "This is the only time you'll ever get a chance to do this scene. It's going to be up there for the rest of your life," Nichols told him. Hoffman adds, "He really meant it. It makes me cry, because he had that kind of passion, and it had that importance. I've never forgotten it."

The only way that directors can have the courage to push actors further is if they believe absolutely, first of all, in the imagined world they are creating, and second of all, in the courage of actors. When Bill Murray recalled that director Wes Anderson "makes me feel different, almost like I'm not obliged to be entertaining. I don't find myself pushing or selling my scenes" — that means that in the case of Murray, going further meant doing less. Actors can have a mask, a signature persona. George Clooney apparently was worried about his performance in *Out of Sight* — he was afraid that it was flat. As it turned out, it was a delicate and expressive performance, perhaps the most expressive performance Clooney has given. In these cases, the directors were able to allow the actors to relax enough to find a simpler, truer *core* below the social mask. Letting oneself deeply relax in front of a camera is a huge risk. And risk is at the center of good acting.

Casting against type is a great way to get actors to take a risk that extends their skills. Because when you cast against type, what you are communicating to the actor is that you see something that others don't. Curtis Hanson on casting Michael Douglas in *The Wonder Boys* (perhaps Douglas' best work): "There is a whole other side to him when you get to know him personally. So I wanted to explore that vulnerable side and also the funnier side."

On the first day of shooting *Who's Afraid of Virginia Woolf?*, Mike Nichols had Elizabeth Taylor repeat her first take (her first entrance down the staircase) sixty times. My guess is that the reason was that he wanted to make it crystal clear from the get-go that ordinary "movie star" acting would not suffice for this demanding role. When William Wyler was directing Laurence Olivier in *Wuthering Heights*, Olivier's first Hollywood movie, the young actor was over-theatrical and full of his own performance. Over and over, take after take, Wyler would say, "That was lousy. Do it again." Olivier wanted to strangle him — until he saw the finished movie. He later credited Wyler with having taught him film acting.

These last two examples in particular are included not as tactics that I think inexperienced directors should have the temerity and arrogance to attempt. But I want you to know how much it *matters*, to good directors and good actors, to get to the heart of good material, to find its truth, and present it to an audience.

WHAT IF THE ACTOR DISAGREES ON INTERPRETATION?

Jack Nicholson says that when he has a difference in interpretation with the director, "my process is always to make a firm argument, wherever the disagreement is, and if I feel I've expressed it, and I feel that it hasn't altered the situation, I do what the director asks to me to do. That's the way I always do it." He goes on to add, "I do make a good argument. That's what I'd want actors to do for me when I direct." This is a very rational approach, and directors should not assume that actors can't be rational about these matters. If each side makes a case for his idea, eventually it will appear that one idea is stronger, better, or truer.

This method only works, however, if there are no other agendas and both the director and actor are open to genuinely listening to each other. In fact, disagreement on interpretation can be an opportunity for a third idea to emerge as a synthesis of the two competing ideas, and win the day. Of course all disagreements are going to be less stressful and more productive if the director, during script analysis ahead of time, has considered more than one possible interpretation.

ALL ACTORS ARE DIFFERENT

"The only language that works is the language you develop between yourself and your actors. You've got to treat every [actor] completely differently... There are as many ways of working with actors as there are actors."
— Sam Mendes

All actors are different. Most actors appreciate praise, and prefer to have their feedback verbalized in a supportive and tactful way. But some prefer a director to be blunt. Steve Zahn said of working with Steven Soderbergh on *Out of Sight*, "He didn't say much to me. He didn't pamper you, [and therefore] I really trusted him. I hate being stroked. I don't need someone to stroke me. I know I'm a good actor."

Different actors respond to different language. Some like to get into the psychology of the character, and others do best with direction that is mostly physical. Some shine when appealed to on the rawest emotional level; others get frightened by that, or feel it is an intrusion. Most actors respond well to the "as if..." or the "it's like when..." adjustments. And the one tool that seems pretty universal is making some connection to the character's objective — asking *what does the character want?*

One of the ways to find out what approach works best with a particular actor is to ask him. It can be a good way to begin a discussion with an actor, anyway, to ask him how he works, with whom he has studied, what he expects from a director. But don't take at face value everything an actor says about these issues. It's even more important to look for subtext, and to be observant of the actor's behavior. An actor may tell you he likes to be left alone, and then turn around and pepper you with questions on every scene. Or, another actor may insist he likes lots of feedback, only to resist and complain about every suggestion the director makes.

Sometimes an actor's preferred approach may not be best for him or for the scene. If an actor asks for coaching and reassurance on every line, it may actually be better for his performance to tell him you have faith that he can find it himself. If an actor who wants to be "left alone" starts acting all by himself, the director must intervene, and get him to engage with the other actors. If an actor says he can get there on his own, but he's not getting there, and you have an idea you think might help, then step in — tactfully and privately, of course. Perhaps by beginning with a question, such as, "How are you doing? Can I help?"

Many directors ask me what to do when one of the actors in a scene gives his best performance on an early take, and the other actor does best after a number of takes. There is no one answer to this question, but for directors who are comfortable with actors, the solution is a matter of common sense. For instance, you might conduct some extra, private rehearsal with the actor who does better in late takes.

The only real way to gain confidence in these matters is through experience. And, by being interested in actors and their craft. Get to know them as people, study how they approach their work. Actors are not alien creatures, just people with unique concerns about how to succeed in a very special kind of work. Even when veterans like Anthony Hopkins, Morgan Freeman, and Robert Duvall insist publicly that they don't want directors intruding on their inner life, that's not a signal for a director to slink away, intimidated. No actor works well unengaged with others on the project. It's just that engagement can take different forms. An actor can have a deep connection that exists in total silence. However, this is rare and demands acute perception on the part of the director. Most of the time, conversation and communication are bridges between the worlds of actor and director.

DIRECTORS WHO HAVE BEEN ACTORS

"John Malkovich [while directing The Dancer Upstairs*] knew exactly what to say, how to approach an actor. I have done seventeen movies now and this is the first time I have been directed by an actor. The difference is so huge because you feel he knows exactly what my problems are."*
— Javier Bardem

"I wanted to direct so that I might direct actors the way I always wanted to be directed, but wasn't often enough. That's why any actor wants to direct."
— Stanley Tucci

It's hard to imagine how anyone could understand an actor's needs and fears without having done some acting themselves. How does Rob Reiner have the guts to say to Meg Ryan, "It's not about you, it's about the other actor"? I'm sure the fact that he's an actor helps give him that authority. Some great directors have actually been acting coaches — Elia Kazan and Sydney Pollock come to mind.

Sidney Lumet and Peter Berg have described the specific benefits of having been actors: 1) trust, and 2) skill. On the issue of trust, Lumet says, "Having been an actor, [I] know precisely why something is difficult. It makes your work with the actors very, very specific. Having been an actor leaves me open to their fears and their insecurities. I'm aware of them. It also gives me great consideration for their privacy. If they're good, they're not going to spare themselves or their emotions. Revealing them is a painful process. But I understand it and respect it. And I think that's why they start to trust me after a very short while."

On the issue of skill, Peter Berg says, "I think an actor has a great advantage directing other actors because he knows how to not be intimidated by acting. Because I'm an actor, I knew how to break in and get into each one of my actors' space in a way that didn't offend or upset them." On the set of *Very Bad Things*, one of the actors was hanging back in a scene that called for a vivid response. Berg was able to speak to the actor on a level of craft, rather than get into an argument about result.

THINKING "LIKE A DIRECTOR"

A director has four responsibilities: 1) to the story; 2) to the audience; 3) to the cast and crew; and 4) to a schedule and budget. Sometimes an "actor-oriented" director gets so enmeshed in the inner lives of the actors that the responsibility to the audience is forgotten. A director who wants to be "actor-oriented" needs to be able to step into the actors' reality — and then step back out, back into an audience reality — in order to make sure that what the actors are doing tells the story.

Not all actors make good directors. Directing requires an objective personality and involves considerable left-brain activity. Actors (as well as writers) are usually very subjective personalities, and predominately right-brained. Sometimes they are so in the moment that it is more draining than they thought it would be to have to be aware of the whole picture. Sometimes actor-directors make the mistake of assuming that other actors work the same way they do. This can prompt them to give direction in some private jargon that is unintelligible to other actors. Actor-directors may even get so married to their own interpretation — the way they would say the line if they were playing the part — that they become as result-oriented as the most amateur director.

If you are considering acting and directing in the same film, be sure you are the only person who can play this part. Be sure your commitment to the subtext is so strong that you don't have to watch yourself. Or, let it be so much fun that you don't care if your acting is good or not.

TECHNICAL DIRECTORS

A little knowledge can be a dangerous thing. Directors tend to be either actor-oriented or technology-oriented. To the director whose background and interests are heavily rooted in motion picture technology, the approaches suggested in this book may be akin working in a foreign country without knowing the language. The adoption of these techniques could

— in some cases — require a complete reorganization of one's entire approach to the filmmaking process. The director should be realistic about what will and will not work in his case. Use common sense. If these actor-oriented processes are not your cup of tea, perhaps it's best to be honest, open, and sincere about your limitations and stay out of the actors' way. They'll do a better job for you on their own than they ever will if you intrude onto their turf without understanding their craft.

THE VIDEO MONITOR

"I love working with directors who deal with the whole process as opposed to just shooting the film. [Soderbergh] never looked at the monitor which I thought was a great thing and unusual. He was always watching the action. He was always watching the interaction of the actors."

— Steve Zahn

"[Alexander Payne] doesn't watch the monitor. It's fun to have a director there when you're doing it."

— Jack Nicholson

"When directors are "a block away [behind the monitors], you're not sure that they're seeing what's really going on, because they're looking at this little screen. With Steven [Soderbergh] being right there with you, it's not hard to believe if he says, 'I got it,' or 'I didn't get it.' You believe him."

— Don Cheadle

"[Milos Forman] would sit right next to the lens and completely concentrate on you so that he cut everything else out of the moment but you. And he was that way each day for six and a half months on Amadeus.*"*

— F. Murray Abraham

The video monitor is a place to hide from the actors. It's the retreat of a director who doesn't know what to look for in the actors' naked faces. It makes no sense to use the video monitor to check the camera framing during a take. It's the job of the director of photography, not the director, to assure the proper framing. The take can be checked later, anyway, on video play-back.

But, there are directors who feel useless if they stand next to the camera. They feel they are in the way and will just bother the actors with their anxiety. So I tell them the same thing I tell smokers who say they can't quit. If you can't, then don't.

ACTORS AS MEAT

"I sometimes think actors are regarded as people you tell to come in, give 'em a chalk mark and tell 'em 'Action!' 'Do this.' 'Do that.' I don't work that way and I don't cast that way."

— Ridley Scott

"I'm retiring from movies next year. Honest to God, I don't want to do it anymore. I'm not happy doing it. Film is a director's medium, it has nothing to do with actors. We are basically puppets, walking around, hitting marks, saying lines. Producers earn all the money, and you get the sense that they hate actors."

— Liam Neeson
(A few days later he said he had been joking.)

"So many directors think of actors as props or set dressing."

— Kelly McGillis

"Sometimes you get the feeling that some film directors just want you to do what they want you to do, and it is frustrating."

— Annette Bening

"[Actors] are outnumbered — they are pressed into conformity by the schedule; by accepted sociability; by heart-warming good mornings and pleasant goodnights; platitudes that take up valuable time; being invited to dinner; cliques of crew that say, 'I like him or I don't like him'; insipid arguments over the content when the scene is good and deathly silence when it's bad; that feeling that one gets when someone is being shrewd with you and does not want to offend you enough to lose his next job."

— John Cassavetes

Directors often relate stories of bad behavior by actors on sets. Sometimes with terror in their voices. But sometimes with glee — as though pleased to have an excuse to blame the actor for the difficulties on their film.

Gina Prince-Bythewood, writer-director of *Love and Basketball*, has said, "On my set, people have to respect the actor's process. I totally respect what actors do. I give them whatever time they need and I never scream out directions from the camera. I take the time to walk up to them and talk to them personally." That's very admirable, but to tell you the truth, the thing that strikes me most about this statement is that it is unusual enough to be reported. That is, that its opposite is so generally accepted as normal behavior.

Guy Pierce commented, "I've worked with directors before who think you're a piece of meat, and I think, 'Ah, I don't have the technical ability to do this.'" I think he is saying something that I know a lot of actors have felt: *I'm not the kind of actor to believably portray a human being when I receive no human contact from the director.*

Actors can sense how directors feel about them and their work; indeed, actors — through gifts and training — are more sensitive than most of us to such nuances. And to their own feelings. Actors are often more expressive about their need for love and respect than those who work in other professions. It's the nature of the beast.

TAKE RESPONSIBILITY FOR CASTING

"I have never felt I made a mistake in casting. Sometimes I have to make it work; but if you just take somebody out of a project, you leave chaos."
— Robert Altman

Once Mike Nichols was asked what he does when he finds himself and an actor are in "different keys." His response: "I don't experience it that way, because my job is to find the key in which we meet. If I have to, I can transpose to some other key. It's usually not a problem because I look for this in casting." When Krzysztof Keiślowski would meet with actors, he would talk to them "about life" — even asking them what they dreamt the night before, and telling them his own dreams. John Cassavetes said, "I sit and talk with them. You just look to see if they are serious about their work and are willing to reveal themselves in some way." Mark Rydell didn't read most of the actors who came in for the role of James Dean for the TV movie *James Dean*. He'd just talk to them, and in particular, ask them about their parents, because that is "the quickest way to find out about a person."

Once the casting is set, you must become completely curious about this new person who has come into your life — even if it's not the person you thought you wanted. You must let go of your idle fantasies of how this actor will read the lines, and instead let yourself wonder about the sure-to-be-surprising ways that the actor's imaginative depths will connect with the imaginative depths of the story.

Finally, the best advice I can give anybody about casting is: Don't cast roles, or performances. Cast relationships. Even if you had to choose from a pre-approved list, even if your first five choices turned you down, once you have a cast, start thinking immediately how to make them an ensemble.

A NOTE ON STARS
Once an experienced actor has signed on your movie, be sure to see all their films. Take, for example, Anthony Hopkins. There is a movie titled *August*, which Anthony Hopkins not only directed and starred in, but for which he wrote the music — and which is set in his native Wales. How could a director possibly know Hopkins, the man and artist, well enough to direct him if he hasn't seen this film? Or Morgan Freeman, in *Street Smart*. Study the actors' performances in their films and television work. See if you can figure out how they are working in the performances you like, and what is missing in the performances you don't like as much. After you've done that, however, forget their previous performances and treat them with "beginner's mind."

Treat them as individuals. Don't think of them as the person who can get you fired. James Caan says about Francis Coppola, working with Marlon Brando on *The Godfather*, "All Francis did was talk to him. Everyone wants to conquer Brando — Francis just talked to him." Jez Butterworth says that at the beginning of photography for *Birthday Girl*, "Nicole [Kidman] and I sort of had a little aside, and I said, 'Look, I've directed lots of actors before, but I've never directed a movie star. Is it any different?' She said no, and that was that, really."

DIRECTORS WHO LOVE ACTORS
"It's all about the actors. The actors trust me, which is good. I let them do what they want, which is fair. Wonderful things happen in their faces; that's why we put a frame around them, like we frame a beautiful painting. The technical demands depend on time and money. But I never let technical demands keep the actors from getting the time they need."
— Alan Rudolph

"One of the fabulous things about my job is that I have stolen a piece of her [Diane Lane in Unfaithful*] that I'll have forever."*
— Adrian Lyne

"Working with actors is what I like best about directing. [I love] providing actors with the opportunity to do their best work. That's what I'm most proud of in the performances, what one might call nakedness."
— Curtis Hanson

"I love actors a lot, to be honest. They're such strange people. They'd do anything for me. It often happens to me that they bring their views, feelings, their attitude to the world. I make use of this, I simply take it. I love them for it. And if you love someone, you try to be close to them."

— Krzysztof Keiślowski

"I just love them so much and I love to write for them because I don't like to see them do bad work somewhere else."

— Paul Thomas Anderson

"A director ultimately can't offer any more to an actor than your love and your friendship."

— Jane Campion

Authority is not a condition, it's a relationship. By loving actors, I don't mean slavish star-fucker adoration — that's offensive and demeaning to everyone. I mean a genuine respect for what actors put themselves through. An appreciation for the level of emotional exposure. I'm talking about a world-view that assumes that people basically are smart and talented, and are happier when they can put the work first and their egos on a back burner. It's true in life that when you expect the best of people, it brings out their best.

Actors really feel loved when they get cast again by the same director. Julianne Moore said, "I'll do an awful lot for Paul [Thomas Anderson] because I've known him so long. I'll go out on a limb because I want to learn something, and I trust that he'll teach me." Many top directors work with the same actors over and over. For creating the trust that leads to a natural and confident authority, there is no substitute for having already been through the fire (as making a movie often is) with someone.

19 | REHEARSAL PRINCIPLES AND TECHNIQUES

"What is this really like? That's the only question. What is it really like when this happens? When someone seduces someone, kills someone."

— Mike Nichols

Many directors enter pre-production with every intention of having rehearsal with the actors, only to find the time scheduled for rehearsal evaporating when the pressures of shooting start to bear down. Don't get me wrong — I'm not agreeing with conventional wisdom that there is no time for rehearsal in film and television. There's always time for rehearsal for those who make it. Most directors, however, have no conception of any useful activity that could possibly take place in a rehearsal. So as soon as some other claim is made on their time and attention, they turn gratefully to the distraction, and rehearsal schedules get left in the dust.

It wasn't always so. Rehearsal, now on its way to becoming a lost art, used to be standard operating procedure. The directors who come from commercials or music video with little knowledge and exposure to actors and rehearsal are a recent phenomenon. Back in the 1930s and '40s there was the studio system; directors learned how to work with actors by directing lower-budget "B" movies until they became proficient enough to be given the "A" material. Many of the great film directors of the '60s, '70s, and '80s came to film from theater or live television drama. They brought with them rehearsal expertise. (To name a few: Mike Nichols, Elia Kazan, John Cassavetes, Robert Altman, John Frankenheimer, William Friedkin, John Schlesinger, George Roy Hill, Ingmar Bergman, Sydney Pollock, Sidney Lumet, Peter Bogdanovich, Arthur Penn.)

Today's consensus that there's no time for rehearsal is a cover-up for the simple reality that directors don't know how to rehearse. Lack of knowledge leads to the fear that rehearsal will make performances worse instead of better; this fear becomes a self-fulfilling prophesy. Because when the director misunderstands the nature and purpose of rehearsal, the performances will deteriorate.

PURPOSE OF REHEARSAL — FARMING NOT HUNTING

When you consider the term "rehearsal," it's actually a poor name for the process. It suggests a repetition, over and over, of a pre-set performance — which, for film, is exactly what it shouldn't be. Perhaps instead of "rehearsal" it should be called "warming up" or "exploration" or "preparing to work." Maybe an even better way to describe it is a chance for the actors to spend "quality time" with the director and with each other. In a productive rehearsal actors and director together *engage in a process* that will continue on the set, when the cameras are rolling, to bring about vibrant performances that bring the story to life. Even for a director who never conducts a formal rehearsal, knowledge of the process and purpose of rehearsal is important. Because "rehearsal" comprises all contact between actor and director, including meetings, auditions, and shooting.

The purpose of rehearsal is not to tie down the performances, but to release them. The result of proper rehearsal is not perfection, but freedom. One of the partners of rehearsal-junkie Fred Astaire said that Astaire would insist on exhaustive practice of dance routines — *until it was not about the feet, but about the romance.* The purpose of rehearsal is to make the scene not about the words, not about the camera shots, but about the relationship, the situation — the *emotional event.* Rehearsal gives the actors time and permission to get deeply involved with the imagined reality of the characters' needs and problems — so that imagined reality can stand up to the distractions of the movie set.

WHAT ACTORS GET OUT OF REHEARSAL

"It's important that actors know that you're not gonna walk away until you're happy or they're happy. You're going to spend time playing these scenes until they spark or until you get some place with them rather than thinking you're going to create something in the editing room."

— Todd Field

For actors, rehearsal has three main purposes. One is the search for insights, breakthroughs, solutions. Such breakthroughs and insights, which bring complexity and depth to a performance, are paradoxically often very simple. The insights link up something primal in the actor to something primal in the script. It feels like a letting go, a stripping down to essentials. At this point the work becomes inventive and intuitive. Michael Richards said, of working on the role of Kramer in *Seinfeld,* "I find you have to work very hard to get to the moments where you surprise yourself — spontaneous moments where something comes through that wasn't in the script, the table reading or any discussions. That's always exciting. It feels holy." Matthew Broderick: "In order for it to be instinctual, you have to do a lot of work."

Second is the chance to meet the other actors at a level below the social mask, to show up as human beings as well as craftsmen — and instead of showing up as products of their publicity.

Third is the opportunity to create the river of emotional life that is the subtext of the written script, and to practice living in it. Rehearsal is a time for warming up the actors' imaginations, warming up the personal connections, warming up the concentration, warming up the relationships, the circumstances, the needs. It's farming, not hunting. So it's not a time to nail down choices so much as to test choices, and practice choices. It's really not about practicing the performance — rather a time to practice making choices, engaging, and taking risks.

WHAT DIRECTORS GET OUT OF REHEARSAL

Rehearsal has practical purposes for the director as well as the actor. Television director Joe Sargent calls rehearsal the chance to do "all the things you can't do in front of a hundred crew people," such as "the experimenting, the searching, the groping," and cultivating "the courage to fail" — all of which "can only happen in the rehearsal period."

In television, as in low budget filmmaking, where often there are one or two takes per set-up, a director needs all the preparation he can get. Sean Penn describes the regular Hollywood shooting plan as "Let's do a few things this way and a few things that way and we'll see what cuts best." He appreciated the thirty-day shooting schedule of *Hurlyburly* because it meant they had to rehearse to find solutions to the scenes, instead of cobbling together some random effective moments.

A film script is an *idea* for a movie. It's a more fully developed idea than a treatment or outline, but it's still an idea for a movie — not the movie itself. "Script analysis" begins the process of *adaptation* of the written document that must take place in order to create the film's story for the audience. Rehearsal is another step in the process of adaptation — it gives the director a chance to test the solutions she has imagined during her script analysis. No matter how well prepared a director is, the imagined solutions often come out quite different when activated by flesh-and-blood actors. This is not a bad thing! Such surprises — whether pleasant or unpleasant — are part of movie-making, which is a collaborative medium. It can feel like a bad thing when such surprises arrive on the set, with no time to consider and deal with them.

Even though established movie stars may not wish to devote their time to rehearsal, it's still better for the film, and thus the director, if they do. Movie stars, who move from project to project, working constantly, need some time and space to completely shed their old performances — and their movie star personas — and adopt a beginner's mind with respect to the project at hand. When a production includes actors of differing levels of experience, rehearsal can help to turn them into an ensemble. The supporting performers, and especially the day players — usually talented and hard-working actors who may be nervous because they don't work often enough — need some interaction with the lead actors, as well as attention from the director, in order to relax enough to be able to deliver their best performances.

It is the director's job to activate and photograph the emotional events of a script. The emotional events of an effective film are more than the sum of each actor's individual performances. If an actor "nails it" in an audition, rehearsal, or even a single recorded take, that one exceptional performance doesn't ensure excellence throughout the entire production. You may only have a single terrific reading, which may even haunt the project and have a negative effect — it might come to represent what the project "could have been." Rehearsal, when done properly, creates a reliable process that can bring the actors back to the playable center of the script over and over. Instead of hunting down perfect performances of each line, a director serves his own interests by creating a situation in which the actors are *working well* rather than chasing after — "nailing" — a performance.

Rehearsal gives a director the chance to go much deeper and become clearer with his script analysis ideas. I find that no matter how many times I have gone over the words of the script on my own, I don't really *know* what my ideas are until I hear the words spoken by the actors. And this is not even counting the new ideas the actors bring to me.

Rehearsal gives the director a chance to practice watching the actors work, noting their respective energy levels and danger signals — information that will be very useful on the set, since every actor is different.

There are two crucial directorial duties that many directors are clueless in carrying out: setting the blocking (physical movement) of scenes; and creating pace and tempo-rhythm. These important tasks are commonly given only cursory attention on the set, and usually left to be "fixed" in the editing room. Rehearsal can be the place for directors to make these choices, thus preventing chaos and despair in editing. The next chapter will deal with these issues.

Just as the actor's skills are challenged in rehearsal, so are the skills of the director. A director should not request or schedule rehearsal on a professional set without adequate knowledge and preparation. Unless the director has had some experience in how to rehearse, via workshops or theater training, the exercise may well backfire. Rehearsal should be fun and exciting, not laborious and tiresome. It should function to keep the director connected to the story and characters at a time when financial and technological concerns tend to overwhelm one's creativity, and it should give the director something to focus on other than idle fantasies of how great the movie is going to be when it comes out. If it isn't pleasurable and compelling enough to do that, then it probably isn't helping the actors either.

THE PARTICULAR TOPICS OF REHEARSAL

Particular topics that rehearsal might cover include:

Connection and trust. One of the most important functions of rehearsal is a chance for actors to make *connection* — that is, to show up as human beings, bond with each other as human beings, relate to the subject matter of the script, and understand the problems of the characters as human problems. So rehearsal properly includes practicing *listening*, practicing engaging, practicing working below the social mask. It's also an opportunity for actors to practice making personal associations to the material. Actors must always work close to the bone, draw from their deepest well, always make choices that affect them personally, and never judge their characters.

Scene Shaping. Scene shaping, addressed in the next chapter, has two components: the emotional structure, which is the subtext choices of through-lines, beats, and most importantly emotional event; and the physical staging or blocking of the characters' activities, movement, and relationship to objects.

Information and Problem Solving. Problems, such as an actor having trouble saying a particular line, will be easier to solve with advance notice, won't they? Resistances, misunderstandings, lack of chemistry between romantic leads — all can be surmounted with some time and intelligent attention. Information — before the cameras roll — is invaluable. This includes information about the actors — how they work, what kind of direction they respond to, their feelings about the script. It also includes information about the script — scenes that don't work, new ideas that come up when you hear the words out loud. A director who looks at rehearsal as an opportunity for information can't go wrong.

Research. The director will have done research into elements of the script that need special attention, such as the history of the Los Angeles "water wars" if he is directing *Chinatown*. The actors may have done research of their own. Rehearsal is an opportunity to exchange such knowledge.

Set up Priorities. If you want to use improvisation on the set, if you want to use warm ups, if you want to use opposites — it's necessary to try these tactics in advance in rehearsal. Suggesting some exotic exercise on the set just before shooting is unsettling to actors, and usually only serves to make them feel you have no faith in them. For example, if listening and engaging is your highest priority (as I hope it is), it's so helpful to have the actors practice engaging before they get to the set. Priorities can get confused under the hot lights, surrounded by impatient crew members, expensive equipment, and dollars melting away with every tick of the clock. Setting and maintaining priorities needs to be a constant commitment.

Let the Actors Work. Actors frequently know how to rehearse, and can often do the work without a lot of interference from the director. They may have several ideas and might appreciate a chance to try them out. A very confident director can watch while skilled actors work things out themselves, stepping in as needed, adding depth with an insightful question or comment, and adding shape with a bit of staging or business.

PRINCIPLES OF REHEARSAL
Following are principles that will help make rehearsal an exercise in intuition instead of a chore.

1) **There is no such thing as "no rehearsal."** If you don't rehearse ahead of shooting, then the rehearsal is in front of the camera. As soon as a scene is repeated for coverage, the performances change and develop, for better or worse. Matthew Modine says he asked Stanley Kubrick why he so often did a lot of takes. Kubrick said, "Jack Nicholson [during shooting for *The Shining*] would come in during the blocking and he'd be learning the lines while he was there. After take 3 or 4 you'd get the Jack

that everybody knows and most directors would be happy with. And then you'd go up to [take] 10 or 15 and he'd be really awful. And then he'd start to understand what the lines were, what the lines meant. And then he'd become unconscious about what he was saying. So by take 30 or take 40 the lines became something else."

Kubrick meant that by take "30 or 40" the actor was no longer thinking about the lines and how to deliver them, but was connected up to their *subtext.* This is the goal of rehearsal, when the filmmaker does not have enough money to shoot forty takes — to take the actors beyond the lines and into the subtext.

2) **Process is king.**
"What you're looking for every day is one little surprise. It's like seeding a cloud and hoping it will rain."

— Mike Nichols

Nichols' theory on rehearsal: Every good day is followed by a lousy day. But — the lousy day is as important as the good day, because on the "lousy" day the unconscious mind is at work. That's how radical it is to believe in process, but it's also how relaxing it is — you don't have to panic on the lousy day, you can even rejoice.

The opposite of dedication to process is fixation on result. When a director is enmeshed in result-oriented thinking, the worst consequence is not the deterioration in communication with actors. If the director's ideas are good, the actors can make the necessary translations from result directions to playable behavior and associations. (Rehearsal gives them time to do this.) If it takes result language to make yourself clear, your best course of action is to admit it: e.g., "I know I'm giving you a result here. I need your help to make it real." And you can always ask, "Is this too much result?"

The worst outcome of result-oriented thinking is that the director's brain can become so rigidly hard-wired to the result in his head that there comes to be a loss in his ability to clearly see the performances in front of him. He may be so set on a certain inflection that he becomes unable to recognize good work that solves the scene even if it clearly reveals itself. Or, the converse may occur. The director may get so focused on the result that in watching the performances, he thinks he has achieved the desired result when the actors haven't gotten there at all.

3) Script Analysis — Be Prepared.
"I come to the set with a plan, but always praying someone will come up with something better."

— Ron Howard

There is no point in holding rehearsals unless you are prepared. When you are genuinely prepared, rehearsal is easy. A director who has done proper script analysis homework ahead of time can relax and enjoy rehearsal and shooting, because the ideas are there, churned up in her imaginative storage banks. She can trust that they will leap to the surface as needed, with the force of intuitive certainty.

By "proper script analysis" I mean that the director has identified the "emotional facts" of the script, has investigated subtext associations and connections, considered possible through-lines for the characters, and — most importantly — has come up with a vision of the emotional event of each scene — together with two or three other possible visions to try if the first one doesn't work.

Script analysis — the cultivation of new ideas — should continue during rehearsal. It's a characteristic of a good director that new ideas emerge during rehearsal.

4) Two kinds of rehearsal.
One is "drilling" rehearsal — that's when some complicated bit of choreography or timing needs to be repeatedly drilled until it becomes second nature, just as actors learn lines until they are second nature. This is more like theater rehearsal, and is only need-ed for film or television in special situations, such as musical numbers, physical comedy, long takes, complicated blocking moves, special tech-nical demands, and of course four-camera sitcom, which is performed in front of a live audience, and therefore should be rehearsed like theater.

The other type is the "fertilizing" rehearsal. It's like organic gardening. In organic gardening, success depends 99% on soil preparation. Rehearsal for most film and television work is all preparation. A great performance in rehearsal can even feel like a failure, because there was no camera to record it. It's not really a failure, as long as you see every-thing that happens in rehearsal as a chance, not to set performances, but to prepare performances. To plant seeds.

5) The technology.
When actors are overwhelmed with technical com-plications, without enough time to practice and get used to it, the acting

will suffer. Period. It's not possible to give actors the freedom they need if the camera is king. Use rehearsal to make the emotional truth of the scene king, and then bring in the cameras to photograph it.

6) **What needs to be rehearsed?** What aspect of the scene do you need to get a head start on before you get to the set? Take, for example, a scene in which there is a gorilla, to whom the characters address lines. If there won't be a real gorilla on the set — that is, if the gorilla's reactions are going to be shot on some other day than the actors' lines — the actors may need to rehearse as if there is a gorilla there, in order to get used to creating the sense of a three-creature scene with only two creatures present. But if the real gorilla is going to be on set with the actors, you don't need to rehearse that aspect — being in the presence of a gorilla will have an affect on the actors that does not need to be rehearsed.

On the other hand, if the characters have a significant relationship with the animal, they may need to rehearse with the gorilla and create that relationship. For scenes in which an actor plays more than one role (as in *Multiplicity* or *Adaptation*), it can be helpful to bring an actor stand-in to rehearse with him.

Ang Lee always schedules a two-week rehearsal period, and thoroughly rehearses all scenes prior to the start of photography. In the preface accompanying the published screenplay for *The Ice Storm*, however, Lee discloses that they chose not to rehearse the scene where Kevin Kline carries the dead child into his parents' home. The central emotional fact of that scene is so deeply compelling that anyone can imagine it, anyone can "go there." The function of rehearsal, to trigger or investigate the imagination, is not needed here.

7) **Rehearsal is not performance.** Don't use rehearsal to check to see if you have a performance. The reason some directors want to get the performance in rehearsal is their own anxiety about whether it's possible to get it. They may also have the notion that once they've gotten pinned it down, they can cross that scene off their list of worries. This condition of *anxiety* gets communicated to the actors and they get the message that they'd better do exactly the same thing when the cameras are there. This makes their performance for the camera a weak approximation of something that worked in rehearsal. This is exactly the kind of directorial mistake that gives rehearsal a bad name.

The reason why we look, in rehearsal, for solutions to the emotional structure of a scene has nothing to do with being "finished." It has to do with creating trust that there is a structure, that the script can be trusted. It has to do with knowing that if we get to the set and the structure does-n't work any more, we know we can find another. When something that worked before stops working, I always say to myself, "at least I know I solved it once. So that means I'll be able to solve it again." **Look at the glass half-full, instead of half-empty.**

8) **Avert despair in the editing suite.** Forget you ever heard the phrase "We can fix it in post." Don't wait until the editing suite to find the solu-tion of the scene, or to create chemistry among the actors. Sydney Pollack has said that while he used to rehearse thoroughly for all his movies, he now only tries to get one fresh and spontaneous reading for each line, because it can all be put together in the editing suite. Krzysztof Keiślows-ki spoke of his technique of "stealing moments" from the performances to edit together. Statements by such masters should not be misinterpreted to mean that a director does not need to know how to solve and shape a scene. Robert Duvall says, about "saving" the scenes in the editing room, "If you don't have it [in the shot], I don't think you can find it [in the editing room]. A chef has to have good produce to make good food."

REHEARSAL PHILOSOPHY — I

One of my students, a volunteer for many years at a suicide prevention hotline, once told me, "If you have empathy and some skills, you can talk down an inebriated man who wants to kill himself and has every reason to do so." *Empathy and some skills* sounded exactly like the requirements for a director running a rehearsal. So I asked him to tell me more about the skills he had been taught. He described the four-stage "pyramid" of a suicide prevention call: the first stage (the foundation, on which one spends the most time), *establish trust*; second stage, *gather information*; third, *explore alternatives*; and fourth (which should take the least amount of time), *end the call*.

This seemed like such an excellent paradigm for the rehearsal process that I have inserted a diagram below. Establishing trust and connection — between actor and director, between actor and material, and among the actors — should take the most time in a film or television rehearsal. It's the first thing you do, but it is not really ever over — a director must check in with actors frequently to make sure they are still on the same page. The next most important function of rehearsal is to gather informa-tion — about how the actors work, their questions and concerns, their ideas and enthusiasms, their resistances, judgments, and gripes, and how to set up procedures for communication on the set. The third, exploring alternatives, in rehearsal terms would be trying out ideas, making choices, getting the scene "off book" (i.e., memorized) and on its feet. The fourth stage, ending the call, means a director needs to be aware when something has been accomplished — and then *stop talking*.

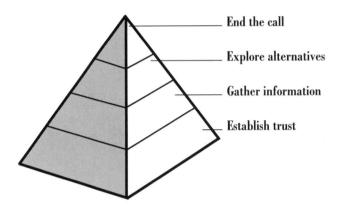

End the call

Explore alternatives

Gather information

Establish trust

REHEARSAL PHILOSOPHY — II

If you are well prepared, rehearsal procedure is as follows: Take the instincts the actors have, define them a bit, not enough to make it intellectual, but enough to make it repeatable, and shape the performance with physical activity and movement. It may be necessary, along the way, to guide the actors in uncovering their instincts. It is never advisable to stuff them with instructions.

Start with the actors and what they already have. We're looking for the choices that connect the actors as human beings. The solution to each scene resides in *engagement* at some human level. The director does script analysis in order to come up with possible ways that engagement will occur. But the adjustment that's "right" for the scene is the one that ultimately works, the one that creates an emotional event in a physical reality. I may have an idea of what choice will get the actor to engage with the material and the other actor, but I am often surprised by the choice that works. That's what I mean by not "really knowing" my ideas until I hear the words spoken by the actors.

"You have to love them for what they're willing to go through in order to get at something that's truthful."
— Francis Ford Coppola

Guide them — or get out of the way — so they can find the deep place. The deep place — the primal place — is the safe place for actors, the place where an actor can become *not worried*. It is only from the deep place that actors *know* that they know what they are doing. If a scene has depth and the actors don't go there, it's a dead spot — a false note — it feels and looks like a lie. Likewise when an actor encounters a moment of truth and doesn't build on it, that feels like a lie too. Let your actors tell their truth.

REHEARSAL PHILOSOPHY — III

Chris Cooper said that of all the joys of working with Meryl Streep (on *Adaptation*) perhaps the most excellent was being exposed to the way Streep is completely forgiving of herself. Her philosophy is, "This doesn't work? Try that!"

BUILD TRUST

It is only possible to fully trust your own intuition when you are working with people you trust and who feel trust for you and for each other. Building trust is a major purpose of rehearsal. Rehearsal is an opportunity for the director and actors to create experiences around the script and to find templates for working together on the set. But more than that, it's an opportunity for director and actors to learn about the characters and story *together* — to make discoveries, insights, and breakthroughs — together. Taking advantage of that opportunity creates a bond that is offered by no other relationship in the realm of art.

Naturally the actors need to get comfortable with each other. Perhaps the characters are siblings — or lovers — and the actors have never met before. Rehearsal can be a chance to explore and make real that relationship, perhaps through improvisation of backstory scenes that are not in the script. Most importantly the actors need to begin listening to each other, putting their concentration on each other rather than on their respective individual performances, to establish with each other the "privacy in public" that will make their characters' relationship believable to the audience.

Elia Kazan said, "The first thing you should do with an actor is get to know him. That's your raw material, what his life is. Before I start with anybody in any important role, I talk to them, for a long time." The principle here is that, since all the actor's work should be personal, the director should avail himself of whatever knowledge can help him give direction that is personal. So that for a scene between two brothers, the director can say to the actor, "This reminds me of something you told me about your relationship with your own brother."

It's very helpful to find out as much as you can about an actor's interests, fears, her life story, her truth — and her resistances. By resistance I mean the dead spot at which the actor can't say the lines unless she either fakes the emotional life of the scene, or emotionally drops out. Where she begins to Act with a capital A. Actors may not themselves know what their resistances are. Ways to smoke out an actor's resistances include 1) asking open-ended questions about her ideas about the character and the script; 2) calling attention to dead spots in the delivery of lines; 3) staging improvisations in rehearsal.

There's no need for a director to delve into the reasons for the actor's resistances. It's a common sense issue. It would be helpful to know if the actor, for instance, has children. If an actor is a parent, you could use, for a scene in which the character is losing patience, an adjustment such as, "as if your son is dawdling and making you late for work." Or, if the character seems preoccupied, the adjustment might be "as if your daughter was crying last night and wouldn't tell you why."

CHEMISTRY

Chemistry among the lead actors is a very important ingredient to the success of a project. Trust can lead to chemistry because actors who trust each other know something about the depth of the other actor's commitment, purity of impulse, and honesty of feelings. These actors recognize each other as humans and fellow artists. They feel they can bring out the best in each other.

Curiosity also generates chemistry. Actors who are curious about each other are interested in each other's response. They are curious about each other's subtext. They challenge each other — what will you do if I do this?

The shared experience of theater training frequently creates an automatic trust among actors. Sam Rockwell talked about working with actors with stage experience in both *The Green Mile* (including Tom Hanks — "a lot of people don't know that") and *Galaxy Quest*, including Tim Allen ("stand-up — don't think that's not stage experience"), Alan Rickman, who had played *Hamlet*, and Tony Shalhoub whom Rockwell had seen in *Waiting for Godot*. "What that [stage experience] brings to the table is people who know how to do homework, which a lot of actors who haven't worked in theater don't know how to do." Stephen Daldry said that while directing Nicole Kidman in *The Hours* he never felt he was "dealing with Nicole Kidman the movie star. We'd rehearse as if we were doing a play. There was a level of mutuality in our approach to the work." All the major roles in *The Hours* were played by actors with stage experience.

According to Mekhi Phifer, director Curtis Hansen began rehearsals for *8 Mile* six weeks before shooting began, by having the young actors go to football games, rap battles, and clubs together. This can be an excellent way to allow actors to share experiences and create a sense of the relationships of the script.

As a practical consequence of building this trust among actors, there can be occasions when the actors take unusual steps to help each other's performance. Before shooting of the scene in *On the Waterfront* in which Terry (Marlon Brando) breaks down her door, Eva Marie Saint expressed embarrassment about playing the scene in a slip. Just before the cameras rolled, Brando came to her and whispered her husband's name; this simple gesture relaxed her completely. Angelica Huston, for the mini-series *Lonesome Dove*, had a scene in which her character reads a letter from Gus, played by Robert Duvall. At each rehearsal, Duvall presented her with a letter — different each time — which he had written himself. And for the shooting of the scene, another new letter. "It gave me my performance," said Huston.

The best way to communicate with actors — or any of the myriad film collaborators — is to have worked with them before. Is it an accident that so many successful filmmaking teams are brothers (e.g., Coen, Hughes, Wachowski, Farrelly, Bui, Zucker)? Or soul-mate friends (that is, friends before they became famous, like Matt Damon and Ben Affleck)? Or that some of the top director-actor pairings have been lovers (Fellini and Masina, Cassavetes and Rowlands, Bergman and Ullman, Woody and Diane, Woody and Mia, William Wyler and Bette Davis)?

So how are you going to make a great movie if you're not working with a brother, sister, lover, or soul-mate friend? Trust, curiosity, shared experience, intimacy, communication short-cuts, and soul-recognition can be developed and nurtured in rehearsal.

USE THE TOOLS

All these tools are also covered elsewhere in the book in greater detail.

Event. Directors have told me that when they come to rehearsal with a vision of what the scene is about and what happens in it, they feel safe and free, able to respond to any question from the actors. It's better yet if in addition to their deeply felt vision of the story and its emotional events, they have also prepared several alternate solutions as well. Each solution should include a set of candidates for beats, through-lines, supported by facts and images of the text. During rehearsal, the main thing the director is looking for is whether in front of the camera an event *will happen*.

Listening. Even if all you accomplish in rehearsal is to set a pattern of listening and engagement, rehearsal will have been worthwhile.

When the actors are not listening to each other, do something about it. It may be possible to suggest an adjustment to the content of the scene which will encourage engagement. In an early scene from *Private Lives* by Noel Coward, the character Amanda has a wonderful line — "Extraordinary how potent cheap music is" — that puts into brilliant focus the feelings the characters are (unwillingly) having for each other. An actress whom I was directing in the scene loved the line, but was becoming self-conscious with it. Finally I advised her, "Don't think of it as a comment on your own emotions — think of her as wanting to console Elyot for the turmoil he must also be feeling." This adjustment worked every time because it engaged her with the other actor. By the way, it might have worked just as well with the opposite adjustment — that she wants to punish him for making her have these unwelcome feelings.

Some language you might use to encourage listening: "Anchor yourself in him." "Let what you are saying land on him." You can also encourage listening by making sure the actors are playing intentions.

Objective/Intention. A choice of verb (intention) can be quite exact, in order to fine-tune a performance — e.g., "Instead of reasoning with her, really plead with her to change her mind." But it can also be used to get in the "ballpark" of the choice — e.g., "Do you think he's accusing and punishing her, or do you think he's reasoning with her, imploring her?" Another way to talk about objective is to ask the actor "what matters to" the character. But the most important thing to remember about the objective is that it should be personal to the relationship, instead of literal to the lines or the plot.

Obstacle. When a scene is bland or flat, look for the obstacle. What will happen if the character doesn't get his objective? How is that of consequence to the character? When the scene is over-acted, also look for the obstacle. But don't forget that in order for an obstacle to work, the actor must make it personal, and experience it in the moment.

Images and Associations. A character's images, whether apparent in the text or implied in the subtext, are keys to her interests and her hopes, fears, dreams, and memories. Via images, a director can encourage an actor to make her performance more believable, or emotionally intense — or more fanciful.

Facts. One of the best ways to begin a rehearsal is by reviewing the facts. Among the "facts" are backstory facts (things that were true before the movie begins) plus the events of the script up to the point of the scene you are working on. This is especially important when you are shooting or rehearsing out of sequence. The following, however, is the crucial caveat — *Do not provide a laundry list of every fact, and do not explain the entire plot.* Limit yourself to **two facts** per scene — find the *emotional facts*, the significant facts, the emotionally pertinent information — the circumstances that might generate behavior in the scene at hand.

Mysterious Lines. Be attentive to the lines that jump out at you, for whatever reason. Encourage the actors to be attuned to such lines and phrases. Sometimes people resist the idea of "mysterious lines" because they think admitting a line is mysterious will make them sound stupid. Foster an atmosphere in rehearsal where mysterious lines are appreciated as paths to the riches of the script and the instincts and intuition of the actors and director. You can go line by line, treating every line as a mysterious line. Or, roam around the mysterious lines randomly, out of order. Approach mysterious lines with this question: What could this line possibly mean? Come up with three possible candidates.

When investigating individual lines, look to see whether a particular line comes out of the character's "new thought," or whether the character is responding to something the other character has said or done. For example, in the *sex, lies, and videotape* scene, when Graham says, "This food is excellent," is he responding to the immediate taste in his mouth? Or is he responding to some remark Ann made before the scene began, perhaps that it was a new recipe, or a disclaimer that she was not sure the dish had come out right? Or is it a *new thought* that changes the subject away from John's carping on his appearance? Such choices add specificity and freshness to the performances.

If a line is repeated, it should mean something different each time it is spoken.

Through-lines and transitions. Transitions are sometimes also called "turning the corners" or "making the leaps." The important thing is that they not be intellectual, but experiential. This is most reliably accomplished if the actors have strong, simple, committed through-lines. If actors are deeply connected to through-lines, then the director can fine-tune particular transitions with a delicate touch. I find the most successful choices for transition subtexts are off-beat and illogical. For instance, in the *Clerks* scene, when Dante recalls that high school was memorable for algebra, bad lunch, and infidelity, there needs to be some transition that takes him there. I happened to have had as my high school algebra teacher a totally Nathaniel Hawthorne-esque New England spinster who dressed in (then unfashionable) black... Well, that's a start.

Beats. You might not need to work on a whole scene; it might only be necessary to address one of the sections, or beats. You might choose to work on the beat that is most difficult emotionally — or you might choose the opposite, to work on a beat without strenuous emotional content, to develop the actors' *texture of life* in the relationships and environment.

Theme. Eleanor Coppola's documentary, *The Making of John Grisham's The Rainmaker*, functions as a textbook on rehearsal techniques. *The Rainmaker*, directed by Francis Coppola, had excellent acting. One technique used in rehearsal was to give direction by identifying the theme, as in, "This scene is about hierarchy."

Adjustments. In *The Rainmaker*, Jon Voight was playing a character that Matt Damon's character found intimidating. The adjustment here was a "freebie." Damon could use his own feelings about Voight, an actor who Damon considered "way above" him. Another adjustment: When Damon's character had to enter the courtroom for his first preliminary hearing and the experienced lawyer who is supposed to help him didn't show up, the acting coach on the set came up with the idea to play the scene "as if" he was a medical student suddenly called upon to deliver a baby. The fascinating observation here is that playing a physician is probably no closer to Damon's real-life experience than playing an attorney — and yet, the adjustment, because it creates a *subtext* reality that is off-kilter to the scene's on-the-nose reality, helped. Committing to a subtext is that freeing to the actor's imagination.

In the *Private Lives* example a few pages earlier, I mentioned two possible adjustments, either "to console Elyot for the turmoil he must also be feeling," or "to punish him for making her have these unwelcome feelings." The character Amanda has both these sides to her personality — a deep well of genuine affection for Elyot, but also an ability to be quite nasty if she feels the urge. A director might use one of these adjustments as a corrective to a performance — for instance, if the performance is getting too brittle and cynical, suggesting that at this moment she might be consoling Elyot for his turmoil rather than concentrating on her own. Or, if the performance were getting sentimental, that this is a perfect time to punish him for making her feel too much.

The "magic as if." The "magic" *as if* is the one that makes the adjustment personal. Every choice an actor makes must be personal and sensory. Personal stories and substitutions help the actor locate a real-world springboard for his imagination.

REHEARSAL TECHNIQUES

Pushing actors. How does a director "push" actors? Yelling or criticizing them is of course neither required nor advisable. What is required is that the director has a deep connection to something primal in the script. And the ability to pay close attention to the actors, to hear their interests and longings as well as their resistances; to hear the dead spot, the false note in their work. A director should listen to the actor's ideas. But if the director has a different idea, one that is deeper and truer to the material, then the director is doing the actor a favor by turning him on to this deeper idea, by offering him the opportunity to stretch.

Find a way in. The purpose of discussion and practice in rehearsal is to find a way into the material that the actors can make their own. It doesn't matter how wonderful your script analysis ideas are if the actors can't find a way into them. That's why a director uses questions to draw out the actors' associations and connections — for example, the questions I asked in the *sex, lies, and videotape* chapter about John's infidelity, and Ann's relationship with her sister.

Engagement — among actors. Rather than ask for conflict, ask for engagement. When you want more "intensity," ask for more engagement. Make sure both actors have objectives. Make sure the objectives engage them with each other — that they have some reason to be vitally concerned with each other. The intention "to ignore" is dangerous because it can create non-engagement. (Instead of "ignoring" another actor, the actor should find some other concern the character could be vitally involved with.)

Engagement — between director and actor. Find your own energy. Actors typically have a lot of energy when they are working well. Match your energy to that of the actors'. Engage with actors. What do the actors need to know about you in order for you to communicate on a feeling level? How do you need to behave in order to live in your own skin and be present as yourself so you can stay in the moment with the actors? Your feelings, your priorities all matter. Even your sense of humor, your need for snacks or music at crucial moments, are pertinent.

Script analysis is really about locating the elements of the script that release energy — both for the director and the actors. Let actors know that it's okay to feel. Let them know this not just with your words, but with your actions, with your feelings.

Be frank and open. Actors really want to know if they are doing what the director wants. I do need to mention here that some of my favorite directors (Cassavetes, Malick, Wyler, Kubrick) are well known for making the actors find the performance themselves, without ever describing what they wanted. In order to work that way, you need to be confident and experienced, and to take responsibility for the frustration the actors might express. Usually, you should have a clear vision and let them know what you think, what you're working on and toward. Instead of describing a directorial vision as, "This is how I see it," it may be preferable to say, "Let me tell you what I'm after here, and see what you think."

You can be totally honest about what's wrong with a performance — even if it's a lack of listening, a choice that's not personal enough, a judgment of the character — as long as your subtext is "I know you can do better."

Keep it simple. Being able to come up with the simple adjustments, simple facts, and simple intentions that go to the heart of a scene or characterization is an art form. It takes great discipline to be spare in your communication with an actor. Start learning now. If you give the actor a laundry list of information, don't be surprised if only one of the items you suggested shows up in his next run-through. The actor's unconscious mind will treat this excess of information like a buffet, and probably select one item from it. Actually that's the best case scenario. Worst case is he may try to do it all, and thus intellectualize his performance. Or, simply tune out everything you are saying. It doesn't hurt for the director to ask, "Am I overloading you with too much information?"

If something doesn't work, try something else. Don't keep pounding on an idea that is not creating a spark.

Working in layers. Don't load the actors up with all your ideas. Be gradual. Try one or two ideas at a time. It takes discipline to stop tinkering and let a scene or a performance breathe. It is central to the notion of rehearsal that one does a little bit at a time, even letting something go for a while that isn't completely right.

Making choices. It's not that you *have* to make choices — you *get* to make choices. A central function of rehearsal is moving toward workable choices — solutions — that create the imagined lives of these characters and allow actors to live in their imagined world. It's not necessary to "nail down" these choices. But it's good to practice making them.

Getting comfortable with being off guard. We want actors to feel confident and excited about their choices, and trusting of each other — but that doesn't mean we want them to sink into a comfort zone.

Play it real. An actor asked George Roy Hill during the first week of shooting *Butch Cassidy and the Sundance Kid*, "You know, I don't know how to play this. Are we making a comedy or a drama or what are we doing here?" Hill replied, "Just play it real, and if it's supposed to be funny, it'll be funny, and if it's supposed to be dramatic, it'll be dramatic." Kathy Bates said of working with writer-director Alexander Payne on *About Schmidt*, "His vision is not middle of the road. It's unusual, and at first I wanted to find out how to create this tone and style that he has in his films. But then I discovered that it was just about trying to make her as real as possible."

Be bold. If the subject is suicide — or sex — don't shy away. Address it boldly and take chances. Get to the root of what the scene is about.

Let the actors find their core. Find that place where they can relax, open up, bloom, let go of defenses, and show the audience something unique. Stars are in a position to insist on this. Jackie Chan, after one of his films which he felt had too many special effects, went to the director of his next film and insisted, "Look, you have to promise me. Fewer explosions. Less violence. Fewer gunfights. Even if you have the gunfights don't show the blood. We want no special effects. Jackie Chan will be the special effects, doing exactly what I am doing in Asia. So...they just let me do it." Actors who are not stars may need some permission from the director to find the "core" they have to offer your project.

The same page. Sometimes it's important for actor and director to share the same thinking about a certain choice. What if, in the *Tender Mercies* scene, the actor were to make the secret choice that Mac's line, "I'm not drunk. I bought a bottle but I didn't get drunk. I poured it all out. I didn't have one drink," is a lie? And what if the director's vision was that this is a story of a couple making a painful but liberating step in honesty and closeness? There would be a problem. An actor's insistence on that choice would interfere with the director's ability to tell the story. Actor and director would need to find some commonality about such a central choice. More than "find" it, they would need to feel it — it would do no good to enforce such an important choice if the actor's feelings were in conflict with this vision.

I want to make it clear, though, that the actor and director would not need to be in agreement about how the actor gets to this central choice. A director's skill to tell the difference between the choices that need mutuality and those that are private and personal to the actor, is essential to a productive rehearsal period. If the director uses the rehearsal period to meddle with the actor's inner life, and to make him distrust his impulses because they are unlike the director's own, rehearsal will make the performances worse instead of better.

Intuition. Directors ask me, "Is it okay to stop actors during a run-through of a scene, or should I always let them run the scene all the way through?" The only answer I can give is, "Sometimes it's better to stop, and sometimes it's better to run the whole scene." Because I have lots of practice, I make these decisions by "instinct." What cues are the actors giving me that advise my unconscious mind either to cut in or to refrain from cutting in? Perhaps I detect frustration, which would make me want to jump in and find out what the problem is. Low energy might also make me want to ask them to pause and investigate. Fakery or lack of connection will almost always make me want to stop.

If, however, there are dead spots or the choices aren't working, but the actors are thinking their way through it, or want to show me something, I let them go on. The actors may need this flawed run-through to discern for themselves what is lacking. Or it might give us something to build on. Or something exciting might be about to happen that I wouldn't want to miss. The call is very subjective.

Build your case on the contributions of the actors. Directors need to bring actors along with the process. If actors are suspicious or reluctant about an idea of the director's, the director should pay attention. He should include the actors in exploration and investigate together with the actors how he came up with that idea, what associations he had, what stories it reminded him of, why he feels that it may be a central solution to the scene.

I have less success when I try to build a case *for* my ideas than when I build a case *against* a resistance or superficial idea that the actor has fallen into. For instance, if a director wants an actor to change her performance and try an opposite, the director will probably need to build a case for this adjustment. An actress in a workshop was playing a character with the objective that she wants to get rid of her sister, so she can grieve alone after the death of their mother. The scene wasn't working because she was "playing the grief" and not connecting to the other actor. The director, not wanting to criticize the actress by telling her the scene was too "heavy," asked her to "try an opposite" and "play it lighter." The actress balked. The direction "play it light" didn't fit the circumstances: the character's mother had just died and the sister had never been properly attentive to the mother. The idea of playing the scene "light" did violence to the actress' connections and associations. I stepped in and suggested the adjustment, "shame your ungrateful sister by hiding your grief and being a charming hostess to her." The performance got lighter, but still had emotional honesty at the center.

Give direction that actors can follow. Try not to tell them to do two things at once, such as, "be coy but business-like" — a direction that gives the actor no information at all, because it is vague and general. Try instead to find a through-line that incorporates both ideas ("coy" and "business-like") and makes the direction specific. For instance, "You can even flirt with him to let him know that he's dealing with someone who knows all the strategies." Or, "Distract him by flirting, so you can take him by surprise and get the better of him in this deal." You see, those are two different adjustments. Which do you want? The actor has a right to know.

A chance to stretch. If the actor disagrees with you, and you feel she could get to the place you want her to go if she made a deeper or stronger emotional commitment, then go for it. Instead of telling the actor his ideas are wrong, approach the situation as an opportunity for the actor to stretch. Let the issue be risk-taking rather than result. Let the concern be truth rather than a difference of opinion. And even if she is giving you something wonderful but you want something else, don't be shy. Just because an actor is doing something wonderful doesn't mean she can't do something else wonderful as well.

Mannerisms. Divesting an actor of a mannerism takes skill and the gift of perception, because bluntly pointing out the mannerism may simply make the actor more self-conscious, and thus aggravate the problem. A director with insight into the reason for the mannerism might be able to help. It might also help to speak in the form of permission rather than criticism — it's true, anyway, that letting go of the mannerism will not shut down the actor, but release him.

Sometimes the underlying function of a mannerism is to hide. If an actor habitually ducks his head during emotional moments, the director might say, "You don't need to duck your head; you can look her in the eye." On the other hand, sometimes the mannerism adds unneeded emphasis, as when an actor nervously repeats lines he feels are important. Again, reassurance may help: "You don't need to emphasize this. Your performance is strong enough, and the words are strong enough. You don't need to repeat this line." If the actor is bobbing his head or darting his eyes distractingly, suggest to him that he can steady his eyeline by making eye contact with the other actor.

Secrets. Keep the actors from gossiping about the characters, making bargains about the emotional life of the scene, and directing each other. Sydney Pollock advises directors to talk to the actors separately, because in real life, no one knows what other people are going to do. Mike Leigh insists on secrecy, never letting the actor know what the other actors are working on. John Cassavetes often gave actors conflicting direction. The purpose of actors having secrets from each other is not trickery or manipulation but the opportunity for actors to engage and have an effect on each other.

After reviewing several possible choices for a scene with an actor, the director can ask to run the scene, saying, "Don't tell me what choice you've made." If an actor says, "I've got something I want to work on," the director doesn't have to ask him what it is before trying it.

Praise. Don't be afraid to praise actors. Don't hold back from telling them, "You're doing great," "I love what you're coming up with," "I'm very happy with the direction we're taking." But watch out for result-oriented praise, such as, "I loved it when you gave that little smirk at the end of that line — do it again, just like that!" which can cause the actor to freeze with fear that he won't be able to duplicate that exact result.

When explaining some understanding that you want an actor to bring to the text, it can help to describe it as an insight that you're sure he could have come up with on his own. When you are not actually happy with an actor's work, you can tell him anything as long as your underlying communication is "I know you can do better." Praise can help even if the work isn't that great. Sometimes praising an actor who is on the way but not there yet can give him confidence, which relaxes him, opens him up, and improves his performance.

Build on the actor's ideas. "Something you just said…" or "Something you just did in that take (or rehearsal) gave me an idea." No matter how fully I have prepared, I always let go of my script analysis preparation and give my total attention to the actors. Ideas come to me while I am working with the actors. The ideas might be coming from the actors, or they might be coming from my earlier preparation — or they might be coming from anywhere in the universe! In any case, if my total attention is on the actors when the idea comes to me, it feels like I got it from them. The principle here is that if the ideas that I came up with in my preparation are suitable for these actors, those ideas will come back to me while I am giving the actors my attention. If my ideas are not suitable for these actors, the ideas won't come to me — which will be just as well anyway.

Plant seeds. Don't argue. It never works to make an actor wrong. There's usually no need anyway for lengthy debate when an actor disagrees with a direction you give. Just having mentioned it will have an effect. It's very likely that she will do it (or something better) a few takes later just because the idea has been planted. I find it helpful to preface something I believe deeply with the words, "Maybe I'm mistaken." (It's always true, anyway — I'm not infallible!) And to sprinkle liberally with "I just had this thought," "I'm not sure it's right," "It might not work."

Ceremony. Shirley Mills, who when she was twelve played one of the children in *The Grapes of Wrath*, recalls that director John Ford would gather the cast once a week during filming "to remind us that the Joads were no bums or hobos. They were God-fearing, decent people who were victims of circumstance." Her description made it sound like a ceremony. The director needs to be able to speak to every member of the cast and crew on the subject of what the film is about. Such expressions need to have some weight, some ceremony to them, or else people become flippant.

Privacy. The actor does not need to disclose her choices to the director or the other actors. Naturally, anything that happens in rehearsal is privileged information, not to be divulged outside of rehearsal.

Stage Directions. Although I question or cross out most stage direction, that doesn't mean the writer shouldn't have put them in — they are useful for agents, producers, and others who must read many scripts a day and need emotional short-cuts to get their gist. And it doesn't mean the director should provide actors with a version of the script expunged of stage directions. Rehearsal is a time when the director can mention to the actors, "We don't need to worry about these stage directions. We're going to find the subtext ourselves. Some of them I have crossed out in my own copy; others I have questions about. Are there any that you were wondering about?"

Trust the script. Each scene that you work on should be approached as if it is the most important scene in the film, the emotional center of the movie. Don't think about whether the scene fits into the spine. If you have done your homework deeply enough, you can trust that it will.

"Check in with me!" Get the actors to let you in. Get them engaged, even if it means having to hear them say things that aren't fun to hear. When there is a problem, ask for details. If they hesitate, say, "I need you to tell me exactly what is bothering you."

Don't oversell your ideas. When a director bounces up to an actor to tell him, "I've got the greatest idea — I know this will work!" an actor may be seized with panic that his execution of the idea won't meet the director's expectation. It's better to be casual, as in, "I thought of something that might be worth trying."

Be inventive. Sam Mendes made a tape of songs — which Annette Bening described as "sort of serious and sort of funny all at the same time" and which included Clint Black's "Desperado" and Bobby Darin's "Don't Rain on My Parade." Mendes gave copies to the cast of *American Beauty* as a way of introducing the tragicomic tone he envisioned for the film.

Rehearsal should be fun, challenging, personal. Keep the investigations idiosyncratic and imaginative, rather than plodding through "by the book." Let your energy and passion show. Let the actors have freedom. Let your rehearsal method be impressionistic rather than methodical. Don't stuff the actors with a boring list of instructions. Make a suggestion and see where it goes. Prefer surprise to perfection.

If it ain't broke, don't fix it. A director needs to be able to see and hear what's going on. The actors may already be doing just what you were about to ask them to do — be able to recognize this and leave them alone. Or they may have come up with something better. Or they may be working well even though they haven't come up with the solution yet. If a director charges in with micro-managing at times like this, any chance for trust between the actor and director will be jeopardized.

Everything you do is direction. If you look down at your notes while mumbling to the actors, that behavior is a form of direction. It communicates non-engagement, with the material and with them. This is likely to have a negative effect on their energy and commitment. In fact, your every move in front of actors during a production is a form of direction.

Step back. Stepping back is a legitimate rehearsal technique. You can't fix other people. Sometimes a director arrives at an impasse with an actor, and it just turns out to be something that's not going to get figured out until later. Sometimes taking energy off a problem gives everyone a chance to relax, let it go, and get back to work.

Don't lie. You need not pretend a direction is optional if it isn't. If a foundation of trust and communication has been built, a director can be quite brief and to the point. If time is short and an actor needs more volume, faster pace, deeper connection, stronger intention, to stand or sit on a particular line — then tell them, without circumlocution, secrets, or ceremony.

Don't ask questions if you don't want to know the answers. The purpose of the "asking questions" technique is not to trick or ambush actors. It is to get information. So no answer is wrong — it's all information, even if only about the actor's resistances or lack of preparation. If you are asking a question with the secret hope that the actor will answer it with the answer you had in mind, don't ask it. Instead just tell them what you want them to do.

Don't use any technique unless you have made it your own. An actor recently told me how irritating it was on the set when a director kept prefacing every direction with "What if...?" It was an unthinking injection of jargon that the director had clearly gotten from a book!

Everything in these rehearsal chapters are samples, not formulas. They will be helpful to you only as an incentive to further study. *You must practice these techniques in order to be able to use them confidently, productively, and safely.* You can't become a better director by following formula or lifting jargon from a book!

DANGER SIGNALS

1) The biggest danger signal is judgment. Somewhere behind any actor's resistance there is a judgment of the character. A director should always be on the lookout for judgments, ready to encourage the actor to look for ways to turn them into energy. One way to acknowledge a judgment is to say to the actor, "I'm sure this must be difficult. You probably don't know anybody like this character." Often as soon as I say that, the actor can begin to think of ways to relate to the character.

2) Be alert to signs that the chemistry among actors is unraveling. Speak to them separately — or together — and be candid. Ask them, "What seems to be the problem? Is it going to get in the way of the work?"

3) Listen for signs that actors are trying to play a result, for instance if you hear the actor lament, "I need to be really betrayed in this scene and I can't find it." Ask the actor to find a "magic as if" or substitution for the betrayal, and then to put his concentration on what he wants the other actor to feel. Assure him that you are monitoring the performance and won't stop until it is good.

4) Notice when actors are resisting being personal in their work. This is a delicate area, and confrontation is unlikely to work. First ask the actor how she sees the character — her interpretation may have not taken into account the stakes. Or, ask her how she works, how she gets to the place needed by the scene. Be inventive. Jog her imagination with images and your own personal stories. If you are personal with your work, you will be able to feel comfortable asking for personal work from actors.

5) Actors can fall into traps — such as failing to trust the choice, and instead playing the line the way they think it should be said. To an inexperienced or poorly trained actor illustrating the lines in this way feels safer, because they can control the line reading. But it's not safer. It's safer to trust the choice, and thereby illustrate the subtext rather than the line. If an actor starts "playing the lines" a director can go over the choices again, to find something the actor connects to more deeply — deeply enough to let go. If this doesn't work, you might be able to tell him to "break up the rhythms."

A similar trap — but less easy to spot — is actors thinking they must know and play the character's logic. Characters are not always logical. An idiosyncratic choice of what the character is doing emotionally will almost always cause the "logic" to fall into place.

6) Stay calm about line problems. When actors, during rehearsal, keep leaving out an important line, treat it as an invitation to explore that line more fully, to make it a "mysterious line." When an actor can't remember a line, there is probably something he doesn't understand or connect to about it. The director may be able to help him find a reality for it.

An actor I know was playing a scientist in a TV movie. The role called for a long scientific explanation that she labored over to no avail. The director and producers kept impressing on her how important it was to get the lines exact and that the scene's information was so important that it couldn't be cut or changed. She never did get it right; when I later saw the show, the scene did not work. A more sympathetic and knowledgeable director could probably have helped the situation by telling the actor that the scene was not about the words, but about the warning or the reassurance — or whatever it was — that they contained. A recognition of the intention of the lines might have helped the young actor put her concentration on her scene partner and might have freed her to say the lines she had struggled to master.

When an actor hates a line and refuses to say it, and you, as the director, don't want to change or lose it, you should communicate clearly why you like it and how it unlocks some important element of the scene or the character. Build your case, recount the stories that give it life for you. If you have rehearsal time, you can give the actor permission not to say it for now, and get back to it later. Of course if dropping or changing the line has little material effect on the scene, you should consider allowing that.

7) Don't be surprised if an actor's question turns out later to mean something different from what it seemed at the time to mean. It's not part of an actor's job to be articulate. Often their concerns are expressed in fragments, whose deeper meaning needs to be coaxed out with questions.

8) Watch for low energy. Rehearsal should be fun.

9) An actor's resistance is a lesson about human behavior — a gift, not a trial. Actors (such as Dustin Hoffman, Russell Crowe) may be called difficult when they have questions about the work. If you like acting that surprises you, then you need to be aware that not all the surprises

are going to be good ones. You need to be prepared for unpleasant surprises. You need to let yourself feel that a negative surprise is better than no surprise! If things go badly in rehearsal at first, and you go through the fire together — and get through it — that can be the best thing that can happen. That's how genuine trust comes into being. This is true in any relationship.

When an actor blows up, it's not necessarily the worst thing that can happen. Sometimes you need to stay calm and ask questions, find out exactly what is wrong. It's not always helpful to try to soothe someone who is upset; it often makes them madder. You need to find out exactly what is wrong. It might be something fixable. If the actor can't or won't be specific about what is bothering him, you can say, "I need you to tell me what is wrong. Is it something about the script? About another actor? Accommodations?" If he keeps pouting about something that seems petty, like the cable hook-up in his trailer not working, I might next ask, "Do you feel you are not being treated with respect? Is it something I've done? Do you feel I've been unfair, or inattentive, or made wrong decisions?"

Of course you must be ready to hear honest answers to such questions, and to listen carefully, ready to face the truth. Sometimes you need to meet an over-emotional person at his own emotional level. Trying to pretend you are not frustrated by the situation is unlikely to help. If you are able to let your anger and frustration show without punishing or berating the other person, it may shift the energy of the situation in a productive way.

Sometimes it's best simply to walk away, take a time-out, as Jim Brooks did on the set of *As Good As It Gets*, an incident described in the last chapter. Sometimes you can ask, "Can we continue to work for now and make an appointment to discuss this later?"

It can be challenging and even stressful to work with creative people. Actors can be temperamental, and sometimes they are testing you to find out if you are strong enough to handle them and be in charge of the movie set and the storytelling. Don't give up. Don't abandon the actors emotionally. When things get tough, hang in there. You can even say it: "I haven't given up!"

SPENDING TIME WILL SAVE YOU TIME
"When a light bulb has burned out, you take time to change it. If an actor is burning out, why not take ten minutes?"
— Francis Ford Coppola

Karen Black, speaking of *Five Easy Pieces*, said, "I think one of the main reasons we were all so good in this picture was because Bob Rafelson gave us the time to be good. If the director has [time] limitations, you can feel it and that will affect your performance. I remember Bob spending an hour on the side of a road with me discussing whether or not my character would say [a certain] single line at the end of the film."

There are no short cuts, not really. I like to use the metaphor of learning a new piece on the piano. Even a very experienced pianist learns a new piece by slowing it way down. The pianist would never try to learn by playing it over and over again at the pace at which it is supposed to be performed. She would play each note very slowly — more slowly than she needs to — in order first to learn the fingering, then to allow the subtext to emerge. Allowing the subtext to emerge is what makes her able to play with feeling.

Someone asked me what to do with an actor in a small role who takes up a lot of time. Give him fifteen minutes of uninterrupted attention and then he probably will relax and leave you alone. This is an example of how spending time will save you time.

Slowing down in the beginning will help you go fast on the set. If you spend the time in the early stages to give people deep attention, to make them feel there is nothing more important in the world than they are at that moment — then, later, when you're under the gun and you have to tell them you need them not to dawdle, they'll be willing to help you out, even sacrifice for you. If you communicate to people that there is all the time in the world, you'll get more done. And then when you genuinely do run out of time, they will help you out because you haven't been crying wolf all along.

If you are a young filmmaker, you are probably blessed with more time than money. You're in luck. Because when it comes to rehearsal and learning how to rehearse, time is more valuable than money. Meet actors; hang out with them; form workshops; direct theater; make short films; learn rehearsal techniques together. The most important advice I can give a filmmaker who has no money is this: If you don't have money, spend time.

WHAT SOME DIRECTORS DO
This is an eclectic collection of quotes and information from interviews I've come across.

Steven Soderberg (interviewed after *Out of Sight*): "I try not to ask actors how they like to work, I try to find out, and that's where rehearsals come in. I try to have a week to ten days of rehearsal, which is really for me, not for them. It's for me to watch them, and get a sense of how they like to be treated, how to communicate with them so that I don't have to figure it out on the set, where I'm not as patient. All the actors are different so you have to treat them accordingly."

John Boorman usually rehearses three weeks, in the afternoons; then he has mornings for the other preparations for the movie. After rehearsal he does a final draft of the script. He only shoots what is in the shot, has a very low film ratio, and uses no improvisation on the set.

Gus Van Sant says improvisation was used extensively in rehearsals for *Good Will Hunting*, and continued while shooting the film. "These guys had lived with these characters for so long and were so immersed in the project that they actually became the people they portrayed." What he means by actors "becoming" the characters they portray is that they become able to improvise subtext with absolute confidence. This confidence gave them the freedom to follow direction; Van Sant says that Matt Daman and Ben Affleck said to him, "You're the director; we'll do whatever you want us to do. We're totally in your hands."

An observer on the set of *The Thin Red Line* reported that **Terrence Malick** limits himself to such comments as, "Take a pause," "Look over at the river," and "Let's do another one." He was also described as loving "scenes going wrong." He lets actors do take after take until their own loss of control becomes the character's.

David Gordon Green: "I definitely want to be 100% satisfied with the page when I'm going into it. I want to know that I believe in the structure, where the film is going and the organic flow of it. But you never know until you get the actors in the room." He rehearses, improvises, rewrites for the actors, even just before shooting a scene.

Jack Nicholson said that **Alexander Payne** doesn't rehearse or change any lines, but "he always takes the actor aside and tells them a little thing and there's a lot of it. There's not a lot of conceptual arguments but a lot of tuning."

Steven Spielberg begins rehearsal on the set by telling actors just to perform the scene any way they want.

A screenwriter described **Stephen Frears'** method thus: First he hashes out, with the writer and producer, in excruciating detail, every nuance of the script. Then, "He walks on the set and says to the actors, 'How do you want to do this?' And the actors come up with all sorts of ideas. He vetoes some, accepts some, and then turns to the cameraman and say, 'Can we accommodate this? Great, let's go.'"

Woody Allen: "All I ask for in an actor is believability. So all I say to them on the set is, 'talk faster,' 'do less,' or 'try to be more believable.'"

Phil Kaufman shot *Quills* in sequence.

Lawrence Kasdan had intense rehearsal for *Body Heat*. He had a month of rehearsal for *The Big Chill*; he wanted the group to get really comfortable with each other. Nowadays he schedules an intense week, with the material, not interrupted by wardrobe and makeup tests. He says he is not looking for performances to be nailed down, but likes to do exploratory work without the pressure of a crew waiting. He asks the actors what's going on, and "makes the connections."

Teresa Wright, who worked with **William Wyler** and **Alfred Hitchcock** in the 1940s and with **Francis Coppola** in 1996 says all three rehearsed a lot, "and the difference from others that did not rehearse as much is quite obvious to me."

For *The Wrong Man*, **Hitchcock** worked privately for a week with Vera Miles, to get her to connect simply and honestly to the emotional life of the wife of an ordinary man suddenly accused of a crime.

Barry Levinson doesn't like to rehearse. But, an actor himself, he takes responsibility for the consequences; that is, he lets the actors do what they want in order to stay completely confident and fresh.

Todd Solondz doesn't rehearse.

Paul Verhoeven on directing sex scenes: "I am extremely open, extremely direct about what I want to see. I tap into my own life — 'This is what this woman did that was so special. Let's try to use that.' And so the element of hypocrisy is gone. I want to discuss this all before, sitting in the trailer. There should be no discussion on the set when people take their clothes off."

Michael Mann likes to rehearse. "I've found it frees me up and frees the actors, so it's more fluid when we shoot." He finds he is able to cut dialogue, as the work becomes more physical. He writes "phantom dialogue" for the actors to use as subtext during rehearsal.

Says **Vondie Curtis-Hall** about rehearsal, "That's how I prefer to work. Then I can really create an environment where the actor feels totally safe."

Richard Linklater has three weeks rehearsal on every movie. "I like actors. I think a lot of directors don't like actors. To me an ideal day would be spent working on a script rehearsing."

Gina Prince-Bythewood: In the first days of rehearsal, she simply observes, and then she and the actors share personal stories to begin the bonding process.

Steve Buscemi: "The way that I like to work is always to see what the actors are going to do first before I say anything, and then take it from there."

Ingmar Bergman: "When I work, it's not important what I'm saying, it's the contact. A good actor is very physical. I can talk to his body, and I know before he knows if his body-mind accepts or doesn't accept what I want. I feel it in my body. To force an actor to do something is silly."

Cuba Gooding says that director **John Singleton** had over two weeks of rehearsal for *Boyz N the Hood*.

Barry Sonnenfeld: "I think the only directions I've ever given are either 'flatter' or 'faster.'"

Mike Figgis: "I am not interested in actors who don't need me. I spend a lot of time talking to them, getting to know them, and loosely discussing the story." He lets actors improvise or not depending on what they like to do.

Robert Duvall, on directing *The Apostle*: "I directed the non-actors in the same way that I did the actors. I stressed to the actors, 'We don't have to get anywhere in the scene. Treat it like a line rehearsal. Just very easy. See where it goes.'"

Sidney Lumet says he doesn't analyze the actors, nor "play the father role." He gets it through technique, through "being a good director," by which I think he means his expertise in creating emotional structure and blocking.

TEACHING ACTING ON THE SET

Lumet says that if an actor doesn't have an acting technique, he teaches them how to play intentions. "I would teach them what we call getting it down to a verb — so that you can *do* something. Don't leave it up here [tapping head]. It's not what you think, it's what you *do* that creates a performance." Ang Lee, in his early movies *The Wedding Banquet* and *Eat Drink Man Woman*, was working with semi-professionals, and put some of them through rigorous acting lessons. Winston Chao called him "stern as a schoolmaster."

Directors Sidney Lumet and Ang Lee, with lots of experience both in acting and in directing theater, as well as passionate belief in their own projects and their own abilities, and high tolerances for confrontation, can get away with teaching acting on the set. I don't recommend it for most directors. If you are working with non-actors, the best advice I can give you is, "Don't ask a non-actor to act."

But if you are going to teach acting on the set, you should stick to one technique, such as verbs (intentions, objectives), or listening, or the "it's like when...," or the "magic as if..."

Improvs and certain rehearsal warm-up techniques may border on having an "acting class" feel to them. For instance, I was present at a rehearsal of a scene in which an older character was mentoring a younger woman. The suggestion was made to try the adjustment "as if" she were talking to her own self at nineteen. The actress loved the idea, but when she tried it, it didn't seem to work. So I suggested she take the time to recall and visualize her face and appearance at nineteen, to recall the enthusiasms and follies of her younger self, and, while face to face with the younger actress, to speak out loud to her younger self for a few moments. And then go into the lines of the scene. This resulted in a very expressive and poignant scene. For a scene in which characters are belittling each other, such as the *Short Cuts* scene between Julianne Moore and Matthew Modine, there could be a warm-up exercise in which the actors take turns belittling each other.

Some actors will balk at such exercises, and feel that a director who suggests them is treating them as if they are not professional. For me it has nothing to do with "professional" or "not professional" — it has only to do with my personal observation that acting is less a mental activity than a physical one. A director who is unsure of whether to try such exercises can always ask the actors how they feel about it.

HOW TO GET REHEARSAL

According to Eric Stoltz, "Most actors would leap at the opportunity to get together [and rehearse] before the pressure is on, even if we aren't getting paid for it. Because the more we know before filming begins, the better prepared we all are, and the better the work is." Actually it's not always that easy to get actors to rehearse. Many actors need to be talked into rehearsal. They need proof that it will be useful. In order to be given rehearsal time by the producers and the actors themselves, you must prove that you can use it efficiently.

If you are confident about rehearsing, one way to talk actors into rehearsing might be to tell them, "On the set I'll have so many distractions; I'll be able to be more focused on you if we have some separate rehearsal." Then you have to find the time for it, and make that a consecrated time and space. Director David Gordon Green finds one way he assures himself time for rehearsal is by always hiring friends to be his crew. That way, "I don't have to look over everyone's shoulder all the time. I can spend more time working with the actors and concentrating on the things it takes to bring everything together."

But I want to mention here again that I don't recommend that directors ask for rehearsal if they have never rehearsed before with professional actors. Rehearsal will make things worse if the unskilled director enforces ideas, talks too much, or lacks vision. In all things, self-knowledge and honesty are your best protection.

20 | SCENE SHAPING

"You have to have come from either live television or the theater to know how to use [rehearsal] well, because you have to know how to block a scene."

— Sidney Lumet

"If I can cast the right people and figure out the things they should be doing in the scene, they don't have to do anything but show up. Nobody has to act."

— Mike Nichols

EMOTIONAL AND PHYSICAL STRUCTURE

During script analysis, a director should have come up with a vision of the emotional structure of each scene — its central emotional event, its individual events and beats, and ideas for the through-lines of the characters. She should, in addition, have considered the setting and objects of each scene, and come up with ideas for movement and activities for the actors. These movements and activities — the physical structure of the scene — should be connected to the emotional structure of the scene.

Certain movement, objects, and activities are embedded in the script. For example, in the *Tender Mercies* scene, Rosa Lee speaks of making soup for Mac. If the scene begins with her in the living room or bedroom, she must move to the kitchen to prepare his soup. Later she mentions a poster which the young musicians left with her. Mac at some point in the scene fetches his sheet music and guitar.

There are still many choices to be made. In connection with the soup preparation, for instance — which drawers or cabinets contain the pan, the spoon, the bowl? And the soup itself — canned (on a shelf), or leftover home cooked (in the fridge)? Is the poster laid out on the kitchen table, or folded up in the living room? When and how do the characters handle the objects? Where do they move and why?

The script gives us some suggestions, in the form of stage directions. For instance, the script says that Rosa Lee is in bed when the scene begins. I usually read a script a number of times without looking at the stage directions at all. Then I go back and read the scene with the stage directions. Reading this particular scene without the stage directions caused me to envision her reclining on the living room couch covered with a throw. The association for me was this: If I were alone, late at night, waiting for news, I might not be able to bring myself to get under the covers of a bed — it would feel like I was giving up. A television is mentioned during the dialogue. Is it possible that she has kept it on, for company, perhaps with the sound muted? I have done that when I was lonely and frightened. Might Mac turn it off for her when he comes in?

On the other hand, maybe getting into bed is an important detail of her character. She has a young child. Routine and normalcy are important for children. Sonny might worry if he got up in the night and found his mother on the couch instead of in bed. Her concern to prevent his anxiety might have prompted her to brush her teeth, wash her face, put on a nightgown, and climb into bed at her usual hour — even if she will only lie there awake all night.

Such physical details create texture of life. They also carry emotional weight. They flesh out the subtext story that the filmmaker is telling. They are physical hooks for the emotional life. They must be imagined *actively*, with the same detail and responsibility as ideas about the emotional life of the scenes and the characters. They are helpful ways to give direction to the actors — more helpful than most intellectual discussion. Does Mac eat the soup Rosa Lee prepares, or does it sit in the bowl while the two of them study the sheet music together?

What if the director envisions the opening of this scene one way, and the actress another? Rehearsal is precisely the opportunity for conflicting ideas to be brought into harmony. The actor can have the chance to try out ways to bring her own inner life to the blocking ideas of the director. The director can have a chance to see the actor's ideas acted out, and come up with ways to incorporate them. One thing I am certain of is that the director is going to be better prepared to handle such a disagreement if he has anticipated ahead of time that both ideas are plausible and legitimate. Don't forget that actors are by nature suggestible. If a new idea — even one opposite to the one they feel committed to — is presented to them with persuasive emotional detail, they may later actually forget that they themselves were not the ones to think of it.

The details of a kitchen say a lot about a family's economic class, as well as taste and interests. What does Rosa Lee's kitchen look like? What does the poster look like? How and where is Mac's sheet music stored? The production designer will of course be involved in such decisions, but the imagining of this family's domestic and creative life must go beyond the execution of a set design. In other words, the purpose of set decoration is not decorative. The props and furniture are part of the characters' lives and they affect the events of their lives.

The director should imagine the physical world of the story as a function of its emotional life. Besides being excellent preparation for directing the actors, this will lead a director to a blocking plan, a shot list, and the storyboards.

THE BLOCKING PLAN

A blocking plan is a three-dimensional vision of the movement and activities of a scene. The notes for a "blocking plan" are usually sketched out from an aerial view. It's different from a storyboard, which is the view from the camera's view-finder. Storyboards should only be created in conjunction with a blocking plan. In other words, the director's idea of what shall be seen through the view-finder and on the screen must bear a relation to the way the human event would take place in three-dimensional reality. Directors whose entire preparation consists of storyboarding will, when they get to the set, have few, if any, ideas about the blocking of a scene except to move the actors around like furniture to fit the plan for the view-finder.

The reason why actors get excited about working with a theater director is that they want to be directed by someone who knows how to structure a story in dramatic terms. "Scene-shaping" is the most serious casualty in the loss of the art of rehearsal. Scene shaping, once thought of as the director's most important skill, is now usually left to the editing room or — worse — the sound track. The proper time to begin scene-shaping is in rehearsal. Continued work on the shape of a scene can still be done on the set, in the editing room, and with the music. But movies will be so much better if the work of scene shaping is begun in rehearsal.

It is crucial to have a blocking plan for episodic television, or any time when a director must work very quickly. Of course a blocking plan is necessary for any scene for which you wish to shoot a "master shot." Without a plan for blocking the scene and shaping its emotional action, any master shot will be unusable. But even if your shot list does not include shooting a full master, you will be a better director if you know how to stage a master. Even if you edit "in the camera" and only shoot snippets at a time, you will benefit hugely from developing the ability to stage and rehearse a scene as a master shot.

The lack of ability to stage and rehearse a scene as a master shot puts a director automatically in "damage control" mode with respect to his shot list. It leads directors into tedious and unnecessary "coverage" of every conceivable angle. Directors who opt for excessive coverage — as well as the producers and executives who insist on it — think that by doing so they are keeping open their options for shaping the scene in the editing room. Actually they are limiting their options. The panic-stricken attempt to cover every possible angle is more likely than not to result in finding oneself in the edit room missing the crucial story-telling footage. A fully imagined subtext story that brings to life the emotional and physical events of the script is your best protection. Otherwise, you are preparing to produce a generic style of miscellaneous shot compositions and talking heads.

WHERE TO GET IDEAS FOR BLOCKING AND MOVEMENT

How do you come up with ideas for blocking? For example, the *Clerks* scene gives Randal some activities (eating his snacks, reading his newspaper), but none to Dante. So choices can be made. Such choices will affect the emotional content of the scene. For instance, Dante could still be collecting debris (left from an earlier incident in the script) from the floor, counter, among the merchandise, or other, less likely places. On the other hand, he could sit or stand behind the counter. Either way — whether he remains stationary in his customary pose, or whether he moves about, cleaning up — will be an expression of his relationship to his station and responsibilities at the store. If he does remain behind the counter, does he look off into space while reminiscing about Caitlin? Or is he focused on Randal? Does he wish he could distract Randal's attention from the newspaper? (A possible objective.)

Ideas for blocking come, of course, from real life. For instance, a scene presented in a workshop depicted a waitress snappishly confronting a customer. The director had staged the scene so that the actress playing the waitress had some business (activity) at the customer's table, then stood still to deliver her line, then walked back to her station. I suggested that the waitress should speak her first line while arranging the items on the table, and her second line while walking away.

I had two reasons for this suggestion. One reason was my recollection from my own waitress days that negative remarks were more likely to be muttered while walking away than to be delivered directly to the offending customer. The other reason was aesthetic. To me it is more satisfying theatrically when actors deliver lines in the middle of activities and movement, rather than when they move, deliver the line, then move again.

One way for a director to develop an aesthetic sense of these matters is to study films. You should look not just at the framing, but at the movement beyond the framing. For example, Elia Kazan's *On the Waterfront* barroom scene, shot in one long take, is well worth studying. Mike Nichols says he learned how to shape scenes for the camera by watching *A Place in the Sun*, over and over. Director Arthur Penn says the shooting plan for the last scene of *Bonnie and Clyde* came to him all at once in a flash of intuition. It is a simple series of human events, culminating in the central emotional event — the last look exchanged between the two protagonists.

It is also useful to study the staging of theater productions. Good theater staging is a stylized version of real life movement — that is, it is based on real life movement, but more concentrated. The characters' need to move has been simplified to its essence — or "gesture." The choreography of Jerome Robbins is a perfect example — he could make dancing look like walking, only more beautiful. As Rita Moreno (*West Side Story*) says, Robbins "choreographed for characters, not for dancers." Wynn Handman, teacher, director, and founder of the American Place Theatre, had this advice — study the paintings of the Great Masters room of the Metropolitan Museum of Art.

My own way of imagining is more kinesthetic than visual, so I often figure out the blocking by walking around the set, speaking the lines as I move, playing all the roles myself.

DOMESTIC EVENT

It is in contemplating ideas for blocking that the concept of "domestic event" comes in handy. The "domestic event" anchors the emotional events in a physical world, and gives a scene "texture of life." For example, in the *sex, lies, and videotape* scene, the characters are eating dinner together. A myriad of details — passing serving plates, pouring wine, buttering bread, clearing plates — can easily be included. Such "domestic" details can illustrate and punctuate the emotional details of the scene.

It's interesting to me that in the published screenplay, Graham rises to help Ann clear the table, whereas in the produced movie, Graham remains seated at the table, looking at his place setting during the "liars and lawyers" confrontation with John. I can't think of any technical necessity that could have impelled this change. It had to come out of exploration that writer-director Soderbergh conducted with the actors.

Soderbergh's interest in and responsiveness to actors' input is surely a major ingredient in his considerable achievements.

"CREW REHEARSAL"
The technical aspects of filmmaking are less difficult for actors if they are connected to the emotional center of their character and the scene. As Meryl Streep has said, "I know I can't make a wrong move if I hold on to knowing what I know is true, what I know is real for me."

Most movie rehearsal is really "crew rehearsal"; its only purpose is to give the technicians their marks and allow them to practice them. The actor is expected to make his words and activities work around the technology. The emotional life of the scene becomes secondary to the technology rather than organic to it. This mechanical approach can be injurious to the intuitive gifts that, now that the camera is about to roll, the actor is most in need of.

THE TOOLS OF SCENE-SHAPING
The tools of scene-shaping are the through-lines of each character, the beats of the scene, and the emotional events — especially the central event. A straightforward approach is to have the character *objectives* define the through-line of the scene, with changes of *intention* (verb) marking the beat changes. It helps the audience follow the story if the transitions (beat changes) are punctuated by emotional movement (change of intention) as well as physical movement (blocking).

For this basic structuring, the actors make choices of their objectives — what each one wants the other character to do or feel. The different intentions that they use to try to get what they want are called by some actors "tactics" or "strategies." Changes of tactics are marked by physical movement. Locating the emotional transitions in physical movements and activities helps the actors keep their transitions simple, real, and fresh.

ORGANIC BLOCKING
Once I get to rehearsal, even though I am prepared with blocking plans, new ideas for blocking — and emotional life — inevitably come out of watching the actors' body language — as well as hearing the actors speak the lines. Often my ideas change completely once I have real physical people right in front of me. This doesn't mean the preparation was wasted. The purpose of preparation is to make me ready for my best ideas to hit in the moment — that is, to make me ready for my intuition to strike.

During a DGA question-and-answer session, Steven Spielberg, responding to the idea of letting the actors create blocking in rehearsal, said that if you let the actors move wherever they want to, they will stand still — even for seven pages of dialogue. The actors-on-couches phenomenon! Yes, actors during rehearsal will often dive for a couch — or other comfort zone. A director who wants to find an actor's true impulses must draw them out. Improvisation can sometimes do this. When actors improvise the scene, or a parallel scene, un-self-consciously, they tap into the intelligence of their bodies, the intelligence of their unconscious connections and associations, in other words, their intuition. The director can steal these intuitions to provide blocking ideas.

Silent improvs can be especially helpful in suggesting ways to create natural movement in a space. The improv can be set up around the pertinent emotional facts — or around the needs of the characters — or around the central emotional event. The director and actors create a physical space. Then the actors live in that space, with those facts, or needs, or event — without speaking. (This also means without using any substitutes for speech, such as gesturing.)

In order for improvisations or other contributions from the actors to be useful, the director must be on the lookout for "actor movement" — that is, theatricalized rather than human versions of walking, sitting, etc. — unless, of course, the character is also an actor.

USING OBJECTS (PROPS) IN REHEARSAL

Let's imagine a scene in which one character is bandaging another character's leg, which has been bitten by a dog. The bandaging is bound to be an element of the emotional relationship. Bringing a bandage or strip of fabric to rehearsal would be very useful. But it might be equally useful to explore the emotional event of one character "taking care of" the other via a metaphor for the activity, such as giving a back rub. If, on the other hand, the proficiency of the bandaging is central to the scene, drilling the bandaging technique might be the most productive use of rehearsal. If the bandaging is supposed to convey both technical proficiency and emotional relationship, it might be a good idea to work on one element at a time — an example of working in layers.

CONNECT PHYSICAL MOVEMENT TO EMOTIONAL EVENTS

A physical direction that goes to the heart of a situation or relationship is the best kind of direction. It is possible to get bogged down in endless discussion about, for example, the nature of two characters' friendship. Sometimes the solution can be found by asking the question: "In the home of this friend, could you put your feet up on the couch?" Then position the actor with feet up — or down — depending on the choice.

The goal is to create movement and position that gives the relationships a sense of predicament. Michael Mann said the awkward placement of a chair during the first meeting between Lowell Bergman (Al Pacino) and Jeffrey Wigand (Russell Crowe) in *The Insider* was critical to the relationship as well as the character development of Wigand.

Physical direction can be a great way to keep from giving the actor an emotional result. For instance, instead of telling the actor her character is depressed, you might say, "Let's try having you slump in your seat when you get this news." Or, "I'd like to begin this scene with you holding your head in your hands. Don't look up until you have to."

Making choices about when — or whether — the characters are looking at each other can be the emotional key to a scene. One character could be looking at the other, who is looking away. The first character could even have the objective "to get him to meet my gaze."

MOVEMENT IN ACTORS

Many actors connect with their best energy — and thus their best performance — when playing characters who move a lot. Examples: Leonardo DiCaprio in *What's Eating Gilbert Grape*; James Dean in *East of Eden*; Marlon Brando in *Streetcar Named Desire*; Kevin Kostner in *Silverado*; Brad Pitt in *Thelma and Louise*; Debra Winger in *Officer and a Gentleman*; Julia Roberts in *Pretty Woman* and *Erin Brockovich*; Jessica Lange in *Blue Sky*; Marilyn Monroe in *The Misfits*. On the other hand, David Duchovny and Gillian Anderson of *The X-Files* were masters of expression with almost no movement whatever. A director can help his own project tremendously by noticing whether an actor does his best work with lots of movement or with little movement, and allowing the characters to be portrayed the way that gives the actor his best energy. For example, Jessica Lange's character in *Tootsie* could have been either a woman who moves a lot or a woman who moves a little — since Lange was playing her, it made sense for the director to see her as a character who moves a lot.

PACING
"You don't necessarily get pace out of fast cutting."

— John Boorman

"I would say 95% of all the direction I've ever given is to say faster."
— Barry Sonnenfeld

The current vogue is for faster and faster cutting. Somehow the notion has taken hold that the only way to create pace is in the editing. This is not true. Many quick-cut movies seem unbearably slow to me — this is because, in spite of the fast cutting, *nothing has happened* on an emotional level. Pace, tempo rhythm, and timing should be rooted in the human events happening between the characters.

Rehearsal rhythm is slower than performance rhythm. Rehearsal is precisely an opportunity to slow down enough to allow subtext to emerge. But eventually the pace has to be tightened up. This tightening up may occur naturally, as the cast gains confidence and freedom. But if it doesn't, a director can say, "I think it has become artificially slow. I think your impulses are to go a little faster. It's stuck in rehearsal rhythm."

Another way to tighten the pace is to take out the "actor pauses." A good director has developed the ability to tell the difference between story pauses and actor pauses. Story pauses — that is, silences during which an emotional event takes place, or texture of life is created — are great. But actor pauses — such as may occur when an actor waits out a pause that has worked before but has lost its emotional content, or when the actor has made an empty, intellectualized decision that "the character would pause" at this moment — are a mark of amateur filmmaking (also soap operas and bad mini series). Don't indulge the actors in actor pauses. Take them out. Sometimes a director can simply say, "Let's tighten it up here. We've got some pauses that used to work but aren't working any longer." But sometimes the director has to take out the actor pauses one by one, finding a separate reason for each take-out.

A way to take out actor pauses is to request that the actors "pick up cues." This means asking the actors to take out the moments in which they wind up for their delivery, in which they get ready to say the line. "Taking out punctuation" is another way to describe this. The reason why picking up cues will make performances more natural and fresh is that in real life we often begin forming our response to another's speech while the other is still speaking.

One advantage to a brisk pace is that the actors can't watch and monitor their performances — they must let go and surrender to the moment. If you want the actors to go faster, you must have more substantive rehearsal than the brief "crew" rehearsal preparatory to setting the lighting. Many actors don't begin learning lines for a scene until during or after rehearsal. A substantive rehearsal can create the safety, connection, and authority among the cast to allow them to pick up cues and pick up pace. Without such rehearsal to explore and develop this authority and connection, it will be nearly impossible to get the actors to pick up the pace on the set.

Objectives help pacing. For instance, if you want the actors to speak quickly and cut each other off, their characters need a reason to be excited enough to do so. Don't get mired in arguments about pace, i.e., when one person declares the scene should be fast, and the other insists it should be slow. Instead talk about the objective.

Improv helps pacing, too. When actors improvise a certain event, it gives them reassurance that that event can take place simply and with dispatch, and without watching their own performance. Volume can also help pace. Speaking more loudly helps give the actor energy. Volume problems are usually really engagement problems.

Especially for comedy, "faster and louder" is always good. It keeps actors from hovering over their performances, and getting too precious with their dramatic moments. If you want it faster, find a human reason. For instance, the characters might be late for an appointment. Or it could be part of the characterizations. Mike Nichols says that *Postcards from the Edge* — while it looks like improv — was all scripted by writer Carrie Fisher. It was in rehearsal that Nichols and the actors determined that *Postcards* was a story about people who talk at the same time. The overlapping of the delivery makes the dialogue seem improvised. Of course you have to get your crew and editing team on board. Peter Berg, who wanted overlapped dialogue for *Very Bad Things*, said, "It's hard to record four guys talking at the same time. It's hard to edit scenes where two guys are talking at the same time and there's improvisation. It's anathema to the crew. But it's much better for the actors."

Actors are routinely told they must pause artificially between every line, in order to increase editing and mixing options. A number of editors have told me this is simply not true. Deliberately leaving spaces between every line *limits* your options, because you are thus locked in to making those cuts after every line of dialogue, ensuring that every scene will play as a series of talking heads.

Not all scenes should have a fast pace, of course. In order for a slow-paced scene to work, its subtext must create the excitement that fast pacing is meant to give. In other words, the actors must be totally in the moment, alive to their sensory life and physical surroundings, with honest feelings, and simple, committed choices.

CREATING THE PICTURE

Staging (which includes choosing the furniture in the room) will have an impact on tone and style. For example, Benjamin's first conversation with Mrs. Robinson in *The Graduate*, in which she asks him to give her a ride home from his parents' party, takes place in his bedroom; she enters claiming to think it was the door to the bathroom. The domestic event is a conversation between a man and an older woman that takes place in a bedroom. This is already a loaded event, but wait — it is a conversation in a bedroom *with a fish tank in it*. The fish tank changes everything; it creates a *tone* — of absurdity? The placement of the fish tank (in the foreground) adds to the comic exaggeration.

The activities of the characters can serve to advance the plot and reveal character. They can also create atmosphere, tone, and pace. An example of a directorial decision that impinges on style is whether to have the events — e.g., confrontations, confessions, seductions, etc. — happen while characters are planted face to face, or while they are engaged in activities.

Choices of activity can at times even serve artistry — as during the scene in *Taxi Driver* when Harvey Keitel, dancing with Jodi Foster, soothes her into staying with him. Or the last, long shot of the brothers sharing breakfast in *Big Night*. These stagings distill commonplace activity into concentrated and revelatory meaning. It's like very good writing.

Sometimes people are surprised to find that my list of top favorite movies can include a film like *I Never Sang for My Father*, with great performances but ordinary camera choices, as well as the work of major visual masters such as Terrence Malick, Carl Dreyer, and Terence Davies. Terrence Malick has said, "An image is not a pretty picture but something that should pierce one through like an arrow and speak in a language all its own." For directors (like Malick, Dreyer, and Davies) who are visual poets, the physical elements are emotional elements at exactly the same moment. Again, this is like the best writing. Shakespeare chose his words for their physical sound and their emotional meaning — equally. "Make me a willow cabin by your gate/And call upon my soul within the house" is unbearably beautiful to say out loud — its meaning and feeling mesh exactly with the sounds of the words. Visual artists can achieve the confluence of meaning and picture too — if they operate at the feeling level.

Once a student countered my suggestion that film directors can learn a lot by directing theater, with this objection: "There are things you can't show in theater. If a character pulls a ring out of his pocket to give to a girl, the audience can't see it unless you over-exaggerate it." I don't agree. The gift of a ring is an emotional event. Film has a technical advantage over theater — an insert of the ring can be shown to the audience. But filming an insert of the ring does not make the couple engaged. The emotional event — that a boy proposes and a girl accepts — must take place between the two actors. If these events *happen*, the audience will "see" the ring even from the last row of the last balcony — or even if the shot is pulled way back, with no insert.

Extend your visual vocabulary to include more master shots, wide shots, two shots. They give the emotional events a singular immediacy. My personal preference as an audience is to see the characters in their surroundings and in their relationships. (To me the insert of the ring is usually an annoying distraction from the real story, which is in the actors' faces.) Plus, I like to make my own choices of what to look at. (So naturally I loved the split-screen, multiple-camera technology of *Timecode*.)

The only reason to use two-shots sparingly is that they have almost too much power. The directorial choice is that certain events are so crucial that the audience should live through them in real time. The two-shot of Brenda Blethyn and Marianne Jean-Baptiste (*Secrets and Lies*) in which their relationship is revealed has so much more power because it happens in real time (the two-shot) rather than in movie time (alternating close-ups). It's the scene being referred to whenever anyone speaks of "*that scene*." The same is true of the two-shot of Billy Crudup and Jennifer Connelly sitting side-by-side on the subway in *Waking the Dead*.

21 | REHEARSAL SCENARIOS

"Sometimes even just two hours a day for a week is enormously beneficial, and will save you precious time and money in the long run. Even if you just sit in a room and answer the actors' questions about the scene, getting that out of the way before you have a hundred crewmembers standing around is helpful. Even if on the day you end up changing what you came up with in rehearsal, the time you spent rehearsing is not wasted. At the very least it gives you a knowledge of who the people are that you're working with, what their sense of humor is and what pisses them off."

— Eric Stoltz

A SIMPLE MODEL FOR A ONE-HOUR-PER-SCENE REHEARSAL

My rehearsal goals are simple — make it real, scene by scene, section by section, event by event. My methods vary a good deal, depending on the script — and the actors — I am dealing with. With regard to the script, my responsibility is to locate the subtext clues and use them to bring to life a physical and emotional reality that the actors can live in and the camera can photograph. With regard to the actors, I function as a whittler more than as a molder — I tend to carve away whatever is not the performance, rather than try to fashion the performances into any particular shape.

At a typical session, actors read the whole scene, slowly, with eye contact. If they are listening to each other and following impulses, I thank them and praise them. If they are pushing or fake, I start asking questions to find out what judgments or preconceptions they have about the role and the script. I mention facts and suggest adjustments that allow alternative interpretations.

Before we get into substantive work on the script, I might engage the actors in simple exercises that bring them below the social mask with each other. Pretty soon we begin to consider choices. I use a two step approach to considering choices: first, open-ended questions to establish ambiguity — eliciting facts, issues, and mysterious lines — firing off questions, riffing with possible answers, free-associating. Once there are a whole lot of ideas and possibilities on the table, we start making some choices.

This is the work of imagining the details of the lives of the characters — which involves adding complexity at the same time as clarifying and simplifying. Always we tap into our personal associations and connections in order to understand and activate the behavior of the characters. Sometimes I push the actors, and sometimes I leave them alone to figure things out themselves. Sometimes I work more extensively with one actor than the other. I encourage each actor to focus on only his own character's needs and concerns, rather than on what any other actor's performance should be or even what the scene should accomplish.

Along the way I deflect their attention from result-oriented ideas, perhaps by saying, "Well, maybe. It might go that way. Or might it not end up such-and-such other way?" Or I may openly question the idea: "What makes you think that?" Anytime they come up with something insightful, specific, or playable, I respond positively, whether or not it matches the ideas I had come up with myself. If their ideas for choices are very different from mine, I might mention that my own thinking and associations had taken me in a different direction, and then we might do some investigations into their and my associations. I may supply some information that has come from my research. I will usually tell stories. Sometimes I wait to suggest my idea later. If their idea is working, my idea may never come up.

We're looking for a choice they can try "on their feet." I like to spend more time "doing" than talking. As soon as we come up with a candidate for a character's through-line, or an understanding that might deepen or illuminate some moment, I say, "Let's try it." After we try a particular choice, I ask them how it felt, and if it gave them any other thoughts. I'm not, however, expecting to find out from their response whether the choice worked or not. It's up to me, as the director, to be able to tell whether we're on the right track or not. The choice that is on the right track is the one that creates engagement between the actors. I want to get at the human relationships and make it a scene about people.

I am constantly listening to the actors' subtext, in two ways: 1) the subtext of the script as it comes to life during the work; and 2) the subtext of their conversation with me and their unexpressed impulses and resistances. I am also paying close attention to their body language. I let their body language tell me when it is time to start adding movement. If they are moving around with the script in their hands, and it looks artificial or forced, I ask them to go through the lines sitting. If they have been sitting and they start to look restless or stuck, I get them moving.

At the time that we start adding movement, we add activities, also called "business." From then on, the emotional life and physical life of the scene are intertwined. And the style and tone of the piece come into play. For stylized material or characters, such as science fiction or period drama, the physical parameters of the stylized world are explored and practiced. For comedy, jokes are developed and set up.

For me, most rehearsal sessions include some improvisation. But I don't plan them ahead of time. I think them up on the spot, whenever I feel it might help the actors tap into the reality of a through-line, beat, or moment. In any case I will probably ask them to work without holding the script as soon as possible. I like to create the notion that it's not about the paper, but about the relationships, the events.

Whether to concentrate on separate beats (sections) or to keep running the whole scene depends to some degree on the nature of the scene, but mostly on what I see in the actors' work. Usually I go back and forth between working the beats and running the scene. Sometimes I work on the first section first, the second section second, etc. — but more often I skip around, stopping and starting a lot, working on individual sections as it seems needed, or as my impulse hits me. Or as requested by the actors. I am looking for things that bother — or interest — the actors. When questions arise, I might work on that section (beat) first. On the other hand I might say, "Yeah, that's the tricky part, isn't it?" and suggest that we work on other parts of the scene first, leaving the troublesome section for later, after we have done some groundwork.

At all times I am responding much more to what is happening right in front of me than to any plan I may have had of what I wanted to accomplish in the rehearsal. I am constantly checking for whether the actors are "pushing" or reaching — these are "false notes," places where they are trying to produce an emotional effect without having made it their own. A false note means the actor has made a choice but has not made it real, personal, and sensory. A "dead spot" similarly means the actor has not made a connection to the subtext. It takes practice, but if you listen and watch with total absorption you will be able to detect the dead spots and false notes. When I am discussing a "dead spot" or "false note" with an actor, I would probably not call it that, but instead call attention to it as a moment that isn't quite working, or that I have a question about. I might ask, "What do you think is going on in this line?" We talk briefly to find the adjustment — or do an improv — to bring the moment to life. I might suggest the actor find a substitution, or do some research. Or I might suggest a subtext, or an "it's like when…"

I am constantly listening for unconscious judgments that the actors are allowing to creep into their work. Often an actor's judgment, or resistance, is based on a misunderstanding of a line. So if an actor mentions, for instance, that her character is impatient and unkind to the people she supervises, I always ask what lines of dialogue suggest to her that interpretation. Perhaps she will point to a line such as, "I'm still waiting for your report." I will probably respond by suggesting, for instance, that a simpler, truer understanding of that line is that the character probably has a supervisor who is blaming her for the lateness of the project.

My own ideas find their expression via a stream of consciousness. I follow impulses, stay in the moment, reveal my innermost thoughts — unless my intuition is telling me the actors need me to be hold back while they explore something on their own. By the end of working with an actor, I expect to feel that I have had a glimpse into *who this person is* — and that I have managed to put some of that onto the screen or stage for the audience.

A tiny checklist for arriving at the simple reality of a scene — a "checklist for believability," if you will — might include the following:
1) Each actor must be talking to someone, about something, out of a *need* to speak (or move). "Talking *to* someone" is *listening*. "Out of a *need* to speak (or move)" means having an *objective* or *intention*. Talking "*about* something" means having something real in one's mind (an image or substitution) for each object, person, and experience referred to by the character in the script.

2) Each actor must be committed to some central core, a primal, private reality that, while inspired by the script, is finally something he alone knows and feels. This is his through-line. This commitment to a central, private reality is what keeps the actors from picking up each other's tone, even while they are surrendering to each other.

3) The choices must engage the actors with each other.

4) Emotional events must *happen* right in front of us (the audience). The director must show the audience *what it's like*, when someone hurts someone, fools someone, brings light into someone's life.

5) The events must occur in a physical reality.

SAMPLE SCENARIOS
A solid two weeks of all-day rehearsals.
I won't spend too much time on this one, because you can probably only get this if you are Sidney Lumet, Ang Lee, Sam Mendes, or Baz Luhrman. You should only attempt it if you have solid experience in conducting rehearsals — and/or an already enthusiastic and dedicated ensemble of actors. Here are some of the things that might take place in a two-week rehearsal:

Have a full-cast reading of the script. Either before or after the reading, there should be introductions. Set the introductions up in such a way that they count for something. Each person should feel free to reveal something more than her credits. You might invite them to share stories of how they relate to the script and characters. There might be discussion of the subject matter and themes of the script.

Rehearse with actors playing major roles, two at a time. The idea is to work on each of the major *relationships*. If the central relationship is a three-person relationship, as in the film *Return to Paradise*, then you'd arrange time to meet with all three (Sheriff, Lewis, and Tony) together, but you might also want separate rehearsal time with Sheriff and Lewis, as well as Sheriff and Tony. You would certainly want separate rehearsal time with Sheriff (the main character) and Beth, the love interest. The purpose of these sessions is less to rehearse scenes than to explore relationships. During the Sheriff-Beth rehearsal time, for example, you might first have a simple read through of all their scenes together, without stopping for discussion until the end.

You might think that in such a long rehearsal period there would be lots of talking. But the opposite is true. One luxury of a long rehearsal period is that you can do lots of "doing" and therefore not so much talking. You can set up improvisations, you can do each scene several different ways, you can work deeply on problematic moments. Or you can take a break from a troublesome scene and come back to it later. Another specific luxury of a long rehearsal period is that seeds of ideas can germinate — they can be left to percolate on the back burner, and can be returned to later.

Rehearse every afternoon while doing other preparation during mornings.

A two to four hour rehearsal every afternoon or evening for five to ten days before shooting can be an enormous help. It's a way to have rehearsals without the stress of the crew waiting around for you. And you still have time in the mornings to attend to other pre-production duties. You would need to be well organized, and you would need to be able to convince the actors that this amount of rehearsal will be well spent.

An article in the IFP/West Newsletter asserted that a great movie has three great scenes, and advised indie filmmakers to put everything into those. You might want to spend this rehearsal time on these three central scenes — or you might want to spend the time on every scene except these three central scenes. Another way to use this time is to schedule an hour's rehearsal for each scene in the script.

Who should attend these sessions? You might want to spend the time on the central relationship. Or you might want to spend two hours each day separately with each of the actors with the biggest roles. Or you might want to call all the actors to each day's rehearsal, to build the ensemble and to stage any scenes with multiple characters.

An hour per day during shooting.
All during the shoot, I strongly recommend at least an hour per day of quality time with director and actors, away from technicians and producers and entourage. Some attention is needed to the logistics of arranging this. Since the set is probably occupied with the lighting crew, you need a small space off the set to rehearse. It's worth it to find a neutral space that is not your office and not an actor's trailer.

Most movie scenes can be pulled together in thirty minutes, if you know how. The main thing to remember is that this is not a time to stuff a performance into the actors; it's a time to warm the actors up, get them connected honestly and personally to each other and the material, and give them confidence in their choices.

As needed.
If you want to stop and work with actors as needed, that is, when there is some problem or question, you must arrange the cooperation of the crew ahead of time. To keep the crew from grumbling and losing faith in you, you need to bring them into your confidence — onto your page — with your plans for what you want to accomplish with the actors. On the other hand, one DP told me that he takes his directors aside and makes them this offer: if the director unexpectedly needs time with the actors, she can give a signal to the DP, who will then announce he needs time for the

lighting. It's a sad commentary how much easier it is to get time to fix lighting than to work with an actor. But an accommodating DP can help. By the way, the actors usually feel anxious and embarrassed when their needs bring about a pause in production, so it's always helpful to them to treat a break for rehearsal as though it was necessary anyway for some other reason.

Ten minutes per scene.
The last ten minutes before shooting a take are a warm-up time, not a time to begin substantive discussions about the scene or the character. Don't spring something complicated on the actors just before shooting. Last minute direction, if you haven't had any prior quality time with the actors, is likely to be experienced by the actors as a source of anxiety. Ask if they have any questions, but keep it very simple, stay relaxed, use the time to communicate to them that you have faith in them, that they should take their time and follow impulses, and that there is all the time in the world.

The exception to this advice is that a director who is extremely competent and confident with actors can use the last ten minutes to deliberately catch the actor off-guard, in order to shake up a performance that has gotten cautious or "over-prepared." This will only work if the director has built trust with the actor.

Zero minutes per scene.
Directors often ask me, how do I direct the scene if there's no time to rehearse? Well, frankly, you don't. If there's no time to rehearse, then there's no time to make substantive adjustments to a performance. Cast well, stay loose, and don't forget — some people prefer no rehearsal.

"TALKING" REHEARSALS
"What I want from a director is courage. What I don't want from a director is too much chatter."

— Sean Penn

Most inexperienced directors either talk too much or talk too little. The ones that talk too little are usually afraid of saying the wrong thing. The ones that talk too much aren't listening to the actors. Actors will always let a director know when he is talking too much. Sometimes with actual words: "I'm getting overloaded." "I didn't follow all that." But if not with words, then with body language: shifting in seats, glazing over in the eyes, sighing, etc. Pay attention to these signals! And when they occur, stop talking.

Talking "just right" takes practice and some discipline to learn. Once you learn it, it's liberating and pleasurable. Knowing the difference between talking that is helpful and talking that is distracting or intrusive will help both directors who talk too much and those who talk too little. Here are some of the purposes of conversation among director and actors:

1) **Set the tone for exploration.** Mike Leigh says that at the first cast meeting, he makes sure to tell the actors that the purpose of rehearsal is to "assemble the raw materials, not create the artifact itself [which will be done when they join up with the crew and the cameras]." He does this to free them from "the idea of having to be interesting, illuminating, funny, or sad," to free them from everything "but having to be real." It is only in this spirit that rehearsal can be valuable, and it's helpful for directors to let the actors know this.

2) **Create association and connection to the subject matter of the script.** Instead of dissecting the psychology of the characters, initiate conversation among the actors on the themes of the script. Kevin Spacey said of working with Sam Mendes on *American Beauty*, "Coming from theater, Sam understands how to utilize a rehearsal period. Sam was open with us about his own upbringing, which opened us up, which allowed us to feel safe to talk to him and all of us about our own lives and our own feelings about families and parents and children and desires and hopes and frustrations. And so we began to build very slowly this trust amongst all of us." Apparently Mendes initiated conversations with the actors on the topics of "families and parents and children and desires and hopes and frustrations" — the themes of the film.

As you see, this involves the technique of "telling stories" discussed in an earlier chapter. It will be far more effective than gossip about the characters' psychology. This technique works on simpler levels as well. If the characters are getting a divorce, for instance, the director might ask the actors about their experiences with divorce. Such disclosures will feel more like a natural part of rehearsal (rather than like an interrogation) if the director begins by talking about his own experiences with divorce, as Spacey describes Mendes doing.

3) **Create a working relationship between actor and director.** When working with established actors, this begins in the casting process, when the director often must convince an actor of sufficient star-power to appear in the project, in order to get the funding. Kevin Spacey said that

he knew after four minutes speaking with Sam Mendes about *American Beauty* that he and the director "had read the same script." Geoffrey Rush originally turned down the role in *Elizabeth*, but Shekhar Kapur came to find him where he was shooting in Prague and "spoke so brilliantly about where he saw the film heading that he totally won me over." Angelica Huston was lukewarm about the role in *The Grifters*. When she met with Stephen Frears, he *apologized* to her for the role — and then she really wanted to do it! Director Jay Roach said about his meeting with Robert De Niro prior to shooting *Meet the Parents*, "The thing that he was most interested in was... to tell him about my life — what was interesting to me and what were my own disasters and dysfunctions. He was interested in my take on the story, but he was much more interested in hearing about my father and my relationship with my wife..."

It sounds like De Niro was evaluating the director's capacity for engagement and self-revelation. It sounds like Spacey, Rush, and Huston were won over by the directors' knowledge, honesty, passion, and insight. This type of discussion is not social chit-chat. It involves disclosure of ideas, experiences, and feelings on the part of the director. A good actor wants to know whether a director is capable of thinking and feeling. Again, telling personal stories will be a crucial way to communicate and create the relationship.

4) **Create an ensemble.** The topics Kevin Spacey says were discussed in the early *American Beauty* rehearsals — families, parents, children, desires, hopes, and frustrations — just happen to be close to the core of human values and concerns. Every script comes down, finally, to such primal issues — e.g., loyalty (*Pulp Fiction*), moral destiny (*Crouching Tiger Hidden Dragon*), sacrifice (*The Straight Story*, *East-West*), the pain of love (*There's Something About Mary*). In rehearsal, a director can gather the actors, either all at once, or in groups. Encouraging discussion on the topics and themes of the script may allow the actors to become more emotionally transparent to each other and enable them to encounter each other below the social mask. Of course it must be made clear that the purpose is "assembling raw materials," not gossip or therapy.

5) **Find out how the actors work.** Besides discussion at the level of human values, there can be discussion at the level of artistic values. You can ask the actors how they like to work, what they love about acting, what problems they anticipate with the script, what their ideas are. Ask lots of questions and listen to the responses.

6) Get on the same page about what there is to accomplish on the set.
Susan Sarandon has said, "I like to rehearse, to sniff around, get comfortable. Also get an idea of what each scene is supposed to accomplish. But I'm a money actor, I can't do it in my living room, can't do it till it's time to do it. But it's important to make sure each scene accomplishes something, otherwise it should come out."

What Sarandon means in the above quote when she speaks about whether a scene "accomplishes something" is identifying its emotional event. Some actors, like Sarandon, want to know the director's plan for the story. Most, however, are only interested in their own characters. Be alert to whether the actor craves to know the intellectual underpinnings of the story or whether she will only find such discussion a distraction from her own work.

7) Establish the humanity of the characters. When discussing the characters with actors, it is less important to nail down why a character does what he does than to establish that such behavior could exist in the world — and to consider a variety of possible reasons why it could exist. Especially if an actor is resisting the character, judging her, or can't understand her, the director needs to find a way to make the character sound like she could exist in the world. By establishing the humanity of a character, a director can guide an actor into an interpretation the actor did not initially connect to.

This discussion will again include recounting true stories. For instance consider Randal, who remarks in the *Clerks* scene, "People say crazy shit during sex. One time, I called this girl 'Mom.'" What is Randal's relationship with his mother, anyway? We know that Randal is a drug dealer with no plans for college or career. Is his mother a stern disciplinarian whom he is rebelling against? Or is she warm and caring — the "soft spot" in his life? This is a good example of a choice that actor and director do not need to agree on. (I'm not even sure that the actor needs to make a choice one way or the other. The line will probably have the most life if the actor substitutes his own mother — whether or not an incident such as Randal describes has ever happened to him!)

I might, however, bring up these possible interpretations with the actor — not to make him nail down a choice, but to establish that the line could come out of the life of a person, not just out of the cleverness of the writer. And I might tell stories about the "bad boys" I know who have sweet and close relationships with their mothers.

Does it sound like the "It could be this…or it could be that" approach could cause endless experimentation and deconstruction leading finally to confusion and frustration? It's really just the opposite, as long as you use common sense. The deconstruction is not the goal, it's a *tool* of choice-making. The philosophy here is that the director presents the actor with the field of options from which to make a choice, and asks the actor to make whatever choice is most truthful. Often an actor only needs one simple, primal clue to give them the key into the core of the character. But such important clues are more likely to surface if one is not trying desperately to hunt them down and "nail" them.

8) **See that the actors have something to go on when they get in front of the cameras.** This means joining them in a discussion of their choices. There are basically two approaches to doing this: (a) find out the actors' ideas and validate them; or (b) tell them your ideas.

Strangely enough, a director can have more control over the performances with the (a) approach. If there is only "talking" rehearsal, without time to try out the ideas on their feet before rolling film, a director can have more confidence that he knows roughly what the performances are going to look like if he simply validates the actor's ideas.

The (b) approach — the director giving actors his ideas in a "talking only" rehearsal, without trying them out — is similar to the John Sayles method I mentioned in the *Goals of Script Analysis* chapter. (Sayles says he sends the actors written backstory for each character.) A director cannot know how his spoken (or written) ideas are going to affect the actor's performance until he sees it performed. The approach of throwing some ideas at the actor and letting her interpret them is going to give the director less control rather than more control. (Not that that's a bad thing! The performances in Sayles' movies, for example, are often wildly idiosyncratic — but in a good way, yes?)

9) **Restrict yourself to two emotional facts.** The purpose of a "talking" rehearsal is not to explain the plot! If the actor has read the script, he knows the plot. If he hasn't read the script, that means he's not interested in the plot. Find **one or two** essential facts that are exciting, that might create behavior, that might make something happen.

10) **Now, here's what not to do in a "talking" rehearsal.** When an actor has strong personal connection to a choice you don't agree with, don't

talk them into an intellectualized version of your idea. Don't tell them what their inner life is. Don't intellectualize the concept or the psychology — anchor all ideas in stories and associations that come from real life. Keep discussions from becoming unhelpfully abstract and intellectual. The touchstone is human relationships, predicaments, needs, memories, hopes, and fears.

Don't talk because you think you should, or to fill the time, or to make people think you are smart. Don't stuff the actors with information and instruction. Pay attention to signals from the actors that they are bored and glazing over — and stop talking immediately. Ask them a question, or change the subject, or — better yet — get them on their feet.

"Talking rehearsal" means talking face-to-face. Telephone conversations between actors and directors who have never met each other do not constitute "quality time."

"ON THEIR FEET" REHEARSALS
"I never did anywhere near this kind of preparation for a film, and it's the most frustrating part of this whole experience [rehearsing a Broadway play] — looking back at the movies I've done and thinking, I could have worked so much harder."

— Chris O'Donnell

Discussion is commonly the only kind of preparation done before shooting a scene. However, many actors prefer working "on their feet" to talking. Why, then, is it so rare? Sometimes actors don't feel comfortable asking for time to work on their feet. There is a widespread notion that it is somehow a mark of professionalism to not need "on feet" rehearsal, i.e., that an actor should be able to "nail it" without rehearsal. Of course they may be afraid that the director won't know how to conduct rehearsal, and the time will be wasted. Or, they may feel the script is too obvious and uninteresting to tolerate much scrutiny and exploration. Some actors feel that it's important not to practice emotions, that they can't perform the emotional content of a scene unless it counts for something, i.e., unless the camera is rolling.

On the other hand, some actors are superstitious and fearful that rehearsal will sap them of their instincts. I don't recommend talking into rehearsal an actor who is sure it won't work — it's all too easy for such negativity to become a self-fulfilling prophesy. But directors will benefit from knowing how to rehearse even if they never get to use these skills. It will increase a director's tolerance for process, and give them information on how actors work. As I mentioned in the section on "talking" rehearsals, a director might ask how an actor likes to work. But it stands to reason that you'll get more reliable information by actually watching them work.

"On feet" rehearsal for film has these goals: 1) initiating a working relationship, finding out how director and actors can spend their "quality time" together, establishing the primacy of process, practicing taking risks; 2) solving the scene by finding emotional structure, physical movement, activities, and pace. The purpose of running a scene or section over and over is that eventually there may be a breakthrough, an insight that would not have otherwise come.

A few thoughts about "on their feet" rehearsal:

The simple reading. Have the actors first do a simple reading of the scene — slowly, with eye contact — before any blocking, before any discussion, and without reading the stage directions. Actors should speak in their own voices, not "in character." This is a chance for the actors to show up as people before they show up as craftsmen. It's a time for the actors to make friends with the words, with the images, with the subtext, and with each other rather than play the roles. It's a trust-building exercise rather than a performance. When actors connect with each other while saying lines of the script, it is different from getting acquainted during social chit chat. By a "simple" reading I mean it should be slow, it should go easy. The actors should be seated opposite each other, making eye contact whenever possible. It should have as its goal allowing the experience of the words out loud in each other's presence, slow enough that connection can begin to each other and to the images in the text.

Activity can be interspersed with conversation. But as soon as there is a spark in the actors' eyes, stop talking and do something — a run-through, or an improv, or some work on a section or moment. But if there is no spark — if the actors' eyes are glazing over — that's also a reason to stop and do something. One of these things is likely to happen fairly soon. In other words, don't talk a long time.

Get them to engage. This is much more important than having agreement on interpretation. It's not part of an actor's job to be articulate. If the things they say about the character don't make sense to the director, what does that matter if the scene is working? It's so easy to get bogged down in useless intellectualization when all that's needed is a reason for the actors to engage with each other.

The purpose of rehearsal is not for the actors to get comfortable with each other's rhythms and responses, but the opposite — to get comfortable with surprising each other, get comfortable with catching each other off guard. If a director has the ability to notice whether the actors are "watching their own performances," or "playing both roles," or not doing work that is personal and risk-taking, that's very helpful. And if, further, the director has the communication skills to call these problems to the actors' attention, that's even better. For example, if an objective that the director and actor have decided on together seems like it should be a good one, but doesn't seem to working, it might need to be made more personal.

One of the most important characteristics of a director who can work comfortably and confidently with actors is the ability to know when an actor is working well but isn't there yet. The directors who don't recognize this often step in prematurely with micro-managing. If a performance seems off to you, in a mystifying way, ask the actor what he is working on. If he says, for instance, "I'm trying to create some reality to these images" or, "I'm still exploring the given circumstances," then it might be wise to let him keep working without interference. But if he says, "Well, the guy is depressed, because his girlfriend left him," then you know it's an interpretation, and if you don't think it's working, you can say, "Why do you think that?" Get him to be specific. "What are the lines or behavior that make you think he's depressed?" From there, you are in position to treat such a line or behavior as a "mysterious" one. This will be so much more helpful than trying to argue him out of his interpretation.

Take, for instance, an actor who says of her character, "I don't think she's honest with herself." When you pinpoint the lines that give her this idea, you may find that it's a place where she replies to a direct question with an indirect answer. You can then say, "What other reasons might a person have for doing that?" Examples: She might want not to hurt the other character's feelings. Or she might not know the answer.

Practice work habits. Practice "permission to fail." Tell your actors never to stop when they misspeak a line. Reinforcing a habit of continuing to work through mistakes creates an atmosphere of permission to fail — an atmosphere essential to creativity. Unfortunately it is customary on movie sets for actors to stop and correct themselves when they flub a line while the camera is rolling. This doesn't make sense. There is already a person on the set — the script supervisor — with the job of noting when a line is said incorrectly. The actor's proper job is to stay in the moment — which means continuing the take, experiencing the stumble as the character's stumble — that is, using it — until the director says cut.

When actors are in the habit of stopping when they make a line mistake, the habit will likely extend to an "emotional mistake" as well. When something unexpected happens emotionally, it will often feel like a mistake to the actor. These "mistakes" are often breakthroughs that are pure magic on screen. If the actor stops, the director — and the audience — stand to lose out on some wonderful stuff. Almost any successful director will tell you that many of the best moments in cinema happen by accident. One purpose of rehearsal is to create the habit of actors never stopping for mistakes. If you don't set this habit in rehearsal, once you are on the set, it will be too late. Getting the actors not to stop for a flubbed line can only be accomplished if you have rehearsals where some work is done "off book" (i.e., with memorized lines). This procedure does not preclude the director cutting the scene for a mistake if he feels it is appropriate.

Don't forget that no matter how skilled and process-oriented the participants are, rehearsal is never guaranteed to steadily improve the performances. It will be up and down, in and out, two steps forward, one step back.

WARM-UPS

By a "warm-up" I mean any kind of off-script exercise designed to get at the subtext of a scene, situation, relationship, or moment. Warm-ups should ideally have a physical component, but they should also connect the actors emotionally to the work at hand. For instance, having the actors arm-wrestle or pillow-fight while saying lines. By the way, a pillow-fight may help with engagement even if in the scene being worked on the characters are not arguing with each other.

Switching roles, allowing actors to interject comments between the lines, playing the opposite — all are possible exercises to help actors get looser and freer. If the scene is going to be played with the characters not looking at each other (e.g., a telephone call), you might rehearse with the actors face to face. Another exercise is to say to one or both actors, "Don't speak your line, or perform your action, unless he really makes you." Another is to speak the subtext: In one of my classes, a director rehearsing the last scene between the wife and husband in *Truly, Madly, Deeply* had each actor say — first out loud, and later silently — the word "Goodbye" before saying each line to each other.

How the director sets up an exercise is as important as the exercise itself. Since such exercises are outside adult social activity — they are more like children's activity — the director who wants to set them up needs to feel comfortable invoking ceremony. And he needs to have had practice performing as well as leading such exercises. It would not be a good idea to surprise the actors with an exercise on the set if no exercises had ever been tried in off-set rehearsals. Be sure always to ask the actors if they are willing to try a warm-up. And be ready to tell them its purpose.

IMPROV

Director Betty Thomas likes to use improv, and has mentioned using it to prepare for *28 Days*. Ken Loach, asked how a professional actor (Adrien Brody) could work with non-professionals in *Bread and Roses*, said, "We had done improvisations before the film started so we knew how we would work, so it was very easy." Mike Nichols says he uses rehearsal as a chance to improvise the backstory, especially the events that characters refer to in the script. I would imagine, for instance, that would include improvising the party at Martha's father's house that is mentioned repeatedly in *Who's Afraid of Virginia Woolf?* As Nichols says, you can't beat improv for creating an imagined reality.

On the other hand, Ian Holm refuses to rehearse with improv — "I can't," he told director Stanley Tucci during preparation for *Joe Gould's Secret*. Michael Richards has said that for the role of Kramer in *Seinfeld*, he would improvise physical business, but never dialogue. "It's my job to bring the character to the language."

My own feeling is that the purpose of improv precisely is to bring the character to the language. I use it myself not to rewrite dialogue, but to rewrite subtext. I find it helpful as a way to encourage and prepare the actors to improvise the emotional subtext on the set. Once on the set, they won't be allowed to improvise words, or movement. They won't even be able to improvise the emotional structure, because in the course of multiple takes and coverage, the characters' objectives —and other elements of emotional structure — are likely to be set as well. (When the actors choose an objective and commit to it for each take, they can stay fresh while giving performances that "match" in the editing room.)

But, even with all this setting of lines, movement, and emotional structure, they can still improvise subtext. For instance, for a scene with no dialogue, rehearse it with improvised dialogue, in order to express and experience the subtext. For a scene with a lot of words, rehearse it in a silent improvisation, without any words — again the purpose is to experience subtext and allow it to be primary.

The scene in *What Women Want* in which Helen Hunt and Mel Gibson mug to a Frank Sinatra tune was tightly choreographed, but after a few takes, writer-director Nancy Meyers asked the actors to "improvise" one take — this turned out to be the take that made it into the film. My understanding of this story is that this take probably still had all the lines and choreography that had been set, but was the best because the subtext was improvised.

"Improvs" are "adjustments" acted out. For instance, *The Rainmaker* adjustment to play Matt Damon's courtroom scene as if it were an emergency room scene. If there were time, it could be acted out as an improvisation, to give it a stronger reality. Sometimes a rehearsal might consist of only improvisation, without any spoken lines at all until the camera is running. I've read that Mike Leigh works that way.

In the chapter on *Rehearsal Principles and Techniques* I used the *Tender Mercies* scene as an example of the difficulties that could occur if the director and actor did not agree on the central choice of whether Mac is telling the truth about having poured out the bottle of whiskey. If there were a lengthy enough rehearsal period, however, it might actually be worthwhile to rehearse the scene with the "wrong" choice that Mac has been drinking, that Rosa Lee can smell it on him. The purpose would not be to prepare to actually shoot the scene that way. The scene played with this opposite choice would be an acted-out experience into both characters' deepest fears. This imaginative investigation of the emotional underpinnings of the script could bring depth and strength to the performances.

David Gordon Green used improvisations in his casting sessions for the female lead in *All the Real Girls*. Rick Schroeder got the job of replacing Jimmy Smits on *NYPD Blue* because of improvs he did with Dennis Franz. The producers realized that the most important element in the recasting of this role would be the actor's chemistry with Franz. By using improvisations, they could see not just how well an actor could read lines, but whether Franz and the new actor could affect each other. A director, during callbacks for the role of a character who tells a ghost story, asked each auditioning actor to tell a story of his own, then read the scene. One thing to remember if you use improv for casting sessions is that the Screen Actors Guild forbids the taping of such sessions. If you have any questions about this issue, contact the Guild.

Writer-director Audrey Wells brought the cast of *Guinevere* to her house to improvise around the dinner scene, because "she knew that the dinner table scenes with the family were going to be very important and difficult." Jean Smart says she is not usually a fan of improv, but found it helpful. "One day she had us just pick anybody at the table and tell them something we wanted to tell them, whether it was a cry for help or something insulting or something funny. It got very intense and was very interesting."

Francis Coppola, during preparation for *The Godfather*, created early rehearsals and improvisations over meals. He also, according to actor James Caan, would create little improvisations and adjustments without telling the actors that he was doing so. For instance, Coppola would "confide" to Caan that somebody was "bothering Talia [the actress Talia Shire, who played Caan's sister]." Caan says that he would then look into the problem and try to fix it. He only realized later that, "the s.o.b. must have done it on purpose!" — that Coppola had invented the "problem" as an exercise to create the protective relationship of Sonny to Connie.

Improvisation is a way to practice active imagining, it's a door to the unconscious, so it is sacred. An improvisation can never be "wrong." It is information. It should not be tweaked and micro-managed until it approximates the result the director had in mind. If some important element of the scene does not show up in an improv — for example if the actor keeps apologizing in the improv even though the character never speaks the words, "I'm sorry" — that's not a failure, it's information about the actor's connection and/or resistance to the script. So it is ably filling the purpose of rehearsal.

HOW LONG TO REHEARSE?

Because I began my acting career in theater, the term "over-rehearsal" doesn't have much meaning to me. I've had the experience of working and working a difficult scene until the breakthrough finally came at three in the morning! And then coming back to rehearsal the next day to work the scene again. So I have iron-clad confidence that even once lost, the emotional content of a performance can always be re-found. Our tools are feelings and imagination, and feelings and imagination can always be resuscitated. It shouldn't hurt to rehearse long hours as long as everyone is free emotionally, and excited about the ideas and the process. The nagging worry of so many film directors that a scene will be over-rehearsed just means that they don't know how to rehearse — and perhaps shouldn't try it.

But since there are time constraints in film production, it's a relief to know that for film it probably isn't necessary to rehearse a long time. Working until the actors "catch a corner" of what they need for a scene, until they have an insight or a breakthrough, or a moment of deep relaxation, or of trust with their fellow actors, or find a movement or activity that releases the emotional content of the scene for them — may be all you need.

22 | JUST BEFORE
THE CAMERA ROLLS

> *"I love putting the movie in the hands of the actors. I am so in awe of what they do."*
>
> — Jonathan Demme

BRINGING THE REHEARSAL WORK ONTO THE SET

Directors have asked me, "When I get to the set, should I just tell the actors to remember what we did in rehearsal, and do that?" Actually, no. Once on the set, you need to re-engage — with beginner's mind. Many things may have happened since rehearsal to distract the actor from the choices and associations that engaged him in rehearsal. But that doesn't mean the rehearsal time was wasted. The rehearsal was a shared history that lets you know you can engage. It makes re-engaging on the set easier.

When something that worked in rehearsal fizzles when the camera rolls, should you say, "Let's try to get back to what we had in rehearsal"? Again, no. You may be able to go back to the objective that worked but not to the performance that worked — the performance is gone. If the loss of connection to the choice is irretrievable, you may need to take the actors aside and work with them. Loosen them up, with exercises, improv, or a pep talk. Or go back to square one and rework and restructure the scene, with questions and new choices. If there is no time to do any of these things, let it go. Try saying, "I trust you. Whatever you've got is going to be fine with me." Or, "Hey, if we can't do it right, let's do it wrong!"

If you have no outside rehearsal, cast well and trust your casting. Keep a relaxed atmosphere on the set, so the actors can do their work without interference.

DO NOT ASK AN ACTOR TO DO JOBS OTHER THAN HIS OWN

Keeping the performances in frame is not just the actor's job. It's the job of the camera operator too. In recent projects Steven Soderbergh has functioned as his own camera operator. This is an interesting trade-off. There are a lot of reasons why it's better for the director to be standing beside the camera during the shot. What is the compensating benefit of being his own cameraman? My theory is that doing it himself is a way to ensure that in camera operation, intelligence and feeling will prevail over mere technical proficiency. I've read that Soderbergh told the assistant cameraman on *Traffic* not to give the actors marks (pieces of tape fastened to the floor to mark the places where the actors are to move).

John Cassavetes once asserted, "It's much easier for an operator to follow action that's free and natural than staged action." Cassavetes goes so far as to declare that qualifications for the job of focus puller should include superior depth perception — which the focus puller should rely on rather than the endless measurements which can make the actors nervous. I mentioned this recently to a camera expert, who demurred quickly: "No, no. A man's job is at stake. What if the performances were great and the shot was out of focus? He'd lose his job."

Conventional wisdom has it that camera operators and focus pullers should only be expected to make precise, prearranged movements at pre-arranged signals. Cassavetes' insistence that everyone on a movie set should perform his job with intelligence, feeling, spontaneity, and trust in his intuition was and still is revolutionary. Can intelligence and feeling be primary values without sacrifice of technical proficiency? It's food for thought, and a worthy challenge, I think.

If you want the crew to give the actors the leeway to allow them to move — or change volume — without meticulous prearrangement, engage the crew ahead of time with what you want to accomplish, and ask their advice on making it work. The challenge may make them feel responsible and creative instead of threatened.

BOREDOM
Rehearsals on set are crew rehearsals. They are utterly useless to the actors. They are tiresome and depleting of actors' energy. As is all the waiting around that actors must do on a set. Waiting around gives actors time to lose their energy, time to intellectualize themselves out of their performance, and time to get invested in ego issues. The biggest enemy of an actor's performance is boredom.

Betty Thomas says she tries to shoot "as quickly as possible. On a comedy, if I spend three hours on every setup, I'm dead." Casting director Debra Zane said that on the set of *Traffic*, the actors almost never went to their trailers. Actors were on the set almost the whole time, because Soderbergh "would move and shoot and move on." Zane says, "Steven likes to catch people in their most organic moments."

Cassavetes noted another danger of tedious crew rehearsals. "The whole crew becomes a kind of audience. If the crew gets bored, the actors feel that it's bad. That's why I want everything to go fast."

THE TRUTH WILL CUT TOGETHER

Don't ask actors to do the editor's job either. Every editor I've ever spoken to has said that what they look for is the spark, the somebody-home in the eyes, the involvement of the actor in the scene even when she is not speaking. And yet, the message received on the set about how to make the editor happy is to not overlap and to make sure everything matches. A good editor can edit around overlaps — it's just more work. Editing around a lack of listening is just as much extra work — maybe more — than editing around overlaps.

TECHNICAL DEMANDS; SOCIAL DEMANDS

People who saw the Marx Brothers perform live in vaudeville say they were even funnier than in their movies, because they were unconstrained by demands of the camera. Milton Berle once told an interviewer that one of the reasons for the success of his physical comedy on live television was the "accidents" that continually happened with falling sets and other snafus during the show. He and the actors always reacted and used the unplanned disasters to take the comedy to a further extreme. He joined the stage carpenters' union so he could personally use a hammer to nail pieces of the set back together during the live commercials. When video tape came along all of this ended because such accidents were edited out. With that advance in technology came the loss of some of the funniest moments in American television comedy.

Annette Bening, who prepares by isolating herself on the set, says the key to movie acting is, "You have to be ready when they are," because everything is ruled by technology. Working with the blue screen makes even greater demands on an actor's concentration. Anne Bancroft: "You can't even think about it. You just have to go with your own inner life because if you start to get involved in all of that, you lose what the scene really is about. You have to stay very connected to the actors who you're playing with and very connected to what you're doing. You have to be more concentrated."

According to Mike Nichols, Jack Nicholson spends time connecting to everyone on the set. He wanders around, talks to the technicians, meets the drivers and all the actors. "He somehow made everyone complicit in what he was doing."

Just as actors need to make the words, the characters, the setting, furniture, and objects, the movement and marks their own, they also need to make the set their own. This may mean doing as Nicholson does, meeting and connecting to everyone. Or it may mean secluding oneself. Being friendly and sociable should not be required of actors. Cassavetes would never encourage small talk, nor abide gossip, on his sets. "I won't tolerate anyone talking about anything but the film, anything but these people, because we're working in such a condensed period of time."

DIFFERENT ACTORS WORK DIFFERENTLY

Liam Neeson put on full costume for a *Rob Roy* scene even though it was a head shot because it was "a demanding shot emotionally" and he would have felt "a bit of a cheat" if he hadn't. Jo Van Fleet, shooting *Wild River*, was told by director Elia Kazan that she needn't apply elaborate hand make-up on a certain day because her hands would not be in the shot; Van Fleet replied, "I'm not doing this for you. I'm doing it for myself."

These choices helped these actors with their concentration, helped them make their connection to the concerns of the imagined world stronger than their concerns for the real world of a busy and anxious movie set. Other actors find a better aid to concentration is to stay completely loose, even silly. Julianne Moore, by her own description, likes to "jabber" with her co-star just before a shot; it relaxes her so she can be in the moment and follow impulses. When she worked with Billy Crudup on *World Traveler*, she found that he likes to prepare alone without distractions.

How can actors have chemistry together when they prepare so differently? If the director makes all the actors feel that whatever method of preparation they use is welcomed and acceptable — that can help.

EMOTIONAL PREPARATION

In *The Rainmaker* documentary Clare Danes said of her preparation for a scene in which she needed to be upset, "I need external things." She requested that crew members yell at her, then for her close-up, she felt she was getting stale, so Coppola got a block of ice for her to sit on. In the same documentary, Matt Damon said he taped a rock to his back for a scene in which his character had been on the bus all night. A student of mine told me that she'd been advised by Karl Malden that if actors are getting nervous, they should put a stone in a shoe. Such physical distractions take the actor's attention away from concerns for whether he is "nailing" his performance — and thus help him stay in the moment.

Actors can easily become, at the last minute, panicky about achieving and maintaining an "emotional preparation." This can mean that they pump up, dredge up, or try to manufacture feelings. When an actor moans, "I'm not feeling anything," I often find that the culprit is strain.

The best pre-scene preparation is sensory. Once I performed in a play (later filmed for television) set in a courtroom. Just before my entrance I would revive a sense memory of the wooden bench in the courthouse hall on which, years earlier, I had waited to be summoned to testify as a witness in a civil case. The memory of the wooden bench of the courthouse, the green cement walls, the echoing linoleum, were all I needed to bring me on stage in a state of emotional readiness.

It's more important for an actor to be emotionally *available* than emotionally *prepared*. A sensory preparation works because anything sensory is physical. But any such sensory preparation should always be relaxed and pleasurable rather than pushed and desperate, even if the feelings of the scene are painful. Even actual physical activity before performing, such as kick-boxing or long walks, can be more useful preparation than emotional self-torture, because it helps an actor get out of his head, into his body, and thus out of the way of his feelings. Jim Carrey has said, "I do scream and yell. But not at anybody. It's not like I'm having a temper tantrum or something like that. It's just getting rid of cobwebs. Sometimes instead of screaming I just go [screwing up his face] sploot, oot, goot."

Sometimes I find the most helpful direction I can give an actor just before a scene is, "Don't let your partner know what you want from him" — because it gives her permission to have a secret. But sometimes the opposite, "Don't try to hide your feelings from your partner," is a more appropriate direction — it helps get the actor out of her head. The other last minute direction that usually works is, "Make sure it's personal."

Angelica Huston tells of the time she was agonizing over her emotional preparation for the wordless memory scene at the end of *The Dead*. Her father, John Huston, came up to her and asked, "How's your horse?"

Angelica says she suddenly realized he didn't want the emotional turmoil she was willing on herself. He wanted her to be a real person with her real concerns.

FREE FALL
"I quite like the idea that though I know what I'm going to do next, I try to sort of un-know it, if you know what I mean."
— Ralph Fiennes

"If you're thinking about your research or you're thinking about what you've decided about certain things, you're not going to be alive in the moment, and really, that's all acting is. When it comes time to get on the set, you have to let go, trust, and free fall. That's why it is so good to work with a director you can trust, so that you know they they'll catch you when you fall."
— Jennifer Jason Leigh

When it comes to emotional preparation, at the very last minute, a state of *unpreparedness* is the best thing. As an actor, I find that just before a performance or a take, I must take a few moments to deliberately forget everything I've been working on. Working in the moment is that radical an experience. Even if the character is tense, the actor should be relaxed. Even if the character is holding his breath, the actor should breathe. If an actor is losing concentration, or hits a false note, the best way to recover is not to pump it up, but to let go. Go into free fall.

When an actor has a great moment, the experience itself is healing, freeing, opening. He wants to have that feeling again, so he tries to figure out what he did or what happened to get him there. This is how actors get superstitious — they must have a chocolate bar a certain number of minutes before the take, or must spend time with their dog, or not spend time with their dog. Such superstitions may even work, simply because once the actor has accomplished them, he can relax.

BEFORE THE TAKE
Make sure the actors are breathing. Actors are often asked to be motionless for a particular camera framing. It's easy for them to assume this means they shouldn't breathe, and to need to be reminded of this crucial life function! Any performance will be impaired by the absence of easy, relaxed breathing. It's a huge help if the director reminds the actor that

it's okay to breathe. It may even be appropriate, if you feel close to the actor, to remind her to relax her face — for movies, relaxing the face muscles is always a good thing.

By the way, it's customary in rehearsal to use an expression such as, "We can start whenever you're ready," instead of "Action." But I actually think it's worth considering whether you might want to start a take that way. I've read that that's what Clint Eastwood does when he's directing. He speaks without jargon, saying, "Let's start," and "Okay we can stop," instead of "Action" and "Cut."

DURING THE TAKE

Editors all know about listening; they are experts at detecting it — they have to be, because if it's not there they have to cut around it to make it look as if it's there. It's not difficult to learn to see whether the actors are listening and engaging when one is looking at rushes. The difficult thing is to see it on the set.

The director's best tool in determining whether she is getting what she needs from the actors, while standing next to the camera on the set, is a full, relaxed concentration. This concentration involves an ability to be present — *in the moment* — as a human being of intelligence and feeling. The reason why directors should study and practice their interaction with actors is to be able to develop their powers of concentration, so that while the camera is rolling, that concentration can be iron-clad even amid the pressures and distractions of a movie set.

Directors sometimes ask whether it's okay to throw direction at the actors while the camera is running. It depends on how it's done. If it's done with love, with a subtext of, "I'm with you, you're doing great, we're close to something great, stay with me," then it might work. If the subtext is, "Hold it! You're ruining film stock. Fix it, will you?" then it probably won't work.

AFTER THE TAKE

Try to stay relaxed and positive with your suggestions about the next take. If there is any anxiety behind your comments, the actors will respond to the anxiety more than the content. Sometimes the best question to ask first is how the actor feels about his work. It's helpful to know if they think it's going well or going badly.

Many good directors consider it helpful to take the pressure off actors, by giving the impression that another take that is needed for performance would have been needed anyway for some technical reason. If the actor is painfully blocked, while you are working on unblocking the moment, do whatever you can to make the actor not the focus of attention. Television director Mick Jackson said he often uses humor, lets himself look foolish, to break the tension of the moment.

GETTING THEM NOT TO "ACT"

Ang Lee is always on the lookout for actors falling into the bad habit of arranging themselves for the camera, and deliberately does things to get the actors off guard — to the point of mischievousness. According to Lee, Hugh Grant is "very smart and knows camera angles better than any of us." While shooting *Sense and Sensibility*, Lee at one point began "speaking English with Chinese grammar while rolling the camera" in order to force Grant to respond genuinely. "That was the take."

Said Sam Mendes, "Kevin [Spacey] knows what he's doing right down to whether or not his eyebrow is raised when he's saying a line. A lot of my job was to take away Kevin's outside eye and make him vulnerable. A lot of what you see in the finished movie are quite late takes when he was just goofing around."

Robert Altman does not always let the actors know when the camera is running.

Paul Thomas Anderson regarding the shooting of *Boogie Nights*: "My job was to keep it simple and stop them from camping it up." It can be good when actors are having fun, but not if they fall into enjoying being an actor, and turn the work into a kind of emotional calisthenics, instead of a genuine connection. Billy Wilder said of Cary Grant that "he knew how to put on a jacket." Wilder meant that Grant could put on a jacket like a man instead of like an actor, while a camera was rolling. Get the actors to do things the way people do them, rather than the way actors do them.

LAST TAKE

A documentary filmmaker told me that he often will start putting equipment away, saying to the subject, "I've got what I need" — and then add, casually, as though as afterthought, "Anything else you want to say?" You guessed it — often the best stuff comes out in this last shot. Some fiction directors, after they get the take they want, give the actors a take to do it "any way they like." Again, this is often the best take — and usually all the lines and all the blocking are still intact.

Many editors and directors have told me that the "one more take for safety" that is almost always shot — is almost never used. One more take "for risk" would be much more likely to have some good stuff on it.

LOOK FOR THE GLASS HALF-FULL

On TV shows, the writer-producers go over the scripts with the director, telling them line-by-line what the performances should be. If the dailies come back with a different line reading, there's hell to pay. Many episodic directors feel invisible to the actors, and depressed about the situation. But they can serve as more than a traffic cop. The actors need a buffer from the rigid result-orientation of many writer-producers. The role of confidante and go-between can be seen as the creative link. Participants in a recent workshop had a good laugh when I described this as a "priestly function." But I believe one can bring a spiritual purpose to any job.

ALL THE TIME IN THE WORLD

The "Are you lookin' at me?" scene in *Taxi Driver* was born of a creative impasse. The shot was ready, but Scorsese and De Niro were not. Finally, Scorsese shut the door and he and De Niro let the technicians wait while they hashed it out.

During the Western Conference Finals of the 1999-2000 season, the Los Angeles Lakers were trailing the Portland Trail Blazers by thirteen points going into the fourth quarter of Game Seven. At the break before the fourth quarter, the announcers listened in on coach Phil Jackson's pep-talk to the team. Jackson's words: "Stay loose. Play your positions." The Lakers fought back and won the NBA Championship.

A film director who trusts his preparation, trusts his intuition, and trusts his actors can say to them when the going gets rough, "Stay loose." This will get better results than pressuring them to nail it. I promise you. The goal is not to nail it but to stay alive.

23 | EPILOGUE

THE ARTIST

"Make sure you're doing it for the love of an idea and not for a lifestyle or so that you could put 'director' next to your name. It has to be an idea you can't get out of your gut. You have to do it for the love of it, not just because it seems like an exciting thing to do. There's got to be something about it, something that you don't talk about to everyone."

— Todd Field

"You always want to stay in touch with the little boy [inside you] because that little boy used to dream of telling stories. It wasn't about contracts or the size of your trailer. It was about the love of being fascinated by stories. So long as you can keep in touch with that and keep it a priority, that keeps you honest and humble."

— Eriq La Salle

"Being an artist is nothing other than the desire, the insane wish to express yourself completely, absolutely. The fact is that filmmaking, although unquestionably predicated on profit and loss like any other industry, cannot survive without individual expression."

— John Cassavetes

"For a young filmmaker, the enemy isn't the studio or the critics, it's self-importance. It takes a great amount of energy to stay hungry, but it's far preferable to self-importance, which is what has brought down nearly every great filmmaker."

— Steven Soderbergh

When Hilary Swank, after her Oscar win for *Boys Don't Cry*, said that she was motivated to take the role of Brandon Teena not by any belief that the role would make her famous, or that such a risk-taking choice was a shrewd career move, but by "the importance of the story" — I believe her. Not because I know anything first-hand about her personal integrity, but because I know that work of that caliber cannot be achieved unless the artist has put the work first.

I read scripts and see movies of people I have met and worked with, and the scripts and finished products are not as funny, not as deep, not as complex, not as intelligent, as I know the people involved in making the movie themselves to be.

I'm trying to write this chapter without sounding too preachy. But the truth is — art matters. For me, the most moving Academy Award acceptance speech ever was Steven Soderbergh's, for best director (*Traffic*), when he said that he dedicated his award to all the people in the world who attempt to do something artistic in their lives.

The proper reason for going into the entertainment business is in order to have the feeling that the thing you do fits perfectly into the dimensions of your imagination. This is different from the drive for fame and fortune, which will make you unhappy. Liberation and connection is what's at stake. It's too painful to go into this business, with all its rejection and backbiting, if all there is at stake for you is money and power. Kathy Bates turned down an audition for the TV pilot of *Three's Company* because "I didn't feel I had developed in my craft enough to withstand the easy money and lack of challenge."

THE AUDIENCE
"Overall, I think audiences are much smarter than what they are getting. Mostly, they are being talked down to."

— Billy Wilder

"You have to attempt to always do quality and see if people like it, rather than just guess what the audience likes."

— Garry Shandling

"I made Shane *for a truck driver in Kansas. Somebody who can't articulate all of his feelings. But someone with a mind and a heart who can respond in the dark."*

— George Stevens

Writer-director Alexander Payne spoke in an interview about the way studio executives condescend to moviegoers. He said the response in Hollywood meetings to any script of intelligence and feeling is typically, "I get it, you get it, but is the audience going to get it?" When producers and execs want writers to excise subtext from their scripts, it's not because they don't understand the writing — they're afraid the audience won't. Krzysztof Keislowski called it "economic censorship — censorship imposed by people who think they know what the audience wants."

Actually, audiences are not stupid. A little lazy, maybe, a little inclined to habit. When movies of substance, like *American Beauty* or *Shakespeare in Love*, get proper advertising support, audiences go to them. Sure, they line up for *Attack of the Clones*. But that doesn't mean they wouldn't prefer a new *Star Wars* episode that had some honest feeling to it. Producer Scott Rudin said it in a newspaper interview: In Hollywood, "there's a general contempt for the audience."

Love the audience. Nourish them, challenge them, treat them with respect. Just as a director must love the characters and love the actors, he should love the audience. Filmmakers and executives who don't love the audience really ought to consider another line of work.

FURTHER STUDY
Film directing of actors is perhaps the only artistic discipline for which there is little or no encouragement to keep a daily or weekly practice with your craft. Musicians, painters, dancers, writers, actors — not to mention anyone who wishes to excel in sports — all practice daily or weekly, no matter how successful and established in their careers.

Don't wait until you are on a movie set, in charge of expensive equipment, a full crew, and a cast of actors, to practice the techniques of this book. Practice them ahead of time, in a setting where money, egos, and your career are not at stake. Some of my former students have set up groups of directors and actors who meet weekly to practice working on scenes together. I have classes in Los Angeles — the Actor-Director Laboratory, and the Script Analysis and Rehearsal Techniques workshop — in which directors can practice with my supervision and feedback. At some point I hope to make some demonstration videos of rehearsal techniques, but there is no substitute for trying it yourself.

Don't put off script analysis. I offer private consultation for directors to prepare for working with actors and to help with script analysis of their project. There are others who offer directorial consultation as well. If you can't afford professional consultation, then put yourself in a room with no telephone and no computer, and lock the door. Ask yourself the difficult questions, give your imagination a work-out, and stay there until you come up with some fresh ideas.

"Any director who doesn't go to acting class is foolish. It's like being a conductor and not knowing what the violin does. Silly. That's your equipment.

That's your raw material, the actors. If you don't understand the nature of creating behavior under imaginary circumstances and how difficult it is to stand on a set and play an intimate scene with people putting tape in front of your nose and moving lights around you, if you don't know how difficult that is, how can you possibly direct actors?"

— Mark Rydell

I do insist that directors who wish to attend the Actor-Director Lab and my workshops in Script Analysis and Rehearsal Techniques need to have taken Acting for Directors first, unless they are actors with professional training and experience. All my teaching of directors is predicated on an approach that comes from inside the character's world, and therefore, inside the actor's experience. By acting himself, the director gains empathy with the actor's process, which helps the director develop a personal communication with the actors. But just as important — the director learns script analysis not just intellectually but by actually having an experience of connecting to a script at the level of its subtext. He goes safely and pleasurably below the social mask to the feeling level, which is the source of intuition.

/////

Eventually all the tools in this book should feel like common sense. Practice them until they do. Or invent your own methods. Have fun. Follow your heart. Be honest with yourself. Let love guide you.

FILMOGRAPHY

12 Angry Men (Sidney Lumet, 1957)
28 Days (Betty Thomas, 2000)
8 Mile (Curtis Hanson, 2002)
A Place in the Sun (George Stevens, 1951)
A Woman Under the Influence (John Cassavetes, 1974)
The Accidental Tourist (Lawrence Kasdan, 1988)
Adaptation (Spike Jonze, 2002)
Affliction (Paul Schrader, 1997)
All the President's Men (Alan J. Pakula, 1976)
All the Real Girls (David Gordon Green, 2003)
American Beauty (Sam Mendes, 1999)
American Buffalo (Michael Corrente, 1996)
Antwone Fisher (Denzel Washington, 2002)
The Apostle (Robert Duvall, 1997)
As Good As It Gets (James L. Brooks, 1997)
Atlantic City (Louis Malle, 1980)
August (Anthony Hopkins, 1996)
Austin Powers (Jay Roach, 1997)
Being John Malkovich (Spike Jonze, 1999)
The Big Chill (Lawrence Kasdan, 1983)
Big Night (Campbell Scott, Stanley Tucci, 1996)
Birthday Girl (Jez Butterworth, 2001)
Blade Runner (Ridley Scott, 1982)
Blue Sky (Tony Richardson, 1994)
Body Heat (Lawrence Kasdan, 1981)
Bonnie and Clyde (Arthur Penn, 1967)
Boogie Nights (Paul Thomas Anderson, 1997)
Box of Moonlight (Tom DiCillo, 1996)
The Boxer (Jim Sheridan, 1997)
Boys Don't Cry (Kimberly Peirce, 1999)
Boyz N the Hood (John Singleton, 1991)
Bread and Roses (Ken Loach, 2000)
Breakfast at Tiffany's (Blake Edwards, 1961)
Butch Cassidy and the Sundance Kid (George Roy Hill, 1969)

Carlito's Way (Brian De Palma, 1993)
Carnal Knowledge (Mike Nichols, 1971)
Cast Away (Robert Zemeckis, 2000)
Casualties of War (Brian De Palma, 1989)
Chasing Amy (Kevin Smith, 1997)
Chinatown (Roman Polanski, 1974)
Choose Me (Alan Rudolph, 1984)
Citizen Kane (Orson Welles, 1941)
Clerks (Kevin Smith, 1994)
The Color Purple (Steven Spielberg, 1985)
Crimes and Misdemeanors (Woody Allen, 1989)
Crimes of the Heart (Bruce Beresford, 1986)
The Crossing Guard (Sean Penn, 1995)
Crouching Tiger Hidden Dragon (Ang Lee, 2000)
Dancer in the Dark (Lars von Trier, 2000)
The Dancer Upstairs (John Malkovich, 2002)
Dancing at Lughnasa (Pat O'Connor, 1998)
Dangerous Liaisons (Stephen Frears, 1988)
The Dead (John Huston, 1987)
Dead Man Walking (Tim Robbins, 1995)
Decalogue (Krzysztof Kieślowski, 1988)
The Deer Hunter (Michael Cimino, 1978)
The Dish (Rob Sitch, 2000)
Dog Day Afternoon (Sidney Lumet, 1975)
East of Eden (Elia Kazan, 1955)
East-West (Régis Wargnier, 1999)
Eat Drink Man Woman (Ang Lee, 1994)
Edward Scissorhands (Tim Burton, 1990)
Elizabeth (Shekhar Kapur, 1998)
Erin Brockovich (Steven Soderbergh, 2000)
Excalibur (John Boorman, 1981)
Eyes Wide Shut (Stanley Kubrick, 1999)
The Falcon and the Snowman (John Schlesinger, 1985)
Far From Heaven (Todd Haynes, 2002)
Fargo (Joel Coen, 1996)
Fat City (John Huston, 1972)
Fatal Attraction (Adrian Lyne, 1987)
Festen / The Celebration (Thomas Vinterberg, 1998)
Five Easy Pieces (Bob Rafelson, 1970)
Flawless (Joel Schumacher, 1999)

Forrest Gump (Robert Zemeckis, 1994)
The Fugitive Kind (Sidney Lumet, 1959)
Galaxy Quest (Dean Parisot, 1999)
Gangs of New York (Martin Scorsese, 2002)
The General (John Boorman, 1998)
Ghostbusters (Ivan Reitman, 1984)
The Godfather (Francis Ford Coppola, 1972)
The Good Girl (Miguel Arteta, 2002)
Good Will Hunting (Gus Van Sant, 1997)
The Graduate (Mike Nichols, 1967)
The Grapes of Wrath (John Ford, 1940)
The Green Mile (Frank Darabont, 1999)
The Grifters (Stephen Frears, 1990)
Groundhog Day (Harold Ramis, 1993)
Guinevere (Audrey Wells, 1999)
Hair (Milos Forman, 1979)
Hannah and Her Sisters (Woody Allen, 1986)
Happiness (Todd Solondz, 1998)
Hit and Runway (Christopher Livingston, 1999)
The Hours (Stephen Daldry, 2002)
House of Games (David Mamet, 1987)
Hurlyburly (Anthony Drazan, 1998)
The Hurricane (Norman Jewison, 1999)
I Never Sang for My Father (Gilbert Cates, 1970)
The Ice Storm (Ang Lee, 1997)
In the Name of the Father (Jim Sheridan, 1993)
Independence Day (Roland Emmerich, 1996)
The Insider (Michael Mann, 1999)
It's a Wonderful Life (Frank Capra, 1946)
James Dean (Mark Rydell, 2001)
Jesus' Son (Alison Maclean, 1999)
Joe Gould's Secret (Stanley Tucci, 2000)
Judgment at Nuremberg (Stanley Kramer, 1961)
L.I.E. (Michael Cuesta, 2001)
The Last of the Mohicans (Michael Mann, 1992)
Leaving Las Vegas (Mike Figgis, 1995)
Life is Beautiful (Roberto Benigni, 1997)
Living in Oblivion (Tom DiCillo, 1995)
Lolita (Stanley Kubrick, 1962)
Lonesome Dove (Simon Wincer, 1989)

Love and Basketball (Gina Prince-Bythewood, 2000)

Magnolia (Paul Thomas Anderson, 1999)

The Making of John Grisham's The Rainmaker (Eleanor Coppola, 1997)

Mallrats (Kevin Smith, 1995)

The Matrix (Andy and Larry Wachowski, 1999)

Meet the Parents (Jay Roach, 2000)

Men in Black (Barry Sonnenfeld, 1997)

Midnight Cowboy (John Schlesinger, 1969)

Midnight Run (Martin Brest, 1988)

Misery (Rob Reiner, 1990)

The Misfits (John Huston, 1961)

Monster's Ball (Marc Forster, 2001)

Mulholland Drive (David Lynch, 2001)

Multiplicity (Harold Ramis, 1996)

My Kingdom (Don Boyd, 2001)

My Left Foot (Jim Sheridan, 1989)

The Negotiator (F. Gary Gray, 1998)

New York, New York (Martin Scorsese, 1977)

Nicholas Nickleby (Douglas McGrath, 2002)

October Sky (Joe Johnston, 1999)

Officer and a Gentleman (Taylor Hackford, 1982)

On Golden Pond (Mark Rydell, 1981)

On the Waterfront (Elia Kazan, 1954)

The Opposite of Sex (Don Roos, 1998)

Ordinary People (Robert Redford, 1980)

Out of Sight (Steven Soderbergh, 1998)

The Pianist (Roman Polanski, 2002)

Platoon (Oliver Stone, 1986)

Portrait of a Lady (Jane Campion, 1996)

Postcards from the Edge (Mike Nichols, 1990)

Pretty Woman (Garry Marshall, 1990)

Primary Colors (Mike Nichols, 1998)

Pulp Fiction (Quentin Tarantino, 1994)

The Quiet American (Phillip Noyce, 2002)

Quills (Philip Kaufman, 2000)

The Rainmaker (Francis Ford Coppola, 1997)

Raising Arizona (Joel Coen, 1987)

Rambling Rose (Martha Coolidge, 1991)

Remains of the Day (James Ivory, 1993)
Return to Paradise (Joseph Ruben, 1998)
RKO 281 (Benjamin Ross, 1999)
Road Trip (Todd Phillips, 2000)
Rob Roy (Michael Caton-Jones, 1995)
The Saint of Fort Washington (Tim Hunter, 1993)
Saving Private Ryan (Steven Spielberg, 1988)
Sawdust and Tinsel (Ingmar Bergman, 1953)
Scenes From a Marriage (Ingmar Bergman, 1973)
Secrets and Lies (Mike Leigh, 1996)
Sense and Sensibility (Ang Lee, 1995)
sex, lies, and videotape (Steve Soderbergh, 1989)
Sexy Beast (Jonathan Glazer, 2000)
Shadow of the Vampire (E. Elias Merhige, 2000)
Shane (George Stevens, 1953)
The Shining (Stanley Kubrick, 1980)
Short Cuts (Robert Altman, 1993)
Silverado (Lawrence Kasdan, 1985)
Simple Men (Hal Hartley, 1992)
The Sixth Sense (M. Night Shyamalan, 1999)
Slap Shot (George Roy Hill, 1977)
Sling Blade (Billy Bob Thornton, 1996)
Smoke (Wayne Wang, 1995)
Solaris (Steven Soderbergh, 2002)
Some Like It Hot (Billy Wilder, 1959)
Sophie's Choice (Alan J. Pakula, 1982)
Star Wars (George Lucas, 1977)
Star Wars: Episode II — Attack of the Clones (George Lucas, 2002)
The Straight Story (David Lynch, 1999)
Street Smart (Jerry Schatzberg, 1987)
Streetcar Named Desire (Elia Kazan, 1951)
The Sweet Hereafter (Atom Egoyan, 1997)
Taxi Driver (Martin Scorsese, 1976)
Tender Mercies (Bruce Beresford, 1983)
Terms of Endearment (James L. Brooks, 1983)
Thelma and Louise (Ridley Scott, 1991)
There's Something About Mary (Bobby and Peter Farrelly, 1998)
The Thin Red Line (Terrence Malick, 1998)

The Three Sisters (Laurence Olivier, 1970) (Paul Bogart, 1966)
Timecode (Mike Figgis, 2000)
To Kill a Mockingbird (Robert Mulligan, 1962)
Tootsie (Sydney Pollack, 1982)
Traffic (Steven Soderbergh, 2000)
Trois couleurs: Bleu (Krzysztof Keiślowski, 1993)
Truly, Madly, Deeply (Anthony Minghella, 1991)
Twilight: Los Angeles (Marc Levin, 2000)
Unfaithful (Adrian Lyne, 2002)
Very Bad Things (Peter Berg, 1998)
Waking Life (Richard Linklater, 2001)
Waking the Dead (Keith Gordon, 2000)
Wanda (Barbara Loden, 1971)
The Wedding Banquet (Ang Lee, 1993)
West Side Story (Jerome Robbins, Robert Wise, 1961)
What Women Want (Nancy Meyers, 2000)
What's Eating Gilbert Grape (Lasse Hallström, 1993)
What's Love Got to Do With It? (Brian Gibson, 1993)
When Harry Met Sally (Rob Reiner, 1989)
Who's Afraid of Virginia Woolf? (Mike Nichols, 1966)
Wild River (Elia Kazan, 1960)
The Wonder Boys (Curtis Hanson, 2000)
World Traveler (Bart Freundlich, 2001)
The Wrong Man (Alfred Hitchcock, 1956)
Wuthering Heights (William Wyler, 1939)
You Can Count on Me (Kenneth Lonergan, 2000)

BIBLIOGRAPHY

Bruder, Cohn, Oinek, Pollack, Previto, Zigler, *A Practical Handbook for the Actor*, Vintage Books 1986

Carney, Ray, *Cassavetes on Cassavetes*, Faber and Faber 2001

Castanada, Carlos, *The Active Side of Infinity*, HarperCollins 1998

Clements, Paul, *The Improvised Play: The Work of Mike Leigh*, Methuen Drama 1983

Crowe, Cameron, *Conversations with Wilder*, Alfred A. Knopf 1999

Egri, Lajos, *The Art of Dramatic Writing*, Simon & Schuster 1972

Fox, Michael J., *Lucky Man: A Memoir*, Hyperion 2002

Herskowitz, Morton, *Emotional Armoring*, Transaction Publishers 2001

Katz, Steven D., *Film Directing Shot by Shot*, Michael Wiese Productions 1991

Schamus, James, *The Ice Storm / screenplay* (Preface by Ang Lee), Newmarket Press 1997

Lumet, Sidney, *Making Movies*, Alfred A. Knopf 1995

Mamet, David, *True and False*, Vintage Books 1999

Meisner, Sanford and Dennis Longwell, *Sanford Meisner on Acting*, Vintage Books 1987

Soderbergh, Steven, *sex, lies, and videotape*, Harper & Row 1990

Smith, Kevin, *Clerks and Chasing Amy*, Hyperion 1998

Stanislavski, Constantin, *An Actor Prepares*, Theatre Arts Books 1936

Stok, Danusia, editor, *Keiślowski on Keiślowski*, Faber and Faber 1993

Thompson, Emma, *The Sense and Sensibility Screenplay and Diaries*, Newmarket Press 1995

Towne, Robert, *Chinatown; The Last Detail: Screenplays*, Grove/Atlantic, Inc. 1997

Travis, Mark, *Directing Feature Films*, Michael Wiese Productions 2002

Weston, Judith, *Directing Actors*, Michael Wiese Productions 1996

ABOUT THE AUTHOR

Judith Weston lives in Los Angeles, where she conducts classes and workshops in the studio she runs with her husband, John Hoskins. For directors, her workshops include Acting for Directors, and advanced workshops in Script Analysis and Rehearsal Techniques. For actors, she teaches ongoing classes in scene study, technique, improvisation, cold reading, and Shakespeare. For actors and directors together, she teaches the Actor-Director Laboratory.

Photo by Susan Schader

She consults privately for directors in pre-production, for projects including studio and independent films as well as television, to help them clarify their directing choices and prepare for casting and rehearsal.

In addition to her Los Angeles workshops for directors and actors, she travels with these workshops, and has taught them in Europe, Canada, and other cities of the US, including New York, San Francisco, and Seattle.

Her first book, *Directing Actors: Creating Memorable Performances for Film and Television*, is widely read by directors, writers, and actors. It has been translated into German, Japanese, Finnish, Korean, and Spanish.

If you wish to study or consult with Judith, or to arrange an on-site workshop, please consult the website, or call or write for more information:

Judith Weston Acting Studio
310 392-2444
www.judithweston.com
judyweston@aol.com

INDEX

Coen, Joel and Ethan, 95
Comedy, 138-139, 274, 300-301, 305
Comfort zone, 5, 274, 316
Communication. *See* Director-actor communication
Connelly, Jennifer, 302
Connery, Sean, 139
Conrad, Joseph, 131
Control. *See also* Damage control
    difference between authority and control, 227-229
Cooper, Chris, 41, 53, 266
Coppola, Eleanore, 271
Coppola, Francis Ford, 46, 206, 253, 265, 271, 283, 286, 320, 324
The "core," 13, 79-80, 204-205, 274, 311
Coward, Noel, 269
Cox, Brian, 52
Creativity, 7, 53, 78, 279, 322
"Crew rehearsal," 296, 322
Crowe, Russell, 82-83, 206, 282, 298
Crudup, Billy, 75, 127, 134, 149, 302, 324
Cruise, Tom, 137, 155, 244
Curtis-Hall, Vondie, 287

D
Dafoe, Willem, 48, 50, 99, 149
Daldry, Stephen, 268
Damage control, 241-242
Damon, Matt, 271, 319, 324
Danes, Clare, 324
D'Angelo, Beverly, 209
Danger signals, 281-283
Darabont, Frank, 103
Davies, Terence, 301
Davis, Geena, 149, 205
Day Lewis, Daniel, 66, 155
Daydreaming, 54-55, 77
De Angelis, Rosemary, 219
De Niro, Robert, 57, 206, 229, 311, 329
Dean, James, 237, 252
Del Toro, Benicio, 93
"Dead spots," 101, 266, 267, 272, 275, 305
Demme, Jonathan, 208, 321
Dench, Judi, 91
Depp, Johnny, 149
Dern, Laura, 55
Devere Smith, Anna, 79
Dillon, Matt, 218
Directing Actors, xvii-xviii, 103
Directing, craft of, 4-5, 28, 229, 258-259
Director-actor bond, xxii, 227-254, 266, 310-311
Director-actor communication, 4, 11, 86, 227-254, 256, 268, 273, 275-280, 283, 309-316
    agreement not always required, 92-94, 111, 113, 204
    importance of information, 238, 259-260, 264, 320

Luke, Derek, 239
Lumet, Sidney, 27, 72, 229, 248, 287-288, 291
Lying, 6, 70-71, 180, 198, 210, 280
Lynch, David, 27, 75, 116
Lyne, Adrian, 54, 253

M
Ma, Yo Yo, 9, 54
MacRainey, Gerald, 43-44
Madden, John, 229, 239
Mahoney, John, 233
Main character, 205-208
Malden, Karl, 325
Malick, Terrence, 285, 301
Malkovich, John, 248
Mamet, David, 66, 95, 98
Mann, Michael, 82-83, 286, 298
Marchand, Nancy, 18-19, 68
Martin, Steve, 72
Marx Brothers, 323
Mastroianni, Marcello, 56
McBride, Chi, 22
McGillis, Kelly, 251
McGregor, Ewan, 239
McKee, Robert, 199-200
McKellen, Ian, 63
Meisner, Sanford, 34, 57, 65, 67, 102, 144
Memory
          facts and, 144
          images and, 128
Mendes, Sam, 24, 68, 72, 90, 246, 279, 310-311, 328
Metaphor, 36, 89, 115, 131, 133
          personal, 14, 23
Meyers, Nancy, 319
Micro-management, 14-15, 80, 99, 107, 241, 316
Miles, Vera, 286
Miller, Dennis, 41
Mills, Shirley, 278
Minghella, Anthony, 227
Mirren, Helen, 235
Mistakes, 61, 316-317
Modine, Matthew, 260, 288
Moliere, 27
Moore, Julianne, 45, 209, 254, 288, 324
Moore, Mary Tyler, 51, 62, 244
Mordden, Ethan, 213
Moreau, Jeanne, 37
Moreno, Rita, 295
Mortality, 31-32, 71
Movement. *See* Blocking, Physical movement, Actors
"Moviola of the mind," 5
Mulwray, Evelyn, 11
Murray, Bill, 31, 245

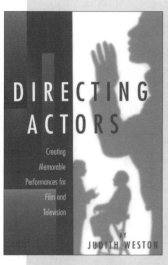

DIRECTING ACTORS
CREATING MEMORABLE PERFORMANCES FOR FILM AND TELEVISION

JUDITH WESTON

BEST SELLER
OVER 32,300 UNITS SOLD!

Directing film or television is a high-stakes occupation. It captures your full attention at every moment, calling on you to commit every resource and stretch yourself to the limit. It's the white-water rafting of entertainment jobs. But for many directors, the excitement they feel about a new project tightens into anxiety when it comes to working with actors.

This book provides a method for establishing creative, collaborative relationships with actors, getting the most out of rehearsals, troubleshooting poor performances, giving briefer directions, and much more. It addresses what actors want from a director, what directors do wrong, and constructively analyzes the director-actor relationship.

"Judith Weston is an extraordinarily gifted teacher."
— David Chase, Emmy Award-Winning Writer,
Director, and Producer
The Sopranos, Northern Exposure, I'll Fly Away

"I believe that working with Judith's ideas and principles has been the most useful time I've spent preparing for my work. I think that if Judith's book were mandatory reading for all directors, the quality of the director-actor process would be transformed, and better drama would result."
— John Patterson, Director
Six Feet Under, CSI: Crime Scene Investigation,
The Practice, Law and Order

"I know a great teacher when I find one! Everything in this book is brilliant and original and true."
— Polly Platt, Producer, Bottle Rocket
Executive Producer, Broadcast News, The War of the Roses

JUDITH WESTON was a professional actor for 20 years and has taught Acting for Directors for over a decade.

$26.95 | 314 PAGES | ORDER # 4RLS | ISBN: 0-941188-24-8

24 HOURS | 1.800.833.5738 | WWW.MWP.COM

FILM DIRECTING: SHOT BY SHOT
VISUALIZING FROM CONCEPT TO SCREEN

STEVEN D. KATZ

BEST SELLER
OVER 161,000 UNITS SOLD!

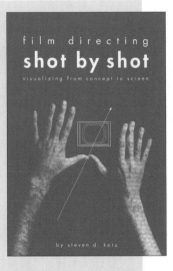

Film Directing: Shot by Shot — with its famous blue cover — is the best-known book on directing and a favorite of professional directors as an on-set quick reference guide.

This international bestseller is a complete catalog of visual techniques and their stylistic implications, enabling working filmmakers to expand their knowledge.

Contains in-depth information on shot composition, staging sequences, visualization tools, framing and composition techniques, camera movement, blocking tracking shots, script analysis, and much more.

Includes over 750 storyboards and illustrations, with never-before-published storyboards from Steven Spielberg's *Empire of the Sun*, Orson Welles' *Citizen Kane*, and Alfred Hitchcock's *The Birds*.

"(To become a director) you have to teach yourself what makes movies good and what makes them bad. John Singleton has been my mentor... he's the one who told me what movies to watch and to read Shot by Shot.*"*
— Ice Cube, New York Times

"A generous number of photos and superb illustrations accompany each concept, many of the graphics being from Katz' own pen... Film Directing: Shot by Shot *is a feast for the eyes."*
— Videomaker Magazine

"... demonstrates the visual techniques of filmmaking by defining the process whereby the director converts storyboards into photographed scenes."
— Back Stage Shoot

"Contains an encyclopedic wealth of information."
— Millimeter Magazine

STEVEN D. KATZ is also the author of *Film Directing: Cinematic Motion.*

$27.95 | 366 PAGES | ORDER # 7RLS | ISBN: 0-941188-10-8

24 HOURS | 1.800.833.5738 | WWW.MWP.COM

SETTING UP YOUR SHOTS
GREAT CAMERA MOVES EVERY FILMMAKER SHOULD KNOW

JEREMY VINEYARD

BEST SELLER
OVER 27,300 UNITS SOLD!

Written in straightforward, non-technical language and laid out in a nonlinear format with self-contained chapters for quick, on-the-set reference, *Setting Up Your Shots* is like a Swiss army knife for filmmakers! Using examples from over 140 popular films, this book provides detailed descriptions of more than 100 camera setups, angles, and techniques — in an easy-to-use horizontal "wide-screen" format.

Setting Up Your Shots is an excellent primer for beginning filmmakers and students of film theory, as well as a handy guide for working filmmakers. If you are a director, a storyboard artist, or an animator, use this book. It is the culmination of hundreds of hours of research.

Contains 150 references to the great shots from your favorite films, including *2001: A Space Odyssey, Blue Velvet, The Matrix, The Usual Suspects,* and *Vertigo.*

"Perfect for any film enthusiast looking for the secrets behind creating film. Because of its simplicity of design and straightforward storyboards, Setting Up Your Shots *is destined to be mandatory reading at film schools throughout the world."*
— *Ross Otterman,* Directed By Magazine

*"*Setting Up Your Shots *is a great book for defining the shots of today. The storyboard examples on every page make it a valuable reference book for directors and DPs alike! This great learning tool should be a boon for writers who want to choose the most effective shot and clearly show it in their boards for the maximum impact."*
— *Paul Clatworthy, Creator,* StoryBoard Artist *and* StoryBoard Quick *Software*

"This book is for both beginning and experienced filmmakers. It's a great reference tool, a quick reminder of the most commonly used shots by the greatest filmmakers of all time."
— *Cory Williams, President, Alternative Productions*

JEREMY VINEYARD is a filmmaker, internationally published author, and screenwriter. He is currently assembling a cast and crew for a crime feature to be shot in 2005.

$19.95 | 132 PAGES | ORDER # 8RLS | ISBN: 0-941188-73-6

24 HOURS | **1.800.833.5738** | WWW.MWP.COM

CINEMATIC STORYTELLING
THE 100 MOST POWERFUL FILM CONVENTIONS EVERY FILMMAKER MUST KNOW

JENNIFER VAN SIJLL

How do directors use screen direction to suggest conflict? How do screenwriters exploit film space to show change? How does editing style determine emotional response?

Many first-time writers and directors do not ask these questions. They forego the huge creative resource of the film medium, defaulting to dialog to tell their screen story. Yet most movies are carried by sound and picture. The industry's most successful writers and directors have mastered the cinematic conventions specific to the medium. They have harnessed non-dialog techniques to create some of the most cinematic moments in movie history.

This book is intended to help writers and directors more fully exploit the medium's inherent storytelling devices. It contains 100 non-dialog techniques that have been used by the industry's top writers and directors. From *Metropolis* and *Citizen Kane* to *Dead Man* and *Kill Bill*, the book illustrates — through 500 frame grabs and 75 script excerpts — how the inherent storytelling devices specific to film were exploited.

You will learn:
- How non-dialog film techniques can advance story.
- How master screenwriters exploit cinematic conventions to create powerful scenarios.

"Cinematic Storytelling *scores a direct hit in terms of concise information and perfectly chosen visuals, and it also searches out... and finds... an emotional core that many books of this nature either miss or are afraid of.*"
— *Kirsten Sheridan, Director,* Disco Pigs; *Co-writer,* In America

"*Here is a uniquely fresh, accessible, and truly original contribution to the field. Jennifer van Sijll takes her readers in a wholly new direction, integrating aspects of screenwriting with all the film crafts in a way I've never before seen. It is essential reading not only for screenwriters but also for filmmakers of every stripe.*"
— *Prof. Richard Walter, UCLA Screenwriting Chairman*

JENNIFER VAN SIJLL has taught film production, film history, and screenwriting. She is currently on the faculty at San Francisco State's Department of Cinema.

$22.95 | 230 PAGES | ORDER # 35RLS | ISBN: 1-932907-05-X

MICHAEL WIESE PRODUCTIONS

Since 1981, Michael Wiese Productions has been dedicated to providing both novice and seasoned filmmakers with vital information on all aspects of filmmaking. We have published more than 70 books, used in over 500 film schools and countless universities, and by hundreds of thousands of filmmakers worldwide.

Our authors are successful industry professionals who spend innumerable hours writing about the hard stuff: budgeting, financing, directing, marketing, and distribution. They believe that if they share their knowledge and experience with others, more high quality films will be produced.

And that has been our mission, now complemented through our new web-based resources. We invite all readers to visit www.mwp.com to receive free tipsheets and sample chapters, participate in forum discussions, obtain product discounts — and even get the opportunity to receive free books, project consulting, and other services offered by our company.

Our goal is, quite simply, to help you reach your goals. That's why we give our readers the most complete portal for filmmaking knowledge available — in the most convenient manner.

We truly hope that our books and web-based resources will empower you to create enduring films that will last for generations to come.

Let us hear from you at anytime.

Sincerely,
Michael Wiese
Publisher, Filmmaker

www.mwp.com

FILM & VIDEO BOOKS

Alone In a Room: *Secrets of Successful Screenwriters*
John Scott Lewinski / $19.95

Cinematic Storytelling: *The 100 Most Powerful Film Conventions Every Filmmaker Must Know* / Jennifer Van Sijll / $22.95

The Complete Independent Movie Marketing Handbook: *Promote, Distribute & Sell Your Film or Video* / Mark Steven Bosko / $39.95

Costume Design 101: *The Art and Business of Costume Design for Film and Television* / Richard La Motte / $19.95

Could It Be a Movie? *How to Get Your Ideas Out of Your Head and Up on the Screen* / Christina Hamlett / $26.95

Crashing Hollywood: *How to Keep Your Integrity Up, Your Clothes On & Still Make It in Hollywood* / Fran Harris / $24.95

Creating Characters: *Let Them Whisper Their Secrets*
Marisa D'Vari / $26.95

The Crime Writer's Reference Guide: *1001 Tips for Writing the Perfect Murder*
Martin Roth / $17.95

Cut by Cut: *Editing Your Film or Video*
Gael Chandler / $35.95

Cut to the Chase: *Forty-Five Years of Editing America's Favorite Movies*
Sam O'Steen as told to Bobbie O'Steen / $24.95

Digital Cinema: *The Hollywood Insider's Guide to the Evolution of Storytelling*
Thom Taylor and Melinda Hsu / $27.95

Digital Editing with Final Cut Pro 4 *(includes 45 minutes of DVD tutorials and sample footage)* / Bruce Mamer and Jason Wallace / $31.95

Digital Filmmaking 101: *An Essential Guide to Producing Low-Budget Movies*
Dale Newton and John Gaspard / $24.95

Digital Moviemaking, 2nd Edition: *All the Skills, Techniques, and Moxie You'll Need to Turn Your Passion into a Career* / Scott Billups / $26.95

Directing Actors: *Creating Memorable Performances for Film and Television*
Judith Weston / $26.95

Directing Feature Films: *The Creative Collaboration Between Directors, Writers, and Actors* / Mark Travis / $26.95

Dream Gear: *Cool & Innovative Tools for Film, Video & TV Professionals*
Catherine Lorenze / $29.95

The Encyclopedia of Underground Movies: *Films from the Fringes of Cinema*
Phil Hall / $26.95

The Eye is Quicker *Film Editing: Making a Good Film Better*
Richard D. Pepperman / $27.95

Film & Video Budgets, 3rd Updated Edition
Deke Simon and Michael Wiese / $26.95

Film Directing: Cinematic Motion, 2nd Edition
Steven D. Katz / $27.95

Film Directing: Shot by Shot, *Visualizing from Concept to Screen*
Steven D. Katz / $27.95

The Film Director's Intuition: *Script Analysis and Rehearsal Techniques*
Judith Weston / $26.95

Film Production Management 101: *The Ultimate Guide for Film and Television Production Management and Coordination* / Deborah S. Patz / $39.95

Filmmaking for Teens: *Pulling Off Your Shorts*
Troy Lanier and Clay Nichols / $18.95

First Time Director: *How to Make Your Breakthrough Movie*
Gil Bettman / $27.95

From Word to Image: *Storyboarding and the Filmmaking Process*
Marcie Begleiter / $26.95

The Hollywood Standard: *The Complete & Authoritative Guide to Script Format and Style* / Christopher Riley / $18.95

The Independent Film and Videomakers Guide, 2nd Edition: *Expanded and Updated* / Michael Wiese / $29.95

Inner Drives: *How to Write & Create Characters Using the Eight Classic Centers of Motivation* / Pamela Jaye Smith / $26.95

Joe Leydon's Guide to Essential Movies You Must See: *If You Read, Write About – or Make Movies* / Joe Leydon / $24.95

Myth and the Movies: *Discovering the Mythic Structure of 50 Unforgettable Films* / Stuart Voytilla / $26.95

On the Edge of a Dream: *Magic & Madness in Bali*
Michael Wiese / $16.95

The Perfect Pitch: *How to Sell Yourself and Your Movie Idea to Hollywood*
Ken Rotcop / $16.95

Psychology for Screenwriters: *Building Conflict in your Script*
William Indick, Ph.D. / $26.95

Save the Cat! *The Last Book on Screenwriting You'll Ever Need*
Blake Snyder / $19.95

Screenwriting 101: *The Essential Craft of Feature Film Writing*
Neill D. Hicks / $16.95

Script Partners: *What Makes Film and TV Writing Teams Work*
Claudia Johnson and Matt Stevens / $24.95

The Script-Selling Game: *A Hollywood Insider's Look at Getting Your Script Sold and Produced* / Kathie Fong Yoneda / $14.95

Setting Up Your Shots: *Great Camera Moves Every Filmmaker Should Know*
Jeremy Vineyard / $19.95

Shaking the Money Tree, 2nd Edition: *How to Get Grants and Donations for Film and Television* / Morrie Warshawski / $26.95

Sound Design: *The Expressive Power of Music, Voice, and Sound Effects in Cinema* / David Sonnenschein / $19.95

Stealing Fire From the Gods: *A Dynamic New Story Model for Writers and Filmmakers* / James Bonnet / $26.95

Storyboarding 101: *A Crash Course in Professional Storyboarding*
James O. Fraioli / $19.95

The Ultimate Filmmaker's Guide to Short Films: *Making It Big in Shorts*
Kim Adelman / $14.95

What Are You Laughing At? *How to Write Funny Screenplays, Stories, and More* / Brad Schreiber / $19.95

The Working Director: *How to Arrive, Thrive & Survive in the Director's Chair*
Charles Wilkinson / $22.95

The Writer's Journey, 2nd Edition: *Mythic Structure for Writers*
Christopher Vogler / $24.95

The Writer's Partner: *1001 Breakthrough Ideas to Stimulate Your Imagination*
Martin Roth / $19.95

Writing the Action Adventure: *The Moment of Truth*
Neill D. Hicks / $14.95

Writing the Comedy Film: *Make 'Em Laugh*
Stuart Voytilla and Scott Petri / $14.95

Writing the Fantasy Film: *Heroes and Journeys in Alternate Realities*
Sable Jak / $26.95

Writing the Killer Treatment: *Selling Your Story Without a Script*
Michael Halperin / $14.95

Writing the Second Act: *Building Conflict and Tension in Your Film Script*
Michael Halperin / $19.95

Writing the Thriller Film: *The Terror Within*
Neill D. Hicks / $14.95

DVD & VIDEOS

Hardware Wars: *DVD*
Written and Directed by Ernie Fosselius / $14.95

Hardware Wars: *Special Edition VHS Video*
Written and Directed by Ernie Fosselius / $9.95

Field of Fish: *VHS Video*
Directed by Steve Tanner and Michael Wiese, Written by Annamaria Murphy / $9.95